MY LIFE
BRETT
LEE

WITH JAMES KNIGHT

MY LIFE

BRETT LEE

WITH JAMES KNIGHT

EBURY
PRESS

An Ebury Press book
Published by Random House Australia Pty Ltd
Level 3, 100 Pacific Highway, North Sydney NSW 2060
www.randomhouse.com.au

First published by Ebury Press in 2011

Addresses for companies within the Random House Group can be found at
www.randomhouse.com.au/offices

National Library of Australia Cataloguing-in-Publication entry (hbk):

Lee, Brett
Brett Lee: my life/Brett Lee and James Knight

978 1 86471 254 4 (hbk)

Lee, Brett.
Cricket players – Australia – Biography.
Cricket – Bowling.
Bowlers – Australia – Biography.

Other Authors/Contributors:
Knight, James, 1967–

796.358092

Cover design by Adam Yazxhi/MAXCO
Front jacket photograph: Jack Atley/Bloomberg/Getty Images
Back jacket photograph: Shaun Botterill/Getty Images
Internal text and picture section design by Midland Typesetters, Australia
Typeset by Midland Typesetters, Australia
Brett Lee career statistics provided by Ross Dundas
Printed in Australia by Griffin Press, an accredited ISO AS/NZS 14001:2004
Environmental Management System printer

10 9 8 7 6 5 4 3 2 1

Random House Australia uses papers that are natural, renewable and recyclable products and
made from wood grown in sustainable forests. The logging and manufacturing processes are
expected to conform to the environmental regulations of the country of origin.

I would like to dedicate this book to my son, Preston, for your unconditional love and for the fact that, at the end of the day, I am just Daddy!

Foreword

Alan Jones

A book about Brett Lee can only be read with a smile on one's face. It seems that in everything Brett has done, he has been an agent of happiness for many. It's my one abiding impression of a remarkable young man.

It is said that children in many ways reflect the value system of their parents. I can confirm that with regard to the three Lee sons, Shane and Brett, both of whom represented Australia in cricket, and Grant, an outstanding musician and scholar who could most probably have done likewise, it's easy to argue that what they have become is a consequence of the steadying and loving influence of Bob and Helen, their parents.

Around the Lees, there's always a smile, a story and a feed! And out of a very simple and uncomplicated upbringing in which, in the contest for authority between Dad and the sons, the sons often won, there can be no surprise at the success that was to eventuate.

In many ways Brett's story is a parental story. Let the kids have a go and they'll find eventually their high water mark. And so it's been with Brett.

Through all the difficulties, he has had the reassurance of a splendid family unit; and through all the triumphs he has never hesitated to share those moments with his family as well.

The statistics tell only part of the story. It was always a source of bemusement to me that when Australia got into trouble in Test cricket it was often Brett's performance that would be questioned, not the team's.

And yet as I used to tell Brett, that was no bad thing. It merely fired him up.

The records show that Brett has triumphed over disappointment, injury and adversity perhaps more than any other athlete I've known. I well remember when in January 2004 in a Test, India v Australia at the SCG, India carted the Australian bowlers in the first innings to the tune of seven declared for 705. Brett took 4-201.

And as the newspaper headlines screamed that truth the next day, the inference was that Brett had received a towelling at the hands of the Indian batsmen. But with a smile on his face, oblivious of the headline, Brett jokingly said to me, 'Well if I got 4-201 the rest of the team must have got 3-504. I think I did alright!' And who could disagree?

I once took Brett and his family to Las Vegas. We went to see David Copperfield. Copperfield started throwing Frisbees into the crowd and I warned Brett not to take one. I may as well have saved my breath. Not only did he take one but, by doing so, Brett then became the subject of several of Copperfield's remarkable illusions.

I couldn't help but feel that Brett could have held his own in that company as well. He could have been the jokester. It would have been a good audience for his humour.

He'd always be asking me why apartments are called apartments when they are all joined together, or why do they call goods that come by car a shipment, but goods that come on a ship, cargo.

Why is a boxing ring square? What do butterflies get in

their stomach when they get nervous? Why do we sterilise lethal injections? He rattles off a million of them.

But over and above all this, it is his modesty that has won over so many people. When Australian country music superstar Lee Kernaghan invited Brett to do a couple of numbers with his band Brett was overwhelmed, yet it was Lee Kernaghan who couldn't believe that this tearaway fast bowler was actually a musician in his own right.

Brett is by any reckoning a remarkable human being, an outstanding Australian and a gifted athlete. And that's what this book is about.

I'm delighted its co-author is James Knight. He has a sensible and sensitive understanding of the role of athletes and yet is capable of objective treatment of the material at his disposal.

Brett has never been in love with himself or his sport but he is in love with life. He is an object lesson to so many other young people that they must seek a world beyond sport if they're to make the transition into the world that sportsmen have rarely inhabited, the world when one day your name is no longer read out.

I have a feeling, though, that if this book were written in 20 years' time, we'd still be saying the same things.

Through all his success and all the attention he's received and the adulation that's been showered upon him in various parts of the world, Brett still returns home and you get a text message which says, 'I'm back. Must catch up.'

When we do, he invariably has the guitar in hand, perhaps a bit of sheet music, a bottle of red and a good voice.

And you know that all the hoopla about international cricket will be cast aside and we will be swept away by his music, the real language of his life which seems to transcend all other considerations.

As a man, an athlete, a son, a parent and a friend, very few people come along like Brett. This book provides an insight into why that is so.

My understanding of Brett Lee derives from many years of friendship and the pleasure that friendship brings. Yet I know my sentiments would be shared by many others. A reading of this autobiography will give a better understanding of why this is the case.

Foreword

Allan Donald

It was at the end of 1999–2000 when this young blond bloke came out of nowhere to announce himself to the cricketing world against India. I remember Ian Chappell saying it could be a very interesting time when Australia bowled because they'd picked this new fast bowler virtually out of nowhere. His name was Brett Lee.

As cricketers, you keep a close eye on what goes on around the world, and South Africa's next tour was going to be in Australia 2000–01, which turned out to be my last. When Brett started his run to deliver his first ball in Test cricket against the Indians I thought to myself, 'This bloke is the real deal.'

He bowled very fast and India had no answers to his real pace, but the thing that stood out for me about Brett was the way he went about his job, not only as a cricketer but as a person. In professional sport the people who get to the top have certain qualities that separate them from the rest, and that is a desire to beat whoever is in front of them so badly. When Brett came into the Australian side, he was in the company of Glenn McGrath, Jason Gillespie and the great Shane Warne. I can't think of a better time to have come into a very good Australian team – with that experience and class around you and being given the freedom to go and blow batters apart.

Young bloke or not, the outstanding factor for me about Brett Lee is that he has taken massive ownership of himself and has shown great leadership with whatever he has done in the team. You simply can't buy that. It comes from having a big ticker and when you combine that with a God-given talent to bowl fast and be humble at the same time, what can go wrong?

It was sad to see the great man retire from Test cricket and he has had big setbacks in terms of injuries, but what he has done time and time again is to come back for more and more. He will be missed – not by many batters, that much I can tell you, but for what he has given the game.

It is a huge honour to have been asked to write this Foreword for Brett. It's something I have never done before, but not for one second did I think I shouldn't be doing it. I know this book is a true reflection of what Brett Lee is all about and I can't wait to read it myself.

It was fantastic to have watched you, mate, and to do battle with you, and well done on a great career. Good luck.

1

It was Christmas Day 2009, early afternoon. I drove into my street with my three-year-old son, Preston, and immediately saw the warning signs: on the far side of the road opposite my home a guy was sitting on a brick fence. He was dressed in a full motorbike outfit with a helmet by his side. He also had a camera with a very long lens. I looked at him, he looked at me. He quickly lifted his camera, but before he could take a picture, I zipped up the road and out of sight around a corner. I then threw a U-turn, pulled a cap tight over my head, and drove back. The photographer sped past the other way.

When Preston and I were safely home, I looked out a front window and saw the guy had returned to the fence. A short while later, my doorbell rang. I looked through the security camera monitor and saw a young blonde woman whose age was difficult to determine through the fuzziness of the screen. I thought it was a set-up: get a photo, throw a few lines over it, and suddenly there'd be gossip in the papers about 'Brett Lee's mystery female'.

I answered the door but stood well back, obscured from the photographer's sight by a hedge.

'Hi Brett, we've never met, but I'm your neighbour,' said

the visitor, who happened to be only a teenage girl. It was true that I didn't know her; I'm a private person and generally keep to myself in the neighbourhood. The girl continued: 'I just thought you should know there's someone out here with a camera who's been trying to jump your back fence. I think he's been trying to get photos of you.'

I thanked her, went back inside, and pulled the blinds down. Preston didn't understand what was going on. I didn't want to worry him, but I knew I had to do something; we'd become prisoners in the house. I sought advice by ringing my cousin and close mate, Luke Buxton, a policeman. I then called the local police and told them what was happening. I felt uncomfortable telling them my name because I didn't want to draw attention to myself. But the police were really helpful and moved the photographer on, banning him from coming into the area for 24 hours. They told me the same bloke had recently done something similar to Nicole Kidman.

The incident made me angry. I understood the photographer had a job to do, but I didn't agree with how he was doing it. However, it did serve another purpose: more than at any other time during my career, I realised I didn't lead an ordinary life. I imagined what it must be like to be the Beckhams or Sachin Tendulkar, and although I was lucky my profile was tiny in comparison with theirs, I had experienced enough to believe that my privacy and rights had been violated.

And why?

I suppose it all began on Boxing Day 1999 when I first walked onto the MCG as an Australian Test cricketer who happened to bowl fast. Even before that moment I'd made a decision to be a 'cricket performer', like an actor, and the playing field was my stage. During every match I wanted to be exuberant, 'amped up'. I wanted to entertain. People could take as many photos as they liked, ask as many questions as they liked. They could cheer me, criticise me, or even have jokes with me. And that's what ended up happening most of the time. I loved it. I thrived on the whole scene: the packed crowds, the atmosphere, and most of all, the challenges. I relished it when the crowds didn't think we could win but somehow we pulled through; I also thrived on the occasions when I bowled on through the heat, or delivered just one more over when everyone thought I was spent. Moments like those inspired and motivated me. At times I wanted to prove to myself I could bowl 155 kilometres an hour all day; or if I was pinned in the ribs while batting, I'd get a dose of 'white line fever' and fight harder for survival than I ever thought possible. Overall, I wanted to show everyone, including myself, that I would give all I had in every single match on every single stage.

But when I left the stage at the end of each day, I was no longer a cricket performer. There were many other areas of my life that were important to me. I could go to a music studio and jam with my mates, or I could slip into a suit and become a salesman at Barclay's Menswear, or I could go home and spend time with my parents, the two most influential people in my life. In other words, I could switch off. Admittedly cricket has been the focal point of my life, but it isn't everything. I love playing the game, but to be honest, I generally find it boring to watch. It's the performer in me; I want to squeeze through the TV and be in the middle of it. I want to be the guy jumping through and getting that '5-for', not the one looking from over the fence.

I've been lucky. Cricket has given me an incredible lifestyle, and as was the case on Christmas Day 2009, I've learnt to take the good with the bad. Sometimes I still sit back and say to myself with disbelief: 'You've played cricket for Australia!'

But I still can't grasp why people are interested in me to the extent that someone would try climbing over my fence to take a photo. Half a lifetime ago it had all been so simple when I was back at school. I was just another student, another kid in the playground having fun. But now it's all so different. Perhaps my status as an apparent celebrity is best summed up by Preston. Often when a complete stranger calls me Brett, my son asks: 'How do they know your name, Daddy?'

It's something I've never got used to. I always find it funny when I see my name appear in the 'Spotted' section of a newspaper: 'Brett Lee was seen at Lane Cove shops' or 'Brett Lee was eating a hamburger in Bondi'. It's ridiculous! But you know the flipside? I'm always interested to see what other people are doing. I suppose it's a strange twist of human nature.

In this book I hope to make you see life through my eyes. As far as the cricket goes, some of you will know my statistics much better than I do; at the time of starting this project I didn't even know who my last Test wicket was. Actually, I still don't know. Throughout my entire career my biggest achievement was something fast bowlers learn to live with: getting over physical stiffness, and rising above the aches and pains that feel like knives stabbing into your joints and muscles. Despite this, somehow you get out of bed the next morning and do it all again. What a way to make a living. A great way.

2

I vividly remember my first trip on a plane. I was 11 years old and had been selected in the NSW PSSA (Primary Schools Sports Association) cricket team to compete at the national championships in Adelaide. My older brother, Shane, had done the same thing a couple of years earlier. Back then, I sat with my younger brother, Grant, in the back of the family Sigma with a caravan in tow while Mum and Dad drove us the 1400 kilometres so we could watch Shane play. The trip took a couple of days. Although I was glad I didn't have to do that again, the thought of flying scared me because I was afraid of heights. I was really nervous after the plane took off, but then I put some headphones on and listened to the song playing on the radio system: 'Don't Worry, Be Happy' by Bobby McFerrin.

I'd like to think those few words sum up my attitude to life. Sure, everyone has their disappointments, but it's important to see the bright side whenever you can. From my earliest memory of sharing a bath with Shane and Grant as kids, to this very day when we're all grown men who've gone on to lead our own lives, family has been central to my happiness. And the two main reasons are 'H' and the 'Doctor': Mum and Dad.

Helen and Bob are two great people who've given me and my brothers every opportunity in life. We call Dad the Doctor because we think he knows everything; he has a really good knack of reading the situation and is often ahead of it. He retired in 2010 after working for 40 years in the same job as a metallurgist at the BHP steelworks in Wollongong, about an hour's drive south of Sydney. Mum and Dad are from working-class stock. Dad's father, William, was a wharfie. He and his wife, Erna, raised Dad and his two brothers in Cairns in far north Queensland, but when times got tough they went on the road for five years, stopping off for William to work in ports like Newcastle and Geelong before finally settling in the 'Gong. By this time Dad was 13 years old. Mum had a similar start: the only sister between two brothers (David and Terry), she was five when her parents, Milton and Iris, decided to call Wollongong home. They'd travelled from Maitland in the Hunter Valley where work opportunities were scarce for Milton, a carpenter.

Seventeen years later, Mum and Dad first met at the weekly Wednesday night dance at the Wollongong RSL Club. They were married little more than a year afterwards on 17 June 1972. They didn't muck about with the next step: Shane was born on 8 August 1973, I came along on 8 November 1976, and Grant was the tailender on 20 November 1978.

I often wonder how Mum and Dad managed looking after three boys aged just five years apart. In some ways the Doctor had the easier job because he could get away to BHP while Mum stayed full-time at the coalface. She was the disciplinarian. We used to get the occasional smack or ruler or wooden spoon on the backside, but that was good for us. Mum was a talented sprinter in her school years, and that gave her an advantage in the early days of raising us because she could mow us down.

I still remember the first time I was able to run away from her without getting caught. I would have been about 13, and after the seriousness of the initial chase down the street, Mum admitted: 'I can't catch you, you little . . .' Then we burst out laughing. Dad was a softer touch. He'd occasionally raise his voice, especially if we were playing too loudly while he was trying to sleep after finishing night shift. But most of the time he just went with the flow.

The Lee boys were far from perfectly behaved, and we pushed the limits as much as we could. When Dad bought a hunting bow he soon discovered his supply of arrows had diminished because I'd shot them into the distance over the back fence. Grant and I eventually snapped the bow and hid the fractured parts under Mum and Dad's bed. Out of sight, out of mind.

Sometimes our strategies worked. Mum recalls once picking up a vase that she hadn't paid much attention to for years. On closer inspection she noticed it had been glued together in several pieces. Then there was the occasion when the neighbour three houses down from us told Dad that we'd broken one of his windows, but he couldn't find any projectile. The Doctor sprung into protective mode, telling the neighbour: 'I don't think the boys could have done it. They've been playing in the driveway, and they couldn't throw a rock or a ball all the way to your house. That would have to be 100 metres!' The neighbour agreed and went home, while Dad came straight to us and asked Shane: 'Right, how did you do it?' I can only say that marbles go a long way when hit by a tennis racket.

Over the years we got into our share of trouble, but we were just boys being boys in a family that has always had a very strong bond. When growing up I thought every family was like ours; it wasn't until I got older that I realised some

7

people weren't as lucky. I can never give enough praise to Mum and Dad.

We lived in a brick home at 8 Winter Avenue, Mount Warrigal, a short drive from Wollongong. Lake Illawarra, numerous beaches, dairy farms, bushland and, of course, our own backyard all became our playgrounds. Mum reckons I was hyperactive right from the start, and by the time I grew to primary school age it was never safe to venture outdoors when I was somewhere about with a bow and arrow, slingshot, or any type of ball.

It wasn't always sport that provided the fun in a household that was full of love and a great deal of tolerance; I don't know how Dad ever put up with me hammering all his screwdrivers so far into the lawn that he had to dig them out with a shovel. Sometimes I didn't think before I acted. Actually that's not quite right: I did think, but probably not enough. Then again, some might say I showed a fast bowler's mental capacity. That was certainly the case when I decided to cut a branch off a pine tree at the side of the house. I was smart enough to realise I needed to protect myself from the pine needles and sap, so I put on a ski jacket, gloves and goggles before climbing the tree. I then began my operation. All went well until I realised I was standing on the branch I was sawing through. I fell over the next door neighbour's fence and whacked into a concrete path. If I hadn't been dressed like the Michelin Man, I reckon I would have been seriously hurt.

Animals played an important part in my upbringing. For years I kept an aviary that included cockatoos, quails, doves and finches. One day I brought home from cricket training a galah that happily sat on my shoulder. But there was one bird I couldn't stand: the Indian myna that was nothing but a pest. I devised a plan that I was confident would eradicate all mynas in the backyard. It was straight out of Wile E. Coyote's book of tricks from the old Road Runner cartoons. I tied a brick to some strong fishing line and suspended it over a tree branch, then I let go of the line to see where the brick would land. After that, I put a piece of bread on the drop zone, and held the line while waiting out of sight in the garage. But, like the coyote, I didn't have any luck; if I told you I reduced the number of mynas by as many as one I'd be exaggerating.

I also once had a turtle that went missing. We all thought it was gone for good until Mum was amazed to hear a knock at the door and find a stranger holding my pet.

'How did you know the turtle belongs here?' asked Mum. The stranger turned over the turtle and revealed I'd painted my name, address and phone number on its shell.

One turtle is easier than one mouse. For those of you in the know, two mice can quickly turn into 10 and more. I had about 80 when Mum became sick of the sight and smell of them. Although I said I cleaned their cage every day, that wasn't good enough for H who insisted I get rid of them. So my response? I let them all go in the garage and 8 Winter Ave had an instant plague.

My Auntie Debbie – the wife of Mum's brother Terry – can also vouch for my fascination with animals. Her family lived on a dairy farm about 15 minutes' drive from home, and a visit there was always a good chance for me to get into mischief with my cousin Luke, who was three years younger than me. We'd plan our days on a whiteboard in Luke's bedroom, and then off we'd go, riding bikes, throwing rocks, kicking balls, just wandering and laughing. We wouldn't even stop for lunch, and generally the only rule of our parents was: 'Just make sure you're home before dark.' On one occasion we arrived back early after a great day, although Auntie Debbie thought otherwise: she walked into the kitchen to find about 25 rabbits sitting on the floor. Luke and I had spent hours catching them. Our methods were simple: throw some fishing net over one hole of a burrow, and send Grandmum Iris's fox terrier, Timmy, down another hole. Sure enough, the rabbits would come out, and Luke and I had justified our positions as fearless hunters. Unfortunately Auntie Debbie freaked out, and we had to let our catches go.

Of all my experiences with nature, none left a greater impression on me than the time I spent with my grandfather William. All the Lee boys knew him as 'Pa' and Erna as 'Ma'. Pa and my uncles Bill and Les taught me how to fish, a pastime that remains one of my favourite escapes. I was about 11 when I first took on the deep sea in one of Pa's two boats. I got pretty sick and started vomiting.

'Keep going, son, it makes great bait,' said Pa.

Pa wasn't a big man, but he was a tough, strong bugger who never complained. He used to pull his boat out into the water one-handed.

I got really excited when I knew we were going fishing. If I was told to be ready by 6.30 in the morning, I'd be up at five o'clock ready to go. I'd be shattered whenever Uncle Les rang up and said: 'It's too windy today, we'll try again tomorrow.'

Pa died from lung cancer several years ago. I miss him. He and Ma lived about four kilometres away from us. I used to ride to their home and listen to Ma play the organ. Whenever they visited our home, a cup of tea and a chat would turn into long sessions of playing pool and table tennis. Simple pleasures can make wonderful memories. It was the same with my maternal grandmother, Iris. I used to fish in a creek behind her house at nearby Corrimal, but I best remember Grandmum for the pavlovas and trifles she made for Christmas dinners. Sadly, Grandad passed away before I was born.

Looking back at those days, one thing is obvious to me: I was an outdoor person. Considering that, it's not surprising sport became part of my everyday life. Soccer, skiing and athletics gave me some of my earliest experiences, but the first sport I really fell for was basketball. Well into my teens I played during breaks at school, and then I'd come home and together with my brothers and cousin Luke would shoot hoops through a ring that Dad had bolted onto a wall at the side of the house.

I also gave rugby league a go; this was really popular during wet weather when mates from the neighbourhood played games on a spare block of land. We'd return home covered in mud, and weren't allowed inside until Mum hosed us down, often in the freezing cold. There was also the time after Shane and I had been watching some footy on TV that my brother had the bright idea that I should tape my ears up like some of the professionals did. So, Shane the boss got some of Dad's electrical tape and wrapped it around me so tightly that I thought my head was going to explode. He then told me to run down a make-believe sideline in the backyard. Seconds later, he took me out with a cover tackle that ended up with both of us smashing a massive hole in the fibro garage. Dad came out, inspected the damage, but said little.

Shane was the typical big brother. He was an imposing figure right from the start, and Grant and I generally did what he said. If there was any doubt about this, I need only recall the day Dad was asleep and Mum had gone to the local shops. H returned to find Shane had locked Grant and me outside. That alone wasn't too bad, but the fact we'd been forced to strip naked was something that showed the Shane Lee touch. He did it just because he could.

As little brothers often do, I put big brother Shane on a pedestal. Therefore, it wasn't surprising that when he started to play cricket I wanted to as well. When Shane first came home and asked to play in the local competition Mum talked him out of it; she thought cricket was boring, a view that probably came from her childhood when she'd spent too many hours fielding balls hit by her brothers. The next year, though, Shane got his way and joined up at Albion Park because registrations had closed at our nearest club, Oak Flats. By the time Shane changed to the Rats (Oak Flats' nickname) the following year, there was no stopping cricket in the Lee household.

I was eight when I first played in a competition. It was Kanga Cricket, a modified game using a soft ball. According to Mum I was at my hyperactive best; I'd bowl, then chase the ball no matter where it went. I can't recall much about it, but how can I forget the other games of the time? We had two venues: a driveway leading to the garage at the side of the house; and the backyard that was initially grass, but Dad eventually paved it after we pleaded with him to find a solution to the boggy patches that hampered us in winter.

We played all year round, year after year. The earliest contests were very one-sided. Shane was the self-appointed captain, coach, umpire, and scorer. He was also a very big cheat. When we played on the driveway, the garage's roller door was the 'wicketkeeper'. Shane used to bat for ages, and often after he nicked a ball, he'd deny it, so I'd run inside and whinge to Mum who was the 'third umpire'. Finally when I did get to bat, Shane would clean me up in a couple of balls, and I'd go crying to Mum again. But as we got older, and Grant also began to play, I got one or two back on big brother. Shane and I were very competitive, and in trying to outdo each other we'd have our share of blues. Grant was always much quieter and accepting.

When the driveway matches were in full swing, we'd open the boundary gates and begin our run-ups on the opposite side of the road. After a look each way to avoid traffic, we'd charge about 15 metres up a slight slope and hurl down a half-taped-up tennis ball. Those sessions introduced me to long run-ups and bowling as fast as I could. The most vicious deliveries were those that hit the rubber joints between the concrete squares; I enjoyed the ones that reared up and hit someone on the throat. The 'wicketkeeper' copped the most punishment; we wore out one roller door, and the second was well on the way to being battered by the time we moved on to bigger venues.

Our backyard cricket, where we didn't have space for run-ups, was different. We used brand new tennis balls on a surface that had really good bounce. Instead of bowling, we threw the balls as hard as we could while imparting various types of spin. I often wore a box and a helmet, and when we sneaked a six-stitcher into play, I used to wear about three or four thigh pads as well. I was scared of the ball and hated getting hit, and still do! As a precaution, we covered the house's windows with foam boogie boards. The whack of a ball into a wall was enough to fire Mum up. Sometimes H showed her bravery by hanging out the washing while balls whizzed past her head; at other times we took off the washing and dumped it on the ground, or folded up the line with the clothes still on it.

Although she never said anything, Mum must have tired of us pinching stockings from her drawer. We'd put a ball in them, suspend them like a pendulum from the clothes line, and practise our batting. The salespeople in the shops at nearby Warilla Grove must have thought Mum had a fetish, considering she seemed to buy stockings every week. At least she didn't say: 'I get them for my sons.' When time allowed, nothing ever really got in the way of us playing. Even at night we simply put on the house's back lights and continued.

We compiled statistics from all the 'home' games we played. First, they were kept on pieces of paper, but when Mum and Dad bought us a Commodore 64 computer our records were much more detailed. Not surprisingly, Shane had the most impressive ratings. This wasn't only because he was bigger and stronger, but also because his cheating served him really well.

After playing Kanga Cricket for a year I joined up with the Oak Flats Rats Under-10s. It might seem strange to say it, but my very first match had a bearing on my future. On a windy morning in Kiama, a coastal town further south, I came flying in to bowl off a long run-up, probably about 15 steps. At that stage I was a skinny kid of average height with big feet that earned me my first nickname, Daffy. Mum remembers my face glowed bright red with all the effort I put in. After just one over I was lucky enough to have six wickets, all bowled by full tosses or yorkers. From that moment on I wanted to be a fast bowler. In another match the same season against Gerringong, some parents complained to my coach Graeme Creighton that I was too quick and it was unfair on the batsman. It would have been easy for Graeme to ask me to slow down, but I am grateful he always encouraged me, even if it meant copping a few blasts from the supporters of rival teams.

I just loved bowling fast. Maybe I had a long run-up because I had so much energy to burn, or maybe I'd been conditioned by bowling so hard to Shane. Whatever the reason, there's no doubt by the time I got to the crease I just wanted to get the ball to the other end flat-out. Even at that age I felt a certain sense of power; it was great fun shattering stumps, especially when the batsmen backed away.

I claimed my first scalp of another kind when I was about 12. At an Oak Flats nets session I bowled a bouncer to a new boy at the club. The ball smacked into his mouth, and from memory, it knocked some teeth out. There was blood everywhere. I was pretty upset. Dad rang up the poor guy's parents and offered to pay the dental bill, but they accepted it was just one of those things. I'll never forget his name: Wesley Croft.

By then, I'd followed Shane's lead and had played for the NSW PSSA team, an honour Grant also went on to achieve. I reckon Grant was easily the best cricketer in the family. When I got a bit older and faster I'd bowl bouncers to him at the local nets. It didn't worry him that I'd bowl no balls; he'd just smoke me! I'm convinced if he'd wanted to go down the cricket route he could have been anything, but he developed another passion that eventually grew on me, and is one of the most important parts of my life today: music.

We used to have an upright piano that we'd crowd around and listen to Mum play at Christmas times. She tried to teach us, but I had a really short attention span and usually went off doing other things. Grant, however, picked it up really quickly. He had a natural ear. One day he heard an ad on TV that had a really catchy jingle. He went to the piano and within minutes he'd copied the tune. Soon enough he was having formal piano lessons, and about 12 months later he was playing classical pieces. Some of my favourite memories are of Dad coming home after work and resting on Shane's bed at the back of the house while Grant played Mozart. There were also the days when he pulled out an Elvis record and lay back to 'Blue Suede Shoes' or 'Love Me Tender'.

The Doctor initially didn't know much about cricket. He played little of it when he was growing up, but he did have a brush with fame when West Indian Wes Hall put on a fast bowling display at his school oval in Cairns. Dad reckons Wes just ambled in, let the ball go and broke two stumps. At the time

15

Hall had come to Queensland to play the 1961–62 Sheffield Shield season.

Dad spent endless afternoons with Shane, Grant and me at the local nets at Panorama Oval which was just a few minutes' drive from home. It was also directly opposite the Balarang Primary School which all three Lee boys attended. Admittedly I wasn't the best of students, but I did have a strong conviction that ensured I worked hard outside of school hours. From the age of 10 I knew I was going to play for Australia. Yes, it was a dream, but I also believed it was my destiny. That probably sounds egotistical, but it's true. It's also very hard to explain; I can only say it was just the way I felt.

The nets became our second home. Dad would drive us down in the Sigma, with Uncle Les often in the front seat, all three boys in the back, and a boot full of cricket gear. At first Dad tried to bowl fast to us. It was a picture you'd never see in a coaching manual: a bloke wearing thongs, faded Stubbies and a T-shirt, running in and double-winding his action before letting the ball go. Meanwhile Uncle Les would stand at the crease and toss up donkey drops. When Dad realised the deliveries weren't the ideal practice for us, he resorted to throwing from half the length of the pitch. Over the years he must have hurled thousands and thousands of balls at us. We used 'corkies' (compound cork balls), the types that, when brand new, left good 'cherries' on the bat. I had a Gray-Nicolls Scoop which only had marks in the middle, giving the impression that I was a good batsman. The truth was I regularly cleaned off all the blemishes on the edges with a rag and a good squirt of Mr Sheen.

I didn't like batting, though. I was so afraid of the ball that I nearly always backed away. Dad responded without any sympathy at all. He'd say sternly: 'You can't do that. Don't step back. Get up and do it again!' 'But I can't,' I'd reply. 'Yes you can. You know you can. Go on, try again.'

I never once heard Dad say: 'Oh bad luck, mate, never mind.' That doesn't mean he forced me or my brothers to do anything, but once he realised we wanted to do as well as we could, he tried to help us the best way he knew how. And while doing this, he learnt more about cricket. He didn't read any coaching manuals but he watched very closely and analysed play whether it was in the nets or Test matches on television. He picked up on simple but important things, like a straight bat had more chance of hitting a ball than a cross bat. Above all else, he instilled a strong sense of self-belief in all of us. We weren't cocky, but because of the Doctor we grew into kids who weren't afraid to back ourselves.

Perhaps it won't be until my own son, Preston, grows a little older that I will truly appreciate all the work that Mum and Dad and many other relations put into raising me and my brothers. When Grant started playing junior cricket the Lee household on Saturday mornings turned into a taxi rank, with boys and bats going in all directions. Sometimes we needed three cars to take us to matches: Mum and Dad would each use theirs, and generally Ma and Pa would provide the third vehicle. No matter where the Lee boys were playing, Mum and Dad thought it was important that some member of the family was always there watching and supporting us.

While doing research for this book, I was reminded by Mum of one story that sums up how much of an effort was made. I can't recall what the exact event was, but at some stage I was playing in a week-long tournament at Waitara Oval in Sydney's northern suburbs. I had to be at the ground at eight o'clock each morning, which meant I had to leave home by about 4.30-ish. Every day Mum drove me up and back, three hours each way.

17

Once we arrived home I had a shower, ate dinner, and went to bed while Mum stayed up to wash my clothes. Then, the next morning she'd be up at about three o'clock to prepare lunches and drinks for the day. I used to take that all for granted, but now, all these years later, I look back and realise how incredibly lucky Shane, Grant and I were.

3

I was in my early teens when I went through the 'homey' period of my life: the baggy jeans, cap on backwards, listening to rap and R&B music and thinking I was really cool. At the time I thought one of my best achievements was winning a dance competition at the Lake Illawarra Blue Light disco. My trophy was a *Tucker's Daughter* CD by Ian Moss. Another notable step through my early adolescence was hanging out at the Dapto Roller Rink with Grant, my cousins Luke and Nathan, and good mate Adam Rainford. The rink placed discount coupons in the local paper, the *Lake Times*, so we used to steal the papers from front yards, cut out the coupons, and have an endless supply of cheap skate hires, hot dogs and Cokes. We did the same for Laser Maze, a game in a partitioned warehouse full of artificial smoke where you shot your opponents with lasers. Always keen for a bargain, we were also regular customers at Pizza Hut for the 'Five dollar, all you can eat' nights. I claimed the record for our group: 17 pieces of ham and pineapple pizza in the one sitting. I felt really sick afterwards.

While gorging pizza showed my competitive nature, ten-pin bowling displayed another characteristic of mine: the need for speed. At the Shellharbour Bowl where Mum, an excellent bowler, once scored a 250 game, I was more interested in hurling the ball fast than knocking over pins. After every release I'd look at the numbers recorded by a speed gun: 40 kilometres an hour was my target. It's funny to think that a few years later a different style of bowling would have me striving for 160 kays. To me, whether it's bowling in ten-pin or cricket, driving a ball down a golf course, serving at tennis, or going for a run, it's all about fastest and furthest. Some friends call me an extremist because there is no middle ground; it's either go flat-out and hard, or not go at all.

By this stage of my teens, cricket had become the focus of my life outside of family. Sometimes when walking home from Oak Flats High, Adam Rainford and I stopped on a hill overlooking the school. We'd spend hours there talking about our dreams. Adam had a lot of patience because he never tired of me saying I wanted to play for Australia. It helped that Shane was doing so well. He was only in Year 8 at Oak Flats High when he was picked as a fast bowling all-rounder in the NSW Combined High Schools second XI. He made the firsts for the four years after that in a period that also saw him picked for the Australian Under-17s and a national Under-19 development squad that included Ricky Ponting. Shane's achievements became an extra motivator for me; whatever big brother did, I wanted to do as well.

There were occasions when I momentarily stepped out of Shane's shadow. One day, while having a net session at a multi-sports centre near our home, Shane and I were invited to fill in for an indoor cricket team that was missing two players. Shane immediately asked if I could open the bowling. I'm sure many of you will know what a brand new indoor ball is like: a hard tennis ball encased in a yellow leather shell that's heavily lacquered. It can swing madly and bust fingers or bruise you badly if it hits you. It was only the first or second delivery of the match when I pushed off the back netting and let one fly. The ball caught the batsman's edge, and smacked into the wicketkeeper's nose. As with the Wesley Croft incident only a year or so earlier, the sight of blood and a guy reeling in pain shocked me. I can't recall playing on.

The country grapevine helped spread the message that I was fast, and a significant moment came while I was a member of the cricket program at the Illawarra Academy of Sport at Wollongong. I was only 13 when the coaching co-ordinator Bruce Jones contacted the head of junior coaching at the NSW Cricket Association, Alan Campbell. I was ear-marked as 'one to watch'.

I was also 13 when I started playing lower grades for Oak Flats in the South Coast men's competition. If my memory serves me right I took two wickets on debut bowling first change against Shellharbour in either seconds or thirds. I batted at number 11, and found that was even too high a position for a kid playing against blokes two and three times his age on bouncy synthetic pitches. I don't think I've ever been more scared of the ball. Mum and Dad ended up pulling me out after a couple of games but I returned the following year.

The men's matches weren't the only time I played above my age. When I first made the Oak Flats High XI, I think in Year 8, I gave away a few years to most of the other guys. It was here I first played in a team with Shane when we took on a touring English side from Petersborough. Shane hammered a century and I took a couple of wickets.

My development moved up a gear after I experienced a growth spurt when I was about 15. In the space of a few months it seemed my body had grown into its size 12 feet. Taller and stronger, I found I was able to bowl much quicker, but there were some worrying signs that accompanied that. Ever since Shane had first taught me to bowl in the backyard, I'd never paid close attention to my action; I simply ran in fast and bowled fast. But after being selected to attend a coaching clinic for young pacemen in Sydney I came under the scrutiny of Dennis Lillee. D. K. Lillee! The Master! Like so many other cricket-mad kids I'd seen the footage of Dennis and Jeff Thomson carving up the world's best batsmen in the 1970s and early '80s. No matter how great the players may be in cricket's future, there will always be a special place for 'Lillee 'n' Thomson'. They had an aura about them. So, to bowl in front of Dennis wasn't only a fantastic opportunity for me, but also nerve-racking. I think I did well because Dennis still remembers that I broke a stump, but more importantly, he gave me advice that I was too young and naive to acknowledge properly. He said I needed to work on my action because it was 'mixed'; at the point of delivery my legs were side-on but my chest was front-on, meaning my hips were counter-rotating and putting extreme pressure on my lower back, which was forced to twist rapidly. Dennis said my action put me in danger of breaking down with back problems within three or four years. I was disappointed I hadn't received a glowing report, yet I returned home and didn't give too much thought to what I'd been told. After all, at 15 we're invincible, aren't we?

One year later I was given reason to think again. It was January 1993, a really exciting time for the Lee family. While Shane was closing in on making his NSW debut in both the limited-overs Mercantile Mutual Cup and Sheffield Shield, I was in Hobart to play for the Blues in the national Under-17 championships. During a pre-carnival camp some of my teammates and I decided to have a throwing competition. I was used to such challenges; I'd already competed at state and Australian titles as a javelin thrower, so maybe I had an advantage. But it proved to be a stupid thing to do because in trying to beat each other we pushed our arms to the limit, and I firmly believe what followed had a huge impact on the rest of my career, including my eventual retirement from Test cricket.

By the time we'd finished the throwing contest my arm was quite sore. I didn't have any problems with it until we were playing a semifinal against Queensland. I chased a ball to the boundary and needed to get in a sharp return because the batsmen were going for a fourth run on a big field. I loaded up, let the ball go, and crack! The sound was so loud that people in the grandstand heard it. I immediately felt pins and needles all the way along my arm which soon puffed up into an angry red colour. Mum and Dad, who were watching, took me straight to hospital. After examining the X-rays, doctors told me I had either snapped or torn a tendon. They said I had to keep my arm in a sling for a month but it didn't need to be plastered. I barely played again that season.

The pain continued after I removed the sling, and even months later the aching woke me up at night. After discussing it with Mum and Dad we assumed a full recovery was just going to take a long time. However, when I was still struggling about a year after I'd suffered the injury, I went and had another X-ray. The result shocked us all: I had a fracture through the ulna, one of the two main bones in the arm. There was complete separation of the bone. That wasn't the only surprise: the new X-rays were virtually identical to the ones I had taken in Hobart. Put simply, my injury had originally been misdiagnosed. Scar tissue had begun to grow through and around the crack, meaning I couldn't fully straighten my arm. In all, I'd lost about 10 degrees of flexibility.

The specialist gave me two choices: I could have the arm rebroken and reset, or I could just put up with it the way it was. I weighed up all the pros and cons with Dad, who suggested further fiddling with the arm could affect my bowling, so we decided not to have the operation. That meant I would have days when the arm was stiff and painful, but it was nothing I couldn't overcome. It also forced me to modify my training, especially weights work where tricep and bicep exercises had to be carefully managed. Now, all these years later I'm still annoyed about the misdiagnosis. I had a number of arm injuries throughout my career, and I still wonder if these were a result of a possible weakness in my arm that might not have been there if I'd initially received correct treatment. The fact I couldn't straighten my arm also played a role in one of the most distressing moments in my career, which we'll come to later.

I'd just started Year 12 when I had the second set of X-rays taken. By then, I had no doubt where my future lay. Two years earlier I did work experience as a carpenter at Martin's Joinery at Oak Flats, and then accepted a job there during summer holidays. Most of my time was spent assembling kitchen cupboards. Who knows if I inherited any carpentry skills from Grandad, but I certainly enjoyed using my hands. I couldn't draw or paint but I loved making things. However, the thought of pursuing this as a career never entered my mind. I only had one preference: I was going to be a professional cricketer, simple as that. I'd already represented NSW Combined High Schools three times, and didn't feel the need to pay much attention to school studies. My biology teacher, Mrs Navin, was one who became understandably frustrated with me. I still remember her exact words after I'd tried to spin a basketball on the top of my finger only to see it knock a whole row of beakers off a shelf. 'If you don't study you're never going to get anywhere in life,' she said.

A few years ago I caught up with my former teacher when I returned to Oak Flats High to talk with students. She said she'd never meant to pick on me. I hugged her and told her I deserved it.

Another teacher was more on my side. In Year 11 I was playing basketball with some mates during the lunch break when a ball from a rival group rolled into our territory. I picked it up and did the only thing we ever did in this situation: I booted it away as far as I could. I didn't give any consideration to the direction, and when the ball rocketed towards a window of the school hall I could only think: 'Oh shit!' It wasn't so much the impending breakage that worried me but my timing was a shocker because the hall was filled with students doing a Higher School Certificate exam. I watched the ball smash the window and knock all the papers off someone's desk. I knew exactly what to do: I bolted away from the crime scene, but a teacher, Mr Trist, still found me.

'Was that you?' he asked.

'Yes, Tristy.'

'All right, get out of here. I'll cover for you.'

Unexpected deeds can happen at unexpected times. Thanks, Tristy.

Towards the end of Year 11, my devotion to cricket steered me further away from school priorities when I joined Campbelltown to play in the Sydney Cricket Association men's grade competition. Shane had been with the 'Ghosts' for a couple of years, so I came to be known as 'Shane Lee's brother' and also earned the nickname 'Bing' in reference to the Bing Lee electrical goods chain of stores. I was nearly 17 years old and to those just getting to know me I was a contradiction, a Dr Jekyll and Mr Hyde. I was quite shy and polite and didn't talk to many people off the field, but when I had a ball in my hand in either a game or at a net session, a switch flicked that turned me into a fired-up, cocky kid who believed he had a gold pass because he could bowl with serious heat. I imagined myself becoming another 'White Lightning', like South Africa's great fast bowler of the time, Allan Donald, who'd become my idol. I loved the way he charged to the wicket, bent his back every single ball, and shook up a lot of batsmen along the way. It was this period that definitely established my reputation as a fast bowler. Until then, I had mostly been sheltered by doing well against guys my own age, but now I had to step up and show I belonged among men in a competition that included Australian and NSW players.

I left an impression at my very first training session, although the memory still sickens me. Bowling at an indoor facility with synthetic pitches, I was given a new ball to try out against first-grade bowler and lower-order batsman Troy Crosland. On about my third delivery I decided to dig one in short; the ball took off and smacked into the side of Troy's head. At first I thought his helmet had saved him, but the ball crashed through the protection and broke his jaw. Not only did I sideline Troy for a considerable time, but his jaw needed wiring and he was forced to suck his food through a straw for several weeks. In a cruel twist I ended up taking Troy's position in the top team; it was a horrible way to begin my grade career.

Causing injuries is an unfortunate product of fast bowling. Over the years, I've broken batsmen's feet, fingers, arms, ribs, jaws and more. I've never enjoyed doing that, but I'd be lying if I said I didn't like scaring batsmen. As a kid finding his way in grade, I thought my best way to survive against the men was to take them on, head on. At that stage I only bowled two lengths: either yorker or bouncer. The other weapon I had – or I thought it was a weapon – was sledging. It was the standard sort of stuff: 'I'm going to knock your head off', or 'You'd better nick one and get out or you'll be taking a trip to hospital'. To the experienced grade players I suppose I could have been viewed as an arrogant little shit. That's why pace was so important to me. If a batsman came out and had a few words to me I'd whizz a few around his head to try to shut him up. I may not have been as tall or as strong as my opponents, but I felt pace gave me power over them.

Sometimes my approach worked, and at other times I looked like an idiot. In one game, I can't remember if it was in my first or second season, I sledged a batsman who happened to be a police officer. I'd barraged him with bouncers and verbals, then gave him a send-off after I got him out. At the end of the day he wanted to start an argument with me as I walked off the field. I apologised by saying I was only having a bit of fun, but this guy was angry. I actually felt intimidated and unsure of what to do until Dad intervened with a clichéd but effective line: 'Come on, mate, he's only a kid and it's just a game.'

Maybe my ego sometimes got the better of me, but on the field I never wanted to back down. It was only experience from playing that eventually taught me where to draw the line. In that first season one of the more famous batsmen I came up against was NSW wicketkeeper Phil Emery, who played for Gordon. He rated me the fastest bowler he'd faced in grade since taking on Test player Geoff Lawson at his peak in the 1980s. I took 4-56 against Gordon, my best haul for the season, but I most remember a wicketless day against a Randwick team that included state players Rod Davison, Martin Haywood and Richard Chee Quee. In about the third over I bowled a good length ball that kicked up and brushed 'Cheeks's glove and he was caught behind. I'd almost run through to the slips cordon in celebration before I realised the umpire had called no ball. I immediately turned to Cheeks and told him: 'You're . . . lucky, and I'll . . . get you next time . . .' I'll leave it up to your imagination to fill in the blanks.

Cheeks hopped back into me by saying I wasn't good enough and should get back to my mark and stop cheating. That made me angry, and it was game on! Cheeks eventually won the battle, but he acknowledged afterwards it was the fastest spell he'd ever faced.

I also sledged 'Moose' (Martin Haywood) after he edged a ball that was dropped in the slips. The next delivery I tried to york him, but my feet slipped at the crease and I ended up launching a waist-high full toss that hit his glove. It broke a bone or two and put Moose out of a few Sheffield Shield games. Some people watching might have thought I was so fired up that I'd meant to bowl that delivery, but I've never purposely sent down a beamer in my life. Unfortunately I was criticised later in my career for launching similar balls during international matches.

Since that grade game, I've become good mates with Moose and Cheeks. That is the greatest part of cricket, or sport in general: no matter how hard a game may be played, its true worth is in the friendships that form off the field. However, as a teenager in a hurry to impress, I didn't fully understand or appreciate that.

Despite the intensity of some contests, there were others that were pure comedy. At such an impressionable age I decided to emulate my fast bowling teammate Matthew 'Mad Dog' McMahon. Although he used to be quick and could intimidate as well as anyone, it was his batting that influenced me. He generally tried to slog the first ball he faced, and not being one to want to hang around and cop any short stuff, I thought that was a very good approach: hit out or get out. So I adopted the strategy of taking guard on or outside leg stump, and giving my opposition bowlers a clear view of my castle. By doing so, I hoped they'd sense an easy kill and aim for the blockhole. But that played into my hands because the moment they let the ball go I'd already be charging down the pitch and ready to swing wildly. The best results were boundaries back over the bowler's head, or edges flying over the slips for four. The flipside led to a long walk back to the stands. I seemed to get away with the tactic for at least a year until Shane revealed what I did on the Channel Nine television program *A Current Affair*, which did a story on the three cricketing Lee brothers. Maybe I imagined it, but from that moment on I swear I didn't receive many first-up full tosses.

I took 14 wickets in my initial season. The Campbelltown 1993–94 yearbook noted I had 'genuine pace which will worry all batsmen in years to come'. Looking back it blows me away to think I played first grade at such a young age; it's an achievement that I'm very, very proud of. It couldn't have been done without my parents who not only came to every match but drove me the hour to and from training at least twice a week. If Dad had been on night shift the trips must have seemed extra long to him. However, he soon worked out a way to counter this, although it's one I don't recommend. My coming of age to the grade ranks also coincided with me learning to drive, so the Doctor thought nothing of hopping into the passenger seat of the old manual Sigma while I got behind the steering wheel. The only problem was that Dad took a pillow with him and was often asleep with his head against the window by the time we left Mount Warrigal. Despite my jitters, we never had any problems, but I do recall getting some disapproving looks from other drivers, especially the day I pulled up at a set of traffic lights to find a truckie staring down at me in disgust. He did have a point because it was pouring rain, and I'd been inching my way through patches of fog.

During that season I was lucky enough to be invited to the Sydney Cricket Ground to be a net bowler for the Australian team the day before a limited-overs international. I couldn't believe who was there: the Waugh twins, Mark Taylor, Ian Healy, Shane Warne, Glenn McGrath and Damien Fleming, among others. I was more nervous than I'd ever been in a match, especially when I stepped out my run-up and stopped level with Craig McDermott who was standing at the top of his mark. I kept stealing looks at him, thinking: 'He is bloody massive!' If that didn't make me anxious enough, the sight of David Boon walking into the net certainly did. When I pushed off for my first delivery my legs felt like jelly. Moments later I felt about a foot tall as the brand new white ball left my hand and hooped straight into the off-side net about halfway towards Boonie. He picked up the ball and gave me a look of disdain as though to say: 'Good job whoever picked this punk!' My next delivery was even worse: I over-compensated for the swing and hit the leg-side net. Shit! Boonie gave me another look that made me feel even smaller.

As I walked back to my mark I was angry and told myself there was no reason to be nervous and I should fire up and have a go. The next ball did the trick: an inswinger on a good length that ripped the pegs out. A few Australian players cracked up: 'He's got ya, Babs!' Boonie kicked his stumps and swore before he flung the ball back at me. I couldn't hide a grin from ear to ear. From that ball on I was fully pumped, and by the end of the session I'd also bowled Mark Waugh. I was smacked a fair few times as well, but why care about that after I'd claimed a couple of Test scalps?

That wasn't the only time in my junior years I came across the elite players. About a year or two later, I was invited to be a general room attendant and runner for the Australian team during one afternoon of a Test match. I was so overwhelmed by getting the opportunity I can't even remember who the opponents were. But I do remember that Steve Waugh gave me one of his shirts to wear. At the end of the day I gave it back to him, but he told me I could keep it. Then, just as I was about to walk away he said: 'No, actually you can give it back to me, because if you work hard enough I reckon you'll get one of your own one day.'

Away from cricket I was a typical teenager fitting in sport, school and social activities, which sometimes required keeping secrets from Mum and Dad. My first hangover came after a night of drinking port and lemonade with Adam Rainford. That drink became my favourite during the school party years. At about this time I also had a new 'hobby'. I'm a bit sketchy on the details; then again, maybe I just don't want to say too much about it for fear of embarrassment. It began when a woman approached me at a local shopping centre and asked me if I'd ever considered doing some modelling. Admittedly, I used to muck around posing for photos taken by Nadine Rainford, Adam's sister. It was just a bit of fun, but it became more serious when I was asked to join an agency. I wasn't keen on the idea after I was told I needed to submit some composition cards that would cost about $200. I refused, but I still ended up getting some work, including a fashion parade on a catwalk in Sydney. My first appearance was in a TV commercial for the shopping centre Shellharbour Square. When the ad appeared on the box I played a 'blink and you miss it' role carrying a container of Valvoline motor oil across the screen at the back of shot. I reckon I was ahead of my time because 15 years later

Valvoline signed up Ricky Ponting to do some commercials with John Laws.

Not long after doing that first ad I was involved in a brochure shoot for the Bradman Museum in Bowral. The photo itself was a wonderful memory because I had to stand dressed in cricket whites next to a statue of Sir Donald. I was very self-conscious when I was asked to adopt particular modelling poses, most of them serious. A few months later I received a signed photo from the man himself: 'To Brett, Best Wishes, Don Bradman.' That was even better than winning the *Tucker's Daughter* CD!

Whether or not I took my modelling seriously, my brief encounters gave me a greater understanding about the importance of presentation. I have always taken pride in the way I've looked. Some might say it's vanity or displaying the tendencies of the so-called metrosexual, but I simply think that a person who presents himself well has some self-respect. As a teenager with little money I had to think smart about the way I did things. Back then, if you had a $15 white JAG T-shirt you were the coolest kid in school. However, 15 bucks wasn't cheap, so I adopted the mindset that I didn't need to have the fashionable brands to look good. After all, most of the time people couldn't even see the brand's tag, so they wouldn't know who was wearing what. As a result, my cousin Luke and I used to go shopping in Kmart to buy all our clothes. It wasn't hard. For example, we'd buy a four-dollar white T-shirt and funk that up by getting an eight-dollar light-blue long-sleeved shirt to put over the top, then we'd roll up the sleeves, undo a couple of buttons and that was it.

My interest in bargain hunting for clothes took on new meaning after I was chosen in the Australian Under-19 team to tour India in early 1994. While away I bought about 15 pairs of jeans. However, I didn't take into account the 11 kilograms

I'd lose on that trip; after I'd returned home and regained the weight I couldn't even do up the zippers, so I gave my sub-continental wardrobe to Luke.

The tour to India was an amazing experience. I was surprised to be picked because I'd only turned 17 a few months earlier, and hadn't even gone to the Australian Under-19 championships from which national teams in that age group were traditionally chosen. I was still eligible to play Under-17s, but somehow it was decided I was ready to take a leap up. So, I boarded a flight for my first overseas trip with players including future Test stars Jason Gillespie, Matt Nicholson, Mike Hussey and Andrew Symonds, and my Campbelltown and future NSW teammate Corey Richards.

It's difficult to describe India and its workings to someone who has never been there. You can see some awful things: beggars affected by leprosy, polio or other sicknesses; and children living in the streets and fossicking from garbage to make a living. There are the sickening smells and invasions of personal space that challenge you from the moment you get through airport customs, and you have to be sensible about what you eat and drink, and what you touch. Alternately, there is so much colour and diversity that you could go back to India every day for as long as you lived and experience something different every single time. In India, anything can happen, and usually does; that's why I love it so much, and will never tire of going there.

Among my memories from that first trip was the time I caught a tuk-tuk – a motorised rickshaw – to training. I can't recall who I was with or in which city we were, but I do clearly remember the music the driver played on his cassette recorder. As we whizzed in and out of traffic with legs and cricket gear hanging out the sides of a vehicle smoking like a green log, there was one particular song that struck me. I asked the driver what it was; he had to repeat his answer a few times, more slowly on each occasion, before I finally heard it properly.

'Muqabala,' he said.

He told me it was a very famous song about men fighting over a woman. Although he was surprised when I asked if I could buy it, he sold it to me for 10 rupees – about 30 cents. In a twist I could never have expected at the time, I sang part of that song 10 years later on the top rating Indian television talk show, *Rendezvous*.

One of my strongest memories from the Under-19 tour is not as pleasant. It was so hot during one match that at the top of my mark I kept satchels of water to drink between deliveries. At the end of the day I headed straight for the showers, not caring that even the coolest water seemed warm. Until that point I'd been careful to drink only purified water, but in a lapse brought on by exhaustion I threw my head back in the shower and opened my mouth wide. Within a couple of swallows I realised my mistake. I immediately put two fingers down my throat and tried to vomit up the water, but that didn't work. A couple of hours later I had a close association with the toilet in my hotel room. I ended up having 38 vomits. I know this because my room-mate Jason Gillespie thoughtfully ticked them off. My normal weight hovered between 80 and 85 kilograms, a long way from the 69 I plummeted to. It was the sickest I've ever been, and I didn't fully recover until some months later when I was back in Australia.

I played in all three 'Tests' on that Under-19 tour; the series was drawn one-all, and my best performance came in the final match in Bombay (now Mumbai) when I took four wickets in each innings. In another game I did something I'm not proud of: I purposely ran through the crease and bowled a ball with the intention of hitting a batsman who'd been frustrating us – and angering me – by hanging around. I collected him under the ribs, he fell, was taken off to receive treatment, and we ended up winning the game. There was no excuse for my behaviour; it showed how immature I still was, and how much I still had to learn about myself and cricket.

My immaturity was much better kept to pranks with my teammates. Unlike in Australia, fireworks can be bought throughout India. I love fireworks, and the prospect of having a constant supply of them was too much to resist. My favourites were the inch-long ones called Crazy Jacks. They made a really big bang like the old Australian Tom Thumbs. I don't think 'Dizzy' – Jason Gillespie – will ever forget the day I sneaked into the bathroom while he was having a shower. A quick strike of a match and a strategic roll of the Crazy Jack ended in a bang which sent Dizzy falling through the shower curtain. I knew I was vulnerable next time I had a shower, but protected myself by locking the door. However, that didn't stop an angry six-foot-six gangly fast bowler seeking revenge. Over the years I've always known when Dizzy is planning mischief because he can't hide a hissing laugh that sounds like a wheezy 'hee-hee-hee'. After I heard that sound when in the shower I knew something was about to happen. I looked towards the door and saw on the slate floor a reflection of Dizzy about to light a Crazy Jack on the other side. I quickly grabbed a towel and twisted it into a makeshift bat. When the fizzing firework came under the door I hit it back with the towel just in time for it to explode at Dizzy's feet. Surprise, surprise, he wasn't happy!

The two-month-long tour was really good for me. Apart from playing cricket in a different country and adapting to its culture, I had to live in a touring environment with guys who seemed so much older and more mature than me. I also had to overcome bouts of homesickness, and crucially, I had to try to fit in Higher School Certificate studies. In an agreement with my principal I took my books with me, but I must admit I barely looked at them. By the time I finished exams later in the year I'd already experienced another place of learning that I was much better suited to.

4

I was in Year 12 when I first went to the Commonwealth Bank Cricket Academy, Australia's nursery for future Test and first class players. I'd been awarded a Tier Two Scholarship which enabled me to spend a fortnight at the live-in facility in Adelaide. My stay was made much easier by Shane being there as a full-time resident. His chief contribution to my curriculum was an invitation to go out on a Saturday night with him and some of his academy mates. Spending time with guys I aspired to be like seemed a great idea to me. We arrived at our chosen venue, The Players Bar, which was part-owned by Australian off-spinner Tim May. Shane and the others walked in without the bouncer giving them a second look, but it was a different story for me who was at the end of the line.

'You got ID?' asked the bouncer.

'No, sorry I left it at home,' I lied.

Being only 17, I didn't actually have an ID, and the fact I hadn't even graduated to peach fuzz on my face made me look even younger. There was no way I was going to be allowed in. Shane and company had already disappeared into the club, leaving me to fend for myself with no ID, no phone and no money. I weighed up my options and decided there was only one thing to do: I ran the 10 or so kilometres back to the academy at Henley Beach, and all the way I was scared I'd be stopped and bashed or something else would happen to me; for a Mount Warrigal boy, Adelaide was a big city.

After returning to my home town I managed to finish the HSC without setting the scoreboard alight! Then I went into the 1994–95 season of grade with Campbelltown, and a number of representative commitments for the Australian Under-19s, NSW Under-19s, and NSW Colts. I also played for the academy against our Kiwi counterparts in Hamilton, New Zealand, in a match that was given first-class status. For the trivia buffs, I took 1-48 and 3-71 in our ten-wicket win.

Although I was very focused on cricket, there were times when my need to be a typical bloke who'd reached the legal drinking age competed with my dedication to sport. Dad, however, had his ways of making sure I didn't stray too far. On the night before one match, I wanted to go out with Adam Rainford.

'What time will you be home?' asked the Doctor.

'About 10.30, 11 at the latest,' I replied.

'No worries then, that's OK. You can have a couple of drinks but just remember your game tomorrow.'

Adam and I eventually arrived home at about 1.30 in the morning. We weren't drunk, but we knew we'd be in trouble if we were caught. We got out of the taxi, and sneaked towards the driveway gate that had a really squeaky latch. We didn't want to make any noise, so we decided to climb the gate, but as we were halfway over it, a voice boomed out: 'Right! What do you think you're doing?!' It was Dad. He'd been waiting in the lounge room for us to come home. It scared the life out of Adam and me, but the Doctor got a good laugh out of it. Not surprisingly I didn't make the same mistake again.

After finishing the season I returned to the Cricket Academy as a full-time student for six months. I felt privileged to think I was following in the footsteps of Shane. In all, there was a long list of stars who'd been there before me: Ricky Ponting, Michael Slater, Shane Warne, Michael Bevan, Greg Blewett, Brendon Julian, Damien Martyn, Andrew Symonds, Michael Kasprowicz and Glenn McGrath. Those players seemed in another world to me; if I'd been told I'd be playing with and against them within a few years, I wouldn't have believed it. The 14-strong class of '95 included four future Test players: myself, Mike Hussey, Jason Gillespie and Matt Nicholson. All but one of the other 10 went on to play first-class cricket.

We had a six-day training week, with Sunday a rest day. Morning sessions were generally for fitness and strength work, while the afternoons were cricket specific. We also had broader classes about life skills such as financial management, media training, and Toastmasters public speaking. Accommodation and food were free, but we were still paid about $60 a month which went towards buying personal items, clothes, and nights out at the weekend. I was keen to add to my bank balance, and so the academy helped arrange a job for me at Pike Constructions. I worked there five days a week. When morning training finished at about 10 o'clock, I'd ride my pushbike 10 or more kilometres to various building sites where I'd dig holes and trenches, and carry equipment for four hours. I'd then ride back for training, and be in bed early most nights because I was so tired. The first week of doing this killed me; my muscles ached and I had blisters on my hands. But I soon got used to it and grew to relish the work because it gave me greater stamina and strength.

Rod Marsh was the academy's head coach, although much of my time was spent under the direction of specialist fast bowling coach, Richard Done, who hammered into all the quicks the importance of 'front arm up, pull it down hard, and follow through'. To me, the most notable improver was Jason Gillespie. On the Under-19 tour to India the previous year he was a gentle seam-up first change bowler, but during his stint at the academy his action seemed to click and almost overnight he was transformed into this really quick bowler who could kick the ball off a good length. His confidence lifted and I reckon he became the most difficult of all players to face at the academy.

My progress was different. Despite the specialist guidance, nine times out of 10 I'd run in and deliver the ball on instinct. There wasn't much thought or structure in my bowling, and that's the way it stayed until I was in my mid-20s, and already in the Test team. My biggest improvement came in my batting. When I went to the academy I was a slogger who backed away from the ball, but Rod Marsh worked and worked on me. At first he said something simple that I'd never really considered: if selectors had to choose between two bowlers of similar ability they'd always go for the one who was the better batsman. Rod spent hours feeding me balls and fine-tuning my technique. I really liked his approach. If I was playing badly he wouldn't hide his thoughts, and alternately if I was doing well he'd be full of encouragement. He was an honest bloke, hard but fair. He also had his own sense of humour, especially when he sprang surprise fitness sessions on a Saturday morning, knowing some of us might have had a late Friday night on the town.

Social outings from the academy led to some unexpected results. One Saturday I went with some of my classmates to a local shopping centre. I had no intention of doing what they had planned, but by the time I rang Mum that night I'd followed their lead.

'What would you think if I ever got an earring?' I asked H.

There was a moment's silence before Mum replied: 'You went and got your ear pierced today, didn't you?'

Nothing else needed to be said. Like so many things we do in our younger years it was just a stage I went through. I wore an earring on and off for a few years. First it was a stud, then a hoop, a Nike swoosh, and finally, a 58, my one-day-international playing number. I don't wear an earring any more, but the hole is still there.

I expected the highlight of the academy year to be a tour of Pakistan in September, but it didn't turn out the way I'd planned. I bowled a lot of overs in really hot conditions, and found the going tougher than in India. It all came to an ugly end in one match when I felt a sudden sting in my back while bowling. I delivered a couple more balls, but the pain worsened to feel like a knife was twisting into my lower spine. It was excruciating. I then started to seize up.

I returned to Australia to see specialists in Adelaide and Wollongong. Scans revealed I had 'hot spots' which were stress fractures or potential ones in the L2 and L3 region of my back. Dennis Lillee's prediction from two years earlier had come true. The upcoming 1995–96 season was meant to signal a new start for me at the northern Sydney club Mosman, after Shane and I had been offered a financial deal to switch from Campbelltown. However, the Whales didn't get much value out of me because I was sidelined for four months, after which I could only play a handful of matches as a batsman in second grade before the season ended. Although I managed to make a half-century it was no consolation for what I was missing out on. This was the first really difficult and challenging period of my career; basically I was out of action at a time when I'd hoped I'd be on the up and up. I was shattered when first told of my recovery period; I'd devoted so much energy and time to my goal of playing for Australia that I wasn't prepared to hear a doctor say: 'You can't play cricket and you can't run.' I kept thinking: 'This isn't meant to happen. How did it happen? Why did it happen?' Up until that point it was as though I'd programmed my mind like a computer to think that playing Test and one-day cricket for my country was the only possible result. The injury made me reassess, and I even wondered if I should have a fall-back plan, such as doing a TAFE course in carpentry.

After three months I was really frustrated. I'd taken up Pilates to help strengthen my core, and on the recommendation of Dennis Lillee, who'd done something similar during his career, I spent hours refining my action by analysing it in front of an old wardrobe mirror in the family garage. However, I still couldn't see an end in sight. Then, something happened that inspired me more than anything had before: on 17 December, Shane made his one-day debut for Australia against the West Indies in Adelaide. It was a great reward for perseverance because Shane had survived his share of battles; after he first played for NSW in the Sheffield Shield and Mercantile Mutual Cups in 1992–93 he was in and out of the team for two seasons before he really found his feet in 1995. After he was picked for Australia there was talk in the media that a true all-rounder had been discovered.

I can remember sitting in the lounge room at home with Mum, Dad and Grant, with all our eyes glued to the TV, when Shane walked out to bat in the Adelaide match. I was so nervous that my palms were sweating, but once Shane got off the mark I had a feeling he'd be sweet. He ended up hitting a rapid 39 and taking Jimmy Adams's wicket. I was rapt for him. On a few occasions afterwards I unashamedly let my pride get the better of me by boasting to anyone and everyone that Shane Lee was my brother.

Shane's success made me realise just how possible it was to go from the backyard to the big time. It renewed my energy and determination. Adam Rainford remembers the afternoon that he, Grant and I were looking through Shane's Australian one-day kit at home. The guys urged me to try on the yellow helmet with the coat of arms badge at the front, but I told them: 'No way. You have to earn that. I'll never put on an Australian one unless it's my own.' Unknowingly, I'd echoed the response of Steve Waugh from a few years earlier when I'd been the Australian room attendant.

I was further fuelled by Grant's achievements. My younger brother, a top order batsman, followed Shane's and my path when he was picked in the NSW Under-17 team. Terrific things were happening all around me, so I convinced myself it wouldn't be long before my luck turned around; my injury was all just part of the journey I had to take if I was to get where I wanted to go.

I was invited back to the academy the next year, 1996. After specialists had given me the all-clear to bowl again, Richard Done worked closely with me as we set about modifying my action. Until that time, I'd looked over my left shoulder at the point of delivery, but this forced my head to fall away, which in turn caused hyperextension of the spine. It was hoped I could get rid of the problem if I changed the position of my front arm, enabling me to look through it and therefore keep my head more upright and balanced. It was a very long and hard process made tougher by the lack of strength in my arms and shoulders; it was very noticeable that when I got tired I went back to the old action. Above all else, I still wanted to bowl as fast as I could.

To break up the routine at the academy we had a bowlers' and batsmen's week with expert guests Ian Chappell and Dennis

Lillee. Although all the players got on well, there was a bit of 'us versus them' during this time. The fast bowlers were me, Andrew Eime (South Australia), Jeremy Allen (Western Australia) and Daniel Horsley (NSW), while the batsmen had Simon Katich and Brad Haddin on their way to Australian selection, and a number of future first-class players including Michael Dighton (WA) and Shawn Craig (Victoria). The rivalry had added heat when it came to a bouncer and hooking session. Dennis told us we had to aim for the badge on each batsman's helmet. Using new balls on synthetic indoor nets, the quicks adopted the attitude: 'Let's have a crack and rip their heads off!' No-one got hurt, but there were a few whinges from the batsmen and Chappelli said some blue words after he saw all of the bowlers over-stepping the front line. It was great fun, although I would have been scared if I'd been at the other end.

After the week was over we went out for a beer with Dennis. If anyone doubts this man has presence you need only have seen him that night to convince you otherwise. We went to Heaven, a nightclub that was absolutely pumping with music and people. Dennis was noticed immediately, and a few fans approached him to have a chat. Word quickly spread until the DJ announced: 'We've got a legend in the house tonight, the Great Dennis Lillee!' The crowd went wild and started chanting: 'Lillee, Lillee, Lillee!' Dennis acknowledged them by walking a couple of steps from the bar onto a gigantic dancefloor where everyone moved back to let him through. He stopped in front of the DJ box, and the music was turned down. He ran his finger along his forehead and gave his trademark flick of sweat, imaginary or otherwise, before he turned around, started to run and launched into his perfect action. After he followed through, he appealed as though he was back on the MCG, with legs bent, and fingers raised in his classic pose. The crowd yelled 'Out!' and umpires' fingers went up everywhere. Dennis walked casually back to the bar. I don't think he or any of us with him had to buy a drink for the rest of the night. The whole scene could have been straight out of a Hollywood movie.

I look back fondly at my academy years. Obviously my development as a cricketer was the focal point of my stints, but as proved to be the case throughout my whole playing career there were many moments away from matches and training that I remember just as strongly, if not more so. During my time in '96 I was a groundsman at the Adelaide Oval. On the advice of previous academy players I found the grand old scoreboard was a really good place to hide for a sleep between training sessions; that was until curator Les Burdett found me. On other occasions I raced work buggies around the oval with other academy mates. It was all good fun, but when my time at the academy was up I was definitely ready to go. After not bowling a single ball in a match for a year I was on a mission to make up for lost time.

5

In late 1996, Panorama Oval at Oak Flats was renamed the Shane Lee Field. I was stoked for my brother who'd been part of Australia's World Cup squad that was beaten by Sri Lanka in the final in Pakistan earlier in the year. At about the same time, Grant also received an accolade, but in his modest way he didn't even tell Mum and Dad about it. In fact they didn't find out until several years later when they attended a function to name the oval at Oak Flats High in my honour. While sitting in the school hall listening to speeches, the Doctor looked at a list on a wall and discovered Grant had been dux of the school.

Unfortunately, I didn't do much in the 1996–97 season to get my name mentioned in the right places. I managed to be picked in the NSW second XI, but most of my playing time was spent with Mosman. After my back injury it was a case of rebuilding momentum, which I initially found hard to accept; I'd always been impatient to get to the next level, but as the season went on, I realised the experience gained from slugging it out for every wicket was all part of my learning.

This education extended away from games where I earned some money with my first independent business venture. I made up flyers with 'Brett Lee's Coaching Clinic' on them, and spent five hours doing a letterbox drop around Mount Warrigal. I'd already done my sums: it cost $20 to hire a net for one-and-a-half hours, and if I coached four kids at once, and charged them 20 bucks each, I could make a profit of $60 per session. With some help from my parents and Mosman – President Ian Finlay was terrific – I was able to buy a brand new Daewoo Cielo with lambskin covers. It copped a fair workout because I was still living at home and making as many as five trips to and from Sydney each week.

My financial position was further helped by another job that promised long-term prospects whether I went on to play for Australia or not. Not long after I'd finished school I received a phone call from Richard Bowman, the joint owner of Barclay's Menswear in Sydney. I remembered him straight away because he'd fitted up the Australian Under-19 team for their tour of India earlier in the year. After explaining he'd got my number through the Australian Cricket Board, Richard wasted no time getting to the point: 'I'm looking to hire a suit salesman and thought you might be interested,' he said.

After overcoming the surprise, I told him I was really keen and that fashion was something I wanted to become more heavily involved in; the days of bargain hunting at Kmart could turn out to be very useful in more ways than I thought.

The next morning I left home bright and early for an interview with Richard. I'll never forget what I wore: a shiny micro-fibre, green-brown, double-breasted, peak-lapel suit; a white silk shirt and a Mickey Mouse tie. It was dreadful, but at the time I thought I looked hot! Although I'd allowed myself plenty of time I didn't consider I'd have a problem finding a park when I finally reached Sydney's CBD; it must have been the Mount Warrigal in me. I drove up and down streets for ages looking for somewhere, and when I finally squeezed into a spot I was already a few minutes late. Worse still, it was pouring rain, and with no cover in sight for a couple of blocks I took the gamble that I wouldn't get too wet if I sprinted. Wrong! By the time I arrived at Shop One on the gallery level of Centrepoint Tower, I was soaking. My suit, my shirt, my hair, my shoes, everything looked a mess. I'd had a shocker!

My appearance made me more nervous, and I thought I'd blown my chances already. I walked in to Barclay's, and met Richard's colleague Melissa Barbaresco; with water dripping off me everywhere I was embarrassed to shake her hand, but she just smiled. And so did Richard when he came out and saw me. I couldn't help thinking he'd judge me on looks alone, but he was so friendly that I soon relaxed enough to sit down and chat without showing too many signs of nerves. Richard said he already employed a young rugby union player, Tom Bowman. Tom, no relation to Richard, was starting to make a name for himself in representative footy and would eventually go on to play for Australia. Because of his commitments he needed to spend more time away from the shop. Richard was happy to give him all the time he needed, but this generosity left a hole in the business. So, Barclay's needed another salesman, and Richard was kind enough to say he was impressed with me when we'd initially met. He took me by surprise when he asked me what my aims in life were. I told him of my cricket ambitions but was worried my back might affect my hopes. Richard took it all in before saying he'd like to give me a go.

Soon afterwards I travelled with Melissa to take an order of uniforms at the Bulli Harness Racing Club on the outskirts of Wollongong. The day after that I was on the shop floor dressed in a smart Barclay's outfit and waiting for my first customer. No sooner had we opened for the day than a man walked in asking for a three-button, single-breasted suit with a notch-lapel in a

Prince of Wales check with a Super 120 high twist fibre. I had no idea; the only fibre I knew of came from breakfast cereal. The man then started to laugh. He was a friend of Richard who thought a stitch-up would be a great way to welcome me.

Over the following weeks everyone at Barclay's helped me tremendously. It was a real family business: Richard; his sister Edwina; their mum, Pam; Eric Fink, the joint owner; his wife, Jacqui; and Melissa. They taught me all the basics about sizes, fitting, fabrics, and sales techniques. I hoped I was picking everything up quite quickly. Even if I wasn't, Richard was always supportive; he said I could have all the time off I needed to pursue my cricket career. I had found a fantastic job and a secure one. I couldn't believe my luck.

By 1996–97, the job ensured I had some very long days: 6.30 am get up; seven o'clock leave home and drive the 80 kilometres to Sydney; eight o'clock try to beat the heaviest inner-city traffic and leave my car in the Domain parking station; 8.30 am walk the 10 minutes to work; work until 5 or 6 pm; then head home, arriving after seven o'clock. Then add the cricket. As a member of the NSW train-on squad I had Tuesday and Thursday afternoon sessions at the SCG that generally didn't finish until sevenish, sometimes eight o'clock. That meant I wouldn't get home until 9.30 or later, after which I'd scoff down Mum's dinner and then go straight to bed to be ready for an early start again the next day. There were plenty of times I was so exhausted I had to fight against falling asleep at the wheel. One night a mudslide blocked traffic at Mount Ousley, the area leading down into Wollongong. I knew Mum would be worried, but I couldn't contact her because I had no mobile phone. I was caught in the mess for hours, and only finally contacted Mum after traffic was moving again. Thankfully she'd heard on the radio what had happened. By then it was well after midnight, but Mum being Mum got up and cooked me lasagne. Sometimes I lightened the load by staying overnight with Shane, who'd moved to Sydney and was renting an apartment at Cremorne on the north shore. But most of the time I liked to get home.

Long hours weren't my only challenge. Car parking at about $15 a day plus petrol and lunch meant I wasn't saving much money. Eventually, I worked out I could put a few dollars away if I left my car for free in the SCG car park, then caught a bus into the city for $1.20. I also started packing my lunch, thanks to Mum.

I look back at that period and think it would kill me if I tried to do it now. I suppose it reflected one of my greatest assets: when I'm in the moment I don't think about anything else. If I'd analysed things too much, maybe I would have thought: 'This is a big effort!' But there was no negative to what I was doing at the time. I just had to do it to get where I wanted to go. In many ways that was my equivalent to university study for other 20-year-olds. My research and assignments were driving, working and training. And if all went well I'd finish with a degree in professional cricket with a sub-major in the fashion business.

The more time I spent at Barclay's, the more confident I became as a salesman who had his tape measure ready as soon as someone walked through the door. This involved changing my way of thinking: initially I thought I was convincing people to part with their money, but I soon swung that mindset to one of knowing I was offering customers a service that they paid for. I really enjoyed it. Most of all, I liked meeting new people and developing stronger friendships with the staff. Richard had been in the business for 20 years, and his family twice as long. I quickly learnt he was a loyal man with an outstanding eye for fashion, a great business brain, and an amazing memory. He helped out Tom and me, and we helped him; it was a great two-way street.

It didn't take me long to realise Richard was also a hilarious bloke who managed to mix his sense of fun with the serious side of business. One second we'd be swearing our heads off telling jokes, and the next second a customer would walk in and Richard would be all prim and proper as though there was no other way: 'Good afternoon sir. How are you?'

Richard was quite short, very strong, and fancied himself as a rugby player. From all reports, he was very good; I imagined he'd had a never-say-die attitude. And he didn't mind playing above his weight! For those of you who are Wallaby fans, you'll remember Tom Bowman as a giant: he was closer to seven feet than six, and weighed about 120 kilograms. When business was slow Richard sometimes challenged Tom to wrestling bouts that ended up with whole racks of suits crashing to the floor, and shirts flying off shelves. It was my job to keep an eye out for customers.

Tom was a classic. Although he was quietly spoken he was so big he could almost scare customers into buying a suit. One day a little Asian man walked in looking for a 92 short fitting. Tom went out the back and returned with a suit that he helped the customer try on. Now, just a tip: once a jacket is on, you should give it a couple of downward tugs to make sure there are good clean lines across the shoulders and chest. Towering over his customer Tom gave two quick pulls and ripped off each sleeve! His customer looked all the way up in fright, and Tom, straight-faced, looked down and said: 'Now you've done that, you'll have to pay for it.' The poor customer didn't know what to think until Tom assured him all was OK. I think the jacket had been a promotional garment that hadn't been stitched properly.

With moments like that it was never hard to go to work, but sometimes it was difficult to leave because my cricket commitments occasionally made me feel guilty. How many other bosses would let you walk out the door at least twice a week at 2 pm? Richard never doubted me. He knew what cricket meant to me, and he was never in the way; he was always supportive and full of encouragement. And he still is. To this day he's one of the main mentors in my life, and I still enjoy going back and working in the store, which has moved to Martin Place and is now named Claude Sebastian.

The knowledge that I had a good job to fall back on gave me the security I needed to really feel confident about giving cricket a crack without worrying about how I'd support myself. Entering the 1997–98 season my aim was to make my debut for NSW, and if I did I thought it was the best way to repay the support that people like Richard had given me.

It took six weeks for my aim to become a reality. After obviously pleasing the right people with a few good grade and state second XI showings, I was chosen to play against Western Australia in a Sheffield Shield match at the SCG in late November. It was the best belated 21st birthday present I could have hoped for. A day or two before the game I was given a brown box containing my baggy blue cap, jumper, tracksuit and training gear. I felt bullet-proof, and Shane's presence in the team added to my excitement. We were back doing what we'd been doing for years, but this time the stage was a lot more intimidating.

I'd never played a game at the SCG. When I'd sat in the Noble Stand and watched Shane play matches at the ground, I used to look at the home team balcony in the Members' Stand and think: 'I'd like to be there one day.' And now I was.

NSW batted first, and coming in at number 10 – Stuart MacGill was wrongly deemed more of a bunny than I was

– I was out caught behind to Brendon Julian for a second-ball duck. The fact the Warriors didn't make too much noise was a clear sign I was considered an easy wicket. As far as batting went I knew I was a long way out of my league. When I first got to the centre and looked at Brendon, Tom Moody, and Jo Angel, I was overawed by their size.

The Blues made only 138, and WA then came out and smashed us. I opened the bowling with Anthony Stuart and was surprised I wasn't nervous. However, my inexperience showed. While Anthony bowled beautifully to grab '7-for', I tried to bowl too quickly and dragged the ball short and wide. Ryan Campbell had a field day against me, belting me over cover and point on his way to a big hundred. Tom Moody was the only wicket I got. My return: 24-2-99-1. WA made 361 and the Blues were in a lot of trouble.

We fared much better in the second dig, scoring 5-477 (declared), thanks to centuries by Rod Davison and Michael Bevan. The Warriors needed 255 to win on a turning deck, and all of a sudden we were right back in the game.

I was much more relaxed with the ball second time round. After only a couple of overs Anthony Stuart and I gave way to our spinners Stuart MacGill and David Freedman who went about working through a top-shelf batting order that had Campbell, Mike Hussey, Justin Langer, Damien Martyn and Adam Gilchrist in their top five. It was close for most of the afternoon until it seemed possible that the Blues could steal the win. It all came down to needing three wickets in the final few overs. It was a really edgy atmosphere that I was excited to be part of. And then my captain, Phil Emery, threw me the ball. I was a little stunned, but was also ready.

Luck was on my side. I bowled Jamie Stewart, and then MacGilla cleaned up Matthew Garnaut to grab his fifth wicket.

The rest of the match was a blur that ended in me racing to hug Shane and my teammates after I bowled Brett Mulder with an inswinging yorker. We won by 60 runs, and I still reflect on that match as one of the more incredible ones I played.

Three weeks later I made my one-day debut for the Blues in the Mercantile Mutual Cup against Canberra at Manuka Oval. Mike Veletta was my one and only wicket in our win. After the game I saw another side of fast bowling when I had a chat with former Test cult figure Merv Hughes at Bobby McGee's bar. It was the first time I'd ever seen anyone put two bottlenecks of Corona beer in their mouth and scull them together.

By that stage I'd moved to Sydney to live. All the driving had started to get to me, and the pressure of cricket commitments made me realise it would be sensible to move closer to the SCG. Plus, I was a young bloke who felt the time was right to leave the nest, start my own life and grow up. It was difficult to leave Mum and Dad, but my time at the academy and various tours had prepared me well.

I rented a unit in inner-city Pyrmont from NSW all-rounder Brad McNamara. Blues opener Rod Davison was my flatmate for the first few months before he moved out and my Campbelltown and academy mate, Corey Richards, moved in. Corey was also in the NSW team at this time. The location was perfect: just a 15 to 20-minute walk to Barclay's, and only 10 to the nightlife scene of Darling Harbour. You can imagine what it was like being a single bloke enjoying life. I was definitely a party boy in my early 20s but I was no different to most people. I was working hard, training hard, and playing hard. My philosophy was that if I devoted so much time to cricket and work, I could afford to have a couple of drinks and enjoy myself. My social life was a release from my everyday life; going to listen to a band, or having a beer with some mates, or looking at eye-candy, was a great way to wind down. I loved it, and I wouldn't change anything I did during that time.

All was going so well in my life that I was excited by every day, and that feeling was magnified just a month after my Shield debut when rumours turned to reality. Although the game against WA was the only first-class match I'd played for the season – and only the second of my career – there were whispers the Australian selectors wanted more of a look at me. I refused to believe it would happen until I received a call saying I'd been picked in the Australia A's for a four-dayer against South Africa in Brisbane. I was amazed. When I initially got picked for first grade I looked around at my teammates and thought they were legends; when I got picked for the Blues I did the same thing; and now I had the chance to play alongside Justin Langer, Matthew Hayden, Stuart Law, Darren Lehmann, Michael Bevan, Adam Gilchrist . . . wow!

However, the higher you climb, the harder you may fall. By the end of the match, which ended just before Christmas, I had little to look forward to in the New Year. The stats said I bowled 48 overs and took two wickets in a draw, but the numbers that counted were L2 and L3. After pushing for too much speed and being ragged with my technique, I'd reopened the stress fractures in my back.

I felt really low. Although I'd eventually convinced myself that my first back injury was all part of my journey, this second injury was much harder to accept. I'd worked so hard to come back, and now I'd returned to where I'd started. It didn't seem fair. The recovery was also more frustrating than first time round. To be blunt, it was a pain in the arse. For three months I wore a brace that went from my bum to my shoulders; I only took it off to have showers. I was so conscious of it that I wore two shirts when I went out socially. My mates quietly made fun of me, saying my movements were so stiff I was like a Ken doll. But away from the jokes, I felt physically trapped, and mentally I was pissed off because the injury had come just when I was starting to make an impression in the right circles. But what could I do? I wanted to stay positive, and told everyone I was going to recover well and be back bowling as fast as ever. But inwardly I had my doubts. I tried hard not to let these get the better of me in what was one of the biggest tests of character I've ever faced. At 21, it would have been easy for me to have said, 'Stuff it, I'll go and do something else,' but in reality what would I do? I'd focused on cricket for years. It's what I knew. It's what I was good at.

After the brace came off I started a tough period of rehabilitation that revolved around working with the NSW squad's physiotherapist, Pat Farhart. I hated the exercises he gave me. For one, I had to lie on the ground with an inflatable bag underneath my back. When the bag blew up it placed pressure on my core which forced me to 'turn my abs on', or as the saying goes, I had to try to 'pull my belly button through my back'. I initially thought it was a tedious and pointless exercise, but together with other core activities and hamstring flexibility exercises, the whole program made me understand how strong I had to be to absorb the stresses of fast bowling. That period also helped me develop a resilient attitude that encouraged me to dismiss the bad moments in my career by looking ahead to the good times I hoped to have. Overcoming adversity has proved to be one of my strongest traits. That probably comes from Dad who has always emphasised the importance of self-belief.

When I was able to bowl again I went to Perth and spent time with Dennis Lillee who'd become my fast-bowling father figure. He was an easy bloke to talk to, someone who understood what I was going through because of the similar back problems he'd had. Throughout my entire career he has been my 'go-to' person whenever I've needed help with my action.

We started by watching videos of me bowling for Australia A. It was obvious I'd tried to bowl too quickly, and in doing so, I'd fallen away at the point of delivery, making my back twist awkwardly. On further analysis Dennis pointed out I still had a mixed action, and the only solution was to rebuild it from the ground up. We experimented with a few different positions in front of a video camera, and eventually developed one that I was comfortable with.

The biggest challenge was to change my back foot from landing side-on at the crease to an angle of about 45 degrees, meaning it was pointing towards fine leg if a right hander was batting. The critical thing was to make sure my hips and shoulders were in the one plane to avoid counter-rotation.

The one unknown in all of this was something I couldn't control. My original back injury came when I was having a growth spurt. Medical research has proven that some sports injuries can be affected by spurts in which the bones grow, but the muscles, tendons and ligaments aren't strong enough to adapt. It was possible this happened to me, and by the time of my second injury my body may still have been playing catch-up with itself, and although technical refinement and strengthening exercises would obviously help me, they wouldn't be the absolute be-all and end-all of cures.

The bottom line was that we weren't put on this earth to run 30 metres, take a long leap, counter-rotate, hyperextend the body, and slam the front foot down at 15 times our own body weights on concrete-like surfaces. Doing that only once sounds stressful enough, but when it might be repeated 120 or more times in a day, it's obvious that fast bowling comes with considerable physical risks. As I continued my rehabilitation I realised I couldn't beat myself up over what had happened. In all likelihood I had to accept serious injuries would happen again before my career was over.

6

Although rehabilitation from injury was my number one priority throughout the 1998 winter, I also found time for a new hobby that would grow to become one of the most significant, influential, and powerful parts of my life: music. Just a few years earlier my experiences of live gigs didn't stretch much further than watching Collette perform 'Ring My Bell' at the Shellharbour Workers Club, and my own efforts at singing were limited to belting out the odd rap tune with Adam Rainford, and those impromptu bursts of joining a chorus on the car radio while driving. But that all changed when I became a bass guitarist in a band that included my brother Shane and our NSW teammates Brad 'Buzzard' McNamara, Gavin 'Riddler' Robertson and Richard 'Cheeks' Chee Quee. And the funny thing is I could not play one chord!

Shane, Riddler and Buzzard first spoke about forming a band while they were in the dressing room after a Sheffield Shield match in 1996–97. About a year earlier Shane had started teaching himself the acoustic guitar after he bought a training CD and a book of chords. He also talked Buzzard into giving the guitar a crack, and the two of them really got the hang of it while they were in England in '97 playing league cricket. There were no worries for Riddler; he came from a musical family and had been playing the drums since he was a teenager.

Towards the end of '97 or in early '98 I went along to one of their jam sessions and left there with a mission: I contacted Grant and said I wanted to buy an acoustic guitar, but he convinced me to get a bass instead. There was no way I was going to go against what my younger brother said because he was the king when it came to music. There's a great story that sums up what music meant to him: when Mum and Dad, as they did with Shane and me, offered Grant some money to help buy his first car, he chose a piano instead. So, with Grant at my side I went in to a music store in Wollongong and came out with a purple bass. At first I wasn't sure of my new toy.

'It only has four strings,' I said to Grant.

'That's because bass guitars normally do only have four strings,' he replied.

The next day I told Shane, Riddler and Buzzard at cricket practice: 'I've got a bass guitar, so I'm joining your band!' I was accepted straight away. No rehearsal, no questions, I'd made the cut because no-one else could play bass. And neither could I at the time, but at least I had the guitar. Grant helped me with the basics, but I found it hard because I didn't have the patience; all I wanted to do was play songs and sing. However, I slowly worked out that the best way to do that was by practising chords for hours and hours. When I was finally able to hold a few tunes I thought I was pretty cool. I was also hooked.

At that stage the band was still missing a lead singer. Cheeks was keen to have a go; he fancied himself as a bit of a rock star and used to muck around singing in the dressing rooms. Music was a strong part of his culture. His mother, who'd been raised in Fiji, used to invite Fijian and Samoan friends to their Sydney home for afternoon sing-alongs.

So, we were all ready. But if we were to be fair dinkum we had to have a name. We all decided it had to be cricket related, and after tossing around 'Hit and Run', 'Caught and Bowled', 'Full Tosses' and similar things, we settled on the backyard favourite 'Six and Out'. Word started to spread about what we were doing, and there was a bit of pressure put on us to play at a fund-raising testimonial roast for Australian and NSW spinner Greg Matthews. At that time we hadn't rehearsed, but we couldn't say no. We only had to play one song, the national anthem. To make it novel we fitted the words to the tune '500 Miles' by The Proclaimers. I only had to manage three chords: E, A, and B. Grant showed me how, and I thought I could do it if I got the timing right. Other than that, I think we ended up having only one rehearsal.

The function was held at Sydney's Regent Hotel in December '98. It was black tie, but we went backstage and put on our NSW one-day tops; Cheeks, being the true rock star, also wore his sunnies. Since we were doing the national anthem we appeared right at the start of the night. We were all really edgy, and kept saying, 'What happens if we're bloody awful?' and 'What happens if someone is pissed off because of what we've done to the anthem?' But we managed to get by without making too many mistakes, and we had a lot of fun.

People didn't say anything too bad about us; I think they were supportive because we were just a novelty act, a cricket band. But after that we became serious. We rehearsed more, including spending four hours at a time at the Sound Level Recording and Rehearsal Studios in Ultimo. We wanted to learn so much and were really enthusiastic about what we were doing. We had our disagreements, but they didn't last long. Our main aim was to enjoy ourselves.

Within a few months we'd worked up a repertoire of about a dozen cover songs, including: 'Blister in the Sun'; 'All the Small Things' by Blink-182; 'Jumpin' Jack Flash'; 'Brown Eyed Girl'; 'Mustang Sally'; and 'Johnny B. Goode'. Eventually, over a period of a couple of years we were comfortable playing 30 or more songs. And we had to be, because we'd progressed from performing three songs at a gig to being the main act at some of Sydney's most popular pubs, like the Castle Hill Tavern, the Crows Nest Hotel, and the Palace in Coogee.

When I first began I was really anxious – shitting myself, actually – before gigs. I practised for hours at home because I didn't want to be open to ridicule on stage. Our first performance away from a cricket audience was at a bar in North Sydney where we had to play three songs at a corporate function. I was so nervous I tried to calm myself by saying: 'What's the worst thing that can happen here? Maybe an amp catches fire.' Sure enough, my amp blew up in a cloud of sparks and smoke during the first song.

The pressure of getting up and performing made me feel more vulnerable than I was on a cricket field. I liked that feeling, I liked being on the edge. I always got excited about playing cricket, but I got just as pumped, or even more so, before going on stage. When we were in a good venue, feeding off the electricity of the people, it was hard to feel we weren't rock stars for a night. If the crowd was having fun, so were we. To see people dancing, singing and carrying on was a tremendous buzz. It put me in a great space. I was just with four mates having an absolute ball. Back then, I was busy but I still had time to do more things outside of cricket than I would have at the peak of my career. It was pretty carefree: go out and play a gig; get up and train my backside off for cricket; have a band rehearsal; have a few drinks at night; go to bed; get up and play cricket; go to bed; get up and do another gig. It was a great life.

I didn't fully realise it at the time, but playing in the band and working at Barclay's gave me substance in life away from cricket. I grew to appreciate that a few years later when cricket demanded so much more of me; although I couldn't play in the band as much, I took a guitar with me on tour, and that's the way it is to this day when I go away. I've graduated from the bass and at last count I have 13 acoustics. When I play the guitar I escape into this fantasy world where I'm alone. There's a song that English musician Newton Faulkner sings called 'Dream Catch Me'. If you listen to its lyrics, that's me. When I'm alone in this fantasy world I can do what I want, and be whatever or whoever I want to be. I'm away from the spotlight, away from the fans, away from my other life. I can lock myself up in a hotel, get room service, and play the guitar for hours and hours. I treasure that feeling when I get so engrossed in what I'm doing that nothing else matters at that moment. I reckon the happiest people in life are those who can find that space to be taken to.

Having the distraction of Six and Out helped me overcome the frustrations of the 1998–99 season when my rehabilitation was followed by rebuilding. The process began while playing grade for Mosman where I concentrated on all the modifications Dennis Lillee and I had made to my action. I was now a front-on bowler, starting with my run-up that was a straight line from the top of my mark all the way to the crease. After bowling off only eight steps to begin with, I slowly increased my run-up until I was comfortable with it at 22 paces; from year to year it generally changed a step or two either way. By early in the New Year I was back to full pace, and no longer worrying about whether or not my back would give way to the increased stress.

I played for the Blues in their last five Sheffield Shield matches for the season. The highlight came when most of the Test players returned for the match against Victoria at the SCG. In our first innings I went out to bat when Shane Warne was bowling. I'd first faced him when he visited the academy and bowled me a wrong 'un that hit me on the hip after I'd tried to cut it. Now, in a match, I again had no idea. Victorian wicketkeeper Darren Berry tried to suck me in when he chirped up from behind the stumps: 'Wouldn't you love to smack Warnie for six? It's something you could tell your grandkids. He's not turning it much. Go on, give it a go. Just two steps down and you can do it.' I didn't fall for it, but I did think about it. In the final game of the season I took my first five-wicket haul in first class cricket, 5-53, against Tasmania at Hobart's Bellerive Oval. All these years later, I can't remember a thing about it.

Soon after that I went on a special tour with the academy to Zimbabwe where we played some really one-sided matches, and I had a competition with my fast-bowling teammate Ashley Noffke. It was an ordinary thing to do, but at the time it was fun: we decided to see how many of our opponents' helmets we could crack. I think our final tally was 16, and it got to the point where the poor buggers we'd 'filled in' had to borrow academy lids.

While the cricket wound down for the season, Six and Out commitments wound up again. Apart from gigs, we took another step up the music ladder when we recorded a three-track CD that was produced by Garth Porter, the keyboard player for the 1970s hit band Sherbet. Garth, a cricket tragic, co-wrote Sherbet's most famous hit, 'Howzat', with bass player Tony Mitchell, and these days writes material for leading country singer Lee Kernaghan. The CD included a song, 'The

Mighty Blues', which we all wrote together. We also got some of our teammates to help with backing vocals.

Shane and I squeezed in recording commitments before heading to Los Angeles to play a promotional one-day series for Australia A against India A in September. We were so wrapped up in being in the USA that we didn't pay attention to us being together in a national team for the first time. Instead, we lapped up cruising in the team mini-bus along Hollywood's Sunset Boulevard. We were like kids on a school excursion, especially when we had our brush with fame and saw actress Helen Hunt drive past us. It's embarrassing to say we bipped the horn and waved at her.

The most unusual sight of the trip was during the cricket. Because of Indian television rights we had to start one game at 7 am. Getting up at the crack of dawn was one problem, but having to overcome the conditions was another thing altogether: for the first ball of the match I virtually pushed off the boundary fence and ran through a fog that made it hard for the guys in slips to see me. I've got no idea how the batsmen saw a single ball in the early overs. What made it worse was a pitch that was diabolical at best. Instead of trying to swing the ball, I held it across the seam and bowled what we called 'spitting cobras' that exploded off good lengths and did everything from getting edges to hitting batsmen in the throat. It was the worst pitch I ever played on. Topping off an unusual day, at the end of the innings we returned to our demountable dressing rooms where Paul Hogan paid us a visit.

We returned home and jumped straight into the 1999–2000 season. I started well for Mosman and picked up a few healthy hauls that impressed NSW chairman of selectors, Alan Campbell, who said I was the fastest bowler in Sydney grade since Jeff Thomson played for Bankstown in the '70s. I tried to lift the pace more for the Blues and was confident I was hovering at 150 kays or above for most of the time. I took two wickets in each of the first three Mercantile Mutual Cup games, and had 12 scalps at 29.5 after three Pura Cup (Sheffield Shield) matches.

While I was looking for consistency for NSW, Australia were playing Pakistan in a three Test series. The day after my third Pura Cup game – a loss to Queensland at the SCG – Corey Richards and I sat in our unit watching Adam Gilchrist and Justin Langer carve up Pakistan on the last day of the second Test in Hobart. I was surprised to hear there'd been some talk in the media that I was a chance for selection in the third and final Test in Perth. Australian captain Steve Waugh had been pushing my cause but I didn't think the selectors could seriously be contemplating me; I'd had a reasonable start to the season but felt I needed to get a few big hauls and maintain consistency before I could realistically hope to be considered. Corey didn't agree with me, and was geeing me up, saying I had a real chance.

About half an hour after Australia won I received a phone call from Richard Watson from the Australian Cricket Board, as it was then known. It was early afternoon, and Richard asked me what I was doing for the rest of the day.

'Not much,' I said.

'Well, you better get some good clothes on because you'll be doing a presser at the NSW Cricket Association offices soon. You've been chosen to go to Perth for the next Test.'

That was the moment my life changed.

I asked Richard to repeat what he'd said. Meanwhile Corey was hanging over my shoulder trying to find out what was happening. After I told him, I heard the fridge door open and that familiar hiss of a beer bottle being opened. While I was still on the phone to Richard, Corey was trying to get me to scull a Corona. As soon as I hung up and received a few slaps on the back from my flatmate, I rang Mum, then Dad who was at work. They were both over the moon, but it still seemed surreal to me. I spent the next half hour making calls to Shane, Grant, my cousin Luke and Adam Rainford. I then rang Richard Bowman at Barclay's who said: 'If you're going to be in front of the media you better come in and we'll fix you up with a brand new suit.'

Despite the fuss that was made of me at the media conference I still didn't believe what was happening. That night I went for a celebratory drink with Shane and some Mosman teammates at The Oaks Hotel in Neutral Bay. When I walked into the pub's courtyard I noticed some people looking at me in a way I'd never experienced before. This was my introduction to being in the public eye. It didn't worry me, and in fact I liked the buzz it gave me. It was recognition that I was on the verge of fulfilling the self-belief and the dream I'd had since I was a boy. At 23, I felt I was starting a new stage of my life.

Linking up with the Australian team was quite weird. I was like a fan who'd won a competition; as most Aussie people did, I knew all the players, but I actually hadn't met them all. I was lucky that there was a strong NSW flavour – the Waughs, Glenn McGrath and Michael Slater – that helped me feel more comfortable.

I was in a battle with 'Kasper' (Michael Kasprowicz) for the third fast bowling spot behind 'Pidgey' (Glenn McGrath) and 'Flem' (Damien Fleming). The opening had come after selectors had dropped Scott Muller. I didn't expect to play because Kasper had experience on his side; he also deserved it because he'd worked hard to get back in after playing his last Test a year earlier. I came to know him as one of the truly good blokes in world cricket, but this didn't mean we didn't go for each other's throats in the final net session before the XI was chosen. We both went flat out for the entire time on practice wickets that had heaps of juice in them. I hit Justin Langer on the foot and 'sniffed up' Ricky Ponting off a full run; there was no holding back in a ball for ball duel. At the end of practice 'Tugga' (Steve Waugh) told me the news I had expected but didn't want to hear: I'd missed out. I was obviously disappointed, but also encouraged by Tugga who said if I kept bowling the same way I'd get my chance before long.

Being 12th man at the WACA Test was actually a blessing because it allowed me to get the feel for being part of an Australian Test team without the pressure of having to perform. The match only lasted three days – Australia won by an innings and 20 runs to clean sweep the series – but that was more than enough time for me to take away some incredible memories.

In the dressing room before play on the first day I spent most of the time sitting quietly by myself and watching everything that was happening around me. I felt a real buzz inside when Justin Langer started brushing his baggy green cap with his hands. Then when Tugga took his cap out and rested it on his kit, I couldn't resist looking at it when I went past to get a drink. Inside it were blood stains from when he'd busted his nose in a collision with Jason Gillespie in Sri Lanka a couple of months earlier. Poor Dizzy broke his leg and was out of action for the season; that injury probably gave me my chance to be in that Perth dressing room, and later make my Test debut. To me, Tugga's cap was the best symbol of what it meant to be an Australian player. It looked as though a dog had chewed it, but in every stitch and faded, frayed panel there were wins, losses, centuries, ducks, wickets, sledges, handshakes, celebrations, dried beer; you name it and that cap had probably seen it. Just thinking about it gave me goosebumps, and I couldn't wait to get my own.

Australia was going to bowl first after losing the toss. Before the team went out Tugga got everyone together and gave a quick talk. He was very matter of fact and there was no hype. He simply said: 'Let's enjoy it, let's play well and do all the things we've spoken about.' 'Punter' (Ricky Ponting) was much more pumped, and was revving the boys up, saying: 'Let's get out there and take them down.' I couldn't have known it at the time, but I was watching the two contrasting styles of leadership that would have a major impact on the directions I took at various times throughout my career.

Just before the players left to go on the field I made a point of wishing Kasper good luck. He went on to do really well, taking seven wickets for the match. Again I couldn't have known how many times we'd be gunning against each other for a spot in the future.

Twelfth man isn't normally the most enjoyable position, but in this match I cherished every moment of it. My main job was running drinks to the bowlers on the boundary. I was really self-conscious the first time I did it; I just wanted to get out and in again without drawing too much attention to myself, but then some guys in the crowd starting yelling my name. I waved to them, they cheered, and I relaxed. I was surprised how many people knew who I was. I was asked to sign some autographs and that made me even more comfortable. Every professional athlete has his own view on signings, and there are times when it's realistically not possible to respond to all requests, but right from my first match as a Blues player I vowed to myself I would make an effort not to disappoint fans, especially children. I remember the first autograph that I got as a boy. It was from

Steve Smith, the Australian opener who played a few Tests and one-dayers in the '80s. He took the time to talk with me, asking me my name, where I was from, and whether I was a bowler or a batsman. He made me feel special; it wasn't so much the signature I treasured, but the experience.

After signing the autographs I headed back towards the dressing room, but I didn't get very far before I faced a predicament. A tennis ball thrown from someone in the crowd had landed about 15 metres inside the boundary, and the fans were shouting at me to get it. I could have pretended not to hear and walked on, but I knew that wouldn't have gone down too well, so in between overs I ran onto the field, picked up the ball and tossed it back over the fence. That got a big cheer. Throughout that first day I enjoyed every time I went around the boundary. The crowd treated me well, and in return I had a small lesson about player–fan relationships; considering how much time fast bowlers spend on the boundary this was to become a necessary part of my playing portfolio.

When you're 12th man one of the hardest jobs is interpreting the signals from teammates when they want something out on the field. Most signals are pretty easy to read, like a tip of the hand towards the mouth for a drink, or a rub of the hand along the arm or over the head for a towel. But in Perth I discovered even the easiest of signals can cause problems. When Punter, on his way to a century, signalled for new gloves I immediately had a worry: yes, I could find some gloves, but the problem was that Punter had seven pairs of them, all numbered differently. I took a gamble and ran out the '3's only for Punter to say he wanted the '4's. He took my mistake well, but asked me to bring out the correct pair after the next over. I nervously rode every one of the following six balls, hoping that Punter wouldn't get out and blame me!

The excitement of the whole Test experience was capped off by the celebrations after we won. Although I was a little unsure if I belonged, everyone stressed I was very much a part of the victory. Some of the guys asked me if I knew the words to the team song, and after I said I did, I was soaked with beer as Justin Langer led us in punching out the famous lines that sent tingles down my spine:

Underneath the Southern Cross I stand,
A sprig of wattle in my hand,
A native of our native land,
Australia, you fuckin' beauty!

I was on a huge high, and yet I hadn't even played; it was hard not to think of what it would be like if I did get the chance.

Luck was on my side because in the following week I got to play twice against Australia's next opponents, India. In a four-dayer for NSW at the SCG I took a 3-for and 4-for, then I grabbed another 4-for for the Prime Minister's XI in a one-dayer in Canberra. The media were continuing to talk up my Test chances, but I missed out on selection for the first Test in Adelaide; instead I played a Shield game against Tasmania in Sydney. The Blues were smacked, but I was happy with my performance, especially in the second innings after I took 3-20 off 18 overs. There was no doubt I was in a purple patch. I knew I was the fastest bowler in Australia, and was confident enough to think I could give any player the hurry up. No batsman likes facing fast bowling. Some deal with it better, and some enjoy the rush it can give them, but no-one would go out every day and say: 'Gee, I really want to face express bowling.' And as a fast bowler that's great to have in the back of your mind. From my junior days all the way through to my experiences with the Blues, I knew there were times when batsmen were absolutely shitting themselves against me. If I was to earn Australian selection I felt I just had to keep doing what I was doing.

I had one more Pura Cup match to impress selectors before the team was chosen for the second Test, the traditional Boxing Day Test in Melbourne, and I couldn't have picked a better venue: it was back to the WACA, which at the time had the fastest pitch in Australia. I was further boosted by the presence of Test players Michael Slater, Mark Waugh, and most importantly, Steve Waugh, who'd get to have a close look at how I was going.

What followed was beyond my expectations. I took four wickets in each innings, and in the second dig, I bowled what I believe were the fastest spells of my career. If there had been a speed gun at the ground I am sure a number of deliveries would have clocked over 160 kilometres an hour. Everything clicked: my run-up, action and follow through all felt smooth, plus there was a breeze behind me and no dodgy foot holes to contend with.

It was one of those great times when I didn't have to over-try to bowl fast. Throughout the peak times of my career, I tended to bowl my quickest consistently when I wasn't actually trying to bowl my quickest. I simply had the natural mindset of being fast and doing well, and the rest just happened. It was all about good rhythm, and it was like that against Western Australia. Both Steve and Mark Waugh said it was the fastest bowling they'd seen, and our wicketkeeper Brad Haddin admitted afterwards that he was genuinely worried for the safety of some of the batsmen. The fact that Brad and the slips cordon were standing outside the 30-metre circle was a fair indicator I was generating some heat. None of us could believe one ball I bowled to Jo Angel; it was a bouncer that took off and half-volleyed into the boundary fence. Jo copped worse later when I came around the wicket and speared a short ball towards his ribs. He tried to fend it away, but a loud crack followed. By the time I reached Jo his right arm was dangling by his side; I'd broken his wrist. Throughout the game I also hit opener Ryan Campbell in the helmet, and enjoyed sniffing up Damien Martyn and Adam Gilchrist.

Sometimes fast bowlers are criticised for intimidating batsmen, and I don't take a step back when I say there were times against the Warriors when I wanted to hit and hurt. I was bowling with anger. I'm sure that approach not only helped me get wickets, but also contributed to other bowlers cleaning up too. Near the finish of the match, when we only needed one wicket to win, Brad Haddin overheard the last two batsmen, Sean Cary and Brad Williams, saying that it was better to get out to Stuart MacGill, who was bowling at the other end, than face me. I still claimed the last wicket for the Blues to win; a great result considering we'd been 130 runs behind on the first innings. Afterwards Tugga said to me: 'That was great. That's exactly what we need.'

Four days later, it was Christmas Eve, and I was back in the Australian XII. News Limited photographer Phil Hillyard, who I was to become good mates with, asked if he could take a shot of me with a baggy green cap on my head. I refused because I wasn't going to touch it until I could wear it properly and no-one could take it away from me. Phil eventually took another photo that painted my thoughts perfectly: it was of me looking at the cap in a Christmas stocking. It was the only gift I wanted.

7

It was nerve-racking being the new kid on the block. Although I'd been part of Australia's XII in Perth I still felt the outsider after I arrived in Melbourne for the Boxing Day Test. That wasn't because the team didn't make me feel welcome; it was, I think, a natural reaction for any player on the brink of stepping up to the top level of any sport. There is always the question you ask yourself: 'Do I belong here?' Honestly, I didn't really care. I just wanted to bowl quickly. If I could ping them at 155 kays an hour, I was ready to play.

On Christmas Eve I consciously spent time alone in my hotel room because I didn't want to pester any of my teammates. Earlier in the day I'd gone for a walk to clear my head, and I ended up running into 'Gilly' – Adam Gilchrist – and his wife, Mel. They asked me if I had any family with me. I told them Shane would be arriving just before the match, but Mum and Dad were staying at home; the Doctor preferred to watch from the comfort of his lounge room. The next morning I woke up to find a gift under my door. It was Eric Clapton's *Unplugged* CD with a card that read:

Happy Christmas Binga. Wishing you a great day and I hope we play lots of Tests together.

Gilly and Mel.

That gesture made me feel as though I did belong. It wouldn't be the last time Gilly would do that little bit extra for me; in the years ahead I would know him as an incredibly thoughtful person who knew how to read others. I was so lucky his note on my Christmas card came true.

But how fast would it happen? After the players and their families all got together to celebrate Christmas in the morning, the squad headed off for training and a meeting in the afternoon. I couldn't stop asking myself: 'Am I going to play tomorrow?' I had one sleep until I found out if I'd been chosen ahead of Kasper, or would it be the same as in Perth? If I'd been given the choice, I would have liked to have known on Christmas Day because it would have settled the nerves. Then again, it might have made me more edgy as I would have stayed awake all night playing the game in my thoughts. It was catch 22.

It was fitting it was Christmas time because I was like an excited child staring at a present under a tree. By game morning I found it almost impossible to keep waiting. Every minute passed so slowly until we headed out of the dressing room for a warm-up. I was last out with Shane Warne, and as we walked down the steps towards the field he wished me luck and said that if I played I should lap up every second. Then he patted me on the backside and whispered to me:

'Good stuff, mate, you're in.'

'What!' I replied.

'You're in. But don't tell anyone. So when Tugga tells you, act surprised.'

I couldn't believe it, and was still stunned after Tugga announced the team at the end of the warm-up. I was going to be Australia's 383rd Test cricketer. Kasper was one of the first to congratulate me. When I was presented with the baggy green cap at a little ceremony on the field, I was so focused on the cap itself that I didn't take notice of who gave it to me. It was former Australian left-arm fast bowler Ian Meckiff, whose career ended after he was called for throwing against South Africa in 1963; that turned out to be quite an omen considering what would happen to me several months later. When I put the cap on the crowd cheered. I didn't want to take it off for the rest of the day.

Despite my selection I still didn't feel quite part of the team. And that didn't change even after I'd found my own spot in a corner of the dressing room between Glenn McGrath and Gilly. At first I held back because I knew players had their particular places at different grounds, and there was no way I was going to jump in quickly and find I'd taken someone like Tugga's seat. It was quite daunting; here I was feeling as though I was back in a kindergarten class waiting to follow the lead of all the big boys. I didn't want to do anything wrong, or give the impression that I thought I was a big shot. I tried to settle in but didn't say much.

Tugga won the toss and we batted first. That definitely helped my nerves because I spent more than two days in the dressing room getting the feel of the mood and observing everyone's behaviour. However, it was a long time because rain meant there were only a couple of hours' play on the first day. What I remember most about that whole experience was my eagerness to take my baggy green back to the hotel and ring Mum and Dad. I slept with the cap beside my bed.

After two days of waiting, my first big moment in Test cricket seemed to come in a hurry. We lost some quick wickets and I was suddenly putting the pads on. While getting ready I saw Australia's scorecard on the television, and I did a double take after I noticed my name; it didn't seem real, but then a surge of adrenalin hit me and I thought: 'Shit, I'm really here, and this is really happening!'

I went out and sat in the team viewing area next to Tugga, who encouraged me by saying I just had to bat the same way I had been during training. I tried not to think too much about it until Warnie, who was batting with Damien Fleming, tried to flick a ball down the leg side off Ajit Agarkar. I reckon nearly every cricketer waiting to bat knows exactly what it's like to feel your heart jump into your mouth the instant you hear an appeal, see the umpire raise his finger, and then realise you can't hide in the dressing room any longer. My heart was thumping like a sledgehammer as I walked out of the players' gate and onto the field. The ground looked massive and for a moment I felt as though every one of the thousands and thousands in the crowd was looking at me. I glanced up at the electronic scoreboard and saw: Brett Lee 0, Runs 0, Average 0. This was one occasion it wasn't wise to charge the first ball!

When I reached the centre, Flem said to me: 'Have a ball mate, enjoy it.' That was the best thing for me; if I'd batted with someone who wanted to instruct me on every delivery I wouldn't have relaxed at all. It took me a few overs to get off the mark with a shaky slap for four through point off Javagal Srinath. Flem said to me drily: 'You're not hitting them too well, are you?' That shot and Flem's humour got me going. By the time I'd made about 15 I started to tee off a bit and also tried matching Flem sledge for sledge; we were having a good laugh and there were times when I actually forgot we were playing a Test. We put on 59 pretty quickly before I hit a return catch to Srinath and was out for 27; it had taken me ages to get that score in first-class cricket, so I was a happy man. More importantly, Australia made 405, a solid start.

We took to the field not long before lunch on the third day. I can't say how much batting first calmed me down for bowling, and the easing of my nerves was further helped by fielding a few balls, including diving to stop a boundary. After every single delivery I looked at Tugga for any sign that he might call me up. I also looked over at Warnie. Really, I spent most of my time looking at the other guys in the team: the way they held themselves, the way they walked between overs, the way they talked to each other between balls. I watched it all, and took it all in; keeping in mind I hadn't played much first-class cricket, this was all so new to me.

I couldn't wait to have a crack with the ball. I'd been quiet in the dressing room, and I felt bowling would be my best chance to express myself and get out all the emotions that I'd bottled up in the lead-up to the match. Despite this anxiousness I was content to bide my time behind Pidgey and Flem, although I wasn't used to bowling first change.

I didn't have to wait long. After just a few overs Tugga did the shoulder shrug at me, the sign to warm up. I wasn't nervous. All the build-up seemed to happen in slow motion. I handed my vest and cap to umpire David Shepherd, then gave the crease area – where I thought my foot would land – a scratch with my spikes. I marked out my run, and tried to take in the final words from Tugga:

Don't change anything, just run in and bowl like you did against Western Australia. Just because you're playing a Test doesn't mean you have to change anything. You'll be fine.

It was a very simple message. Like Flem had done with my batting, Tugga knew it was best not to give me too many things to think about. I'm not saying I wouldn't have been able to handle that, but it's just what was best for me at that time. In truth, I wasn't anywhere near as tactical about my bowling at that stage of my career as I would be later. I just wanted to come in, let the ball rip, and try putting it in a spot where I thought I could get a wicket; there certainly wasn't much science to my bowling, and I hadn't yet learnt to watch batsmen closely and analyse their strengths and weaknesses. Apart from my speed, I knew the surprise factor could help me; the Indians had seen a bit of me in lead-up matches, but I was still very new to them.

Standing at the top of my mark about to bowl my first delivery was one of the proudest moments of my life. I still get tingles thinking about it now. The crowd cheered when they heard my name, but I tried to block them out as I took a deep breath and charged in. I can't actually remember my first three deliveries; just to have landed them on the cut stuff was an achievement. A five-over-old ball and grey skies helped the chances for swing. All I tried to do was bring the ball back into the left-hander Sadagoppan Ramesh. I ran in for my fourth delivery, and before I realised what I was doing I was bumping past Justin Langer at bat pad and racing towards a celebrating slips cordon. Ramesh had edged a good length ball onto his stumps, and I was running around like a madman. I'd got a Test wicket. A bloody Test wicket! Shit! Gilly and Slats (Michael Slater) hugged me, Tugga and Warnie shook my hand, and Junior (Mark Waugh), who didn't like a lot of 'man-love', gave me a pat on the back. Once all that happened, I thought: 'Well, there's no reason why I can't get more wickets.'

I got another one in my second spell. It came too easily when Rahul Dravid flashed at a wide one and Gilly took the catch. Although I felt comfortable enough I was still a bit more tense than usual, and it wasn't until my third spell, when the ball started reverse swinging, that I really started enjoying myself. In my eyes all the pressure was off me. For the first time I could see on a speed gun how fast I was bowling. To see the numbers flash up on the scoreboard was one thing, but to hear people in the crowd talking about it really got me going: 'He's bowling at 154.8 kays an hour!' I heard them because I was only a few metres away when I was fielding on the boundary. I had to laugh at the difference between being in front of the Members Stand and the outer crowd. In one area I'd hear, 'He's bowling with decent pace,' and in the other there'd be: 'Shit, that's quick!'

Before going on, it's appropriate to head back to my Mount Warrigal childhood. During backyard games a good whip off the legs, usually by Shane, often meant another tennis ball was added to the dozens on top of the roof or in the gutter of the house of our neighbour Maureen. One day, Shane decided I should go and collect them all. After big brother gave me a boost, I climbed up a pole and scuttled onto the roof where I saw an oasis of 50 or more balls. Many of them had been up there for a year or more, so the fur was burnt off on the sides facing the sun, while those in the gutter were bald on one side and wet on the other.

Although I didn't know it at the time, those balls introduced me to bowling 'spit rock', or a type of reverse swing. Holding the wet side towards leg, I practised inswinging yorkers. Years later Shane showed me how old cricket balls weighted on one side with spit could bend the same way. It was something he'd picked up from Mike Whitney and Wayne Holdsworth at NSW training. The principle was that the ball had similar properties to a lawn bowl with bias. Shane and I had experimented with it for the Blues and Mosman.

There was also another way of 'reversing', by keeping one side of the ball rough and dry, and the other as smooth as possible. In this, the theory was that air travelled more quickly over the smooth side and created a drag effect. Like conventional swing there was some mystery to it because there were days when it just wouldn't work, and others when the ball started to go unexpectedly. Unlike conventional swing, the ball swung much later, making it even tougher to play. When it worked, it was one of the most, if not *the* most lethal weapon of the fast bowling trade. I felt I could knock over any batsman in the world with reverse swing. That's not being arrogant; I just believed I had the ability and pace to be very difficult to play, especially for a tail-end batsman. So, when the ball started moving against the Indians, I knew I had a good chance of picking up more wickets.

I heard someone from the crowd say: 'He could get five. Five on debut! How good would that be?' Until then, I hadn't thought about a 5-for; I was just out there having fun. India were 5-167 when I started the fifth over of my third spell. First ball, I went for the spit-rock yorker that ended up being a shin-high full toss that swung in late and bowled Mannava Prasad. Next ball I went for the yorker again, and this time I got it spot on, hitting Ajit Agarkar on the foot. I appealed, the slips cordon appealed, and I reckon about 50,000 at the ground went up as well; Shane was in the crowd with his Mosman teammates Andrew Yates and Craig Hughes. He told me later he reckoned he was first out of his seat and spilled his beer. 'Shep' – umpire Shepherd – put his finger up, and I was on a hat-trick. I didn't want that moment to end, but part of me was wanting to race off the field and ring Mum and Dad. When I went back to my mark Tugga jogged up from gully to have a word. I was too pumped to remember what he said; nor did I know what field I had. I knew what I was going to do with my next delivery: if I'd been two times lucky, well, why not three? The noise was deafening as I ran in while fans belted the advertising boards around the boundary fence. I let the ball go, and it just wasn't to be. Javagal Srinath pushed a widish one to cover, and I smiled. I wasn't disappointed. How could I be? If I could bottle up a mixture of a natural high to sell, I would have chosen that moment.

Three balls later I sniffed Srinath and the ball popped off his gloves to Mark Waugh in the slips. I turned around and appealed while running back and into the hugs of my teammates. The crowd was roaring and I was dreaming. On the replay on the scoreboard I saw myself saying, 'Far out, I've got 5-for!', or words to that effect. It was clear as day. Tugga came up and shook my hand and said: 'Well done.' He didn't show any great emotion, but I think quietly he was happy because his support for me had been justified. I was glad I'd proved him right; I would rather have let myself down than Tugga. I then walked back to third man, took my cap off and thanked the crowd who were on their feet. It was a great moment, definitely one of the best of my career.

I ended up with 5-47 off 18 overs and I got a couple more wickets in the second innings. We won by 180 runs, Australia's sixth straight Test victory. But there was one batsman I couldn't get out: Sachin Tendulkar. He got a century in the first innings and a 50 in the second. I was amazed how good he was. When he came out to bat I felt the energy lift in the field and crowd. Any fans of the comedy movie *Spinal Tap* might understand my efforts against Sachin in this way: you have a volume level of one to 10, 10 being the loudest, but then you have an 11, which is for super loud. I found I tried to do the same when I bowled to Sachin; I looked to find an extra notch that I didn't know I had. I don't really know how it happened, but it just did. I did the same against Brian Lara later in my career.

Extra notch or not, it made no difference against Sachin. No matter how fast I bowled, he seemed to have all the time in the world, and he had incredible wrists that could turn the ball on any angle, especially from outside off through midwicket and backward square leg. There was simply no margin for error in my bowling. I had to pitch on a good length on a fourth and fifth stump line in that corridor of uncertainty. Anything away from this was generally runs. He was just too good.

Despite my success in the Test I still hung back when it came to the winner's traditional grabbing of stumps at the end of the match. As we walked off Pidgey put his arm around me and congratulated me. Then, I felt a tap on the shoulder, and I turned to find Justin Langer pushing a stump into my hand. It was a Gilly-like gesture that made me feel as though I'd really graduated to being part of the team.

I enjoyed the celebrations in the dressing room, especially one moment that might surprise some of you: after treasuring my pristine baggy green, I couldn't wait to get some beer spilled on it. I wanted character, and to me the older your cap looked, the more respected you were. Tugga set the benchmark; his tattered baggy green was one reason why he was so revered. When the moment finally came and someone drenched me, I felt great, even though the beer stung my eyes. It's funny how that occasion, and others like it in the future, affected me, especially in Tests when I'd be out fielding in the sun and the stench of stale ale would follow me everywhere. That night I started a habit that stayed with me throughout my career: no matter how drunk I was after a celebration, I always knew where my baggy green was right up until the time I returned to the team hotel and put it in the safe in my room.

We moved on to Sydney for the third Test. Having matches only a few days apart didn't allow me much time to think about what I'd achieved on debut. That was a good thing because it would have been easy for me to put pressure on myself if I'd sat back and wondered: 'Well, I've got a 5-for but what happens if I don't do that next time?' Instead, I just tried to stay in the mood. I took six more wickets, and in a touch of deja vu, Javagal Srinath survived another hat-trick ball. We won by an innings and plenty in only three days.

There's always something extra special about playing on your home ground. The first time I came on to bowl the crowd went crazy, and after I'd run in for my hat-trick attempt Tugga said it was the loudest cheer he'd ever heard during a game. The most exciting part of all was the knowledge that Mum and Dad were there, although they had a few problems on the first morning. I'd given them tickets for the Members Stand, but they didn't realise it was first in, best dressed, and by the time they arrived they couldn't find a seat. So, the Doctor decided to sit on his esky at the bottom of the Australian players' walkway right next to the entry onto the field. It didn't worry him at all and he told Mum he was 'quite happy'. Inevitably, a security guard came along and told Dad he had to move, but the Doctor wasn't too keen to budge. The issue was finally sorted after Dad revealed he was my father, prompting the guard to take my parents to a private box where they enjoyed free food and drink all day. The Doctor was pleased with himself.

The match had a unique twist for me. How many Australian players have been given two brand new caps for their first two Tests? To mark the new millennium we wore special skull caps that were replicas of those worn in 1900. This time there was

The two greats who forced me to find '11' on the *Spinal Tap* scale! My friends Brian Lara and Sachin Tendulkar, both capable of playing shots that frustrated, yet amazed me.

© *Newspix/Phil Hillyard;* © *Hamish Blair/Getty Images*

It's impossible to go out in public in India without drawing a crowd. A simple run with my mate Mark Raisbeck in Goa, 2010, quickly turned into: 'Hello, Mr Brett! One snap, please!'
© *James Knight*

My career has taken me in unexpected directions, not least singing a duet with Indian legend Asha Bhosle.
© *Newspix/Sam Mooy*

My boss at Kings XI Punjab, Preity Zinta, during the 2010 IPL season.
© *Graham Crouch/IPL/Getty Images*

The smiles of Indian children are priceless. Taken on location at a TV shoot in Goa, 2010.

On tour with White Shoe Theory, Pune, India, 2010. Jak Housden (left), Mick Vawdon (centre) and Kere Buchanan (rear) aren't holding anything back!
© *James Knight*

To me, Neil Finn (Crowded House and Split Enz) is music royalty.

Not a bad technique from Prince William on his visit to meet residents of Flowerdale, a community hit by Victoria's 'Black Saturday' bushfires.
© *Samir Hussein/WireImage*

An Australian soccer champion and a bloke who treats me like family. My Weet-Bix brother, Tim Cahill.

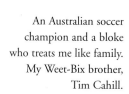

The great D. K. Lillee and the Fast Bowling Cartel (FBC). From the left of the photo: Glenn McGrath, me, D. K. himself, Michael Kasprowicz and Jason Gillespie.

Here's Neil Maxwell and his wife, Rachel. Maxi isn't just my manager – I have no doubt I wouldn't have gone as far in my career if it wasn't for his support, belief and never-ending loyalty and friendship.
© *Newspix/Richard Dobson*

My mentor, Alan Jones. Like Maxi, AJ has helped shape who I've become. He is so often the first person I turn to for advice when things are tough.

'H' and the Doctor – Mum and Dad. I love them so much.

Shane, Mum, me and my younger brother, Grant. This is as good a time as any to apologise to Mum and Dad for all the grey hairs we must have given them!

A more recent photo of the Lee boys.

My little man and best friend, Preston. He makes me look forward to every single day and has made me understand how precious life is. I look forward to the journey ahead with you, mate.

no beer spray on the treasure, and the cap now takes pride of place in a glass box in my study.

The winning celebrations were massive. At first we stayed in the dressing room where I spent ages sitting with Pidgey, chatting about Test cricket and what it was to be an Australian player. I did that a lot in my early days, listening to all the other guys talk about their experiences. Their main advice was nearly always the same: 'Have fun, and believe in yourself.' Warnie gave me one of the most valuable tips. He said Test cricket was just like playing grade with only the very, very best of grade players, or playing a Sheffield Shield match with only the very, very best of Shield players. Yes, the pressure was greater, but there was no need to over-complicate your game just because you were playing at the highest level.

Back then there was a different structure in the dressing room after a game. There certainly wasn't the same level of media management; it was generally the captain and the star performer who'd handle the interviews, and they'd be back before celebrations really got going. But by the end of my career the captain could be out of the room for the first half hour after the match, and there'd be three or so other guys who'd done well also fronting the media. So, straight away we'd have a third of the players missing. I'm not complaining, but it did separate the team. We really didn't settle down for a drink together until about an hour after the game, if not longer. And by then it was easy to have lost that initial glow.

As was the case after the Sydney Test, there was nothing better than coming off after the game, waving to the crowd one minute, and the next hearing the *psssht* of a cap pulled off a beer bottle. It was all part of the team game, an important part: scull the first beer, then sit around with your mates and have a laugh and a joke. The difference between my early Tests and my last ones was enormous. I think they've even banned beer now for the first half hour or so after a match. I don't agree with that. You have to enjoy yourself as well.

A foggy memory leaves some details sketchy, but I think it was a few hours after the win – it was certainly after we'd sung the team song – when we heard a knock, knock, knock from under the floor of the dressing room. I had no idea what it was, but it was obviously a common happening because someone said: 'Righto, it's time.' We all went out the front of the dressing room, down the walk past the members' seats, took a sharp right at the bottom, and another right took us under a staircase, through a door, and into a low-roofed room where the knocking had come from.

Pidgey started sledging Justin Langer. 'Is this where you live?' he kept asking him. JL was the only one who didn't have to duck.

Finally the mystery was revealed to me. It was time to have a drink with the cellarmen who worked below the Members Stand. They asked me to sign a white door that had been autographed by other players over the years. Then we cracked open the beers and enjoyed one of the lesser known traditions of playing at the SCG.

Somewhere along the line, the team, with most of us wearing our skull caps, had a game of tag on the ground. I was still in my whites when I got back to the hotel several hours after the match. I wanted to wear those clothes as long as I could. Here I was, walking around with the Australian emblem on my chest, and I didn't want that moment to pass.

There was double reason for me to celebrate that night because I was told I'd been chosen in the Australian squad for the one-day tournament, the Carlton & United Series, involving India and Pakistan. And that wasn't all: my brother

Shane had been picked too. I thought of all the dents in the roller door, and smiled. Shane had been my guide through the cricket ranks; from playing at Oak Flats High, to grade, to NSW and Australia A's, he'd always been there to make my transition easier. Now we were on the brink of playing together at the highest level. Neither of us thought much about how my rapid rise had seen me jump ahead of Shane; we were simply back together again, and that's what counted.

In the build-up to the series, there was a lot of media hype about two sets of brothers, the Waughs and the Lees, being in the one team. All that mattered to Shane and me was getting out on to the field together. In the lead-up I was asked what number I'd like to have on my back. If I could have, I would have gone for eight because it's always been my favourite number: I was born on the eighth, and I grew up at 8 Winter Avenue. However, Brendon Julian already had claims on that, and my second favourite number was five, which Steve Waugh had. So, I did the mix and match and went for 58.

I was chosen to make my debut in the first match against Pakistan in Brisbane, but unfortunately Shane was 12th man. I bowled second change behind Pidgey, swing bowler Adam Dale, and Andrew Symonds. I finished with 0-39 off 10 overs which included two no-balls and three wides, and I was bowled by Abdul Razzaq for two. Not one for the scrapbooks, especially when Australia lost a low-scorer. Nevertheless, the atmosphere of 35,000 fans demanding instant action gave me the taste for a game that suited my philosophy of being a performer as much as a cricketer. I had a gut feeling good times lay ahead.

The next match gave me the best moment of my career. It didn't matter that I didn't take a wicket because the sense of occasion far outweighed personal achievement. We played India in front of 70,000-plus fans at the MCG, and as we walked out onto the field before the match, I could only look at the number 20 on the back of the player in front of me. Then I looked at the name: Shane Lee. I stood next to Shane for the national anthem, and realised that no matter what happened in the future, this moment could never be taken away from us, or our family. To play cricket for your country is an incredible honour; to play cricket for your country with your brother is simply happiness.

For some strange reason the occasion made me think of lunch during a grade game in Sydney when Mum and Dad had bought a couple of chickens, and our teammates flocked over because they knew the Lees put on a good feed. I'd bowled badly that morning, and H had told me: 'Why don't you just pitch the ball up further and get a nick?' My teammates laughed and I'd felt a little embarrassed at Mum's simple approach. Now, with Shane at my side at the MCG, such memories reminded me of how lucky we were to have had such a loving upbringing.

Shane had a handy match, knocking a quick 22 at the death, and taking a wicket, while I again couldn't break through. We won by 28 runs. My first one-day international scalp came in the next match against India in Sydney: Devang Gandhi caught by Michael Bevan for six. That is as much as I can tell you about it!

The whole series was a blur of matches, airports, hotels and training sessions. It was an important part of my education as a professional cricketer. Touring life was all so new and exciting to me that I had no reason to be deflated by it, but I accepted how tiring and relentless it could seem for the 'been there, done that' guys in the team like the Waughs.

My real breakthrough moment came in my sixth game when I took 5-27 in a huge win against India in Adelaide on Australia Day. The Indians were in miserable form, and it seemed they already had their minds on going home. Two matches later Shane and I hugged each other after we'd managed our first wicket together: Azhar Mahmood, caught Shane, bowled me. That was in the second match of the best-of-three final series against Pakistan. We won 2–0.

Shane and I both had pleasing campaigns. We took 16 scalps each, three behind the leading wicket-taker, Glenn McGrath. Shane also batted well. We ended up playing 17 matches together before Shane slipped out of the selectors' minds about 18 months later. I have no doubt he should have played Test cricket. He definitely had the talent. It would have been fantastic to have worn baggy greens together, but some things just aren't meant to be. Shane played 45 one-dayers for Australia. I'm very proud of him, as is our whole family.

I loved the whole feel of the one-dayers: playing under lights; being in the so-called pyjamas in front of packed houses; bowling short spells; having the odd swipe and hope as a batsman; and relishing the chance to be a performer, an entertainer. Always aware of the hype, I fed off the energy of the crowds. Sometimes I did that too much, and that led to me becoming too excited and erratic. But most of the time the atmosphere helped me, and hopefully I helped pump the crowd up as well through my bowling. What better stage could I want?

In analysing my career, it's fair to say that one-day cricket has come a lot easier to me. Possibly I grasp the game a lot better than Test cricket. In Tests, a batsman generally has time and the fast bowler has to be patient and be prepared to work on plans that may take overs and overs, if not hours to work. My immediate nature is to attack, even if that means going for a few runs. In one-dayers my preference for attack is met by the batsman's need to score as quickly as possible, and that creates more chances to get wickets. From that initial Carlton & United

Series I always felt I had a good chance of taking wickets when any batsman tried to step it up against me. Alternately, I had to work much harder in Tests to find out what suited me and the plans of the team.

After playing just two Tests and nine one-dayers in my initial international season I didn't have a worry in the world. I capped off the dream by being named the Sir Donald Bradman Young Cricketer of the Year at the inaugural Allan Border Medal presentation night in Melbourne. I was on a high and living very much in the moment. Thankfully, there were some other people around me who saw beyond the moment and their importance to me was only just beginning.

8

If I had any doubt my life was changing after playing for Australia, I needed only go for a walk along the street or into a shop to buy a coffee. Suddenly, I was being recognised and stopped by people wanting to chat with me. Complete strangers were coming up to me and saying things like: 'Great stuff. You're so quick. How fast do you reckon you can go?'; 'I like it when you bowl bouncers'; or 'Gee, I'd hate to face you'. It was all good fun and certainly nice to hear.

The increase in my public profile didn't stop there, as I began receiving offers from companies to endorse their products. Shane and I were being managed by Shane's former NSW teammate, all-rounder Neil Maxwell, who'd returned to Australia after a stint as marketing director for New Zealand Cricket. Before that, he'd learnt so much about the running of the game while working as an administrator under the guidance of the legendary chief executive of NSW Cricket, the late Bob Radford. I'd first met 'Maxi' while he was playing for the Blues several years earlier. He recalls the occasion better than me: it was during a state practice when players were trialling yellow balls for potential use in day–night Sheffield Shield matches. Maxi remembers taking note of me because I clean bowled Steve Waugh, which he reckons he hadn't seen anyone do at state training. I was just a teenager. Maxi tried to give me the nickname 'Flora' because Shane had already been christened 'Meadow', in relation to the margarine brand. Thankfully that name didn't stick.

Prior to Maxi, Shane and I had had stints with two other Sydney managers, Peter Culbert and Warren Craig, but the fits weren't right. So, at about the time I began playing for Australia, Shane asked Maxi for guidance, and the two of them went around interviewing prospective managers, which Maxi reckoned was great because they got a lot of free lunches. However, Maxi and Shane weren't confident they'd found a suitable person. As a result, Maxi agreed to do it himself. This was a big step for him because he hadn't done that type of work and he didn't know whether he'd be good at it or would enjoy it. All these years later, I can say he has been both a brilliant manager and a very good friend.

Good management of the modern-day athlete is essential. I live in the age of professional sport, and despite the views of some critics who believe the purity and romance of cricket have surrendered to the players' quest for money, I'm not ashamed to say I recognise the importance of being a businessman. When the word 'endorsement' is mentioned the thing that springs to my mind is: 'Image is everything.' Whether on the field or off it, it's important how you behave and present yourself. This isn't only a matter of knowing right from wrong in a common-sense approach to life, but images also determine marketability. Right from the start of my career for NSW I was conscious of this. My parents, Shane, and Richard Bowman at Barclay's Menswear had all offered me valuable advice, and when Maxi came into the picture my views only strengthened. Yes, I wanted to endorse products, but I wouldn't race into any deal because it would simply help my bank balance.

The first big offer came from an alcohol company. I'd only just started playing for Australia, and was flabbergasted that a business wanted to commit to a multi-year deal worth about $300,000 a year. It could have set me up as a millionaire in no time, but I told Maxi the image wasn't what I wanted. Maxi agreed, which was to his credit because it would have been easy for him to push the deal on me and take 15 to 20 per cent of the cut. That was an important moment for both of us because it said a lot about Maxi's integrity and personality. At that stage I think the only deal I had in place was one that enabled me to get product from a sunglasses company.

Soon after, we were approached by Derick Frere of Star Advertising, who wanted to align me with the Sanitarium Health Food Company. I knew straight away the fit was perfect for me. It was a wholesome Australian business that identified strongly with children. Like so many other Aussies, I'd grown up on Sanitarium's most famous product, Weet-Bix, and was happy to be positioned in the market as a 'Weet-Bix kid'. It gelled perfectly with the strategy that Maxi and I had already developed to place me in the health and fitness area. Maxi was so new to player management that he admitted he 'didn't have a clue' about what any potential deal was worth. He did some research, but as much as anything he went on gut feel. We agreed to a television commercial deal worth about $100,000.

The ad was filmed at North Sydney Oval, and was based around the theme: 'Brett Lee does seven Weet-Bix. How many do you do?' All I had to do was run in and bowl, and through the creativity of television, a bolt of lightning followed the ball until it smashed into exploding stumps. I lobbed up to the shoot unaware of how much was involved. Certainly I hadn't expected to have a make-up lady especially assigned to me. I reckon a few of my teammates will laugh about that, considering they've always joked I'm a metro man who's very precious about my hair. I thought the whole experience was fantastic. I know a lot of athletes who don't enjoy fulfilling their sponsorship commitments, but I loved it. It gave me a small taste of television, and once again, just like being on the field and playing for real, I felt as though I was a performer.

After the commercial went to air, my mates rang up and called me the Weet-Bix Kid, and people had a reason beyond cricket to stop me in the street. I liked that. I also received letters from boys and girls telling me how many Weet-Bix they ate; some boasted they could beat me, and even challenged me to competitions.

Doing that deal was one of the best calls away from cricket I've ever made. I'm still involved with Sanitarium and am indebted to many people over the years, especially Christina Hawkins, the first marketing manager I had an association with. Always friendly and supportive, Christina took a risk in signing me because it was a rarity for an individual to be aligned with the Weet-Bix brand. Over the 2004–05 summer, Sanitarium actually renamed one in every six of their Weet-Bix products 'Brett Bix'. It was the first time in their 76-year history that they'd done anything like that. I'm so grateful Christina and her colleagues took the initial chance with me, and I hope Sanitarium is as well.

I was surprised how quickly other opportunities came across Maxi's table. One minute I was bowling a lightning bolt, then the next I was driving a new BMW Z3. The arrangement with a dealership at Rushcutters Bay was too good to be believed. All I had to do was drive the sports car around, and after I'd done about 10,000 kilometres, I'd take it back in and I'd be given a new one in a different colour. It was sensational. There I was: 23 years old, driving with the car top pulled back and the sunnies on. How cool! And they were giving me the car for nothing!

I don't want to sound flashy; I'm simply giving you an idea of the perks of professional sport. Of course I enjoyed it, but I don't think it went to my head. No matter what people have given me or what endorsements have been made, I've never thought: 'Hey, I'm a superstar, so I can walk around with my head in the air.' That is so far from the truth that it's probably the other way around. I love all the spoils that go with my position, but I haven't found it hard to keep my feet on the ground. The people closest to me wouldn't let me carry on like a wanker.

In the years since the Weet-Bix deal, and many other endorsements that have made me wealthy, some strangers have said to me, 'You're a spoilt brat!' or 'You don't deserve what you've got!' In those cases, because I'm not a confrontational guy, I've generally told them, 'Yeah, I know, but I'm getting paid to do something I love, so that's pretty cool, isn't it?' However, most people who stop me are full of encouragement, just like they were at the start of my career.

I've been really lucky with Maxi. Like him, I was very green at the start of our relationship, but we were both adamant about one thing: I'd look after what happened on the field, and he'd take care of off the field; I'd separate the two aspects of my life massively. I have no doubt if I had become heavily involved in Maxi's day to day work, it would have affected my cricket. I trust Maxi. He has a job to do. It's a great arrangement.

Maxi wasn't the only new person to come into my inner circle at the start of my career. Initially I didn't know what to think when Six and Out member and NSW player Gavin Robertson rang me to say radio talkback host Alan Jones wanted to interview me. Gavin was a good friend of Alan's.

At that stage I didn't want to give out my phone number to anyone in the media because I'd been warned by other players that once one journalist had a number every journo had the number. Whether this was true or not, I was certainly cautious. Gavin assured me all would be fine, so I agreed. Alan, one of the most influential media commentators in Australia, had been Sydney's top rating breakfast announcer for years. At the time he was working for 2UE, although he switched to 2GB a couple of years later. Because of his reputation I considered him an intimidating figure, but he was really nice to me during the interview, and we agreed to catch up soon afterwards.

When we finally met we clicked straight away. He was an avid sports fan who'd achieved great success as coach of the 1984 Grand Slam-winning Wallabies, and he'd also been in charge of the Balmain rugby league team in the early 1990s. I was taken by his knowledge about anything and everything, sport and otherwise. I also came to know him as a very generous and kind man. He didn't only become my good friend, but, together with my dad, he became a mentor who I'd turn to at various times throughout my career. I became a lot more street smart because of AJ. Right from the start, he taught me how the world worked and how different types of people behaved in different ways. Most of all, he encouraged me to never stop being hungry. He'd say things like: 'Don't be happy with a 3-for or a 4-for, get yourself five or more.' He even said I could get a Test hundred! I never thought I could do that, but AJ gave me self-belief and helped bring out the best in me.

I'd won the lottery having people such as Maxi and AJ behind me. I knew that sooner or later I'd hit some rough patches, and having trusted people to turn to gave me comfort and confidence.

9

My first international Test and one-day tour was to New Zealand from February to April 2000. I wasn't to know until several months later just what a bearing this trip would have on my career.

The tour started with a six-match one-day series which Australia won 4–1, with one washout. There are so many one-day games played that they blend into each other, and unless something incredible or unusual happens, I don't remember the details of most of them. However, there were a couple of incidents in this series that I'll never forget. First, in the opening game at Wellington's Basin Reserve I took one of my flukiest-ever catches. I was down at a squarish fine leg when Chris Cairns top edged a pull off Glenn McGrath. I thought the ball was going to go pretty fine and at best I might have been able to stop a boundary. I sprinted towards the sightscreen and was surprised to see the ball carrying further in the swirling wind than I'd initially judged. I kept bolting until I realised I'd overrun the likely landing spot, so I put the brakes on and threw out my left hand behind me. Some-how the ball stuck. Chris Cairns had walked under a ladder that day.

My second memory is the result of just one ball I bowled during the third match, a day–nighter, at Carisbrook, Dunedin. Of all the crowds I played in front of, few were as angry and badly behaved as this one. You could say they were feral. Dunedin is a university town, and the students seemingly came in their thousands to cheer their team and heap rubbish on us. The Black Caps were chasing a big target, and their last realistic hope of reaching it was a partnership between all-rounder Chris Harris and wicketkeeper Adam Parore. I'd copped some punishment earlier in the innings and was keen to make amends. After keeping the ball up for a while I dropped one in short that took off and forced Adam to throw his head back. Unfortunately for him, his helmet fell off and knocked the stumps.

I thought it was a legitimate wicket and Adam started walking off without reacting, but then he saw the umpires conferring. A delivery over shoulder height was a no-ball, but the umpires were comfortable with their decision, and the game should have continued as normal. But when replays on the big screen were shown, the crowd reacted. Players learn to live with boos and jeers, but when things like cans and pieces of wood are hurled onto the field it's another matter altogether. Some people were even throwing lit pieces of paper and cardboard cartons.

At the end of the over I went down to fine leg and received an absolute earful, and then I was hit in the back of the head by a plum. I turned around and saw only three security guards among the masses. I'd had enough, so I joined all the other outfielders who ran into the middle. The game eventually stopped for several minutes while all the rubbish was cleared. All the players were either annoyed or angry. I was actually frightened because this was a new experience, one that I never wanted to repeat, but at various times throughout my career it would be. There will never ever be an excuse for that type of behaviour.

We won the match, and on our way back to the team hotel we stopped in at a McDonald's that was crowded with cricket fans making their way home. Some of them gave us a hard time. One guy, who was dressed in an old Adidas shirt, tried to get under Matthew Hayden's skin, but 'Haydos' told him to pull his head in. The next morning we discovered one of the tyres on the team bus had been slashed. A small knife and note signed by 'Adidas Three Stripes' was found. Our manager, Steve Bernard, reported it to the police, and we had no further troubles. It's disappointing that sport should ever come to that.

After the one-day series we played a Test warm-up against provincial side Northern Districts in Hamilton. Forget how many wickets I did or didn't take; one umpire, Dave Quested, will certainly remember me for a wrong reason. He reported me for running through the crease and trying to hurt number 11 batsman Bruce Martin late on the first day. I've never been a cheat, and the implication that I was in this game still makes me angry. Sure, I was trying to intimidate Martin by getting into his ribs, but that was it. Fast bowlers are allowed to do this, aren't they? Unfortunately, the evidence of my boot's spike marks wasn't good for me: I'd stuffed up my run-up and landed about a foot over the popping crease.

Umpire Quested warned me, and I immediately apologised. But it didn't end there. After the day's play was over, Quested took a tape back onto the field and measured my indiscretion. He then told the media. I was stunned, and my position wasn't helped by team management's decision not to allow me to comment. After the match I apologised to Martin who accepted it was an accident. Years later, the incident was brought up again by some sections of the media when I was in the firing line for bowling a beamer to Brendon McCullum. Both experiences underlined to me how important it was to take the good with the bad. The public spotlight can be a great place to be, but it can also be very fickle. I didn't realise that as much as I would later in my career.

It was best to forget about the controversy and get stuck into the three Tests, where my good form from the Indian series continued, and I collected 18 wickets in Australia's clean sweep. Several moments stood out for me. On the opening day of the first Test at Eden Park, Auckland, bowling conditions had been good all day on a pitch with inconsistent bounce. We'd been rolled for a modest total, and needed to hit back hard. I came on second change, and after Damien Martyn took a screamer to help me get rid of Craig Spearman, the Kiwis sent in Craig Wiseman as a nightwatchman. They were three down with a couple of overs to go.

In the last, Wiseman came on strike against me with only three balls left. Tugga ran up to me and told me the plan was simple: he was going to put in a bat pad, and leave the batsman sweating on a short one. I was to give him what he expected, and then pitch the next two up. I bowled the bouncer. No luck. Next ball, a play and miss to a full, wide one. So, one ball to go. Tugga came up to me again and asked what my plan was. There was only one thought: yorker. I charged in, got the ball on the spot swinging in, Wiseman played too late, and the stumps were rocked. It's a great feeling when a plan comes off.

For me, the biggest moment of the match came in the second innings after Wiseman brushed an attempted sweep up in the air for Gilly to take the catch. It was Warnie's 356th wicket, beating Dennis Lillee's Australian record. Warnie put his hand in the air and acknowledged the crowd and his teammates. So much has been said and written about him over the years; some people love him, some hate him, others laugh at him, and there are others who accept him for what he is and isn't. I look back on my time with Warnie and think what a privilege it was to be alongside one of the greatest players in cricket history. He wasn't just a cricketer; he was a superstar, a rock star.

Although my knowledge and interest in other sports is small, I reckon few athletes in any type of game have had as much of an impact as Warnie had. After all, he started a whole generation of kids wanting to bowl like him at a time when leg spinning was considered a dying art. Whenever he came on to bowl, I was like so many people in the crowd: I expected something to happen. Warnie had charisma and an aura around him that allowed him to intimidate batsman from the moment he was at the top of his mark. He often gave the impression that the batsman was lucky to survive every single delivery. Yes, he sledged a bit, but I reckon he could play with batsmen's minds just by looking at them; with a glare or even a smile he could say: 'You know I got you out last time, and you know I'm going to get you this time. Why waste your time trying?' It wasn't arrogance, it was just Warnie.

He was also a 'cricket nuffy' who could talk and talk and talk about the game. He knew every batsman, stat and player. Outsiders may have thought he was just a freak who lobbed up and bowled a good leggie, but he was much more than that. He thought deeply about cricket, and was so on top of his own game that he knew exactly what he needed to do to succeed. I don't think I'll ever see another player like him. Definitely one of a kind.

In the second Test at the Basin Reserve I opened the bowling for Australia for the first time, and took two wickets within two overs. As the innings went on I came across one of the best batsmen I ever bowled to. Chris Cairns mightn't have the greatest stats, but he was an amazing player. He came to the crease with his team really struggling, so his answer was to go on the all-out attack. He smashed a century, and belted me. I was hit for some big sixes in my career, but few could match those in windy Wellington. I was bowling rapidly, with a hurricane behind me, when I decided to sniff Chris. He let the ball go, and in my follow through I glared at him, which in hindsight was a mistake. The next ball I bounced him again, and he had a go at hooking it. At first I thought he got a top edge, but that changed after the ball sailed over the fence, out of the ground, over a roundabout, and went rolling down the road. It took at least a couple of minutes to get it back. Mark Waugh said: 'That's massive!'

The next over I went charging in with the vision of ripping the poles out. I pitched the ball up and Chris launched a rocket straight back over my head. It was a huge hit against the wind. Another six. To make me feel even smaller, Chris winked at me as though he was asking: 'So what are you going to do now, kid?' I actually really enjoyed it. There are few better sights in world cricket than a batsman willing to take up the challenge against a fast bowler. It's great to be part of it, and it's great for the crowd. Chris got a half century in the second innings as well. Cairns two, Lee nil!

The final Test in Hamilton gave me my most satisfying return for the series: 5-77 and 3-46. My dismissal of Craig McMillan in the first innings reflected my fortunes in the five Tests I'd played to that point. Craig was batting really well and I was beginning to wonder how I was ever going to get through him. As I was walking back to my mark, Michael Slater, who was standing at mid-off, told me he wanted a wicket with the next ball. He even specified he wanted a caught behind, and asked me how I was going to do it. We made a joke of it before I said I'd get the wicket by bowling wide of the crease and sending down a wide one to chase. Everything went according to plan: an ordinary delivery, an ordinary shot, and a simple catch for Gilly. Slats and I ran to each other and burst out laughing.

I think I intimidated New Zealand more than any other team I played against. This wasn't because I went out of my way to fire up when I bowled to them. In fact, they became the team I most enjoyed playing because they were such a good bunch of fellas. Over the years I developed many friendships with the Kiwis, none more than with Stephen Fleming, who was captain on the 2000 tour. Right from the first time I met him he seemed like a top bloke, the type everyone on both teams liked and respected. There have been few people who've represented their country with better values and spirit than Flem.

The start to my international career was a fantasy: 31 wickets at 16.06 in five Tests. I knew the golden run would break at some stage, so it was best to enjoy it while it lasted. The fun I was having was boosted by the media's and public's interest in my pace. After the New Zealand tour we headed to South Africa for a three-match one-day series. In the final contest at the Wanderers Stadium in Johannesburg I clocked two balls at over 156 kilometres an hour, one to Andrew Hall, the other to Jacques Kallis. They were considered the quickest by an Australian since Jeff Thomson pushed around the 160 k mark (100 miles an hour) in the 1970s. With Pakistan's Shoaib Akhtar also bowling at about the same speed, the media started to hype up Lee vs Akhtar and the battle to reach the 100 mile barrier. I didn't mind talking it up because I thought it generated interest, and behind it all, I knew I could do it. Breaking the barrier was just going to be one of those things I'd never be able to pinpoint. If or when it happened, it would be a case of everything clicking for me. It was exciting to be part of it.

It was also exhilarating to think that I'd gone from being considered a fast bowler to an express bowler. Although some in the media equated the 160 k mark to the four-minute mile, I preferred to think of it in sprinting terms. How many people had run under 10 seconds for the 100 metres? To me, it was incredible to think that of all the millions of people who'd played cricket throughout history, I was one of only a handful who could do something that nearly everyone else couldn't, no matter how hard they tried.

But there was a catch. A big one. Forget Sachin Tendulkar and Brian Lara; the hardest person I ever played against was myself, or more precisely, my body. Keeping in mind I'd already bowled for seven years at about 140-plus kilometres an hour before my Test debut, the cumulative stress on me was significant. That's especially so when you consider I was still growing for some of that time. Shoulder, back, hips, knees and feet all under the hammer ball after ball. And that's just the bones. I pulled up sore after every day of bowling right from the start of my Test career. I'd already had my back and arm problems, and reality told me I'd inevitably have other worries and potentially serious injuries as time went on.

About 15 overs into my debut Test I knew I had problems when I started feeling pain in my left ankle every time I landed it on the delivery stride. I already had aches in my right foot. This pain was magnified when I landed in foot holes towards the end of the match. As I had long done, I relied on strapping to help me through. Plus, I have a high pain threshold which mostly allowed me to adopt my 80 per cent rule: basically if my body was 20 per cent niggles and pains, I was still fit enough to play. From my junior representative days onwards, my interpretation of 'feeling fit' was often feeling good enough to get the best out of what my body could give. People on the outside don't understand this. So, let me repeat what I've said earlier: we were not put on this earth to bowl fast.

By the time I reached South Africa for the one-dayers, I was in agony in both ankles near the Achilles tendons. No-one in the team or support staff knew how bad I was. I got through the first two matches, at times with tears in my eyes, but on the morning of the series-deciding last game I could barely get out of bed. I knew I was in real trouble, but convinced myself that one more match wouldn't hurt me. I also took into account the lonely place you can go to when you're injured. Your replacement comes in, does his job, and you can be quickly forgotten. I didn't want to wish any possible replacement ill luck, but I certainly didn't want to give them a chance either. So, I was going to play, no matter what.

Prior to going out to bowl I prepared in a way that isn't advisable to others, although it was within allowable legal limits: I took two tablets each of Voltaren and Panadeine Forte, and to prevent any possible drowsiness I downed two cans of Red Bull. When I bowled I felt like Carl Lewis steaming in. Who knows if that contributed to me clocking the 156 k deliveries, but at least I couldn't feel a thing in my feet. I took three wickets, but we lost, thanks to some smart batting from Mark Boucher and Lance Klusener.

In the dressing room afterwards the painkillers wore off, and by the time I went to bed there was a constant throbbing in both feet. The next morning I stood up and the pain shot all the way to my knees. I looked down to find both ankles had swollen right up. I returned to Sydney and saw orthopaedic surgeon Kim Slater, who told me I had a posterior ankle impingement in both feet. In simple terms it was bone on bone caused through plantar flexion, or the landing of the foot, which created so much pressure that the bones at my ankle were squeezed together. Soon afterwards I went under the knife at the Mater Hospital. Kim cut away some bone and took out two floating spurs in my left foot and one in my right. These spurs were little pieces of bone that had chipped off through years of wear and tear. I was in a wheelchair the first day after surgery, then on crutches for a few days before I was allowed to put pressure on my feet and begin a recovery over several weeks. It was frustrating, but I couldn't hold off any longer. As it turned out, I couldn't have chosen a better time because the Australian team's next commitment was three months away.

The break gave me a chance to return to Barclay's Menswear for a few days' work here and there and also get in some serious rehearsals with Six and Out. Throughout our development as a band we'd been guided by a number of people, including our manager, Luke Harris, who also played in a band called Funhouse with Phil Bowley and Mick Vawdon. These guys were great, and the Six and Out contingent and our mates were regulars at their gigs in Sydney. They always had a big following at inner-city pubs like Scruffy Murphy's. Funhouse became our 'Bradman Group', setting the benchmark for us to try to reach. Phil was an amazing guitarist, Luke was awesome on the drums, and Mick played bass guitar and had one of the best voices I'd ever heard live. He also came from a sporting background, having been a junior Australian representative rugby league player. He and I became great mates. I taught him about cricket, and he did the same with me about music.

Of all the people involved in our music no-one was more influential than Garth Porter. After helping us earlier with our three-track CD, he backed up to work with us on a full album. We set to work in his studio during the winter of 2000.

We also invited some other prominent people to help us, including Daryl Braithwaite, Steve Waugh and Channel Nine sports commentator Ray Warren. My brother Grant, and cousin Luke, who'd taken up the guitar at about the same time I did, also gave a hand. The end result was a 12-track CD that included cover versions of 'Howzat'; 'The Nips Are Getting Bigger' (Mental as Anything); 'Just Keep Walking' (INXS); 'Psycho Killer' (Talking Heads); 'Eagle Rock' (Daddy Cool); and Paul Kelly's 'Dumb Things', in which we changed the words to make it a cricket-related song. The CD also had five originals written by Garth, and his country music buddies Troy Cassar-Daley and Colin Buchanan.

The originals were mostly subjects we could have fun with. 'Cyclone Sally' was about a female fan with tattoos, a tracksuit, cattle-truck cologne and a bucket of KFC. 'I've Been Dropped' told the story of a washed-up cricketer, while 'It's Over' was a serious song about a broken relationship. The two we knew were going to make a publicity splash were 'Can't Bowl, Can't Throw' and 'Eleven'.

'Can't Bowl, Can't Throw' played off the line that had caused controversy the previous season after Warnie was accused of muttering the words about fast bowler Scott Muller near a stump microphone during the Hobart Test against Pakistan. That was the second and last of Scott's two Tests, and I replaced him in the Australian squad. Channel Nine cameraman Joe Previtera eventually admitted he'd made the jibe. Our song was in no way meant to make fun of Scott. We just used the line to build a chorus theme around a lighthearted cricket song.

We also made a video clip that took two days to shoot. I played the role of a hopeless schoolboy who bowled the ball into the sides of nets, and couldn't catch a cold. That was easy enough, but the highlight came when we shot some scenes one night at an inner-city pub in Sydney. The record company, EMI, invited employees and friends to be extras in the crowd that also had 'real' people who were briefed before we started. We had to play the song about 15 times until the producers had enough different camera angles. It was when someone threw a bra over Shane's guitar that I thought to myself for the first time: 'Far out, we really are a band!' The video ended up getting on *Rage*, the long-running music program on ABC-TV. I thought that was cool.

'Eleven' was a more serious song, capturing moments in cricket through history. These are the words:

Baggy green, Test in creams
SCG, childhood dreams
Bodyline, 99.9
Windies tied, Hansie lied

McGilvray's call, underarm ball
McCosker's jaw, twins of Waugh
Healy stumps, blaster thumps
Lillee bumps, Howzat ump

Chorus:
It's the power of eleven
It's the spill of emotion
It's more than a game
A history aflame
It's the pride of a nation
Our spirits in motion
It's the roar of the crowd
Singin' out loud
Yeah, Whoa

Channel Nine ended up using the chorus for its promotion of the 2000–01 season.

The whole CD production spanned about three months. Everything in my life was going brilliantly. Sure, the ankle surgery had slowed me down, but considering I didn't miss any cricket, I didn't have anything to be concerned about. I was floating through every day. But it all came crashing down in a way I could never have expected. Despite the highs that music gave me, this period also included an episode that made me sick with worry, and it still pisses me off. It was a result of something that happened during the New Zealand tour.

10

During the 2000 winter I took a break from recording commitments with Six and Out to go to England on a business trip with Neil Maxwell. It was a chance to meet and greet prospective sponsors before Australia's Ashes tour the following year. It also coincided with the Wisden Cricketer of the Year Awards in London. Although we received an invitation, I didn't want to go. I told Maxi I preferred to get away from all things cricket related, but he was adamant I should attend. After an argument Maxi got his way, which was a blessing because of what happened: I was awarded the Young Cricketer of the Year that was presented by Sir Richard Hadlee and Courtney Walsh. I was stunned. I wasn't at all confident with public speaking, but I managed to stumble through a few thank-you words before I went back to my table and quietly asked Maxi: 'Do you think they [Hadlee and Walsh] would mind if I asked them to have a photo with me?' Of course they were more than happy to do so, but that still didn't stop me from feeling meek in their presence.

Afterwards, Maxi and I joined some others from the function to go to a jazz club. I still had my trophy with me, and I reckon to this day I'm the only one who's ever checked a

Waterford Crystal bowl in to the club's cloak room. That night further strengthened my bond with Maxi. I thought about my reluctance, if not stubbornness, earlier in the evening, and in assessing this I told Maxi: 'If you ever need me to do something, and you're *really* serious about it, remember this night.'

Maxi has a really good approach to player management which he attributes to something his mentor, Bob Radford, told him while they were working together at the NSW Cricket Association: 'You only go into the change room when the players have lost. People know how to have fun when they've won, but they need support when they're down.'

How true those words were just a few days after the Wisden function. We arrived back in Australia, and no sooner had we landed than Maxi told me we had to attend a meeting with Australian Cricket Board Chief Executive Malcolm Speed in the afternoon at the SCG. I presumed it was about contract negotiations, so I didn't ask any questions. But when Maxi and I met again a couple of hours later, he looked really worried.

'What's wrong?' I asked.

'Binga, there've been a few problems with you.'

'What do you mean?'

'Mate, you've been reported for throwing.'

The words didn't sink in until Maxi explained the whole situation. I'd been mentioned by umpires Venkat and Jayaprakash in the match reports for the first and third Tests in New Zealand. These in turn were passed on to the International Cricket Council by match referee Mike Denness. All I could initially say to Maxi was: 'This is bullshit!'

We met Malcolm Speed who was incredibly supportive. He told us I'd have to defend myself via a telephone hook-up with a panel of 10 'experts' who were members of the ICC. Malcolm said it was critical that we held a media conference as soon as possible to show we had nothing to hide. Before doing this, Maxi and I decided to speak with the boss of the Australian Cricketers' Association, Tim May. It was then agreed we'd hold a presser the following day.

That night, I was pretty shaken up by the time I returned to the Pyrmont flat I was sharing with Corey Richards. I walked around in a fog for a couple of hours unable to come to terms with what was happening. I believed I didn't have a problem, but it wasn't me that I had to convince. The thought of the potential repercussions hit me. I was furious. If someone was calling me a chucker, they were calling me a cheat. My view on that stays the same to this day. I don't give a damn what I do in life, but I don't cheat. End of story. I don't take drugs, I don't ignore the rules, and I don't manipulate people to gain advantage. I am not a cheat!

I calmed down a bit after I received a phone call from Steve Waugh who said that as far as he was concerned I had nothing to worry about. He told me not to listen to all the fuss that would follow, and suggested my only concern was about taking wickets. His support gave me a lot of confidence, and from that moment I was determined to try to stay positive. The next day Tugga and Malcolm Speed were at my side during the media conference at the SCG. It was a gut-wrenching experience, especially while I waited for what I expected would be a blitz of negative questions. However, I was surprised how supportive the journalists proved to be; they didn't push me too hard. I told them I believed I didn't have a problem, and that the whole issue went back to the time I broke my arm at the Australian Under-17 carnival in Hobart. Ever since then, I'd been unable to straighten my arm. Examining my action with the naked eye you wouldn't have to look twice to know my arm was bent, but this wasn't illegal. Under the laws of the game the problem came if an arm was seen to straighten during the delivery process. But I just couldn't physically do this, so how could I have a problem?

I was relieved when the presser was over, but the mental torment was only just beginning because I had three weeks to wait before the telephone hook-up. It was the toughest time of my career. Normally, a player would say injuries are the most trying things to overcome, but I'd take recovery from surgery over a chucking controversy any day. Realistically, I was facing a life sentence. It was a strange place to be. On one hand I knew beyond all possible doubt that I was innocent and felt I couldn't be judged any other way, but what happened if I was? It would have broken my career because a physical ailment that I couldn't change would have prevented me from trying to modify my action. In that case, it was career over.

I was humbled by how much support I got. Apart from friends and family, I received letters and emails from fans across the world. I was also stopped in the street by people wishing me good luck and telling me how much they enjoyed watching me. One night I received a call from Shane Warne who was in England playing county cricket for Hampshire. He'd recently had a lot on his plate after being involved in a phone-sex scandal. After I asked him how he was, he answered: 'Mate, where do I start?' The topic soon turned to me, and Warnie told me to stay strong and ignore the critics. Even Prime Minister John Howard defended me on television. But that didn't hide me from everything. Below is part of one email that Maxi's office received from an anonymous sender:

Think about it Brett when you next go to a restaurant. it is now your turn 'cos the Waiter/Waitress will come up to you (To Take your order) & say: 'Now what would the chucker like to order.'

I laughed it off and threw myself into Six and Out's recording sessions. Not for the first or last time music was one of my saviours.

I'll never forget 'D-Day'. It was 1 August. Maxi and I flew to Melbourne and headed for the ACB offices near the MCG. We met Dennis Lillee who I'd asked to be my expert witness – Maxi, Malcolm Speed and Tim May would also help represent me.

Despite assurances from Dennis that I'd be cleared, it was only natural for me to feel bloody nervous. We all went into a small room, and I couldn't take my eyes off a speaker phone on a table. It was strange to think that on other lines around the world there were people I'd never met who'd be deciding my future. There was also a whiteboard with each panel member's name written on it. I can only recall those of Sunil Gavaskar and Michael Holding. We'd decided we were going to put a tick next to the names of the people who said I was clear; I needed six to be given the green light to play again.

Each member had been given footage of about five overs I'd bowled during the matches I'd been reported in. The members spoke in turn, asking me various questions like, 'What do you think of your action?' and 'Why did you change from bowling side-on to front-on?' I felt my heart rate rising and falling, depending on whether I heard good or bad comments, and I really had to stop myself from thinking, 'Will I or won't I play again?' Some members of the panel voiced real concerns that they didn't know whether I threw or not. In hindsight I'm sure a key moment came when Dennis launched into a five-minute burst that destroyed any argument at all that I could possibly have an illegal action. He bluntly told them the whole issue was a joke.

The process took about an hour, maybe an hour-and-a-half. A few ticks went up on the board, but I had no way of knowing what would happen when Gavaskar, who was head of the panel, told us he'd ring back as soon as he could with a verdict. Fifteen minutes later Malcolm Speed answered the call and his smile gave away the result. I'd been cleared unanimously.

There's only one word to sum up my feelings: relief. That night, Maxi and I went out and had more than a few drinks to celebrate. I was very grateful for the support of Malcolm Speed who was very professional in his approach to the situation, but overall the whole process was amateurish. For such a serious issue the hearing should have happened with all the appropriate people in the one room. More footage from as many angles as possible should have been shown to allow complete technical analysis. The panel members should also have had an intricate understanding of the processes of fast bowling. Not all of them did. It still surprises me how there are so-called experts who don't know that wrist positions and body angles change for various deliveries. Maxi and I thought the whole affair was hit and miss, which was concerning to say the very least, considering my future and my livelihood were at stake.

In the years since then, I've periodically been tormented by the chucking issue. It's the old saying: 'Throw enough mud and some of it will stick.' That pisses me off. I've never thrown a ball when bowling, but I've still had the odd commentator or journo implying that my action is dodgy. Then it's written in the paper: 'allegedly throws the ball'. People don't read the 'allegedly'. They don't read 'could possibly throw'; they only read the implications of guilt. That's been annoying because I'll forever have to contend with the chucker's tag. It's especially

Brett Lee

been the case on tour. The English and South African crowds
have been the worst. Admittedly, most of them are making fun,
but they base their jokes on something incredibly serious. The
whole issue still grates me.

11

I was only in fourth class when the West Indies were carving up the cricket world on their way to a record 11 straight Test wins in 1984. The statistics didn't mean anything to me, but the names from this period certainly did: Joel Garner, Michael Holding, Malcolm Marshall. Going back even further I remember watching footage of Andy Roberts and Colin Croft. Then in later years, when I was going through high school and starting out in senior cricket, Courtney Walsh and Curtly Ambrose were the kings. It's unbelievable to think that all those fast bowlers, among others, came from a handful of islands that seemed an impossibly long way away when looked at through the eyes of a boy.

The 2000–01 season in Australia showed how times had changed. Thirty-eight-year-old Courtney, at that stage the most successful fast bowler of all time, was into the final period of his career, and he couldn't stop the Windies from losing to us 5-0. Along the way Australia set a new winning streak in Test cricket, and we also bowed to our own great paceman Pidgey McGrath.

Glenn was definitely the best fast bowler I played with or against. He was so good because he nearly always found a way to succeed at the big moments. That was shown in the series against the Windies where he took it upon himself to destroy Brian Lara. There was some talk that 'The Prince' had a leg injury, but you can't take any of the gloss off what Pidgey did to him. He dismissed him three times in the series, and tellingly they were the first three times Brian walked out to bat. The very first dismissal was all class: the ball pitched on off stump, Brian followed it, nicked it, and Adam Gilchrist did the rest. The Prince's first three scores were 0, 4 and 0. Think about how brilliant you have to be to shatter the confidence of a freak like Lara. Later, Justin Langer told me that when he was fielding at bat pad in the first innings, Brian had said to him: 'This is no fun anymore being out here batting.'

We won the first match in Brisbane by an innings and 126 runs inside three days, and equalled the Windies' record of consecutive Test wins. It was the Glenn McGrath show. Pidgey's match return was 10-27 off 33 overs. If you got those figures in schoolboy cricket you'd be wondering about the opposition.

After bowling anywhere from opening to second change in my previous Tests, it was great to get the nod as Pidgey's new-ball partner. When we bowled together, particularly throughout the early stages of my career, he had a terrific calming effect on me. I'd be flinging yorkers and bumpers, trying to get a wicket every ball, while Pidgey would run in and be content to build the pressure with maidens. Although we were very different bowlers, I learnt so much from him about patience and working on plans.

I managed to take four wickets for the match without feeling any ankle pain. The game also provided a welcome turnaround for my batting. Since my first Test I hadn't reached double figures. When I went to the crease we already had a good lead but were a long way from being convincing. I joined Gilly who reminded me of the 'achievement contracts' the Australian players had agreed to before the game. They were the idea of our coach, John Buchanan, who took a very analytical approach to the game. I'd signed off on facing 80 balls, a huge ask for a tailender.

After being nervous at the start, I got on a roll, and my confidence was further helped by Gilly who mixed serious conversations with lots of jokes. It probably helped that he had so much natural talent that he didn't have to bog himself down with too many technical thoughts; when in the mood he could pretty well slap any ball he wanted to. The more runs we got, the more Gilly made me laugh by pointing out people in the crowd, poking fun at himself, and challenging me to play various shots.

We put on 61 in pretty quick time before Gilly was out, and Stuart MacGill joined me. You could call MacGilla 'Robocop' because he was so stiff in his movements, and his helmet and bat added to the picture. I didn't think we'd last for too long, but before we knew it we were involved in one of those partnerships that would have frustrated me if I'd been bowling. We mixed some good shots with some straight-out flukes. I was pretty relaxed about it all until I realised I was getting more runs than I imagined. Then Robocop added to the pressure after he said to me: 'I promise I won't get out before you get your 50.' I was on 47 at the time. Two runs later it seemed as though I'd been on 49 for ages. Finally, I pushed a ball off Nixon McLean into the covers and Robocop took off, so I felt I had no choice but to go as well. I can't tell you who picked the ball up, but I can say I next saw it flying past me as I dived for the crease. I made my ground, the ball went for four overthrows and I'd got my first Test 50. My first six soon followed when I somehow managed to hit Marlon Black back over his head.

Robocop and I put on 50 before he was run out. I reached 62 and fulfilled Buck's contract to the letter by facing 80 balls. It all came to an end when Pidgey was cleaned up by Courtney Walsh for a duck. I can't recall my final partner's reaction after getting out but I don't think I'd be far from the mark if I said he walked off the field sledging himself. Throughout my career Pidgey was the funniest bloke of all to bat with, and I remember times when he'd come down for a chat between overs and say things like: 'I'm a dickhead. How'd I miss that last one by two feet?' It was great humour.

When it came to his bowling, he knew exactly what he was doing *all* the time. He showed that in the best possible way in the second Test in Perth. The build-up to the match had been full of media hype because Australia was on the brink of a record 12 consecutive wins, and my return to the notoriously fast and bouncy WACA pitch meant I fielded a lot of questions about how fast I thought I could bowl. I spoke with both Steve Waugh and John Buchanan about this, and we all decided I just had to keep bowling as I had been. If my speed pushed up, well, that was my good fortune.

The opening of the Test was one of the most exhilarating I was ever involved in. Tugga won the toss and went against the norm by sending the Windies in. I struck it lucky in my first over when I trapped Daren Ganga LBW. Then in my fifth over I got rid of Ramnaresh Sarwan, caught by Michael Slater in the covers. But all the main action had happened the over before. Pidgey had started it with 298 Test wickets. Three balls later he had 299 after Sherwin Campbell edged one to Ricky Ponting at first slip. So, in walked Brian Lara. In the build-up to the match Pidgey mentioned in the media how he would love to knock over The Prince for his 300th scalp. As only Pidgey could do, he talked it up that Lara was his bunny.

There was a real edge in the air as he ran in to bowl. He gripped the ball in 'Caddyshack' fashion, a delivery named after English paceman Andy Caddick who, when bowling to lefties, often held the seam at an angle towards first or second slip. The idea was that if the ball hit the seam it would jag away. Not every delivery did, but when it worked and was on line, it was a difficult ball to play. Pidgey pitched it perfectly on middle and leg, the ball jagged, Lara got a thick edge to it and MacGilla took a juggling catch on his knees at fourth slip. Three hundred Test wickets, and now on a hat-trick; it was as though Pidgey was executing his own script.

Another leftie, Jimmy Adams, was next in. Now, what would Pidgey do? When on a hat-trick a lot of different thoughts can race through your mind, but generally it's best to think about bowling a ball with the highest probability of getting a wicket. That means you aim for the stumps and hope to bring in LBW, caught or bowled into play. But Pidgey thought differently, and this difference helped define his greatness. I don't know what Jimmy was expecting, but I doubt he would have prepared himself for a short one that squared him up. He couldn't do anything more than pop up a simple catch to Justin Langer at bat pad. It was brilliant McGrath!

The Windies recovered slightly but they were never in the hunt after a Mark Waugh century steered us to a 200-run first innings lead. If you liken players to cars, Junior – Mark Waugh – was a Rolls Royce; he always looked pristine with his clean whites, collar up, and immaculate hair. Just wheel him out of the garage when needed. He also had the best catching hands of anyone I played with – just ahead of Shane Warne and Ricky Ponting – and his batting was a pleasure to watch.

Best of all, he had a dry sense of humour. I reckon one of the funniest quirks of cricket is the habit of the incoming batsman meeting the batsman already at the wicket before facing the first ball. Unless there is some really important tactic or something dodgy going on with the pitch, there's nothing really cricket related that needs saying. You generally don't need too much of 'Keep going, mate, keep watching the ball, watch hard' and so on. It goes without saying you have to do that. But when I walked out to join Junior in this Test, I could have done with a bit of reassurance because the Windies had just taken the second new ball and I was so anxious that my eyes must have looked like overcoat buttons. So, I met Junior and expected to hear some comforting words, but all I got was: 'They're bowling bloody rapid out here. Bloody quick. Good luck.' Then he turned around and went back to his crease.

We rolled the Windies cheaply again for another innings victory. I took 5-61, and was on a hat-trick for the third time in my Test career. I couldn't emulate Pidgey, but I sneaked into the history pages in another way by getting the final wicket, Walsh LBW, that triggered the celebrations for our record win. Twelve in a row. The team packed into a tight huddle and Ricky Ponting unexpectedly started shouting the team song. I felt goosebumps while we all yelled at the tops of our voices. As we walked off after doing a victory lap Tugga told me something that would ring too true too soon: 'Binga, enjoy this while you can because at some stage it will stop.'

That night we celebrated hard. I was one of several players still in my whites and wearing the baggy green when we reached the Leederville Hotel, one of a handful of pubs and nightclubs I *think* we went to. We sang the team song to the crowd who went bananas. Afterwards I seem to recall a couple of players running down the street with sparks flying from their spikes. As my career went on, those types of moments happened less and less. Back then there wasn't as much media and weren't as many people with mobile-phone cameras watching every move. We certainly weren't judged as much as players are now.

The next morning Tugga's words from the previous day echoed in my thoughts after I woke up and felt stiffness in my back. I actually knew something wasn't right during the Windies' second innings. I'd reached down to pick up something in the dressing room when I felt a pinch on the lower left side of my back. Team physiotherapist Errol Alcott advised me to take an ice bath and do some stretches. He then rubbed Deep Heat into the area, and the pain eased. I didn't think about it when I went back out to bowl, but I didn't do myself any favours. Some foot holes on the pitch had forced me to go wider on the crease, and that put a lot more strain on my back because I had to twist to push the ball back in.

The end result was that I headed back to Sydney for a scan that showed a slight line through my L3 vertebra. It was a warning sign that a stress fracture wouldn't be far away unless I rested. There was no definitive moment when I sustained the injury. I may not have even done it during the Perth Test; more than likely it was from the fast bowler's continual workload. Imagine getting a plastic ruler and bending it. Soon enough a few surface cracks will appear but the ruler won't necessarily break. But keep bending, and the lines become deeper until the ruler eventually snaps.

I was out for six weeks and missed the rest of the Tests. It was very tough to cope with, and I initially tormented myself by asking: 'Why am I going through this?' Despite the feelings of insecurity that injuries can cause, I was relieved after I had a good chat with Steve Waugh. He didn't want me to rush back because he wanted me to be primed for a four Test tour of India at the end of the Australian summer. He thought my ability to bowl reverse swing would be critical. So, although I was on the sidelines I was motivated by the fact I was still part of the captain's plan.

I wasn't allowed to do any hard physical exercise during the first three weeks of recovery, after which I started soft sand running each morning at Sydney's Balmoral Beach. My back continually grew stronger until I was given the all clear to bowl again just before the beginning of the one-day series with the West Indies and Zimbabwe.

I struggled for rhythm in my first couple of matches, and then I had the worry of feeling a twinge in my back that was thankfully nothing more than muscle pain. By the time I arrived in Perth for my fourth game, I was starting to feel more confident, especially after picking up a 4-for against the West Indies in Adelaide.

But the WACA wasn't kind to me. Coming on as second change against Zimbabwe I got tapped around at eight runs an over which turned out to be the least of my problems. I was fielding at fine leg when a ball was hit between me and Ricky Ponting at deep midwicket. Punter chased it down and flicked it back to me. I turned and loaded up for a flat throw into the wind. As I let the ball go, I heard a crack. Worse still, I felt it too, right near my elbow. My arm went blue, and pins and needles followed. I didn't want anyone to think I was soft, especially since I'd just come back from injury, so I stayed on the field. Another ball came my way and this time I bowled it back in. I tried not to look at my arm because it felt as though it had ripped apart at the elbow. The pain was up there with anything I'd ever experienced.

In a case of Murphy's Law I noticed Tugga giving me the signal to warm-up to bowl. I didn't have the guts to tell him what had happened; in my confused state I thought that somehow I could get through it. My first few deliveries came out as powder puffs, no more than 130 or so kays. I bowled two very slow overs, and then in my third I chased down a drive and tried pinging the ball back to Gilly with a sidearm throw. If ever there was a moment I could have screamed, that was it. As I walked back to my mark I stopped and pretended to do up my shoes to give me a chance to recover from the shock and pain. I had tears in my eyes. By the end of the over I knew I was in a hopeless position: 1-72 off nine overs and a cooked arm! Tugga, who was worried I'd reinjured my back, asked me what was wrong. I told him: 'I think I've snapped my arm in half.'

In the dressing room I was examined by Errol Alcott and team doctor Trefor James. With just the slightest pull on my arm I felt the bones shifting. It nearly sent me through the roof. Trefor confirmed the worst; at the very least my arm was broken. I then went into another room by myself and was so angry that I smashed my left fist into a wall. To this day, I reckon I actually chipped a piece of bone off the knuckle. I was taken to a hospital where X-rays revealed I'd snapped my ulna and severed the medial ligament and flexor tendon. The damage was extraordinary, considering it had come from a throw. I was booked in to be operated on by leading surgeon Greg Hoy in Melbourne the next day.

If that wasn't depressing enough, I had one final moment that confirmed I should have stayed in bed that day. On the night-time flight out of Perth with Errol Alcott, I was pretty high on painkillers and managed to relax a bit with my bandaged arm propped up. I'd just fallen asleep when I was whacked on the point of the elbow by a trolley pushed by a stewardess. Not for the first time in a matter of hours I held back a scream.

So, in what was to become an all too common part of my career, I was wheeled in to a theatre and sucked into a black hole. When I woke, my ulna had two screws in it and a piece of grafted bone that had been taken from my hip. The medial ligament was reattached, and some floating bone that may have been there since I broke my arm in the Under-17 accident in Hobart was also removed. I was in considerable pain for a few days, and was grateful to be given hits of morphine. In a really thoughtful gesture Neil Maxwell sent down one of his staff to keep me company while I was in hospital. Dominic Thornely was an up-and-coming NSW all-rounder who I'd met six years earlier when I'd gone to watch my brother Shane play an invitational match against England at Bradman Oval in Bowral. Dom had been employed by Maxi as a cadet to learn the ropes. He ended up spending most of his time organising my diary and servicing our clients. We became very close mates, and I really appreciated his support while I was recovering, even though I must have vomited in front of him a few times while fighting off the effects of the anaesthetic.

The setback reinforced my need to accept injuries as an occupational hazard, and despite media speculation that I would struggle to regain my pace while apparently having such a dodgy body, I never doubted I'd come back as well as ever. However, the injury meant I was no chance of going on the Test tour to India which was only a few weeks away. I can't deny it was very disappointing, especially when the three-match series turned out to be one of the best in history. India won 2–1, and confirmed their growing status in the modern era. Instead, I was left to count the days until the start of the Ashes tour in May. I was told my arm would heal in about eight weeks, and for the first three I wore a special traction brace that had its angle reduced every week.

It wasn't long after the brace was removed that I had one of those moments that gave my mates some cannon fodder.

I'd been nominated for *Cleo* magazine's 'Bachelor of the Year', a competition I treated as a bit of fun. The whole concept of being called 'sexy' embarrassed me. However, I suppose it was better to be thought of in that way than not being thought of at all; I've always tried to look fit and presentable, and then it's up to others to judge me. When it came time for the photo shoot I expected I could lob up in casual gear, pose for a few snaps, then head on my way. But the organisers had other ideas, and I had to model with my shirt off. I felt very uncomfortable, but overall it was a bit of a laugh. I ended up coming runner-up to David Whitehill, who my mates were quick to remind me was a dolphin trainer.

The *Cleo* award wasn't the strangest recognition I received. About a year earlier my mate Adam Rainford rang me to say he'd just passed a newsagency that had a board outside saying: 'Injury worry for Brett Lee.' It immediately got Adam's attention because I was 100 per cent fit at the time. On closer inspection he discovered the name in question belonged to a dog. As it turned out, it wasn't just any dog. By May 2001, Brett Lee was known as a small, ugly, black thing with one testicle that was blitzing its rivals in the most famous greyhound races in Australia. The titles meant nothing to me, but apparently any dog that could win the Interstate Challenge, Adelaide and Australian Cups, Maturity Classic, Golden Egg and Warrnambool Classic was the greyhound equivalent of Phar Lap. I met it and posed for photo shoots with it in Victoria. I remain quite chuffed to think the dog was named after me and is in the Australian Greyhound Racing Association's Hall of Fame. At one time it was part-owned by Australian Rules great Tony Lockett. Unfortunately it was put down in 2010, but not before it served another purpose that attracted headlines that made me grin: 'Brett Lee semen worth thousands.'

As the countdown to the Ashes entered its final month, I resumed bowling off a shortened run-up under the supervision of good mate and NSW team physiotherapist Pat Farhart. I was happy with my progress and my mood was further helped by a significant step forward in another part of my professional life: on 1 May, the Brett Lee clothing label was launched by model and author Tara Moss at a function at Barclay's Menswear.

The plan had been cemented over several months. At first I'd jokingly asked Barclay's owner Richard Bowman about the prospects of doing a label. His reaction surprised me: 'Well it's funny you should say that because I've been having a really good think and would like to run something by you.'

It all started from there. Richard had already influenced me tremendously. If I liken him to a cricket coach, he hadn't just taught me how to bowl fast; he'd also taught me about in-swingers, leg cutters, slower balls, how to bat, how to field, how to deal with the media. In terms of a fashion business this meant booking in and ordering items, and learning about margins, break-even points, rent, sales and staff. That was all while also getting the feel for different fashion styles and trends across the world, especially in Europe, which was six months ahead of Australia.

In doing our research before we started the label, Richard and I looked through hundreds, if not thousands, of fabrics. I also did discreet trials by wearing unbranded suits or shirts to see what types of comments I'd get from friends and the general public. I knew I couldn't please everyone, but if someone went out of their way to say something I took the feedback constructively. I also spent time at social functions looking at what other people were wearing. From that, I took away ideas.

Right from the start I was adamant I didn't want any sporting attire in the range. Perhaps things would change in the future, but at that stage I wanted a clear line between fashion and sport because I thought that brought out a difference in me. I certainly didn't want to be promoting a pair of cricket pants. So we settled on a range that included suits, coats, unisex T-shirts, jeans and polo tops. They were at the mid to lower end when compared with brands like Hugo Boss and Valentino.

Call it ego, or simply common sense, but I didn't want the venture to be a failure because I thought that would reflect poorly on me. Furthermore, I was conscious of not only putting my name to a piece of clothing, but being actively involved behind the brand. I wasn't going to endorse something without knowing why, or having an interest in the product; I wanted part of me to come through in what was sold.

Now, with the brand a decade old, I'm proud of what has been achieved. The label remains exclusive to the Barclay's business which, as I've mentioned, is now part of the Claude Sebastian department store. The greatest compliment I can get for my clothing is when an overseas visitor who knows nothing about cricket buys something and really likes it.

There was one occasion when an African–American came into the store when I was working between cricket tours. He chose one of my suits and kept saying: 'That's cool, man!' At the time I was breaking in a pair of Hugo Boss shoes made from stingray skin, and I had a matching belt. After the customer noticed them he said: 'Man, I really like your kicks, they are serious wheels.'

'Yeah, I've only been wearing them for three hours, but they're feeling good,' I replied.

He asked if the shop had any pairs in his size, 12 US. I told him there were only four pairs in the country, and although I tried fitting him into an available smaller size, he was out of luck. Then he asked me what size I was wearing.

'12 US,' I said.

He got quite excited and convinced me to let him try my shoes on. They fitted perfectly, and that made him even more pumped. Before I knew it he was saying: 'I'll buy the suit and a shirt but only if I can buy your shoes as well.'

'You want me to sell you *my* shoes?'

'Yes, sir. And I want the belt as well.'

Of all the things Richard Bowman and his staff had taught me, I'd never been prepared for a customer who only just stopped short of wanting to take the shirt off my back. After a little consideration I agreed, and we settled on a price we were both happy with. He walked out saying it was the best customer service he'd ever received; he even came back later to thank us, and strolled past the shop smiling and flashing his shoes. The greatest thing was that he had no idea who I was or that I had my own label. He probably went back to the US and told his friends about the day he bought the poor sales assistant's shoes and belt. Maybe he might come back one day. Repeat business is good business, and that's what I believe Barclay's has done well, and that in turn has helped me and my label.

Who knows where the fashion business will take me in the future, but I do have ideas. David Beckham is someone I'd like to emulate in some ways. I am by no means comparing myself to Beckham, but I have learnt from what he has done. He reached the top of his sport, the people loved him, he remains a good-looking rooster, and he has the knack of looking sharp and presenting a great image for his own attire. Whether it's due to him or the people behind him, he and his aligned brands have been very smartly and professionally positioned.

After the launch of my clothing label, there was only one thing I needed to round off a perfect May 2001. It came when the specialists said I'd fully recovered from my arm injury and was fit to take part in what is every Australian cricketer's dream: an Ashes tour.

12

I have the enviable knack of being able to sleep for entire flights, whether they are across the country or the world. That's what I hoped would happen when I boarded a plane to go to England to join up with the Australian team for a one-day series ahead of the Ashes. The rest of the players had already gone, but I'd been delayed because of a filming commitment for Sanitarium with my brother Shane, and Australian rugby players George Gregan and Matt Burke. After receiving special approval from the ACB, Sanitarium agreed to get me to England as soon as possible once the filming had finished. I didn't protest because it meant flying first class, something I'd never experienced.

I thought all the other passengers looked surprised when they saw this 24-year-old guy heading towards the pointy end of the plane. After I found my seat, I couldn't believe how many gadgets and buttons there were, and by the time we were in the air I was still struggling to work out what all of them did. I'd heard, or perhaps I'd seen it in movies, that the chairs went all the way back like beds, so I was very keen to find the right button and get to work banging out the zeds. I pressed what I thought was the appropriate button, but even with a slight rocking from me the back of the seat didn't budge. I tried again. Nothing happened. I tried a bit harder. Still nothing. I was getting frustrated and began to think my whole first-class experience would be wrecked by a dud chair that stayed upright. I thought of calling staff for assistance but how silly would that look? After all, fast bowlers already had a big enough reputation for stupidity. Not wanting to look like an idiot, I pressed the button once more and rocked back as hard as I could.

Crack!

Suddenly the chair folded back like an opened book, and I was hurled over it before landing at the feet of the two stunned people sitting behind me. It sounded as though a gun had gone off, and an attendant was quickly on the scene. All I could do was lie on the floor with a puzzled look on my face.

'I've got no idea what happened. The chair just broke,' I said. I was too embarrassed to tell the truth.

Luckily there was one spare seat, which the attendant directed me to. Before she went back to her other duties I asked her as casually as I could: 'Do you mind please just checking this chair works OK?' I paid careful attention to which button she pushed. Yep, it was different from the one I'd tried in the other chair, and just another fast bowler's moment. After that, I settled down and slept most of the way to Heathrow.

Not long before I'd left, there'd been some media speculation that I'd be the first player in history to earn $1 million a season from an ACB contract. It followed a four-year agreement between the ACB and the Australian Cricketers' Association that stated Australia's highest paid player would reach the mark within two years. Since I'd enjoyed a successful start to my career I was one of the names that popped up as leading the way.

Money is a trap for players, especially young ones just starting out. It's all too easy to think: 'Hey, this game is great! I'll get a few runs or some wickets, and make some big bucks. How cool is that!' The emphasis can easily switch from performing for enjoyment to making a quick grab and hoping the performing for enjoyment is still there. I hope it didn't affect me in that way. Certainly, the further I went in my career, the more conscious I was of earning a living, but I don't recall it being a big issue for me in 2001. Yes, I thought the prospects of what I could earn were awesome, but I would have played for Australia for nothing. The money was just a bonus, a lovely bonus. It was best the ACB didn't know this!

Despite the riches, there was one area that was of growing concern to Neil Maxwell in particular. He believed 'marketability' should have been taken into account with player contracts. He argued the ACB was increasing its exposure, appeal and therefore revenue through the use of players in advertisements and promotions that the players weren't being paid for. He used me as an example during the 2000–01 season when I played a lead role in TV commercials for one of the ACB's biggest sponsors, Ansett Airlines. At that stage, players received a compensatory payment for 'team spirit'. This annoyed Maxi for some years, and I'm sure his campaigning played a significant part in the introduction of a marketing component in the modern-day contracts in which each player is individually ranked. However, none of that was on my mind as I prepared for the Ashes.

The early part of the tour was full of surprises for me. Among them was the night that team physio Pat Farhart and I were driving near the pretty town of Arundel in the south of England. Patty, who was behind the wheel, was so struck by the rural scenery that he commented: 'How good is this country? If we were driving in Australia we would have been hit by a roo by now. Lucky there's nothing here that can do that.' Almost as soon as he said it, a deer bolted out of some bushes. We

T-boned it, then it skidded on its hooves all the way off the road, flipped off some grass, and ran away.

That experience was a long way from the surprise attacks from locals we'd been warned about: prior to the tour, team management had alerted us to the tricks of the English news-papers and paparazzi. We were told of such tactics as the 'planting' of women at social functions, hotels and bars. Being a single guy I wasn't necessarily worried, but it was good to be made aware of the possibilities of being caught in traps. Of course, anything like that could be a distraction and potentially affect the team's performance. Worse still, it could seriously damage a player's reputation and his relationships.

The biggest of all early tour surprises for me came on the morning of Australia's opening match of the NatWest one-day series against Pakistan in Cardiff. Although I was with the squad I wasn't actually an official playing member at that time. It was planned I'd continue recovering from my arm injury by easing into a workload during net sessions. I was bowling off about eight steps, and felt I was coming along nicely. If all went well I'd be fit enough to be considered for the first Test which was nearly a month away. That all changed when Steve Waugh approached me at breakfast just hours before the match with Pakistan.

'Have you got your yellows?' he asked.

'No.'

'Well, you better find some because you're playing.'

Nathan Bracken, Damien Fleming and Jason Gillespie all had injuries, leaving Glenn McGrath as the only fit paceman. I didn't want to let Tugga or the team down, so I said I was right to play, although I shouldn't have. Team manager Steve Bernard sorted out a shirt for me to wear, and I borrowed a pair of Warnie's pants.

Pakistan captain Waqar Younis won the toss and decided to bat. As I walked out on to the Sophia Gardens field I quietly panicked because I didn't even know how long my run-up was. It had been four months since I'd come off a full run, and generally my distance to the crease changed slightly from year to year. Considering the preparation I'd had, I was like a car being put from first gear straight to fifth. It didn't feel right at all. There's nowhere to hide when you're an opening bowler, and I was certainly exposed. Despite that, I managed to get Shahid Afridi to nick a ball to Mark Waugh in the slips in the second over, but after that I got belted and finished with 1-85 off 10 overs, the most expensive return by an Australian in a one-dayer at that time. In the same match Shoaib Akhtar jumped ahead of me in the race to the 160 k barrier after he clocked 157.2 kays.

Australia won the match, and we backed up again the next day to beat England at Bristol. I managed to gain a bit more rhythm and took a couple of wickets, but in reality I was still a long way from being in game shape. All that was forgotten when we were 'Bound for Glory', or in other words, left cricket behind and headed to Huddersfield to be VIPs at a Bon Jovi concert. If I could be anything else in life I reckon I'd choose to be a rock star. The energy at big concerts is a world away from everyday life. There's the excitement and expectation when the fans flow in. Then the band comes onto the stage, the crowd roars, and with as little as 'hello' from the lead singer there's enough electricity in the crowd to light up a city.

When the music starts, the beat vibrates through your body and lifts you to another place. It's magical, it's amazing, it's almost out of this world. If I compare it to cricket, I think of running in to bowl in front of a crazy packed house during a day–nighter, then multiply the buzz tenfold.

With our passes we were allowed onto a platform at the side

of the stage for a few songs. We were just metres away from the action. One of my greatest memories of the whole tour came when lead guitarist Richie Sambora came over and high-fived me. I happily admit I was a groupie, but I wasn't alone; when I looked around me I saw my teammates losing themselves in the moment. No-one was happier than Michael Slater who was such a fan he'd even had the trademark Bon Jovi Superman tattooed on a shoulder. Slats was in heaven.

It was back to cricket mode when we moved to Nottingham to play Pakistan at Trent Bridge. Unfortunately my day was spoilt by idiots. There are some things you don't expect to happen on a cricket field, and one of them is having a firecracker go off next to your head. I was fielding at fine leg late in Pakistan's innings. I'd become used to hearing bungers being set off in the stands during the match, and had even seen paramedics attending to a boy who'd been hit by a fizzer, but when I saw something out of the corner of my eye flash past, and a loud bang followed, I had no intention of staying where I was. It scared me, and I immediately worried that other crackers were going to be tossed. I ran in and told Tugga. Michael Bevan, who'd been boundary sweeping, also said he'd nearly been hit. Tugga spoke with the umpires and everyone agreed we'd leave the field until calm was restored.

On our return it was much calmer; hopefully the fools responsible were found and booted out at the very least. After the game, which we lost, I was asked by some journalists how I felt. I said I feared for my life. In hindsight that was probably an exaggeration but it did show how on edge I was. Some people suggested there might have been racial reasons behind it, but I think I was just in the wrong place at the wrong time in front of a very excitable crowd that had fans who acted first, then thought later.

The incident made me realise how vulnerable cricketers are. We play on an open arena, at times within an arm's length of spectators. All it takes is one idiot and you never know what could happen. An exploding firecracker is enough to blind someone, but one day it could be worse. Just a few months after this incident, 9-11 happened in the United States. I'm not knowledgeable enough to comment on the political effects, other than to say the world shifted that day, and with that, popular sports events attended by the masses had to become more vigilant. I stress again, all it takes is one idiot. I accept that any sporting team could be targeted, especially when on tour, but it can also happen in our own backyard. It's the world we live in.

Another incident happened after we won the final against Pakistan at Lord's. We were standing on the Pavilion balcony during the presentation when a full can of beer was thrown from someone in the crowd below us. It just missed Inzamam-ul-Haq and smacked into the side of Michael Bevan's face. I was standing right next to 'Bevo' and he immediately asked me if I could see any blood. That was enough for Tugga to call us away and we had the rest of the presentation indoors. Again, just one idiot.

I took 2-20 off eight overs in the final, the best I'd bowled since my return. I then played against Essex at Chelmsford in one of only two warm-up matches before the first Test at Edgbaston. I only recall my batting. On the final day of a game that was yawning towards a draw, our second innings coincided with the television broadcast from Australia of a State of Origin rugby league match between NSW and Queensland. These matches are huge affairs that fire up passion on both sides of the border, and also in the Australian cricket team. Mark Waugh was really keen on supporting his beloved Blues, and it seemed there was no way he wanted to miss it. However, he had the problem of being the next in to bat when the Origin game was about to begin. He solved it by telling me I could take his place as long as I didn't get out for 80 minutes, the length of the game. As it turned out I got among the runs and finished with 79, before my eyes lit up like saucers at a delivery from off-spinner Peter Such, and I was stumped.

I was chosen in the Test team ahead of Damien Fleming. Back then, the captain and vice-captain, Tugga and Gilly, made the decisions in consultation with the chairman of selectors, Trevor Hohns. The lead-up to the Test coincided with the run-in to the Wimbledon tennis championships. As a promotional event I met the world's fastest server, Greg Rusedski. I bowled a few balls to him which he forehanded back with a bat, and then I tried to return a couple of his serves. No chance! He'd been clocked at 147 miles (235 kilometres) an hour, but he said he kept his bullets to me to a gentle 200 kays. It's no wonder tennis players have so many shoulder injuries; the stress must be intense, and I couldn't help thinking about the comparisons between serving and bowling.

My own haste and immaturity affected my opening Ashes performance. I contributed little to our innings win in the first Test; my biggest personal achievement came when I claimed my first English scalp, Mark Butcher caught by Gilly after I'd come around the wicket. Back to bowling first change behind Pidgey and Dizzy, I found I was still searching for rhythm, and struggled to bowl the fuller length needed on the slower English decks.

It also took some time getting used to the Duke ball that felt very different to the Kookaburra ball used in Australia. I was able to get a better grip on the Kookaburra seam because the stitching was a lot rougher, whereas the Duke almost slipped out of the hand because of its heavy lacquer. English bowlers might say differently. Basically, it was all a matter of familiarity, and although I could swing the Duke, I couldn't get my hand behind it well at the point of delivery. Above all else, though, I struggled with my elbow. I didn't realise how much time I needed to come back from the injury until I was under pressure to perform. I was still getting my strength back, and the confidence that went with it. This was a problem throughout the whole series. Looking back, I would have loved another month or two to get ready, but at the time I thought I was right, and that's the call I unwisely made.

We moved a step closer to retaining the Ashes after an eight wicket win in the second Test at Lord's. Although I'd been 'christened' at the home of cricket in the one-day final against Pakistan, the full aura and mystique of Lord's didn't hit me until the Test. When playing at various grounds around the world, whether it's the MCG, Wanderers Stadium or Feroz Shah Kotla, it's impossible not to feel the energy and buzz in the crowd; but at Lord's it's different. I'd been told by other players about the unique atmosphere, but I still didn't believe it until I experienced it for myself when Pidgey bowled the first ball of the match. As he started from the top of his mark there was the expected noise, but just before delivery everyone went quiet as though they were all holding their breaths. It was complete silence from about three steps out. A moment frozen in time. It was surreal.

As with other grounds I noticed a difference between sections of the crowd. When I was fielding in front of the Pavilion where all the egg-and-bacon-tie members sat, the hardest thing was trying to avoid being hit in the back of the head by corks exploding from Champagne bottles. I honestly reckon some of the members had a competition to see how far out onto the field they could fire their missiles. Together with the *phwwts* of the popping corks there were a lot of polite claps, 'jolly good's and even the occasional 'dear chap'. Meanwhile, at the other end of the field near the George Jetson spaceship, otherwise known as the media box, I got called every name under the sun.

It was impossible not to be swept away by the history and grandeur of the famous Long Room and the dressing room where so many generations of players had all been before me. Among thoughts of Bradman and Sir Garfield Sobers and so on, there was a lesser known name that deserved its own special place on an honour board: Pete the room attendant. He was a great Welsh fella who turned into an Aussie when we arrived. The whole team loved having him around. To me, it's the often overlooked things that can make a place feel so special.

Of all the names, one stands alone: the Queen. The teams were presented to her on the field and then we went into the Long Room and had an extended tea with her on a rain-interrupted first day. I couldn't believe it when she sat next to me. She firstly apologised about the weather. Still overawed, I replied: 'Well, that's not your fault.' I didn't know what to talk about, primarily because I was worried about saying the wrong thing. I asked her a couple of questions, including what would have been the 'go to' for many nervous players over the years: 'Do you like cricket?' She told me she liked watching it at Lord's because of the atmosphere. Once the apprehension wore off, I felt as though I was talking to my grandmother.

It would be wrong of me not to mention one other feature of Lord's that sticks in my mind from 2001. That is, the shower heads in the dressing room were as big as soccer balls! I'd heard teammates mention: 'You haven't had a shower until you've had a shower at Lord's.' It was true; it was like standing under a waterfall.

Again my role in the match was small. In a contest dominated by the brilliant Pidgey who took eight wickets, I claimed only two, the same number I'd managed at Edgbaston. In the post-match media conference Tugga was asked whether he was worried about my form. He was supportive, and even suggested my spell to Graham Thorpe in the second innings was one of the highlights of the match. I enjoyed that duel. Initially Tugga had wanted me to stick it up the captain, Michael Atherton, with some short stuff. Atherton pulled me for four early on, and that got me more fired up and I really tried to launch into him. Then when the strike was turned over, Thorpe baited me by saying: 'Mate, you're slow. Is that the best you can do?'

I shot a few words back at him, and it was well and truly on between us. It was nothing serious or controversial; it was just good hard cricket with plenty of emotion and the mental games that go with it. I ended up breaking a bone or two in his right hand when a ball jammed his glove against the handle. Soon afterwards, I trapped him LBW. It was a pleasing psychological victory.

My small returns – one wicket in each innings – continued in the third Test at Nottingham where we again won comfortably and claimed the Ashes for a seventh consecutive time, an Australian record. This time it was done with Gilly as our captain because Tugga had torn a calf muscle and would only return for the final Test of the series. Dressing-room celebrations lasted several hours. I partied as hard as any in the team, but inwardly there was disappointment I hadn't played much of a role.

Cricket can be a very strange sport. It's based around a team, yet it's very much made up of individual performances. It can be argued these performances come in for closer scrutiny than in other team sports because the individual is in the spotlight for much longer. Just look at it this way: in a game of football or netball the spotlight moves from player to player within seconds, but in cricket, the one batsman or bowler can be the focus of most of the attention for hours on end. This is where cricket is different, and although I'm no expert, I wonder if a football player who's had a bad match in a winning team is as likely to be noticed as a cricketer in the same position. The pressure on the cricketer is increased by statistics. Any of us can look back at scorecards and see who the dominant players have been in any match, and yet it may be one catch, one shot, or one delivery from someone else that had a major impact on the result. Unfortunately for me, whatever way I examined my performances, I hadn't done as well as I should have.

That's the way it continued for the last two Tests. By the end of the series, which we won 4–1, I'd grabbed only nine wickets at an average of 55.11. It was a good reality check and lesson for me after my achievements in my earlier series. All around me there'd been some incredible performers: Pidgey took 32 wickets, Warnie 31, and Dizzy bowled some superb spells on his way to getting 19 scalps, while Tugga, Junior, Gilly and Damien Martyn all played some great knocks. Everyone contributed, except me. I'd bowled at 80 per cent of my pace and got smacked. I felt embarrassed.

I was grateful the team stuck by me. Tugga never stopped supporting me, and in an environment where it's easy to worry about yourself first, a number of players continually reassured me. I was also helped by the backing from home. It was wonderful to come off the field after a tough day and find positive messages on my phone. Alan Jones was one who kept in really good contact. I was always lifted when I saw texts like: 'It's past midnight and I'm sitting here watching you bowl. You've got one in the bag, and when I wake up I want to see a few more next to your name. Believe in yourself.' That not only taught me about Alan's unwavering loyalty, but showed how little he slept because he'd be up by 2.30 am to start preparing for his radio program. Over the years, AJ and I have communicated with each other nearly every day no matter where we are.

I also relied on my own philosophy to help me through. I actually imagined I was on a long surf session. My early successes had shown how terrific it felt to be on a peak, taking wickets, winning, seemingly doing everything right, and feeling invincible, tall, proud and happy. But I knew the next wave I caught could leave me gasping for air and scrambling to stay afloat while everything seemed to be against me. Not that I was waiting to fail, but I understood how the game worked and I knew the lows were inevitable, especially if I was lucky enough to have a long career. I tried to convince myself that the lows made the highs even more worthwhile.

Apart from the reasons I mentioned earlier, there was another factor that affected my performances. The crowds definitely got to me. I was often called a 'chucker', and although that didn't worry me as such, there were times when I got wrapped up in trying to prove myself to the knockers. I have a pretty strong, if not stubborn personality, and when things aren't going my way I try to take the problem head-on. So, when people in the crowd said things like, 'We thought you were quick, but you're a joke', my response was to think, 'Well, I'll show you!' As a result, my plans for line and length were thrown out the window in my bid to bowl as fast as I could. The fact that my elbow stopped me from generating the pace I should have frustrated me more. Yep, I put my hand up and say the crowds beat me in the mind games.

I did take the occasional points victory in the cross-fence sledging wars. I remember one guy who really hopped into me about being a chucker. After ignoring him for a while I backed myself to match him in the verbals and asked him to stand up. The English crowds can be very witty and once they get a bite from the player, it's game on. It was a cold day, and I was wearing a jumper with the sleeves pulled over my hands. The baiter played on this and said: 'Not only are you a shit bowler, but that jumper is way too big for you.' I hit back with: 'That's the same thing they say about your missus.' He sat down straight away and was cheerfully nailed by his mates. He got a little red faced.

As for the England players, I enjoyed taking them on. I thought they were a cocky sort of bunch but a fun side to play. Tugga and the more experienced guys in our team stressed how England had a mental weakness and could crack when things were against them. It has changed now, but back then I believe we were definitely the tougher team upstairs. We had a 'never give up' attitude where, no matter what position we were in, we never accepted, 'well, we're buggered here'. But England did. I could sense it, and so could the rest of my teammates.

I got on well with the England players, and I wouldn't say there was a bad bloke among them, but there are a few I'd like to single out. I really admired wicketkeeper Alec Stewart. He was a true fighter, a gutsy player. He was the epitome of a guy who deserved to win a series against Australia. At the time I didn't feel sorry for him, but in hindsight it's sad he didn't get the chance to bask in Ashes glory.

No-one could top fast bowler Darren Gough as an out-and-out character. He was a good guy to have a laugh with. He used to be funny to watch, and showed the value of entertaining as well as playing. He'd comically drag his feet around and say: 'Fookin' Test cricket, this is shit!' Then he'd get the ball and bowl the house down with a cheeky glint in his eye. It's so important cricket continues to have such characters. It would be so boring without them, but I do worry the sport is losing its 'love-em, hate-em' personalities. I'll say more about that later.

Throughout the series Australia's players didn't go into England's dressing room much because we wanted to have a hard edge and not become too close to our rivals. However, there were some really good times when we did get together, and I didn't enjoy anything more than the few jam sessions I had with Mark Butcher, who loved his music and playing the guitar.

'Butch' introduced me to a little club in London called Ten Room. It was co-owned by the world famous jazz musician and composer, John Altman, who was a cricket tragic. Among other things he'd composed the soundtrack for *Titanic* and had arranged the Monty Python classic 'Always Look on the Bright Side of Life'. He was also a brilliant saxophone player who'd played with Van Morrison, Bob Marley, Jimi Hendrix, Eric Clapton, Sting . . . the list goes on and on. The first time we went there, Butch got up and belted out a song. I was very impressed. But Altman was the star; he'd wander through the crowd with his sax, and be in deep conversation with someone, but would always have one ear on the music, and when it was his turn to play he'd never miss a cue. I had a game with him where I'd sing a note and John would immediately copy it. I jumped from high to low and in between, and John nailed every one. We became good friends throughout the tour. I have Mark Butcher to thank for that. If cricket became extinct tomorrow, I wouldn't be that worried, but if I lost my music I'd be shattered.

On the field my biggest memory of Butch was his sensational 173 not out in the fourth Test at Headingley when England chased down 315 to win by six wickets. He hit us all over the park, and although it was frustrating and annoying when someone took us apart, I must admit Butch's batting was great to watch. Like it or not, we had to accept and appreciate we were being outclassed. It was one of the most dominant innings played against us during my Test career.

It was probably fitting that my tour finished the way it started. On the final day of the series at The Oval, I was bowling wide on the crease to Darren Gough when I felt a twinge on the left side of my lower rib cage. It was later diagnosed as a muscle strain, but after my return to Australia scans revealed I'd chipped off part of my rib cage. It was another case of impingement similar to my ankle injuries: on my bowling follow-through, there was so much stress that my bottom rib was being squashed by my hip. Yet again I was in recovery mode, putting me in doubt for Australia's home series against New Zealand. And yet again, I was unknowingly about to have another brush with officialdom.

13

One of the strangest things I've ever heard is that high-profile athletes are role models. Think about it: just because a person bowls fast, or kicks a ball well, or can play a great serve-volley game doesn't mean they should be put up on a pedestal as an example for everyone to copy. That's ridiculous. All of us in society have our skills, talents, morals and beliefs that we can learn from. To me, role models are those people you have regular contact with who may shape your behaviour, or at least make you think about what you're doing. They are parents, brothers, sisters, teachers, coaches, next-door neighbours, best friends. As for high-profile athletes? Yes, they can influence behaviour, and you only have to visit a schoolyard to see kids imitating Ricky Ponting or Tim Cahill to realise the power of professional sport, but surely it is up to the parents, coaches, teachers etc to tell the kids whether the behaviour of the athletes they're copying is right or wrong, and for what reasons.

I've known many sportspeople who'd rather keep to themselves and steer away from the public. They don't want the media exposure or the massive public following. They just want to play their games, then go home, or go out and have a beer with their mates, without having to think about their sport or the people watching them. Alternately, there are guys who want to use their profile to try to make a difference. However, it's unfair to expect everyone to be like that.

I don't class myself as being any different from the next guy. I know there are kids out there who idolise me, or want to have the same action as me, or celebrate wickets in the same fashion I do. I think that's wonderful, and it reminds me of when I was younger and wanted to be like Allan Donald. I suppose it's human nature, especially in the age of mass media exposure. But please, let's draw the line before calling me a role model.

I say all this because of the times I was criticised for my behaviour on the field, and my position as a role model was questioned in the public domain. The third Test of the 2001–02 season against New Zealand in Perth gave me my initial taste of this. I'd had a good start to the series, especially in the opening Test in Brisbane where I'd followed a first innings 63 with a 5-for and a Man of the Match award. Actually, Man of the Match trophies can become dust-collectors, but it's still nice to be considered the best performer in any game. I was just as pleased I'd fully recovered from my rib injury after I was forced to miss the opening Pura Cup match of the season.

The third Test had become the series decider after the first two matches were drawn. It wasn't looking good for us after we'd lost the toss and the Kiwis smashed us; Lou Vincent, Stephen Fleming, Nathan Astle and Adam Parore all made centuries in a massive nine declared for 534. We struggled in our chase and when I joined Warnie we still needed 60-odd to avoid the follow-on with only three wickets left. I copped a barrage of short stuff from Shane Bond who was bowling some serious wheels. He tried to wind me up by saying: 'You're happy to dish it out when you're bowling, but you can't hack it now, can you?'

I put his barb at the back of my mind and concentrated on helping Warnie, who was seeing the ball really well. He was hilarious to bat with because he'd tell me in advance what he was going to do, like, 'I'm going to smack this pie thrower out of the park,' or 'If Martin drops one short I'll put it over square leg.' I thought he treated his batting the same way he did his bowling; he had that presence that said he could take anyone down if he wanted to. Yet, I don't think he realised how good he was with the bat. It was much tougher for me. I ground it out for an hour and a half before Daniel Vettori snared me for 17.

By that time we'd avoided the follow-on, so I felt I'd done a reasonable job. Back in the dressing room I joined my teammates riding Warnie's fortunes. The way he was smoking the bowling we joked he was going to get a hundred, and we wondered how he might celebrate. Would he raise his bat and then get on with it? Or would he take his helmet off and bow? Maybe he'd do a fist pump? With Warnie it was impossible to know.

What eventually happened revealed a lot about the Warne character. He worked his way to 99, and was facing Vettori, a left-arm spinner. All he had to do was work the ball away, push it off his pads, or drop it at his feet and steal the single, but Warnie being Warnie went for the soap-opera moment and tried to smack a six over midwicket. As he hit it, the words in the dressing room were basically: 'Shit, he's stuffed it up!' The ball hung in the air for ages before Mark Richardson took a screamer in the deep, and Warnie trudged off as though someone had let the air out of his tyres. He was filthy when he returned to the dressing room; he kept bagging himself and saying what he should have done. It was a weird feeling for the rest of us because we didn't know whether to laugh or be sympathetic. Warnie did have a right to feel hard done by: replays showed

Vettori's wicket-taking delivery was a definite no-ball that the umpire didn't pick up.

The theatre of Warnie's innings was the introduction to my brush with officialdom and the start of my slip from being a so-called role model. It happened late on the fourth day as the Kiwis were winding down their second innings; they were already 400 in front when their number 10 walked out to bat. It was Shane Bond. I was bowling and thought it was time for some payback. Firstly, let me say Bondy and I had a good relationship and we got on very well off the field. My fast-bowling rival was a copper, so I knew he was a tough fella, but that didn't mean I was going to allow him to intimidate me on the field. We respected each other, and accepted we'd have cracks at each other when playing. It was all part of it.

It was 'on' between us right from the start. It all started after I bowled a ball and Bondy stared at me. I stared back and might have said something to him. He replied and then started baiting me, saying I was too slow to get him out. That fired me up. By then, I was tired. I'd bowled nearly 50 overs for the match and couldn't wait to have a rest. Like my teammates, I just wanted to get off the field and didn't want a cocky tailender holding us up.

Bondy didn't last long before I ripped his poles out, and in the heat of the moment I lost my temper, pointed him to the dressing room and told him to 'Fuck off!' It was my fourth wicket for the innings and eighth for the match. I most remember the incident because of what followed. Tugga tapped me on the shoulder and said in his typical dry way: 'Well bowled, Binga. That has just cost you 10 grand!' It wasn't until then that I thought: 'Oh no, what have I done?' With that wicket, New Zealand declared, and my focus switched to watching what turned out to be an exciting run chase. We finished with 7-381, 59 short of the target. Another draw.

After the match I went and apologised to Bondy, who shrugged off the episode without a care. There was no bad blood at all. But that wasn't the end of it because I was summoned to appear in front of the match referee, Jackie Hendriks. Just as an aside, at the time of doing research for this book I thought the referee was Clive Lloyd, so it shows you how the mind can mix one game with another.

Jackie told me I'd been mentioned in the match report of umpires Darrell Hair and Ian Robinson. He then said what I'd been expecting: 'You know I have to fine you.' I told him I'd been baited, but knew that was no excuse, and I had to learn to control my emotions. The penalty was fair enough: $8250, which was 75 per cent of my match fee. I was angry. Not because of the money, but because I'd let myself, my family, and my friends down. Then again, I challenge anyone to be a cleanskin all their lives.

I put the issue behind me, but it surfaced again two weeks later during the first Test against South Africa in Adelaide. It was my first time taking on the Proteas in the long form of the game, and if my experiences against them in one-dayers were anything to go by, I was prepared for a tough series. The South Africans were closer to the Australian mindset than any other team. They didn't mind copping a few knocks and believed they could win from almost any situation. I was excited about playing them, and was eager to make my presence felt as a fast bowler as early as I could.

We won the toss, batted and made a healthy score, thanks to centuries by Justin Langer and Damien Martyn. Although our performance put us on top, we had to work hard for the runs against a pace-heavy attack of Shaun Pollock, Nantie Hayward,

Makhaya Ntini, Jacques Kallis and Lance Klusener. Many of Australia's batsmen had been sniffed up, perhaps more than they should have been, especially by Hayward. I also wore a few short ones, but got great pleasure out of hanging tough in another good partnership with Warnie. Whenever I copped one, I thought: 'My chance will come.' I kept that mindset when we went out to bowl in the first innings; I was really fired up to defend my teammates and show we could match South Africa's aggression.

As they so often did, Warnie and Pidgey dominated, taking eight wickets between them. I took two – Neil McKenzie and Claude Henderson – but I only had myself to blame when neither was given out because they were off no balls. That annoyed me, but in no way were my frustrations responsible for my attitude when Hayward joined Ntini for the last wicket. Point blank, I wanted to send both of them a clear message, and I made the decision without informing Tugga or any of my other teammates that I wouldn't even try to get them out. It was tit for tat. Gone were the days of the fast bowlers' union when the unwritten law was that you didn't bounce a tailender. My philosophy was simple: 'I'm going to take you out before you take me out.'

I hit Ntini in the helmet two times in a row, and then went after Hayward with two more bouncers. I didn't care that he was batting outside leg stump and moving further away; I could have put one on off stump and knocked him over but I followed his nose. I said to him after one of the deliveries: 'I actually don't want to get you out, so you better tread on your stumps because you'll be out here a while until I hurt you.' It was full on. It was also a message to other fast bowlers around the world that if I was going to cop a heap of bouncers, then they'd better be prepared for 'get squares'. I may have presented a bad boy image, but fast bowlers aren't meant to roll out the welcome mat and say: 'I hope you enjoy your stay – here's a nice half-volley for you.' What I did was use a legitimate fast bowling weapon, and if I'd crossed the line, wouldn't the umpires have stepped in?

For those in the media and the public who criticised me afterwards, well, I can handle that. Everyone has opinions. The big question is: 'Would I change what I did?' No, not at all. No-one got their knickers in a knot if I bowled bouncers to a top batsman. If I was having a battle with Brian Lara it was considered a great contest, but all of a sudden it was considered bad form when it was at the tail. I firmly believe that my forfeiting of Ntini's and Hayward's wickets enhanced my wicket-taking capabilities throughout my career. It was all to do with reputation. From that moment on I knew tailenders would come out to face me knowing they had more to fear than losing their wicket. Australia went on to win the match by 246 runs and the last two batsmen out were Ntini and Hayward. I got them both. Afterwards I spoke with them about the incident. If they'd chosen to make an issue of it I would have been disappointed, but they accepted it as part of the game.

The criticism of me didn't stop with my bowling, as some people also took offence at how I celebrated my wickets. In the media it was written that I 'crowed', and I even had strangers stop and tell me that I was over the top. My response to them was always the same: 'Well if I'm celebrating, at least it shows I'm taking wickets.'

I love taking wickets, and, as with other parts of my game, I want to enjoy the moment. I never know when I will claim my last scalp, so each one I get is one to cherish. This hasn't only applied to playing for Australia, but also for NSW, Mosman, Campbelltown, and even before that. From my earliest years of playing I've instinctively celebrated. It's just what I do. I only realised to what extent I was doing it after I watched some highlights of me playing for Australia. Some of the celebrations made me think: 'Oh, you idiot. What were you doing then? What were you thinking, you goose!' But most of the time my leaps and clicks of the heels, or charges down the pitch with a finger raised, are spontaneous expressions of the way I feel. Surely there is nothing wrong with that! My displays reflect an important part of who I am and emphasise my view that I'm a performer and entertainer as much as I'm a cricketer. I'd have a dull old time if I couldn't shown my emotions, and the game would be worse off too if it didn't have that aspect of theatre.

Funnily, one of my celebrations has drawn particular comment and has come to be known as the 'chainsaw', because apparently it resembles me pulling a cord as though trying to start a machine. I can't remember when I did it for the first time, but I do know that if anyone had seen me in my early days at Mosman's Allan Border Oval, I could have been pulling the cord way back then. The only thing was, though, I wasn't starting a machine. In fact, that celebration does have a definite meaning to it: I'm giving a knockout punch as though I'm hitting someone to the ground. Maybe that seems a bit violent, but I'm not the first fast bowler – and I won't be the last – to show aggression. I haven't bothered correcting anyone who calls it the chainsaw, and it actually makes me laugh. I mean, why would I take a wicket and start up a chainsaw? What, am I bowling in a forest?

Despite some hype that the series with South Africa was a 'heavyweight title fight', Australia won 3–0. Pidgey and Warnie led the wicket-takers while Matthew Hayden and Damien Martyn had great series with the bat. So did Justin Langer who I was really pleased for. JL had been in and out of the Test side, but since he'd replaced Michael Slater for the final Ashes Test, he'd been in red hot form, peeling off five centuries and two 50s. I really admired him for his sheer determination.

He'd played a bigger role in my development than he could ever know. He was so encouraging and had the ability to psych me up and make me feel good about myself. For example, he knew that one of my checkpoints as a fast bowler was 'staying tall', so he'd come up to me with his half-strut, half-shuffle, and fire in his eyes, and say: 'Look at the size of those light towers! That's how tall you are! Come on, get as tall as those light towers!' That worked with me, and afterwards if I got a wicket, he'd grab me and say: 'See what you can do!' JL wasn't only so valuable because of his batting, but he could inspire and motivate others. I fed off his enthusiasm, knowledge, energy and mental toughness.

The 2001–02 home season had one more incident that I was criticised for. It happened in Australia's last match of the VB one-day series against South Africa in Perth. I'd already played one of those innings I wish I could have put in my pocket and reproduced anywhere – 51 off 36 balls, including six, four, six, four, six (26) off Allan Donald's last five balls. He joked with me afterwards it was an ordinary way to treat a boyhood hero.

We made a decent score, then Jacques Kallis led the chase, and while he was at the crease the South Africans were in with a good chance. One of Jacques's greatest shots was his guiding of the ball over slips off a fast bowler; he'd step back, give himself room, and with a perfectly timed angling of the bat he could steal himself a boundary, if not a six. I was always conscious of this when I was bowling to him.

On this particular day, I steamed in to bowl and was so focused on Jacques's movements that I only watched his feet for an early sign of what he might do. I noticed him moving away, and I instantly thought I should try to cramp him. So, I followed him with a bouncer that went through to the keeper, and it was only at that stage I realised he was holding up his hand and saying: 'Stop!' Apparently a seagull had flown across the pitch and distracted him, but I'd seen nothing of that. From a distance it could have looked quite ugly, as though I was out to hit Jacques. I immediately apologised and told him what I'd thought he was going to do. He wasn't at all angry, just shocked. There was nothing in it but afterwards my sportsmanship was again brought into question by the media. In one report by the *Sydney Morning Herald*'s Trevor Marshallsea, it was suggested some people may have had an image of me as 'a golden-haired boy charging in with blood dripping from his fangs'.

This may seem like a tired line of defence used by many athletes in different sports, but it's much easier to make a comment or judgement when you're watching from afar. When you're in the match it's different. Again, I was comfortable with what I did.

Australia won the WACA match but for only the third time in 23 years we didn't qualify for the finals. It turned out to be Steve Waugh's last one-day international. At the time, I wasn't aware how much of an impact that would have on me.

The summer of controversies was another part of the learning curve for me. By then, I'd accepted that high-profile people spent a good deal of their lives in goldfish bowls. Warnie had taught me this. He had a very big influence on me, and in return I think he enjoyed me hanging off his coat-tails. He liked being with the young guys coming through, and we spent a lot of time together going out, having dinners, just getting to know each other socially away from the team environment. But whenever we did, you could bet that we wouldn't be alone for long before someone would want Warnie to sign an autograph, or pose for a photo, or have a chat about anything and everything. Earlier in the season I'd gone with him to Melbourne's Crown Casino, and as we walked along I heard people whispering: 'That's Shane Warne and he's with Brett Lee.' It felt very strange to me, and was something I was still getting used to.

The further I went in my career, the more I realised that I couldn't stop doing things just because I might draw attention to myself. At first, I used to be a little hesitant if I went out to a pub and ended up being invited to play an impromptu song with a band. I knew my every move would be monitored, and what would people think? But I wasn't doing anything wrong. I was just getting up and enjoying myself. Provided I wasn't out drunk the night before a game or during one, I had as much right to be there as the next person. I made the decision that as long as I wasn't doing anything that would shame Mum and Dad, I should be able to have some fun without worrying about public judgement.

Just two weeks after the Australian summer, we were in South Africa for a further three Tests and seven one-dayers. We won the Test series 2–1 in a contest remembered as much as anything for Gilly's extraordinary batting. He scored two centuries, including 204 not out off 213 balls in the first Test in Johannesburg; it was the most enjoyable Test innings I've ever seen. And in what was more a media story than anything else, I overtook Shoaib Akhtar in the pace race after being timed at 157.4 kilometres an hour in the second Test in Cape Town.

The use of speed took on new meaning for me in the one-dayers when Ricky Ponting became captain. After being raised on Steve Waugh's belief that I was first and foremost a wicket-taker, it was difficult and confusing to find out I had to become more economical. Ricky and I never really spoke about my role at that stage; unfortunately it was relayed through the media a fair bit. I would rather have been told personally than to read about what I was meant to do, but that was just Ricky's captaincy style.

Statistically he did have a point because I was the most expensive of the frontline bowlers in the South African series, going for nearly six an over, one-and-a-half runs more than Glenn McGrath. But on the flipside, I had the best strike rate, picking up a wicket every three-and-a-half overs compared to Pidgey's five. As we know, the heavy use of statistics in cricket means pretty well anything can be read into them. In my defence, I believe there were times my pace and aggression contributed to bowlers getting wickets at the other end. I might have finished an opening spell with figures like 1-26 off five overs, yet I'd done a good job because I got rid of a key batsman that created a flow-on effect for other dismissals.

Furthermore, my economy rate wasn't helped by my sheer speed, which meant more than a few nicks flew over or through the slips for boundaries. That may seem like an excuse, but I justify it by saying my type of bowling was less conducive to being economical than the style of someone like Pidgey. I thought Ricky's request for me to tighten up didn't support the way I bowled, but I obviously had to accept it and work on it.

Whether Ricky was right or not, or for that matter, whether I was right or not, Australia had a comfortable series win. It was only 11 months until the World Cup in South Africa, Kenya and Zimbabwe, so every one-dayer was considered an important part of our build-up.

I was glad when the series was over. It was the end of an intense summer, and time for me to go home and enjoy the simple pleasures of family, mates and jam sessions. But one controversy was still to surface. About a month after the tour, Graeme Smith, who'd made his debut in the second Test and had gone on to play the third Test and a number of the one-dayers, spoke out in South Africa's *Sports Illustrated* magazine about the sledging he'd received from Australia's players. He especially pointed the finger at Matthew Hayden, but there was a long list of others accused: Shane Warne, Glenn McGrath, Justin Langer, Ricky Ponting, Adam Gilchrist, Mark Waugh, and last but not least, me.

Graeme said I'd threatened to kill him after we had a mid-pitch collision. That is true, and I think I said it a few times during his debut Test innings. At that stage I thought he was arrogant. Even before he'd played a Test he'd talked himself up in the media. Then, after he'd top-edged me for four and smiled at me, I hated the bloke. He was a cocky shit who deserved to have his poles ripped out, but only after I put a ball through his grill first. My impressions of him remained the same throughout the tour, but in future matches against him I got to know him as a really good bloke and we became good friends.

Sledging, or 'mental disintegration' as Steve Waugh called it, is part of the game. Yes, we were full of chirp against the South Africans, but they said their fair share of things back at us. Neil McKenzie had a crack in a sly way, Lance Klusener could talk as well as he clubbed bowlers, and Mark Boucher certainly wasn't afraid to say what he thought. But after the game, all was forgotten. It was just hard, very tough cricket.

Nine times out of 10 I tried to make my sledges funny. It was all about putting a batsman off his game, and I thought humour was a good way to do this because it could break concentration. Later on in my career, when I was starting to learn Hindi, I enjoyed some banter with the Indians. The television cameras would close in on me saying something and perhaps the commentators would make comment. Meanwhile, out in the middle I'd be struggling to keep a straight face after telling Sachin Tendulkar: 'Could you hurry up and bring me a glass of cold water.' I've never been involved in sledging that I believe stepped over the line. Certainly I've never stood – and never will – for racial slurs, but away from that I see nothing wrong with going down and swearing at a batsman or cracking the odd joke.

So does this affect the public's perception of me as a 'role model'? I'll leave that for others to decide, as well as the interpretation of what a role model is and should be. I can only say that I've tried my best to represent myself in a way I'm proud of. Outside of cricket I love making people feel good about themselves. This often comes through charity work. I get approached regularly to help various organisations, and although they all do wonderful jobs, it's not possible for me to help them all.

As a result, I've primarily chosen a charity that's close to my heart. The Adventist Development Relief Agency (ADRA) supports kids and teenagers who battle depression and social problems such as drugs, alcohol and broken home lives. Over the years my brother Shane and I have spent time with some of the kids at camps, and raised hundreds of thousands of dollars for them. They, like everyone else, need people who care for them. One of the reasons I'm passionate about this goes back to my early teenage years when a mate I played cricket with committed suicide. His death wrecked his family. The tragedy taught me that you often don't know what people are going through in their lives until something tragic or dramatic happens.

My profile has given me a great opportunity to help others. In doing so, I support the words of one of the kindest and most generous men I've ever met, Alan Jones. He reckons giving is the most selfish thing you can do because it makes you feel good about yourself.

14

The first three things I used to pack whenever I went on tour were my baggy green, a guitar and bowling shoes. However, for one particular trip in the winter of 2002 the most valuable item I had to take was my own body. Together with Neil Maxwell, his work colleague Chris Muldoon, and Gatorade representative, Joshua Black, I went to Chicago for a series of special fitness tests at the Gatorade Sports Science Institute.

I hadn't been doing much training in the lead-up, so I was worried about how I'd perform. To reassure myself, I went for an hour's run the day before the tests. It wasn't the most sensible thing to do, but it did set my mind at ease. The first test involved a series of runs at increasing speed and angle on a treadmill to determine my Vo2 max, a reading that shows the body's ability to use oxygen during exercise. I did quite well, and then moved on to a sweat test. This was an hour-long session during which I rode a stationary bike at moderate speed in a laboratory that maintained the temperature at 27°C with 70 per cent humidity to reflect a typical summer's day in Sydney. After about half an hour some of my sweat was collected in a plastic bag placed around my arm. At the end, it was shown I'd lost a little more than a litre of fluid with a higher than normal concentration of salt, making me a 'salty sweater'. Salt loss can cause cramping, a problem I'd regularly had, especially in the final hour or so of a whole day in the field.

The most interesting test was the final one, a power test. I switched to another stationary bike which I rode flat out at 30 second intervals. The readings showed that my highest output, measured in watts, was about twice that of an average person. It showed that all my strength and drive came through my legs and backside, which was typical for a fast bowler. I was told my readings were similar to those of a sprint cyclist.

Once the testing was out of the way we had time to be tourists. Chicago is the home of one of the greatest athletes of all, Bulls basketball legend Michael Jordan, but I came to know it for its lack of knowledge about cricket. One day we filmed an ad at a suburban baseball field after the producer asked about 20 locals if I could have a game with them. They were all cool about that, but were surprised when I turned down the offer of wearing a mitt. During warm-ups, I dived in the outfield and took a 'specky' catch. The other players ran over to look at my hand, thinking it would have been red and stinging. I tried to explain to them the differences between cricket and baseball, and how cricketers didn't use mitts. They couldn't believe it, and they were even more amazed when I told them I bowled or 'kind of pitched' 100 mile-an-hour balls that bounced.

But none of that compared with what happened a day so later. I don't know how it was arranged, but I managed to receive an invitation to throw the first pitch at a White Sox game. The Sox, together with the Cubs, were Chicago's two Major League Baseball teams. I did some research and discovered the 'first pitch' was an honour that often went to politicians, including presidents, and movie stars. As soon as I found that out, I was nervous.

Maxi and I were given a running sheet for the day. It all seemed pretty straightforward, but even the best laid plans couldn't account for what happened. After being picked up from our hotel in a limousine we got stuck in a traffic jam on our way to Comiskey Park, the Sox's home field. Maxi and I began to panic. All I wanted to do was get to the game, calmly do my bit and have a chat to some of the players, but by the time we arrived there was no chance of taking anything slowly. I was rushed by a Sox representative through a grandstand and straight out onto the field. A guy in a golf cart drove over to me and showed me a box of balls from which I had to choose one. I was then introduced to Mark Buehrle, a Sox pitcher who, as was traditional, had a quick word with me before moving to the catcher's position to take my pitch. At the same time as we shook hands, the voice of the ground announcer boomed over the PA:

Ladies and gentlemen, our special guest and opening pitcher today comes all the way from Australia. Let's hear it for Brett Lee. He's a bowler.

Any hope I had of anyone understanding what I did was lost the moment an animation on the big screen popped up and depicted a ten-pin bowler knocking over skittles. I felt really embarrassed, and more so after Mark Buehrle asked me: 'So if you're a bowler, are you going to roll the ball in to me?' There was no time, and probably no use trying to explain cricket, so I told Mark I'd do my best to throw the ball over-arm.

He seemed happy enough, but when he went to the catcher's area, he sat down and showed only casual interest, as though it was going to be a walk in the park catching a pitch from a ten-pin bowler. On my way to the pitcher's mound I did a few quick stretches; I hadn't warmed up properly and was worried what I could do to my arm, but the occasion had me pretty pumped up, so no matter what the results, I wasn't going to hold back.

I was surprised how high the mound was. I'd never stood on one in my life. I certainly didn't assess the need to throw the ball on a downward angle as pitchers are meant to do. Instead, I launched into a flat cricket-like throw that sent the ball shooting over the catcher's head. Almost in shock Mark Buehrle put his mitt up just in time to stop the ball smashing into a camera being set up by a professional photographer. I walked back to Mark who shook my hand again and said: 'Hey man, you had some pep on that one!' I then headed into the stands where a number of fans patted me on the back and joked: 'You don't throw too bad for a ten-pin bowler.'

When back home in Australia, I had some time to work on a new musical interest. A year earlier, my brother Grant and I moved into a house that I bought at Lane Cove on Sydney's north shore. Grant, by then an accountant, was still very much the muso who played keyboards in a pub band called The Gas. In lieu of charging him rent, which I never would have done anyway, I told him he could earn his keep if he played the piano to me most nights. The problem is we didn't have one. So, even before I'd bought the house, we went searching virtually every piano shop in Sydney. Grant would hop onto a stool, play a few notes, and then move onto another piano, often surprising the salespeople with how good he was. Finally, at a shop in Mosman, Grant found one that made him say after hitting just a few notes: 'That's it!' He didn't make things easy for me because it was a Bosendorfer 1950s antique grand piano, seven-foot-four long, with ivory keys, three extra bass keys, more width, more volume, better sound than the standard piano, and it cost about $60,000! But I still bought it.

The first room we put it in had a sofa as well. It was wonderful. I'd come in, turn the lights down, lie on the sofa, and listen to Grant play Mozart. Wind the clock back to a few years earlier and it was the Doctor doing the same thing at Mount Warrigal. With Grant's help I learnt a few tunes. The piano would never replace my love for the guitar – by that time I had several of them – but it was a beautiful instrument that, like everything else in music, allowed me to get lost in the moment.

Whether it was listening to Mozart, jamming, playing gigs with Six and Out or strumming at home by myself, I have no doubt music helped my cricket. By the time Australia started the 2002–03 summer I was really excited. That was in no small part due to it being my first home Ashes series. Before we reached that point, Australia played in the most bizarre matches I was ever a part of. After only reaching the semifinals of the ICC Champions Trophy tournament in Kenya, we warmed up – or should I say overheated – with a three-Test series against Pakistan.

The first strange thing about this contest was that it was played on neutral territory. It was meant to be hosted by Pakistan, but unfortunately the country was politically unstable after the US invasion of Afghanistan a year earlier. The first Test was played in Colombo, Sri Lanka. It turned out to be a great match, thanks to one of the best spells of fast bowling with either the new or old ball I've ever seen. Some players, and the authorities too, questioned Shoaib Akhtar's action over the years, but putting that aside, it was incredible to see what he could do with the ball when everything clicked. Bowling reverse swing with a 20-over-old rock, he picked up five wickets in 15 balls to wreck our second innings and suddenly give Pakistan an outside chance of winning.

At one stage he was on a hat-trick after bowling Ricky Ponting and Mark Waugh. Steve Waugh survived it, but was LBW the next delivery. Shoaib's fourth scalp was a fast-bowling classic: a yorker that swung in from around the wicket and smashed the stumps before Gilly could get his bat down. That brought me to the crease, but luckily it was the end of the over. When I did finally face him, the Rawalpindi Express went for another yorker, but as can happen, the ball came out at the wrong angle and I copped a beamer that hit me flush on the hip bone. I thought the left side of my waist had been blown off by a shotgun, and I momentarily lost all feeling in my left leg. I was pissed off because I thought I'd been purposely targeted, but Shoaib apologised straight away before adding: 'I'll knock you over next ball.' Still pretty angry, I replied: 'And don't forget you have to bat next innings!' I fell to off-spinner Saqlain Mushtaq soon afterwards. Shoaib finished with 5-21 off eight overs after picking up Warnie, LBW, to round off his efforts.

It was a devastating spell. Shoaib had that rare ability to find another level beyond the norm. Forget for a moment what he could do with the ball, his slinging action alone made him a nightmare to face. Whereas batsmen had a good sight of the ball through the run-up and delivery with most bowlers, Shoaib obscured the ball behind him with his action. Any bowler who does this has a distinct advantage because a batsman can't pick up the ball until very late. It's the same with Shaun Tait, Sri Lanka's Lasith Malinga, and West Indian Fidel Edwards. Then, when you added the speed and the late swinging ball, you had a lethal weapon.

There were no better exponents of reverse swing in the world than Shoaib Akhtar. Over the years I spoke with him numerous times about his own techniques. I also had chats with Wasim Akram, another brilliant bowler who could get even the oldest balls to move around. Generally, subcontinent bowlers are very conscious of keeping the ball dry, as opposed to my 'spit rock' approach. Wasim said his team used to have one designated shiner, and when returning the ball to him or the bowler, players tried to catch it seam up to avoid wetting either side of it.

The other part of the process has always been controversial. Reverse swing relies on the ball being 'roughed up' on one side, while the other side is 'protected', meaning it is kept as smooth as possible to present a textural opposite. The roughing occurs through natural wear and tear and can be enhanced by fielders returning the ball on the bounce to the keeper. But there are also less legitimate methods. I've known certain players to come in to bowl while scratching the ball hidden in their cupped hands. I've also heard of bottle-tops being used and at least one bowler used to bite the ball. The most extreme example is the story of a wicketkeeper who superglued little rocks to his gloves which he brushed the ball against.

I have no reason at all to suggest anything untoward happened during the Colombo Test, but whatever the reasons for the ball moving so far during the match – at times it swung up to a foot – batsmen the world over should be grateful Shoaib couldn't produce that form whenever he wanted. If he could have, there'd certainly have been some lower averages in stats columns.

When it did come time for Shoaib to bat I got some revenge and smacked him on the grill of the helmet as Australia were closing in on a 41-run win. For a while, Pakistan were well in the hunt until Warnie picked up some key wickets on the final morning, and then Pidgey and Dizzy cleaned up with the second new ball.

Now to the bizarre part of the series: the second and third Tests were played in Sharjah in the United Arab Emirates in front of nearly empty stadiums in temperatures that were farcically hot. If I'd thought of it at the time, I reckon I could have fried eggs on my forehead. The second Test in particular was a joke, with temperatures reaching 57°C out in the middle. I don't think there has ever been a worse toss to lose, and Tugga lost it! After bowling just one over I was spent, gasping for air, and wondering how I was going to manage to bowl again. I went straight to fine leg, sculled a bottle of Gatorade and poured a bottle of water over my head. I can remember Pidgey going up to bowl his second over and saying to Tugga: 'If you don't take me off here, I'm going to die!'

Early on, our fitness coach, Jock Campbell, came down to fine leg and asked me how I was going. I was so out of it that I asked him when we were going fishing. I had heatstroke within half an hour and didn't know where I was. Probably the best example of the conditions was a slow-motion replay of sweat spraying from paceman Andy Bichel's front boot when it slammed down on the popping crease. At lunch I jumped straight into an ice bath in the dressing room, and steam came off me. Someone could have died that day, or become seriously ill. They were the worst conditions I ever played in. Ever!

But that wasn't the most unusual part of the match. Although we played on a flat, slow pitch, the game lasted only two days, and yet we managed to win by an innings. In their first dig Pakistan folded for only 59, their lowest Test score, and the next day they rewrote the records again, making only 53. Matthew Hayden scored more than them by himself with 119, a really gutsy innings considering he spent seven hours slow-roasting in an oven.

I don't know what to say about Pakistan's performance. I had no reason to suspect anything at the time, and still don't. However, I can understand some fans could be suspicious in light of allegations against some Pakistan players over the years. I'll leave that for other people to make judgements on. I'd like to think it was just one of those odd occasions that can, and do happen.

We won the final Test by an innings as well, but this time the match lasted four days, and we returned to relative Arctic-like temperatures in the 40s. I had a disappointing series, taking only five wickets at 46. But I wasn't concerned. The Ashes were looming, and on home soil I had high expectations.

15

Alan Jones knew what was wrong as soon as I rang him. 'You've been dropped, haven't you?' he said.

For the first time in 24 Tests I was on the outer, and wouldn't play in the Ashes opener against England. Sure, I'd had a lean series against Pakistan, but the phone call from chairman of selectors Trevor Hohns was still unexpected. He told me I'd lost my spot to Jason Gillespie. I'd been on the cricket scene long enough to realise any player's position wasn't set in concrete and being dropped was simply an occupational hazard, but that didn't stop me from feeling angry.

I wanted to hit back immediately and prove that Hohns and his fellow selectors Allan Border, David Boon and Andrew Hilditch were wrong. Alan Jones, who'd learnt to read me as well as anyone, had a novel idea: he suggested that I imagined the heads of the selectors on top of the stumps when I returned to play for NSW in a Pura Cup game against Tasmania at the SCG.

'You're going to knock those heads out of the ground time and again,' said AJ.

AJ is a master motivator whose stories really hit their mark with me. One of my favourites is his recollection of the time he was coaching the Wallabies, who'd come in for some pretty bad press. On the day of a Test, AJ said he went to the hotel foyer and collected all the newspapers, so his team couldn't read them. Then on the way to the ground he read out some of the headlines and stories to help stir his players.

I was certainly fired up by AJ's words against the Tasmanians. I took 5-63 and 5-86, my initial ten-wicket haul in a first-class match. Then, in the next game at the SCG starting four days later, I claimed 7-114 and 4-66 against South Australia. The selectors' heads had copped a hammering and I felt I'd done all I could to force my way back into the Test team. Australia had won the first two Tests in Brisbane and Adelaide, and although it would have been easy to retain the same 11 for the third game, the fact that it was at Perth got me across the line. In consultation with Steve Waugh, the selectors decided to go for my pace. Andy Bichel was the unfortunate guy who made way for me. 'Bich' was one of the hardest-working blokes I ever played with, and was also good fun to be around, but although I felt sorry for him, I was grateful I'd been given another chance so soon.

The pressure was on me, especially when some of the pre-match talk predictably focused on how fast I'd bowl and whether I could regain the pace some critics said I'd lost. Tugga added to the hype when he predicted batsmen could get hurt. Unfortunately for Alex Tudor, that came true in the second innings when we were moving in for the kill and the retention of the Ashes. I'd taken three wickets in the first innings when England folded for 185. We replied with 456, and by late on day three, we were three wickets away from wrapping up the Poms for a little over 200 when Alex came out to bat.

I'd already grabbed Marcus Trescothick caught behind, and, motivated by keeping my place in the team, I wanted to assert my authority over every single batsman. That meant I didn't mind a bit of violence. I took the second new ball and told Alec Stewart at the non-striker's end: 'Tell him [Alex Tudor] to tread on his stumps, otherwise I'm going to kill him!' There's no doubt I wanted to intimidate Alex. I still had the shits with the selectors, I had my tail up, was bowling downwind at 150 kays an hour, and was in a groove.

I planned to dig a short one in and hope for a catch off the gloves to Gilly, or one of four slips, or Justin Langer at bat pad. But the end result was distressing: the ball skidded through the gap at the top of the grill on Alex's helmet and slammed into his eye. The sound made a sickening noise like two pieces of wood being belted together. I ran straight to Alex who was staggering and clutching his head. I nearly vomited when I saw the amount of blood spurting from his wound. He retired hurt and soon afterwards I nearly hit Steve Harmison with another bouncer before I cleaned him up, and with that, Australia reclaimed the Ashes. I went off the field and instead of going to the Australian dressing room I headed for the doctor's area, where I found Alex receiving stitches. He was surprised when I apologised because he saw nothing wrong with what I'd done.

When you look at it from a purely mathematical viewpoint, facing fast bowling is daunting. At my peak it took only about 0.4 of a second for the ball to leave my hand and reach the batsman. In that space of time the batsman didn't only have to pick up the delivery but he had to decide what he wanted to do with it, and act on his decision. If anyone is in doubt about how quick that response needs to be, I suggest you click a stopwatch and see what you can do in less than half a second. That's one reason why I respect Ricky Ponting so much as a batsman. One of the hardest things I've found as a fast bowler is being able to practise in the nets what I want to do out on the field. For example, when a batsman wants to work on his cover drive, he gets throw-downs in that area. But as a bowler, how do you practise your bouncers without the fear of hurting your teammates? Punter is the only person I know who didn't mind having a session against the bouncer. There were dozens of occasions when I said to him: 'Mind if I work on some short stuff?' He never said 'no' or complained, and we had some great 'game-on' battles that I believe prepared both us well for what happened in the middle.

We went on to win the Ashes 4–1 after we had another victory in Melbourne, before England knocked us over at the SCG. The last Test provided a personal milestone when I bowled Trescothick to claim my 100th Test wicket. There was also a much more significant century that prompted one of the most emotional moments I ever witnessed on a sports field.

It was late on day two and Australia was five down, with Tugga and Gilly in control. Andy Bichel and I were the next two in. As I sat on the players' balcony, I wondered what I'd do if I had to bat that evening. It wasn't so much Australia's position that made me think, but the fact that Tugga was in a race against the clock. He'd been under scrutiny for much of the season. The selectors said they couldn't guarantee his spot and the media questioned if he was playing his final Test. Many critics had written him off; the poor bugger was being nailed at every turn, and after only scoring two 50s all summer, he was under immense pressure.

I really felt for him when he walked out to bat. Despite his knockers, it seemed everyone in the packed crowd was on his side as they cheered him off the mark and clapped virtually every run he made. By halfway through the final session he was closing in on 50. It had been a pretty watchful innings, but after drinks he smoked some boundaries and, all of a sudden,

I was like so many other people watching and thinking: 'Shit, he's a chance of a century before the close of play.' And that made me nervous. What would I do if I had to go out and bat with Tugga in the 90s, and me under pressure to give him the strike? I kept my fingers crossed that Gilly didn't get out.

Off-spinner Richard Dawson came in to bowl the last over. Tugga was on 95. He couldn't get a run off the first three balls, and with each missed chance the tension grew. I was so focused on what was happening on the pitch that I couldn't tell you what the crowd was doing, but I imagine most were holding their breath like I was. After the fourth ball, I felt a rush of disappointment because Tugga was off strike after running three from a drive through point.

Now, all the pressure was on Gilly. I reckon if the fifth ball had been a half tracker that could have been hit into orbit, Gilly would have just worked it into a gap for a single. And that's exactly what he did as he found a hole through midwicket. So, Tugga was back on strike: one ball to go, two runs needed. England captain Nasser Hussein added to the theatre by having a long chat with Dawson, after which they brought the field in. This was a time when the thrills of Test cricket far outweighed anything a one-dayer or T20 match could offer. Then, the moment came: a full fast ball outside off stump, a cover drive, a boundary, and Tugga with both arms raised in the air as though he'd just won the world heavyweight boxing crown. I felt tingles watching it and hearing the crowd roar. Everyone around me was yelling and cheering. This wasn't only a great moment in sport, but a great moment in life.

The whole team was pumped when Tugga returned to the dressing room. We were full of questions: 'How was it?'; 'Did you think you'd get it?'; 'Did you guess what he was going to bowl?' There were plenty of claps, hugs and high fives. I most remember the look on Tugga's face. You'd rarely get a smile from him when he was on the field, but in the privacy of the team environment, he had this sly, cheeky grin on his face that said: 'Yeah, that was pretty cool!'

Afterwards I did a cross for the Nova radio station, and the crowd was still really loud in the background. The vibe was something very special, and I heard it said later that complete strangers shouted each other beers in the Members' Bar.

It must have been a strange time for Tugga, because despite the speculation over his Test future, there was a tremendous push from some sections of the media and the public for him to return to Australia's one-day team. But, as we often hear in sport, there's little place for sentiment, and Tugga couldn't fight back.

After our disappointments in the limited-overs format the previous season, we made amends by losing only one of nine games throughout the VB Series with England and Sri Lanka. I had a pleasing return, topping the wicket-takers' list with 18 scalps. The highlight came when I took 5-30 against England in the second final at the MCG. The night was capped off after I was announced both player of the match and the series.

I hadn't had the most normal of preparations heading into the last few matches. Only a couple of days earlier, my brother Shane and I were invited to throw and hit a few baseballs in front of some talent scouts from the American Major League Baseball club, the Arizona Diamondbacks. Not knowing how seriously to take the apparent 'trial', we went down to a Lane Cove oval, and discovered we were to be timed by a speed gun. I don't think I impressed too much but I reckon if Shane had wanted to pursue baseball further, he might have made a go of it. He had a really strong arm and could belt the ball a long, long way. Unfortunately, he was struggling to overcome a chronic knee injury that had troubled him for a couple of seasons. He'd last played for Australia nearly two years earlier during an away series in India, and by the end of the 2002–03 season, he decided enough was enough and retired from all forms of the game. He was only 29. Yes I'm biased, but I stand my ground when I say he was one of the most naturally gifted cricketers I ever played with.

What he missed in Test cricket, Shane made up for in one-day internationals by being a member of Australia's World Cup winning 1999 squad and the '96 squad that finished runner-up. I was stoked to follow in his footsteps when I was chosen for the 2003 tournament in South Africa, Kenya and Zimbabwe. In the lead-up I trained as hard as I ever had. Under the direction of Australia's fitness conditioner, Jock Campbell, I adopted some unusual training techniques, including running with a parachute behind me to improve my strength and power. I was 83 kilograms, a few lighter than usual. I may have looked wafer thin, but I felt super strong. Soon enough, another form of weight loss gained all the attention in what was a rocky start to Australia's World Cup defence.

16

When something serious or unusual happens in the Australian team, the Chinese whispers start. Not everyone in the team may know much, but it doesn't stop the murmurs between players. That was the case soon after we'd arrived in South Africa for the start of the World Cup. I knew nothing more than 'Warnie is involved', but judging by the strange atmosphere around the players I suspected the news wouldn't be good.

A team meeting was called in our Johannesburg hotel where Warnie addressed everyone. He looked really tired and on edge, and started to fight back tears. He told us he'd tested positive to a banned substance, a diuretic that he'd used in a bid to make him look slimmer by getting rid of excess water. He was adamant he'd never taken a steroid or any other performance-enhancing drug. He apologised to everyone, and then said he'd leave for Australia the next day.

I was shocked. Two things came to mind. Firstly, it was a wake-up call for what I put in my own body. I'd always been very careful, but rest assured, I began double-checking labels on every painkiller and cold and headache tablet that I considered taking. Secondly, I couldn't stop myself from thinking: 'Shit, this is Warnie. This can't be happening. We're in trouble now!'

It was the second big blow to our campaign because injury had already ended Nathan Bracken's tournament. 'Bracks', who had incredible variety, had proven to be one of the most effective one-day bowlers in the world. It would have been easy for the rest of the team to be affected by the dramas, but Punter, Gilly and Haydos were instrumental in keeping us focused. They all had similar messages: we couldn't worry about what had happened, we still had a great squad and it was up to ourselves to prove we could succeed.

Our first game against Pakistan at Wanderers Stadium gave us tremendous confidence, especially for one bloke who I would've had in my team every single time I played for Australia. Unfortunately, not everyone thought the same way and this bloke was under pressure heading into the World Cup. Andrew Symonds was his own man. As a player, he never complicated anything or analysed his game too much. He simply went out and had a crack, whether batting, bowling or fielding. He had some monumental failures, but when he struck form, as he did against Pakistan, there was no more valuable cricketer, and no-one worth watching more. 'Symo' was a rarity; not only was he a match-winner but he put bums on seats.

After being sent in to bat we were in trouble at 4-86, before Symo turned the game on its head with 143 not out off 139 balls. He had one of those days when it all clicked. Forearm jabs over midwicket, inside-out slices over cover, flat-bat slaps past the umpire. We made 310 and rolled Pakistan for 228, with Ian Harvey picking up four wickets.

Now back to Symo. Although some of his actions and misdemeanours caused him trouble over the years and surely contributed to his premature decision to quit playing, I can't stress enough how much of a joy he was to have in the team. Yes, there were times when he annoyed the hell out of me and other teammates, but that's because he loved being a stirrer. It also worked both ways because Symo left himself open as a target on more times than I can remember. Earlier in his career his clumsiness prompted Mark Waugh to nickname him 'Jethro' after the TV character in *The Beverly Hillbillies*. But that wasn't the biggest ammunition he gave us.

There were countless famous Symo moments. One of my favourites is the time he read the sign of the hotel in which we were staying, The Rendezvous, and then told someone on the phone that he could be contacted at the 'Rond-ez-vooz'; and then there was the legendary occasion when he bought a ticket in a raffle for a car. When the ticket-seller told him the prize would be drawn on the 31st of the month, he confidently told her: 'Well, you'll be expecting a call from me on the 32nd.' There's also the story about him driving past Sydney's Randwick Racecourse and asking his teammates if that was where the Melbourne Cup was held; I'll give him the benefit of the doubt and say that one didn't happen.

At team meetings the players could be in the middle of an intense discussion when suddenly Symo would say something that would crack everyone up. He was one-of-a-kind. If I can jump forward to the cricket being played today, I'm positive the game would be better off if it had more players like Symo. He was a character. Cricket needs those types of players more than ever.

It was another player's turn to shine in our second Pool A match at Centurion Park, Pretoria. Jason Gillespie was magnificent against India, taking 3-13 off 10 overs. I also got 3-for, but was in the shadow of Dizzy who barely bowled a bad ball. What was tipped as being one of the most exciting preliminary matches turned into a thrashing: after rolling India for 126 we lost only one wicket in knocking off the runs.

We continued our good form with wins over Zimbabwe and Namibia before an amazing individual performance helped us home against England at St George's Park, Port Elizabeth. One of the great things about being a bowler in one-day cricket is that you often get the chance to have a bat as well, and if you do well with one aspect of your game it often flows into the other, because you're not only confident but have a feel for the pitch and the ground. Just ask Andy Bichel who had a game the rest of us could only dream of having. He took 7-20, and then with Australia in big trouble he scored 34 not out in a 73-run stand with Michael Bevan (74 not out) that steered us to a two-wicket win with two balls to spare. I went wicketless, but I did leave some mark when a delivery was clocked at 160.7 kilometres an hour, my fastest ball at that stage of my career. Shoaib Akhtar had earlier outshone me with a 161.3 k bullet, also against the Poms.

We notched up our next win against Sri Lanka in the second stage of the competition, a Super Six match at Centurion. Although my statistical contribution was three wickets, perhaps my most telling moment came when the dangerman Sanath Jayasuriya retired hurt for one after I'd hit him with a short ball that broke his left thumb. I never counted how many batsmen I injured during my career, but I'm guessing there would be dozens of broken bones.

The next game was surprisingly one-sided considering how it looked halfway through our innings. New Zealand captain Stephen Fleming sent us in on a St George's Park pitch that had really good carry. Shane Bond bowled the house down, taking 6-23. We were in strife at 7-84 before our saviours against England did it again: Bev and Bich both scored half-centuries to get us to 9-208. Right at the end I fluked a couple of sixes in a row off Jacob Oram, including one after I fell away and somehow managed to get enough on the ball to send it over third man. Sometimes it's the little things that can make a significant difference, and that shot alone told me my luck was in for the day.

After Pidgey took three quick wickets to put the Kiwis on the back foot, I came back for a second spell to find the ball hooping around 'spit rock' more than it had in any of the previous games in the tournament. One ball turned out to be one of the best I've ever bowled in one-day cricket. Coming around the wicket I went wide of the crease and angled the ball in, before it swung away to take out the left-handed Oram's off stump. It was exactly what I wanted to do. By then I was on a roll, having already dismissed Fleming and Brendon McCullum, and by the time I caught and bowled Shane Bond to finish the match I had 5-42. We won by 96 runs, an incredible margin considering we seemed down and out when we were batting.

At Kingsmead, Durban, we beat Kenya who'd surprised nearly everyone by getting through to the Super Six stage. To this day Gilly doesn't mind rubbing it in about what happened to me in this match. My contribution rested on three particular deliveries in only my second over. The first rose sharply to hit Kennedy Otieno on the elbow. Initially I saw only his pain as he writhed on the pitch, and it wasn't until I reached him that I saw the ball had hit the stumps. The very next delivery to Brijal Patel was full. It drew a defensive edge and Punter took a diving catch at second slip. I knew nothing about the incoming batsman David Obuya. All I was thinking was: 'How good would it be to get a hat-trick in a World Cup?' There was no indecision about what I'd bowl: it had to be full and straight. If Obuya missed, I would hit. Simple as that.

I fired in a 155 kilometre-an-hour yorker that somehow Obuya managed to dig out. Or that's what I immediately thought. But a split second later the ball flew up and hit the top of the stumps. I was stunned. Shit, I had a hattie! For some crazy reason I sprinted off to Pidgey way down at fine leg. I was swept away by adrenalin. It was one of those moments that will stay with me for the rest of my life. People might argue it was no big deal because it was only against Kenya, but so what? After all, you still have to put the ball in the right spot.

I finished with 3-14 off eight overs, and much to Gilly's amusement I didn't get Man of the Match. That honour went to Kenyan left-arm orthodox spinner Aasif Karim who admittedly bowled exceptionally well to take 3-7 off 8.2 overs. Although I'm not one for awards, being overlooked did bring me down to earth a bit.

With 15 wins on the trot we had good reason to feel invincible heading into a semifinal against Sri Lanka at St George's Park. However, not for the first time in the tournament our batting efforts left us on a cliff's edge. 7-212 was hardly a comfortable score, and it would have been much worse if it wasn't for some more brilliance from Symo with an unbeaten 91. Rain affected Sri Lanka's chase and forced the umpires to show their knowledge of astrophysics by turning to the complicated Duckworth–Lewis method for revising run rates. The new target was 172 off 38.1 overs.

If there was one ground during the tournament that felt like home to me, it was definitely St George's Park. I felt Australia, playing our third match at the venue in only 16 days, had a distinct advantage. We knew how the pitch played and, personally, I loved bowling on it because it gave the pace bowlers good support. I'd clocked my fastest delivery there and felt primed to bowl just as quickly against the Sri Lankans.

Right from my first over I was conscious of my speed because the results of every delivery were flashed up on the big screen. 150, 152, 154 kays . . . I felt great and was further lifted by the crowd that let out 'ooh's and 'aah's nearly every time my numbers flashed up. By my second over I'd struck a great rhythm and was rewarded with another of my favourite wickets: I bowled Marvan Atapattu through the gate with an off-cutter at 160 clicks.

I could never have expected to get such a thrill from taking a wicket at such pace. I may be wrong, but I think it was – and probably still is – the fastest recorded wicket-taking ball in history. That delivery helped set us on our way, and with all the bowlers fulfilling their roles to the letter, we restricted Sri Lanka to 7-123.

As much as the victory may be remembered, the match will be known more for one action by Gilly. He had smashed his way to 22 when he went for a sweep against Aravinda de Silva. The ball popped up and wicketkeeper Kumar Sangakkara took an easy catch. But what had the ball hit? Umpire Rudi Koertzen shook his head, and that normally would have been the end of it. Gilly paused for a moment, and then started to walk off. In the dressing room a number of players yelled: 'No, go back, you're not out.'

We presumed Gilly had misread Rudi, but then we realised what he was doing. He'd given himself out; he was walking. And that was a standstill moment that defined Gilly as both a player and a person. I still don't know why he chose that time to do what he did, but I respect him for it. It did, however, mean that he had to walk from that day on. He would only set himself up for criticism as a hypocrite if he only occasionally chose to give himself out.

For about an hour after his actions, there was a lot of chat in the dressing room about whether he'd done the right thing.

Could he have cost us the match? Why on earth did he do it in a World Cup semifinal? Why didn't he first do it for Western Australia when there wasn't as much at stake? More than anything it made me question what I would do.

My view didn't change and it stayed the same throughout my career: I could get all three of my stumps ripped out of the ground and I'd still wait for the umpire to put his finger up. There were so many times I had caught behinds given not out off my bowling that I think standing my ground after nicking a faint catch helped even the ledger. I didn't consider that cheating; it was simply putting the responsibility on the umpire to do his job. Whether a batsman walks or not is a personal decision. I have no problem either way, as long as each player is consistent.

Nine wins in a row at the World Cup. Could we make it 10 by winning the final at Wanderers Stadium? The night before the match I sat in my hotel room after having my regulation pre-game meal of pasta, probably spaghetti bolognese or chicken penne. I was just about to go to bed when there was a knock on my door. It surprised me; I wasn't expecting any teammates and I hadn't called for any room service. Other than that, what else could it be? Security was so tight that no-one else could get through. There were heavy police patrols outside the hotel, and anyone entering the foyer had to be swabbed for explosives. I opened the door to find my cousin Luke Buxton and friend Luke Harris.

'Hi, Binga, just thought we'd come across and watch the final,' said my cousin matter-of-factly.

They'd only just flown in from Australia. It's not the usual thing to have two mates crashing on your floor the night before such an important game, but what a lift it gave me. I was really touched by their efforts.

The next day Indian captain Sourav Ganguly surprised many when he sent Australia in after winning the toss. His decision was a compliment to our bowling attack: after our quicks had wrecked the Indian line-up in our preliminary match, it wasn't hard to think that Sourav was worried we could do it again. Nevertheless, his decision was questionable on what I thought was definitely a 300-plus wicket. In fact, the Johannesburg altitude made the ball fly further than normal, so 350 was a more acceptable total. Our batsmen didn't disappoint. Gilly started the show with a half-century, Haydos offered good support with 30-odd, then Punter and 'Marto' – Damien Martyn – went on a smash-fest. Punter was unbelievable. He hit eight sixes in an unbeaten 140 off 121 balls, while Marto finished 88 not out off 84 balls. They put on 234 in 30 overs.

India needed 360 to win. At the innings change-over Punter stressed we couldn't be complacent, because if there was one team in the world that could embarrass us, it was a team that included Tendulkar, Virender Sehwag, Rahul Dravid, Sourav Ganguly and Yuvraj Singh. It took only five balls for Pidgey to deliver the biggest blow of the innings: after pulling the fourth ball for four, Sachin Tendulkar tried to do it again the next delivery but only managed to sky it straight back to Pidgey. That was the crucial wicket that gave us the psychological edge. Soon afterwards, I picked up Ganguly after he'd skied an attempted pull to Darren Lehmann at mid-on. However, there were still two worries: Virender Sehwag, who was teeing off, and the weather.

We needed to bowl 25 overs to constitute a match, otherwise we'd have to return the following day and do it all again. When I was fielding on the boundary I watched a bank of black clouds roll in, much to the excitement of the Indian fans in the crowd. They were dancing and yelling at me: 'Mr Brett, it's going to rain. We will come back tomorrow and you are going to lose!'

I looked up after every single ball but thankfully we only had one brief interruption for rain, which made no difference to the overs we had to bowl. As for Sehwag? He continued to smash until he reached 82, then he took on Darren Lehmann at mid-on. 'Boof' mightn't have been the most agile player in the field but he had a great arm, and when he hit the stumps with Sehwag well out, we knew we just had to keep our heads and we'd be on our way to victory. I took one more wicket, bowling Javagal Srinath, and fittingly Pidgey took the last when Zaheer Khan skied one straight to Boof. India all out for 234.

It wasn't until after the initial celebrations and trophy presentation that the enormity of what we'd achieved finally hit me and I said to myself: 'Shit, we've just won the World Cup.' The two Lukes who'd come from Australia joined the team in the dressing room. Some of my random memories of our hours of celebrations include Bich with the Aussie flag tied around his neck and hanging off his shoulders, and Jimmy Maher doing the 'worm', which was basically a wriggle on his stomach all the way from the pitch to the boundary. That, of course, happened after more than a fair few beers! We sang the team song out in the middle late that night. Fantastic! I couldn't have been happier. I felt I bowled up there with the best throughout the series. I took 22 wickets, just one behind the leading wicket-taker, Sri Lanka's Chaminda Vaas. Pidgey finished with 21.

We had little time to bask in our efforts because we headed straight to the West Indies where we stretched our unbeaten run to 21 one-dayers, before it came to an end in Trinidad during a seven-match series. It was a world record that still stands at the time of writing this book, and will take a phenomenal team to beat it.

We won the series 4–3. Although I did quite well, my main memory – which was luckily not to be something I couldn't remember – happened during a training session. In what is a warning to all players, don't forget the golden rule: if you're bowling, never turn your back on the net when walking back to your mark. When I did this before the sixth one-dayer in Grenada, a quick 'watch out' from several players came too late for me to avoid being smacked in the head by a fully bludgeoned slap from Jimmy Maher. I lost all feeling in my legs and hit the ground dazed. At first I felt embarrassed and wanted to get up quickly, but my wonky legs wouldn't let me. I was taken back to the dressing room where I recovered from some slight concussion. I don't know how boxers get knocked about the head for a living!

The one-dayers followed four Tests which gave me my first experience of playing in the Caribbean. Windies grounds have unique carnival atmospheres: steel bands playing; recorded music thumping in the stands; girls dancing; blokes drinking rum straight out of the bottle; the waft of marijuana smoke across the field; palm trees; the way the sun emits a distinct fading light in the late afternoon. I loved it. In many ways it was like a nightclub in the day. After playing each day, I often went and strummed my guitar pool-side at our hotel. This was my type of tour. Even some of the pools left a lasting impression on me because they had swim-up bars. I made a mental note of those and now have something similar at my Sydney home.

There was one other endearing trait that made me feel as though I belonged: the West Indians love to watch fast bowling. It was very early on in the tour when the team arrived at a hotel and a receptionist asked me: 'Are you here to bowl some licks?' People on the street, even policemen, asked me the same thing. 'Licks' was the lingo for fast deliveries, and I seemed to be liked by the locals right from the very start for the mere fact that my job was to 'lick de batsmen up, marn'.

The tour began on a sad note for us all. Glenn McGrath had stayed behind to be with his wife, Jane, who'd been diagnosed with breast cancer. When I heard the news, reality struck. I was lucky to be a professional cricketer travelling the world, but in the scheme of things, bowling a ball didn't seem that important. I rang and texted Pidgey to offer my support. He joined us for the final two Tests, knowing the entire team was behind him during a very tough time.

Pidgey's absence put more pressure on me and the other fast bowlers, Jason Gillespie and Andy Bichel. It was something I tried not to think about; I preferred to focus on enjoying the moment, and if I did that, I was confident the results would come. Stuart MacGill also had a tough mission replacing Warnie, who'd been suspended by the ACB for a year for his diuretic misdemeanour.

There were many reasons why I loved playing Test cricket, and one of them was best underlined by what happened in the Second Test at Port of Spain, Trinidad, home of 'The Prince', Brian Lara. I hadn't seen the best of Brian when I first played the West Indies in Australia in 2000–01, but I got a much better appreciation of what he could do after he scored a century in the opening Test in Georgetown, Guyana. We won that match, but The Prince's 110 was a sign we'd have to be at our best to keep him in his place.

When he came to the crease in the second innings of the Trinidad Test, the Windies needed to bat for nearly a day-and-a-half to hold on for a draw. Their target of 407 was out of the question. At the end of day four, The Prince was 50-odd not out. He'd already scored 91 in the first innings. On the final morning he had this look about him that said: 'Bad luck, you're not going to get me out.' I was brought into the attack about an hour into the session after Jason Gillespie and Brad Hogg had failed to make a breakthrough. The Prince was 88, and I was hell-bent on stopping him getting his century.

The pitch was dry and cracking, but was still playing very well. I struck a rhythm straight away, and within an over or two I felt I was bowling as consistently fast as at any time in my career. I knew this because I was making The Prince rush his shots. He started to jump around and flinch a bit, making me think: 'I have a chance here.' So, I tried to pick up the pace even more; like when I bowled to Sachin Tendulkar, this was a *Spinal Tap* moment when I turned the efforts up to 11. A few balls zinged past The Prince's head, and the crowd went wild. Even from the middle I heard individual voices yelling: 'Lick him up, marn!' Every time I went down to fine leg there was more of the same with each sentence accompanied by clicking fingers and the scent of ganja. Elsewhere, others were screaming: 'Lara is going to lick you up, Lee!' There were licks going left, right and centre!

It was quite surreal. Every time I bowled I felt as though I was entering a tunnel. I heard the crowd and knew there were fieldsmen there, but all I could see was Brian Lara. There was nothing or no-one else in my sights. I was so engrossed in the battle that nothing else in the world mattered. I didn't say much to The Prince at all. I knew if he was disrespected or verballed he'd chirp up, but that was the wrong thing to make him do. He could take it personally and, let's put it this way, the guy had scored a 500, so he knew how to bat for a long, long time. Instead, I gave him a few death stares to let him know I was up for the challenge. I tried to be right in his face.

It was an amazing place to be. He'd miss a ball or flinch, play one away, work a single . . . I wanted him to slave over every run, and he was definitely making me work extra hard for his wicket.

In the end I didn't get him out, but I was pleased he didn't reach his hundred off me. He brought that up with a boundary off MacGilla. I bowled seven overs straight, and had only two fours hit off me, which Ramnaresh Sarwan managed on only the final two balls of my spell. My return: 0-23. This was a classic example of statistics not telling the story.

The Prince scored 122 before he fell to MacGilla. Australia won by 118 runs; again the numbers hid what happened. Afterwards, The Prince and I shared a beer and swapped shirts. On the one he gave me, he wrote: 'That's the most intense spell of fast bowling I've ever faced. It was a pleasure.' That was one of the main reasons I loved Test cricket. It wasn't to get a shirt from a rival; it was the meaning behind the shirt. Furthermore, the battle helped me realise something that remains very important to me: some cricketers don't make friends against the teams they play, but I made a lot of mates, including batsmen who I knocked over or hurt. My duel with Brian Lara cemented a friendship that I'll always cherish. In addition to all of that, I hope The Prince and I entertained everyone who was watching, especially those at the ground. After all, they're the people who players and administrators need to treasure.

Brian Lara was one of the two most technically and physically gifted batsmen I ever played against. It will surprise no-one to know the other was Sachin Tendulkar. Sachin had a lot more structure with his technique, while Brian had the West Indian flamboyance. They both had great eyes, and were both very light on their feet. I mentioned earlier that Sachin had incredible wrists that could turn the ball on any angle. Brian could also do this, but it was more his whole hands and body that allowed him to have similar diversity of shot selection. It was as though he almost danced into positions, some of which no-one else could ever hope to achieve.

As with Sachin, if I bowled a fifth or sixth stump line to Brian, he could just as easily work me to fine leg as to third man. I don't know how he did it. Depending on the mood he was in, he could hit the ball to wherever in the field he wanted. There was no really good length where I thought I could permanently tie him down. If I executed a plan perfectly I could always restrict a batsman nine times out of ten, but with Brian it was different. When he was on fire the perfect line to him would have been about a millimetre inside the return crease where he couldn't reach the ball!

There were times when bowling to either Sachin or Brian that I'd get smacked for four and I'd think: 'You prick! But gee, that's a bloody great shot!' Some of the most common examples were when they worked me at an angle through cover, backward point or midwicket off good length balls that I considered near perfect in line. VVS Laxman was another who could do that to me.

But the classic example was their ability to hit the ball harder on the up than I'd delivered it. Whether the ball raced through covers or straight back past me, this was the ultimate way to disrespect a fast bowler; a full face of the bat just coming down and smacking my best to the boundary. The final insult was when I lifted my head and saw Sachin or Brian looking contentedly at me as though they were thinking: 'That felt good for me, how do you feel?' Then I'd walk back to my mark and ask myself: 'What am I expected to do now? I don't know where to bowl. I honestly do not know.' I'd come up with another plan or think of a delivery that I'd want to try. Sometimes it worked, but on other occasions I ran in to bowl knowing I was up against players who were in a different league to me. They were just too good. There was never a part of me that gave in, but I admit there were occasions against Brian and Sachin when I thought: 'I'm not good enough to get you out today.'

Who was the better of the two? It's too close to call. Perhaps Sachin's bat seemed wider to me – about three foot wide, in fact – but either way, both batsmen could make others look as though they were trying to score runs with pencils. When on song, they made scoring runs look oh so easy.

There's another player I need to throw in to the mix. His performances during the West Indies series were every bit as good as Brian Lara's. Ricky Ponting scored three centuries, including a double in the second Test. Punter will certainly go down as one of the best batsmen ever, and would have succeeded in any era. The most valuable players are ones who can step up when it's needed most. Punter has done this throughout his career. When watching him bat in the Caribbean I was grateful I wasn't bowling against him. His pull shot, the best in world cricket, was murderous, and his performances were one of the foundations for our 3–1 series win.

The Tests finished on a downer for us after the Windies, inspired by centuries from Shivnarine Chanderpaul and Sarwan, chased down a world record 418 to win the last match at St John's, Antigua. Overall, though, the tour was a pleasing team return, and I was satisfied after claiming 17 scalps, the same number as Jason Gillespie, and three behind Stuart MacGill, the leading wicket-taker. I'd bounced back well after losing my Test spot at the start of the Australian summer. I was only three years into my international career, but felt I was maturing as a bowler. I still needed to be more consistent and relied too much on the bouncer–yorker lengths, but at 26 years of age I was still a work in progress. I was excited about what lay ahead both on and off the field, especially since I was about to enter a new stage of my career that stretched well beyond the boundary.

17

It was chaos. Cameras were just centimetres from my face, and there were so many flashes going off that I was blinking as much as a rat caught in a flour tin. Thirty, 40, 50 reporters were jostling for position, all hoping to catch my eye and ask for 'a one-on-one exclusive!'. I'd just arrived in Mumbai after signing a deal to become the ambassador for Timex watches in India. It was obviously a risk for the company to have a cricketer who hadn't even played a Test in India to be the 'face of the brand'. Furthermore, I was a white foreigner, but Timex was confident I was the 'right fit' and would appeal to the Indian market. If my first media conference was anything to go by, I had at least ensured the prospect of a headline or two in a few papers and on TV news bulletins.

I was ushered to a table and was formally introduced amidst the whirr of camera shutters and never-ending flashes. After a moment's calm I waited for my first question from the pack. A well-dressed man with a very serious look on his face was first to fire in:

'Brett, you have a dog. What is with that?'

Of all the questions I'd been expecting, this certainly wasn't one of them. I replied, 'I'm sorry, I don't have a dog. I don't own a dog, mate. No dog, sorry to disappoint you. I don't know what to say. You've got me with that one.'

Silence followed, after which I noticed a look of bemusement on the reporter's face, but he quickly regained composure and jumped to another topic: 'So what do you think about India playing Australia?'

It turned into a long and draining conference that included dozens of one-on-one interviews which taught me a valuable lesson about Indian reporters that still applies today. When they pre-empt their interviews by saying, 'Just three or four questions please,' that can be translated as: 'I am going to ask you all the questions I can before you are sick of me!' And when they say, 'OK, this is my last question,' that is generally followed by 'OK, this is my *very* last question,' and then 'OK, this is my *very, very* last question,' and then . . . I'm sure you get the idea. The last question normally stretches over about five questions. I can only laugh, and over the years I've tried to have fun with the interviews. I've seen all sorts of things to make me smile: reporters tripping over cameras; others clambering over the backs of each other to get a better view; those who've gone for a spill and landed as though they've just been dumped on the bottom of a rugby ruck. It's crazy, it's bizarre, it's hilarious, it's India. I love it.

The role with Timex was another important step for me outside of playing cricket. After developing some strong and long-lasting sponsorship relationships for me in Australia, Neil Maxwell thought India was worth exploring for other opportunities. Australian cricketers were very popular in this part of the world, and in the case of some, such as Steve Waugh, this popularity led to considerable business opportunities. At first Maxi believed it would be a case of 'prostituting me' and taking anything we got, but after receiving the offer from Timex we realised with a smarter approach I could be positioned long-term in one of the biggest and most potentially lucrative markets in the world. Add to that my affection for India that began on my Under-19 trip in 1994, and it seemed a great chance to establish commercial relationships that I'd enjoy long after my cricket career was finished.

These days I'm still an ambassador for Timex, and I also have similar roles with Pearls, a multi-faceted company that has interests ranging from building infrastructure projects to the media; Pain Relief, a muscle cream; Venky's, the largest supplier of poultry foods across India; and Castrol. My duties include public appearances; store openings; guest speaking at official functions; launching new products; modelling for TV advertisements and magazines; and all the other standard things that need to be done in the commercial world.

All this has meant I'm a frequent visitor to India; since the initial Timex deal I've been back to the subcontinent more than 40 times on business trips that usually last about a week. Just like many cricket matches, memories from these trips have blended into each other, so instead of trying to pinpoint exactly when each moment happened, it's best just to give you a sample of stories from across the years that will hopefully paint the picture of what my corporate visits to India have been like.

Firstly, I've had some very funny experiences working for Timex. On magazine shoots I've worn bandanas while sitting on motorbikes, hung onto and abseiled off a studio-made cliff, and dressed up in a *Matrix*-like outfit. On more formal occasions I've launched several watches at functions where I've had to get up on a stage or a runway and walk along wearing such bizarre clothes as a red leather motorbike jacket with the sleeves rolled up to reveal the product in the spotlight. The very first time I did that I was accompanied by deafening music and then, just a few steps into my appearance, I thought I'd been blown up after a confetti bomb exploded in front of me.

I'm convinced that at least every second Indian is a pyromaniac. Those who are have something in common with me. On one of my earliest trips to Mumbai I asked some police officers who were looking after my security if they could go and buy me some firecrackers. When they asked me how many I wanted, I told them 'four or five', meaning single ones. They returned with five bags bursting with about 100 crackers, many of them bigger than bottles.

I asked the cops where we could go to let them off. They waggled their heads and said, 'No problem, we organise.' We hopped in a car and drove off. It was late afternoon peak hour with horns blaring and kids weaving between the traffic selling everything from magazines to pencils, toy fans, and watermelon slices. We stopped by the side of the road near a beach, where some officers got out and blocked off the traffic. Other cops nearby joined in and there were soon about 20 taking part. The guys who'd bought the crackers took me to the beach but insisted I stay back a reasonable distance while they lit the wicks. They told me they didn't want me to blow myself up. A comforting thought! Meanwhile, all the people in the blocked traffic either sat in their cars or got out and became spectators too. They all cheered and yelled. No-one complained; everyone seemed happy to be there. After the fireworks finished, I waved to the hundreds around me, and then got back in the car with the cops, and we drove away, leaving other officers to start the traffic again. It ran so smoothly it was as though it happened every day. As the saying goes, 'It could only happen in India!'

In such a cricket-mad country, security is often needed for high-profile players. I don't want to sound like a precious superstar, but from the moment I step off the plane in India

I'm grabbed by people wanting autographs or asking me to look this way or that for 'just one snap please!'. No-one means any harm, but it's comforting to know I can call on protection if the situation becomes too overbearing.

There have been occasions when I've appeared for either Timex or New Balance that shop windows have been broken by the crush of onlookers on the outside. I've even once had to stand on a table and ask everyone to move to prevent injuries from happening. It's amazing how quickly crowds can gather. As soon as one person sees me, rest assured the word spreads fast, and within minutes there can be hundreds if not thousands cramming for a look.

There was one incident, I think in Delhi, where Maxi and I tried to 'escape' through the back entrance of a shop. As soon as we slipped behind a curtain, the fans were on to our plan. We bolted through a passage that was only a shoulder-width wide and headed for a street where we were told a car would be waiting for us. It was, but the driver had pulled up near another alley at the other end of the street. By this stage, hundreds had raced around from the front of the store and were heading towards us. All Maxi and I could do was laugh, and, of course, run! We didn't have security on this occasion, and somehow we had to make our way through the masses. As Maxi and I reached the swarm I started to get grabbed and pulled, flowers were thrown at me, and I felt fingers in my pockets where scraps of paper with poems and phone numbers were being shoved. I kept laughing; I didn't feel at all threatened, but it was a real struggle to reach the car.

When we finally did, sweat was pouring down our faces. As we drove away, Maxi and I went through my pockets and decided we'd randomly pick a phone number to ring. I borrowed the driver's phone, so whoever I was going to call wouldn't have my private number. After a few rings, I heard the voice of a youngish girl.

'Hello,' she said.

'Hi, it's Brett Lee.'

'Who?'

'It's Brett Lee. You gave me your number.'

I then heard a thud and the phone went dead at the other end. I rang back a few minutes later and the girl told me: 'I'm sorry about before, but when I heard it was you, I fainted.'

On another occasion, when I did have security with me, I thought I'd have a bit of fun with my two bodyguards. They were both mountains of men, about six-foot-four-ish with gym-sculpted bodies. They were very friendly and polite to me. When I first met them they began their work only after getting autographs and photos with me. One of their main jobs was to walk me through crowds where they had a tendency to hold my hands; it was just the Indian way, but it did take me a while to get used to it. Basically, unless I was in my own hotel room they wouldn't allow me to go anywhere by myself.

One day I decided to go for a walk – I can't recall in what city – and the bodyguards dutifully came along. There I was in my shorts, training shirt and sneakers accompanied by these two huge blokes striding out in their black shoes, black trousers and tight black shirts. After starting at a slow pace I soon thought I'd see how fit my two new mates were, so I began to jog. They kept up, with their keys rattling in their pockets. I cranked up the speed, and within the space of a few hundred metres I was running flat-chat with my 'heavies' trying their best to keep up. After another few hundred metres they began to fall back until one slowed right down and yelled: 'I am sorry, sir, but I am dying!'

The enthusiasm of the security guards I've had over the years has been matched by hotel staff. When travelling in

Australia I might get one or two genuine knocks on my door per day from housekeeping, but in India it might be 30 or more interruptions, primarily because someone wants to meet me. Bringing up a fruit platter is always a favourite tactic. It's nearly always a man who'll come in and present me with a collection of every type of fruit imaginable. The conversation that follows goes something like this:

'Some fruit for you, Mr Brett.'
'Thank you very much, this fruit looks very nice.'
'Yes, sir, it is brilliant fruit.'
'Thank you.'

After a little pause, the man will continue:

'Mr Brett, can I please have one snap with you?'
'Of course.'

And then the man goes out and brings in a friend or two, or returns in a couple of minutes with a little group. I know the drill well. I face my room's window so we're not shooting into the light, we gather for 'one snap' from *each* of the visitors' cameras or cell phones, we shake hands, and then we all say goodbye.

Once news spreads of this, there is a steady flow of door knocks and fruit platters. This can even happen at midnight after I've been filming all day and am exhausted. I'll open the door with my hair looking as though it's been brushed by a balloon, and there they are, smiling at me. It doesn't matter at all if I've turned on the 'Do Not Disturb' light, and if there is security on the floor a guard may even put down his gun and ask for a photograph as well. One of my favourite encounters was the time a waiter came up to deliver some room service I'd ordered. I opened the door, he grinned and asked for my autograph, then he frowned after he realised he'd forgotten my food.

The best advice I can give anyone going to India is to make sure you pack your sense of fun and good humour. Although it can be frustrating, I look back fondly at many of the things that have happened to me. On one trip I took my favourite pair of jeans with me; they had a fashionable designer stain on them and were worth $300. I put them in to a hotel laundry service, and they returned crisply ironed, minus the stain, and were about four sizes too small. For a moment I was angry, but then I realised the people who'd washed them had simply wanted to help me. They must have thought: 'They are Brett Lee's pants, so we have to get them clean and get the nasty stain out!' So they scrubbed and scrubbed and scrubbed.

For devotion to service it would be hard to top the time I rang the concierge and asked if he knew somewhere local where I could buy some guitar strings. Half an hour later he rang back and asked if I needed bass or acoustic strings; he'd obviously made a few calls. I told him I needed acoustic, and he hung up after saying, 'Not a problem, Mr Brett.' Another hour passed without any news, then another hour and another. Finally, about seven hours later, someone came to my door with half a dozen strings. He told me he'd been out searching the whole day for them. He said it was his pleasure to help me. He refused to be paid, but I eventually persuaded him to take some money. I gave him about 1500 rupees, the equivalent at the time of about $50. It was a considerable sum of money for him, probably a couple of months' wages.

So many of the Indians I've met are very eager to please. Although I'll keep most of my cricket stories separate, it's fitting to mention one here while we're talking about hotel staff. On one of the Australian team's stays in a hotel whose name it's perhaps best not to mention here, the smiling general manager insisted we go to a function room to celebrate one of the players' birthdays. We arrived to find a chocolate cake placed on a table. The manager began to sing 'Happy Birthday' – in a horrible B flat – when a cockroach suddenly scurried out of the cake. Quick as a flash, the manager grabbed it and put it in his mouth, much to the disbelief of all the players, who immediately said: 'That was a cockroach!' The manager denied this, and in a bizarre act he then opened his mouth and invited everyone to have a close inspection. The funny thing is, everyone did.

'See, no cockroach. A piece of chocolate fell from the cake. No cockroach, no cockroach,' he said. No-one believed him and the cake went untouched.

I've seen the manager a few times since that happened, and I always say to him: 'It was a cockroach, wasn't it?' He's never admitted it.

Incidents like that could be straight out of a Monty Python movie, as could the morning that Maxi and I were picked up in Mumbai in a really stylish BMW. In the back, the car was like a lounge room with a DVD screen and speakers. We asked the driver if he could put some music on. He happily pressed a button or two, and suddenly a porno movie came on that was at, should I say, a very climactic stage. The driver frantically stopped it and must have apologised to us 100 times. He said he had no idea how the disc had got there. Again, only in India!

Overall, the initial Timex deal opened the door to a number of business relationships that I'll be involved with for many years to come. Furthermore, I've benefited from other incredible opportunities, including acting in Bollywood and the expansion of my music, which I'll discuss later. The Timex deal also exposed me to an extraordinary country that I'll never tire of visiting. More than anything, it's hard not to fall in love with the people. The co-author of this book, James Knight, told me that one of his favourite sayings comes from a man he once met in Calcutta: 'We Indians are poor of pocket but rich in heart.' How very true.

India is a place where I feel different. In Australia people may recognise, idolise or hate me. They do in India as well, but the level of obsession and the sheer volume of people make it difficult to comprehend. It's in India I really feel like a superstar. I hope it hasn't affected me. At the time of preparing this book, I'm in the early stages of establishing a charity in India that will provide musical opportunities for children. It's difficult to say too much about it because it's a work in progress, but in short I've chosen music as a way to help because I know it can both stimulate and inspire, and hopefully the children who benefit will gain joy from their involvement, no matter what their predicaments in life might be.

As a final word before moving on, I'd like to thank Ekta from Delhi, who sent me an email a year or so ago via Neil Maxwell's offices. It truly humbled me. Below is an edited version of it.

A couple of days back I had gone for some work to Connaught Place (CP) – one of the best and most expensive markets in Delhi. After having lunch I was heading to my car when I got intercepted by a beggar. This has always been one of the harshest realities of CP where one can see extreme poverty residing just outside the shops belonging to some of the best brands in the world. Mostly people shoo them away but I've always been a bit of a hopeless case in such situations. Initially I always gave money, but with time I realised that such kids are managed by gangs and they end up getting nothing. So I give them food.

The beggar was a girl of about 12–13yrs. As usual I asked her if she wanted anything to eat as we were standing just opposite McDonalds. But she said that she wanted money and not food. I was surprised as usually kids are too happy to take the food. I asked why she wanted the money to which she said that she wanted to buy something. I had taken out Rs.50 (about $AUD1.25) to pay for the parking, so I handed her the same. I was shocked when she said (in Hindi): 'I don't want this much. Ten rupees will do.'

For the first time in my life, a beggar was returning me money. I was totally speechless. Since it was getting late I decided to leave, telling her to keep the money. But she insisted that I take back the extra money and instead help her buy whatever she wanted to because she expected the vendor would shoo her away. I asked where would I have to go and she pointed towards a magazine stand across the street. Honestly, I accompanied her purely out of curiosity to see what an illiterate girl could want from a magazine stand.

When we reached there I asked what she wanted and she said a poster. So I told the vendor to give her whichever poster she wanted. I had assumed that in all probability she would ask for a Bollywood actor's poster. But when she said Brett Lee, I honestly thought that I had heard something wrong. I asked if she was sure and she replied in the affirmative. I asked her if she knew who he was and she just said: 'Obviously I do, he plays cricket, India loses because of him and I like him very much, my brother told me his name . . . but don't you know him?'

If this encounter wasn't already interesting enough it was topped by someone asking a cricket freak like me if I didn't know who Brett Lee was! Anyways, I just smiled and told the vendor to give me the biggest poster. (He had it in three sizes, the smallest was postcard size.) Again the girl insisted that I take back 40 rupees and buy the smallest one which was for 10 rupees. I got a little fed up and just snapped that why the heck was she so concerned about my money. She just looked up at me and said: 'With 40 rupees you'll be able to feed your whole family for three days and I don't have a home to put up this poster, I'll carry the photograph in my pocket.' At that point of time I couldn't hold back my tears. The girl's innocence and the realisation as to how lucky I am was just too overwhelming.

Anyways I handed her the postcard and out of curiosity asked what would she do with the picture and she said very plainly: 'I'll keep the pic with me, whenever I'm sad I'll look at it and get happy as I really like him and his face is the only thing that can bring a smile to my face.'

I had always known that Brett was loved in India but understood the true extent of it that day. Why is it so? I really don't know. I guess it's just his personality, honesty, lovable nature and love for the Indian people that comes through. I've never been a fan of anyone in my life, but now I am of Brett Lee. I hope to be lucky enough to meet him someday . . . and even if I don't, then I know that he will continue doing what he's really good at . . . playing cricket and bringing a smile to people's faces . . . be it Australians or Indians, rich or poor!

18

Apart from beginning my corporate commitments in India, I used the 2003 winter to prepare for unusually scheduled Tests and one-dayers against Bangladesh in northern Australia in July and August. As much as the benefits of soft-sand running and weights made me feel I was ready to roll against Bangladesh, it was a social event that really motivated me.

I'm not a big fan of black-tie occasions, but I look back at a dinner in Sydney as one of the more enjoyable and meaningful formal occasions of my playing career. A hundred and fifty of Australia's surviving Test cricketers – apparently there were only about 200 alive at the time – gathered to be presented with numbered replicas of the baggy green. I remember walking into a hotel function room and being overwhelmed by this mass of greatness. It was inspiring to put names to faces, shake hands, and swap stories.

Of all the people I met, none left a greater impression than the oldest surviving player, Bill Brown, an opening batsman during the Bradman era. He was a few weeks short of his 91st birthday, and still had enormous enthusiasm and energy. What a dear man, an absolute gentleman. I think it was a journalist who asked him what he would have done if he'd had to face my bowling. Bill replied: 'I would faint!'

We had a beer together in a pub just before the function and he told me about the boat trips the Australian team took to England in the 1930s and 40s. I found it hard to imagine spending three or more months at sea, and said I wouldn't have been able to manage because I'd get sick. Bill just smiled.

Moments like that made me realise what a proud tradition Australian cricket has. I felt privileged to think that maybe one day I might be an older cricketer having a conversation with a young up-and-comer. Hopefully the tradition will live forever. Bill died in 2008 at the age of 95. His presence and character represented an era that should never be forgotten.

As expected, Australia won both Tests and all three one-dayers against Bangladesh. My favourite memory of those contests was a coaching session I had with Bangladesh's bowlers a day or so before the one-dayers began. I was invited by their team management, and although it may have seemed strange for an opponent to be helping out his rivals, I thought nothing of it. They were a nice bunch of guys feeling their way in international cricket. Administrators and players from across the world have a responsibility to foster such players if cricket is to prosper.

The Australian summer came round quickly. Ahead of a much-awaited home series against India, we played two Tests with Zimbabwe which we won convincingly. The first in Perth will be remembered for Matthew Hayden's 380, the highest Test score by an Australian. I picked up four wickets for the game, but much more significantly, injuries early in the second innings to Jason Gillespie and Stuart MacGill – Glenn McGrath with an ankle injury was already missing from the team – put a lot of pressure on the remaining bowlers. I bowled 35 overs and

Andy Bichel just a few less. I've already spoken about the strain of being a paceman, and with only three days' rest between Tests, there was always a higher than usual chance something would go wrong. And it did.

In the second Test in Sydney, we lost the toss and bowled first. I was a little hesitant entering the game because I felt sore on the left side of my abdomen. I hoped it was just general stiffness, but from very early on in my first spell I knew I wasn't right. I managed 23 overs, but enough was enough; my soreness became a torn muscle and the prognosis was that I'd be out of action for about a month. That meant I was sidelined for a one-day series in India, and had only six weeks to be ready for the first Test against the Indians in Brisbane. However, there was a blessing to come from the lay-off: after consulting team management it was decided I would have 'clean-out' surgery on my left ankle at the same time. Kim Slater again did the operation. I owe much to him; if it wasn't for his brilliance I wouldn't have played as many Tests as I did.

My recovery from both setbacks went well; the muscle healed within three weeks, and within a month I was back testing out my ankle with full-paced runs. I thought I was still in with a chance of being fit for the Gabba Test, and said so in an interview for *The Sydney Morning Herald*. I acknowledged I wasn't a 'dead-set certainty' of playing but that was what I was aiming for. If that plan failed, I said I'd target the second Test. I thought much of it depended on whether I'd be right to play a one-dayer against Tasmania about five days before the first Test. I considered I was fit, and well and truly on my way back.

But then I got a phone call. I was at Alan Jones's place at the time, and I put the call on loudspeaker. It was Australia's Chairman of Selectors, Trevor Hohns. He said he'd seen the quote in the paper and asked me what was happening. He added: 'I thought we were working towards a plan.' The selectors' plan was to see me back playing in a couple of Tests' time; first I was expected to ease back into playing for NSW. I told 'Cracker' (Hohns) I thought I could jump ahead and be ready for the first Test. We argued the point, but neither of us made any concessions. I got the feeling Cracker was worried that if I came back early I'd make the selectors look silly. Perhaps that was an over-reaction, but it was the way I felt. As it was, I missed the game against Tasmania, and didn't play in the first two Tests.

During that time there were a couple of events away from cricket that proved welcome distractions for me. The major one was bizarre and totally unexpected. To any English rugby fan reading this, 22 November 2003 will be remembered as the day Jonny Wilkinson booted a field goal in extra time to nab the Aussies in the World Cup final in Sydney. Although I don't often attend sports events, I was at the Olympic Stadium for that game, but it was what happened afterwards, well past midnight, that was much more memorable.

I was having a drink with Damien Martyn at the Cargo Bar at Darling Harbour when a bloke wearing a suit approached me.

'Excuse me, Mr Lee,' he said in a very official voice.

I immediately wondered if I'd done anything wrong. The suit continued: 'Sir, Prince Harry has requested a drink with you.'

I thought he was pulling my leg, and the first words that came out of my mouth were: 'Yeah, mate, and where are the Queen's corgis?'

He laughed, said he was serious, and told me to look into a private room away from the main crowded area. I turned my head and, yep, the prince was there.

'Don't worry about the private area. Tell him to come on over here,' I told the suit.

Sure enough, a couple of minutes later Harry walked through the public area accompanied by some security, I think police officers in suits. We shook hands and he introduced himself with a bit of Aussie-ness: 'G'day, mate!'

He was in a really happy mood. He'd been to the change-rooms after England had won, and I reckon a few beers and champagne might have been downed. Whatever the case, he was up for more, and offered to buy me and Marto drinks. I insisted I should get them because Harry was a guest in our country. He didn't seem to mind that, but what on earth could I buy a prince? The conversation that followed went along the lines of:

'What would you like?' I asked.
'I don't mind. Let's get funky, let's have a go,' Harry replied.
'Well, I've got this mate who's got this drink called a car-bomb.'
'I love it! Let's do it!'

I'm sure Harry had no idea what it was. For the record, it's three quarters of a pint of Guinness with a shot glass of Kahlua, Jameson's and Baileys that is dropped or 'bombed' in. He loved it! Here he was, one of the world's most famous people, sculling a pretty savage concoction watched on by a crowd, but he didn't care at all. He was just a 19-year-old bloke doing what 19-year-old blokes do when they have a night on the town. Meanwhile, I was sculling the drink too in what became a race. All I could think was: 'This is great, I'm drinking with the prince!' After beating me to bottoms up, Harry said: 'England wins again!'

We had a few more drinks together, during which people got photos of us arm-in-arm like mates. I had to pinch myself. We also had a chat about cricket; he was kind enough to say he thought I was a really good player.

A few years later, I also had the pleasure of meeting Prince William, though in much more serious circumstances, when he visited victims of 'Black Saturday', the horrendous Victorian bushfires that killed 173 people. He was very polite and down to earth. Just like his brother. A bloody good bloke.

Two weeks before I met Prince Harry, while I was in the middle of my injury rehabilitation, I had my 27th birthday. Again, there was a surprise in store. My family and a few close mates had come to my home. We were sitting at the bar at the edge of my pool when someone said I wasn't allowed to turn around. I obviously knew something was happening, and for a moment I was thinking: 'What happens if there's a stripper? Shit, Mum and Dad are here!'

I asked my mates what was going on, but no-one told me anything. After about half an hour of secrecy, I heard a male voice say: 'Happy birthday, Brett.' I turned around to see one of Australia's best musicians, Diesel, set up with all his equipment. While I was still coming to terms with the shock, Diesel launched into one of his most famous songs, 'Fifteen Feet Of Snow', followed by 'Tip Of My Tongue'. My brother Shane, Gavin Robertson and a few others had chipped in to buy me the private performance. It was magical. The show lasted 40 minutes, maybe more. There would have been about 30 people at the party, another 15 or so hanging over the back fence, and others were listening from the balcony of a neighbour's place. To this day I hear of people talking about 'the day Diesel played in Lane Cove'. But next to no-one knows whose house it was.

After my rehabilitation I finally returned to playing in a one-dayer, then a Pura Cup match against Victoria in Melbourne. The latter, which we lost narrowly, coincided with the second Test in Adelaide. It turned out to be a good workout for me:

I bowled 44 overs at good pace and picked up a few wickets. I was also really satisfied with my batting in the first innings when I kept getting bounced on a green top. I finished 74 not out after sharing a useful stand with Brad Haddin. As a bowler, whether it's in junior cricket or all the way to Tests, it's a nice feeling to get runs.

As much as anything, the match was memorable for me because of an incident in Victoria's first innings. I was heading back to fine leg after bowling an over, but was in a world of my own and well out of position when Jason Arnberger got a good piece of a bouncer from Stuart Clark. I belatedly saw the ball in the air and immediately thought it was going for six. Then I reassessed and realised I was half a chance of taking a catch. So I took off, sprinting finer around the boundary. The ball dropped quicker than I thought, forcing me to make a sudden jump between steps, throw my right arm at full stretch above my head, and hope for the best. Somehow the ball stuck and I was more stunned than anybody, although many of my teammates said it was the arsiest catch they'd seen in their lives.

A couple of days later I bowled 50 overs and took six wickets, including a 5-for, in a draw against Tasmania at the SCG. Hoping I'd proved my fitness and form to selectors, I was relieved when I was called back into the Australian team for the third Test, the Boxing Day match at the MCG. In some ways it seemed everything old was new again: I was back where I'd started my career four years earlier. However, this time the circumstances were very different. In 1999–00 Australia had dominated the Indians, but in 2003–04 we were down 1–0 after losing in Adelaide. Plus, there was no McGrath or Warne, and injuries to others meant we had a very inexperienced attack: Nathan Bracken was playing only his second Test, and Brad Williams, his third.

Personally, the biggest difference between the two series was my position in the team. During my debut summer I couldn't do anything wrong and the general fascination with my pace shot me skywards quickly. Four years later, though, some journalists were questioning if I'd lost my speed and were suggesting I didn't have the same wicket-taking impact as I had earlier in my career; others said my run with injuries had affected me; while there were some who thought batsmen were just getting used to me. And then there were the people in the street – everyone seemed to have an opinion.

In the pre-match media conference Steve Waugh was asked about my position. He believed I still had genuine pace, but acknowledged 'out-and-out' fast bowlers were at their quickest when young. He also said I had to step up and 'assume the mantle of the strike bowler' in the absence of Pidgey and Dizzy. All the talk and pressure affected me, and I felt as though I was hanging on by a thread. It was hard to believe I was only one Test into a comeback, and had done so well at the World Cup earlier in the year. Yes it's a cliché, but any athlete is only as good as their last game or performance.

I copped some hammering on the opening day of the Melbourne Test. Then again, every bowler did. After winning the toss and batting India were 4-329 by stumps. Their hero was Virender Sehwag who was brutal. When he is firing, there are few more dangerous players in the game. I hit him twice on the helmet early on in his innings, but he refused to be intimidated and got the better of me as time went on. He belted 195 off 230-odd balls.

My only joy for the day came when Sachin Tendulkar edged his very first ball to Gilly. By then, the Indians were nearly 300, and I was first to admit I hadn't done my job as a strike bowler. Although I'd pushed above 150 kays, I'd mostly bowled too short and also had no-ball problems. Luckily, I got an early breakthrough the next morning when I claimed Sourav Ganguly, and that triggered a collapse: India lost 6-16 to be all out 366. A double century by Ricky Ponting and a ton to Matthew Hayden swept us to a 192 run lead, a position that allowed us to dominate the rest of the Test on our way to a nine-wicket win.

I took two more wickets in the second innings for a match return of 4-200 off 49 overs. I hadn't delivered the goods, and when the media talk continued about me, I didn't need to be a rocket scientist to know my spot was in jeopardy. As one reporter put it, had I become the 'great white hype'?

I entered the fourth Test in Sydney with points to prove. It was no ordinary match; not only was it the last in the series, but it was Steve Waugh's final Test. For other reasons it turned out to be the saddest of my whole career.

On the morning of the first day I woke up feeling very strange; I wasn't sick as such, but I didn't feel well either. It was weird. I knew something was wrong, but I couldn't put my finger on it. I tried to put it out of my mind in the dressing room before the start. There'd been plenty of talk in the team about how we wanted to give Tugga the best possible send-off, but after he returned from losing the toss he stressed the match wasn't about him. He told us: 'Thanks for your thoughts, guys, but this is just like every other Test match. We have to go out and win it.'

Dizzy, who'd come back from a groin strain, opened the attack with me on a pitch with some bounce but nevertheless it looked a great batting track. We got some early swing and seam and with a bit more luck could have picked up both Sehwag and Aakash Chopra, who played and missed a few times in the opening overs. But then I struck problems that all started with a good delivery, a fast outswinger that Chopra edged straight through to Gilly. It was a no-ball. Shit! The very next delivery Chopra edged one to gully where Simon Katich dropped the catch. A couple of overs later Sehwag slapped me for 18 off an over, including a six over backward point off another no-ball.

The openers put on 123 before Dizzy claimed Sehwag, and soon afterwards I cleaned up Chopra with a 'jaffa', a fast inswinging yorker. By the time Dizzy trapped Rahul Dravid LBW, India were 3-194 and we knew we had to lift the intensity to try to get Sachin Tendulkar and VVS Laxman out before they got set. A day later they were still there, and our chances of giving Tugga a winning send-off were shot. It was bloody hard enough trying to deal with only one of those two batsmen, but put them together in the form and mood they were in, and that was enough to give any bowler and captain migraines.

I've already spoken about Sachin's brilliance, but on his day VVS was every bit as incredible. Like Sachin, his wrist work meant he could place balls to a number of different spots in the field, and his timing and ability to hit the ball on the up were as good as any player in the game, and surely throughout history too. I remember once bowling a bouncer to him in another game and sledging him light-heartedly by suggesting VVS meant 'Very, Very Scared', but there was none of that at the SCG.

At the start of the second day, my weird feeling had worsened to a feeling of discomfort in the stomach. I told team physio Errol Alcott that something definitely wasn't right, but it was nothing I couldn't manage. I went onto the field where Sachin and Very, Very Special added to my pain, hitting me for a handful of fours in my first few overs. After bowling 15 no-balls in 21 overs on the first day, I readjusted my run-up so my front foot was landing well behind the popping crease, but this affected my rhythm. For most of the day I bowled too full or too short and my pace was at times in the 130s.

Sachin and VVS were unbelievable. They had a 353-run partnership that finally ended when Dizzy bowled 'Laxey' for 178. I yorked Ganguly for my second wicket, and then Parthiv Patel teed off. By stumps India were 5-650. It was a really quiet dressing room. Normally after such ordinary days, I consciously didn't dwell on them. The hours outside of play were for going out with friends or teammates or finding an escape through my guitar. But this day was different; I didn't feel in the mood to do anything. I'd earlier spoken on the phone to Mum and Dad who, knowing the pressure I was under, tried to be positive and encouraging. However, I sensed something was wrong.

On the team bus on the way back to the hotel, I rang Shane and asked: 'What's going on?' My brother told me Grandmum (Mum's mum) had died. I knew that my strange feelings for the previous two days had been related to this. Sitting at the back of the bus I didn't think it was the right time to find out too much, so I told Shane I'd ring him back. I hung up, and immediately felt pissed off that Mum and Dad hadn't told me, but then I realised they were just trying to protect me at what was a vulnerable time for me.

Back at the hotel, I got off the bus and saw Neil Maxwell. I welled up immediately and told him and Adam Gilchrist what had happened. Gilly invited us up to his room where his wife, Mel, and her sister were. Gilly and Mel hugged me and asked me if I wanted a cup of tea. I can't remember much of what was said, although I do know Gilly kept repeating: 'Stay as long as you like, mate.' Yet again, Gilly had shown he was the guy who did that little bit extra. He was always there; always thoughtful. He had a great understanding of how people ticked.

I eventually went back to my room and rang Mum and Dad. It was a really tough time, and without looking for excuses, my mind wasn't on the game when it continued the next morning. Although his team had a pile of runs, Ganguly didn't declare overnight. I got rid of Patel and Ajit Agarkar, and had a thought I could have done without: 'Shit, if I get another wicket now, I'll be on the SCG honour board for the most expensive 5-for. I actually didn't want another scalp. I presumed the Indians would declare after reaching 700, but even after they did Ganguly wasn't making any moves. I then thought they were waiting for Sachin to reach his 250. At the time he was 14 short. There were huge numbers everywhere on the scoreboard. I began my 40th over. Sachin flicked the first ball for four, and there was a cheer from the main Indian section of the crowd as I had the unfortunate 'honour' of seeing 200 go up against my name. Two balls later Ganguly declared; it seemed to me he wasn't waiting for Sachin's 250 but my double century. 39.3 overs, five maidens, 201 runs, four wickets: the most expensive return of my career.

India made 7-705. The match ended in a draw, and not surprisingly the result was overshadowed by Tugga's retirement. For a while it looked as though he was going to finish with a fairytale century, but he holed out off Anil Kumble when he was 80. After the match the dressing room was more crowded than I could ever remember it; well wishers were coming and going, all heading to and from Tugga. It seemed hours before the team was left alone, and although we hadn't won, Punter broke with tradition and launched into the team song with Tugga standing on a table next to him.

The celebrations continued that night at a party organised by Steve's manager. I thanked Tugga for his support and guidance. I was just one of a long line of players who owed him so much.

I knew I'd miss him. His presence, knowledge, mental and physical toughness, loyalty, ability to inspire, and his friendship all made him a very special person. In a small reflection of his character, he wrote letters and gave gifts to many players. He sent me one of his books with a personal message inside.

Tugga was a player I never wanted to let down. In the early days of my career I was intimidated by him, and even now when I meet him socially he still has an aura that demands he is in charge. One of the things I knew I'd miss about him most was the sight of him sitting in the dressing room having a Southern Comfort and Coke while chatting in a corner with Justin Langer, Matthew Hayden or any of the other longer-lasting players in the team. He'd often have a sly grin on his face, as though he was just about to tell a joke. It was something that was often overlooked about Tugga: his sense of humour. So many people away from the team thought he was just a tough bastard, but he was also a funny guy to be around. I thoroughly enjoyed his company.

The emotion and hype surrounding Tugga momentarily shoved aside my thoughts about my own performance in the Test. I'd been pasted in the second innings, finishing with 0-75 off 12.2 overs. I was devastated with the way I'd played. However, in my defence, in the two matches since coming back from injury I was confused about what I had to do. That was in no way a criticism of Tugga's captaincy, but a result of who we were missing. I'd tried to be the spearhead of the attack *and* the stock bowler *and* the bloke who went out there and tried to blast batsmen out in three-over spells. When throwing all those things together, I felt as though it was a case of 'jack of all trades, master of none'. The people who really counted remained loyal to me. After the Test I was in a pub with my brother Grant when a stranger told me I was 'shit' because I got 4-201. Grant, being the accountant, shot back: 'Yeah, that means the rest of the bowlers got 3-504!' Despite that, the bottom line was that I hadn't bowled well, and I had to cop whatever followed.

As strange as it may sound, I was relieved to be dropped to 13th man for the first two matches of the one-day series against India and Zimbabwe. After initially wondering what would happen to me, I began to think: 'Great, now I can have some time to sort myself out.' All the pressure had suddenly and unexpectedly been lifted by the thing that any professional sportsperson dreads. I told myself: 'Cool, it's finally happened. Now I can deal with it and move on.' There's no doubt that hanging on by a thread was actually harder for me than being dropped.

I rang Dennis Lillee and asked him for advice. He'd noticed my front arm wasn't as high as it should have been, and he also gave me a few suggestions about stopping my no-ball problems. I couldn't fix those overnight, but at least I was conscious of them and could develop a recovery strategy. Throughout the remainder of the season I spoke with 'the great man' on several occasions.

I came back into the team for the third one-dayer against Zimbabwe in Hobart, and was pleased with my pace and control after picking up 1-29 off 10 overs. That feeling was short-lived because two days later against India I was belted for the most expensive limited overs return on Australian soil: 0-83 off 10 overs. I didn't think I bowled as badly as the figures suggested. I wasn't great, but there were other matches in which I'd played worse and picked up two or more wickets for not many.

I was a victim of the 'snowball effect'. After I'd had a few disappointing games close together, I allowed the negative to dominate my thoughts. Everywhere I turned I thought other people were looking down at me: the newspaper journalists who thought they knew it all; the TV presenters who thought they were so important because they read autocues; the reporter on the other side of the world who picked up the story and was immediately an authority on it; and the general public who I thought had *all* seen me play badly, and *all* wanted me sacked.

Because I was in a false environment where so many lived, breathed and swore by the game, it was all too easy to be swallowed up and forget there was a real world outside. Even when people came up to me and told me they liked the way I played, I thought: 'I know I'm shit. Why are these people taking the piss out of me?' I felt down and out, and when a player is like that, he may feel pressure that isn't actually there. I know I did during that time, but I also tried my hardest to fight it. With the support of my family and Alan Jones I tried to convince myself that I didn't have to be in the negative space. Yes, I knew there were people questioning my form and spot in the team, but if I walked into a coffee shop and felt as though everyone was looking at me, I told myself they were doing so because I was an Australian cricketer, not because they'd seen me belted over the park and were collectively thinking I was hopeless. Most of the time the vast majority of people wouldn't have known what had happened, or wouldn't have cared. I tried to take strength from that.

However, it was impossible to steer away from all the media talk going into my next one-day game against India at the SCG. I had one more chance. No excuses, no questions asked: I simply had to perform. There was tremendous emotion surrounding the game because former Australian player, commentator and coach of Victoria, David Hookes, had died three days earlier after an altercation with a hotel bouncer in Melbourne. His death was shattering news because he was part of 'the family', the Australian cricket family.

Like many other kids I'd seen the footage of him hitting five consecutive boundaries off Tony Greig in the 1977 Centenary Test. He had the reputation of being a very aggressive player. I knew him most as a broadcaster who always said what he felt; I respected him for that. I didn't always agree with him, but I admired the strength of his convictions. I always got on well with him, and we shared the occasional beer. All the guys in our team were really upset, and we all wore black armbands. We vowed we'd 'do something special for Hookesy' in the match.

After winning the toss and batting on a good deck, India rattled up 4-296, with both VVS Laxman and Yuvraj Singh getting centuries. Although I'd been a little inconsistent I was satisfied with my return: 2-46 off nine overs. The game had a few twists and turns, including a rain delay that reduced our target to 225 from 34 overs. Gilly hammered 95 and put us on the way, but we slipped in the final stages.

With one over to go we needed 11 to win with two wickets in hand. Andy Bichel and I were at the crease, and neither of us had faced more than a few balls. Right-arm medium pacer Lakshmipathy Balaji was the bowler. Bich and I worked singles off the first two balls, and I hit a full-toss for two off the third. The equation: seven to win off three. It was impossible for me not to be swept along by the excitement. This is one of the great advantages one-day cricket has over Tests: the atmosphere of a close finish under lights in front of a packed house is hard to top. Balaji ran in, and although I wasn't trying to second guess where he'd bowl the ball, I had a feeling he would pitch it up, perhaps going for a yorker. As it turned out, it was full and outside off, right in my hitting zone. I swung hard, sliced it, watched the ball fly and heard the crowd roar. The ball sailed over cover, over the fence and into the crowd in front of the Bill O'Reilly Stand. I gave a little fist pump before Bich came down with his 'game face' on. He hit me in the chest and told me to stay focused.

'Come on, Binga, we still need one, we need one,' he said, pumping me up.

Ganguly brought his whole team into the ring. From memory, I think Bich and I had decided we'd pretty well run on the next ball wherever I hit it. It was full, I slapped it to cover again, there was a misfield, and we shot through for the winning single. After I made my ground I kept running with my bat in the air, and then I realised I should turn around and find Bich. I hugged him as though we'd just won the World Cup. It was a sudden release of emotions that had built up over the previous three weeks.

As we walked off, our fitness coach, Andrew May, who'd been sitting on the boundary line, held up an esky lid. On it, he'd written: 'We won.' I dedicated my performance and the win to Hookesy. The next day I was the hero in the media. Just 24 hours earlier, I was the world's worst player, but then with just one shot I'd turned my reputation around; for a day, anyway. Neil Maxwell got the back page of the *Daily Telegraph* framed for me. It was a picture of me hitting the six, complete with the headline: 'Masterstroke – Lee's Towering Six Sets Up Stunning Win.' Underneath that, Maxi wrote: 'Remember what they said yesterday.'

I thought it was one of the best gifts I'd ever received. It was an important moment in my cricketing education that taught me not to get caught up in the highs and lows of media opinion. Four years into my career I'd realised just how fickle my sport could be, and that reinforced my need to cherish the good times because there were definitely enough bad times waiting to kick me.

I played in all of Australia's last five matches. I felt as though I was back to my best after I took 3-22 off 10 overs against India in our final preliminary game in Perth. Then I took two wickets in each of the two finals, also against the Indians. In the second final in Sydney, I had another one of those 'arsey' moments in the field: standing only several metres from the bat at short fine leg I held onto a rocket clipped by Virender Sehwag off Jason Gillespie. It's all just for argument's sake, but I reckon that could well have been the best catch I've ever taken. A few overs later I caught Sachin Tendulkar in the same position, again off Dizzy. It was a good way to finish the summer; after my earlier disappointments it was reassuring to know I'd helped contribute to Australia's series win.

The season finished on an unusual high for me, and hopefully for one other particular person too. As I'd become used to, I received a lot of requests from charities to help them in various ways. It was impossible to help them all, but I tried to do what I could, when I could. I was single at the time and after talking with Maxi I thought it would be wonderful to do something out of the ordinary for the Allan Border Medal night. So, we contacted the Make-A-Wish Foundation, an organisation that tries to make wishes come true for seriously ill children. That's how I came to meet 14-year-old Sarah Genuis, a leukaemia sufferer from Melbourne. What happened next is best told by Sarah. The following is part of an email she wrote to my official web site, Brett-Lee.net, soon after her experience, which included a front-page story in Melbourne's *Herald Sun*:

One morning in February, a lady from The Make-A-Wish Foundation rang me and asked if I'm a supporter of cricket.

I told her the honest truth, I wasn't much of a supporter but I understood it. After I told her that, she asked me if I know Brett Lee. I said, 'Of course he's the gorgeous blond on the cricket team.' She laughed and continued, 'Well he has asked us to find a girl to be his date for the Allan Border Medal and we figured that you and him had so much in common with music and everything that you would be perfect for this.' I was in shock. I was screaming. I never imagined for myself to meet a celebrity and walk the red carpet with him. She updated me and told me all the information. The last thing she said was, 'On Thursday you will meet him and get to know each other so you know him well on the night.'

When that Thursday came I wasn't shy or nervous but excited and cheerful. I met him at the hotel he was staying at, Quay West, and waited in the lobby for him to arrive. I was the first to spot him. He looked so tall, gorgeous and the smile he gave me was the best of all. He gave me a hug and we talked for a bit. He asked me if I was nervous and I responded, 'No just very excited.' Then the photographer and the journalist arrived. The journalist asked me a few questions and after that we went near the Yarra River to take photos.

Brett Lee is a great guy to talk to. You feel very comfortable around him. As we took the photos he would look up and smile. It was the best feeling. I felt very special. Then the photographer and the journalist left, letting me know that my article was going to be on the front page. I was very excited. The day ended with Brett Lee, my mum and myself sitting in the lobby, drinking lemonade and having a chat about the night. We had a laugh and let each other know we were very excited about the night. One thing that really touched me was that he told me I was going to be fine with my illness and I just have to think positive. I was thankful to have heard that from his mouth and to have a person around who is so sure about my health.

That photo on the front page touched a lot of people's hearts because the next day I got a call from The Make-A-Wish Foundation asking if they could give my home number to a lady who wanted to help. I accepted and soon after I received a call from a beautiful lady, Rachael, who worked at a shop, Body Art, and organized everything for the Allan Border Medal. Shops around her work also wanted to help out too. They provided jewellery, a handbag, shoes, a dress, and Rachael was a make-up artist and was going to do my make-up for the night. It was just so beautiful to see how much people really care and I thank her to this day because I wouldn't have looked as beautiful as I did if it weren't for Rachael and all the other generous people.

On the morning of the special day, I went to choose my dress, jewellery, bag and shoes with Rachael. Straight after, she began to do my make-up. I was so happy with the way it turned out. Then I went and got my hair done and that turned out great too. As time went by I was getting more and more excited.

Just in case you didn't know, The Make-A-Wish Foundation also organised for my family and I to have a night at Crown. So when we were packed and ready we headed off to Crown. When we arrived we waited to meet a lady from The Make-A-Wish Foundation, Adrianne. We all walked to Brett Lee's hotel and waited for him to arrive. After 15 minutes he arrived in his interesting suit. It was one from his own designer label, Brett Lee. It had threads all over the suit looking like it was inside out. It was interesting and he liked to be different and I liked that myself. He loved my dress and made me feel very beautiful. Then my family left and I met all the cricket players. Gillespie is so tall but very friendly. Then our car arrived to take us to Crown. We were in the car with Ricky Ponting and his wife. They spoke to me, and Ricky was very nice.

When we arrived we had to stay in a room and got arranged into order of couples. Then we got led to the red carpet and can you believe it, Brett Lee held my hand. They took so many photos and we had a great time. Then we got led backstage of the Palladium, and we were called to the stage and got shown to our seats. As we walked on stage there was so much applause. It was so fun.

As I got to my seat, Brett Lee pulled the seat out for me. We got to know each other a lot. We spoke about our hobbies and he signed my autograph book and so did most of the cricketers but Brett Lee's message touched me the most. He wrote how I'm an inspiration for being so positive and still smiling no matter how down I am. At the end he wrote, 'Mates Forever.' I found it so sweet.

At 9.30 I had to meet my parents outside the Palladium because the Make-A-Wish Foundation thought I would get bored but I wasn't at all. But I did as I was told. Straight after Shannon Noll finished singing I had to go and Brett Lee walked me out. I hugged him and said, 'Thank you so much for this experience.' He said, 'It was my pleasure.' He took my mobile number and promised me we would keep in touch. He said I was his lucky charm and it made me so happy.

From that day, I realised miracles do happen because Brett Lee is mine. He's so positive and makes me a positive person too and that's how I think he has fought all his tough times. He gives me hope and courage and I really love him. I know that that dream has passed but it hasn't left me because Brett Lee has changed me. He made me realise that no matter how tough life gets, never give up and that's how I think each day and that's why I know I will fight this disease. So thank you Brett Lee for everything, you really are an inspiration.

That night was wonderful. It was one of those moments when my joy came from seeing the joy of other people. Sarah looked lovely. She wore a beautiful dress and had made so much effort to sparkle. But above all, her personality shone through; she was so positive and enthusiastic. Her circumstances put everything into perspective for me. At the end of the day cricket is just a game; sometimes I think those close to it can forget that. We must remember that it's what happens outside the boundaries that really counts. Sarah and I still keep in touch, and I've caught up with her a few times when I've gone to Melbourne. She's doing really well. As much as she may thank me, I thank her for the opportunity to meet someone so special.

19

Bloody injuries! Although I'd accepted they were an occupational hazard, I couldn't help feeling luck was playing a cruel joke on me when I broke down before the first Test against Sri Lanka at Galle in March 2004. I'd been hot and cold in the one-day series against Sri Lanka – which we won 3–2 – but all the signs were positive in Australia's warm-up match to the Test against a President's XI in Colombo. It was a critical game for me. Shane Warne had returned from suspension, and on Sri Lanka's spinner-friendly wickets, it was likely he and Stuart MacGill would both be in the Test team. That meant Australia would only take in two quicks.

Pidgey was still out injured, and with Jason Gillespie a certain starter, I was in a bowl-off with Michael Kasprowicz. I thought I'd confirmed my selection when I took 4-29 in the first innings, including two wickets in my first over. Not only had I bowled quickly, but I got a lot of swing. However, all too familiar pain in my left ankle troubled me, and in the second dig every single delivery killed me. After I'd taken a wicket with my final ball to finish with five for the match, I confessed to Ricky Ponting that I was 'gone'.

'What do you mean?' he asked.

'My ankle is stuffed. I'm kidding myself. It's the same thing again.'

I hobbled off the field, and kept walking past some journos who wanted to know what was wrong; I was too annoyed to talk to them. I was soon back in Sydney recovering from another round of Kim Slater surgery. I have no doubt my heavy workload after coming back from my abdominal strain in October 2003 contributed to my problem. In just a four-week period between December and January I clicked over 194 overs in two Pura Cup games and two Tests. That's 50 a match, 25 an innings. The workload issue for bowlers is always going to be a problem. Cricketers are paid good money to play, and both administrators and the fans expect them to play. So, play we do. Who knows how my body will be in the years ahead. I do know that if I went to a new physio tomorrow and had to fill out a card of my skeleton that reflected all the problems I had during my career, I reckon I'd colour in everything but my head.

It took about three to four months before I was back into the full swing of training again. After missing the away series to Sri Lanka, I was sidelined for two further Tests against the Sri Lankans in northern Australia, and some one-dayers in Zimbabwe. I aimed to be back for a few one-day series, including the ICC Champions Trophy in England, before what I considered would be one of the most important tours of my career: a four-Test campaign in India in October '04. I'd still to play a Test on Indian soil, and was hell-bent on making a great impression when I got the chance.

One of the most important parts of my rehabilitation was a session I had with Dennis Lillee at Brisbane's Allan Border Field. Considering all the no-ball problems I'd had during the 2003–04 season, it was obvious my run-up and approach immediately before delivery needed work. After charging in off

about 30 metres for most of my career, I wondered if a shorter run-up would be more successful in allowing me to strike a good rhythm, and also be more efficient. Dennis responded to this by asking me to run in and bowl with my eyes shut; when I felt I was at the right point to deliver the ball, I did. I went through the process about 20 times before I was hitting pretty well the same delivery spot every time, give or take a few inches. The whole distance was a couple of metres shorter than it had been, and I adopted that as my new run-up length.

I fine-tuned the run-up further after I paid my own way to India to spend a few days at the MRF Pace Bowling Foundation in Chennai. I was very keen to learn more about subcontinent conditions, especially how the ball reacted after it scuffed up on the dry, baked pitches. The more I knew, the more I hoped I'd be at an advantage in the Tests that were only two months away. In addition to playing two games with a touring Australian Academy team, I benefited from working with former Indian quick Javagal Srinath.

Although most of my focus was on my comeback, there was one monumental distraction at that time: a court case against high-profile entrepreneur Kovelan Bangaru. My brother Shane, Neil Maxwell, Michael Slater and I had all invested various amounts of money, totalling about $2 million, in property development ventures proposed by Bangaru and his company Streetwise. I became involved after listening to a proposal put to me by Bangaru in his Sydney office in July 2003. Bangaru suggested my profile could be used to market an equity loans project to build 200 houses which could be sold 'deposit free'. In return for a considerable investment, I could take a 15 per cent share.

I went away and discussed the proposal with Maxi and Shane. By that stage Shane and Slats were already involved in a different venture. With Maxi's help I did some research and decided it was a sound business. In August I signed a memorandum of understanding subject to approval by Cricket Australia (it had changed its name from the Australian Cricket Board in July 2003), which needed to give the green light to any endorsements undertaken by its contracted players. I invested $981,000.

Cutting a long story short, we (Maxi, Slats, Shane and others) all became concerned about how our investments were being used. So, we took court action to freeze Bangaru's assets and retrieve our money. The process ended up taking about two years. During that time it was discovered that Bangaru had signed documents and cheques on my behalf, and hadn't invested my money in the agreed project, but had used it in other ways and was collecting interest on it.

It was a stressful time, especially for Maxi, who felt morally responsible because he'd introduced me to the venture and had advised me. In a reflection of his character he spoke with his wife, Rachel, and decided if the worst happened and we couldn't get any money back, he'd offer to sell his house to repay the money I'd lost. That showed the strength of the man. However, I would never have asked for that. Eventually we got most of the money back, but were hit heavily by legal bills. In all, I lost over $300,000. I felt cheated and let down. It was a great life lesson for me, an expensive lesson too.

Sadly, I was taught how little I could trust outsiders. That is a horrible view to have, but in my case I have to be extremely careful. Over the years I've met others who've wanted to align with me solely because I have money. Now I look back at the whole Bangaru episode and realise that Maxi, Shane, Slats and I were the lucky ones because we could afford to take court action. The ventures involved many everyday people, mum and dad investors who lost large sums of money.

In 2005, Bangaru fled to the USA after his company collapsed. He left behind investors and banks that were owed many millions. In 2007, he was arrested in the States and put in jail while the appropriate authorities negotiated his extradition to Australia. In December 2010, he was sentenced to eight-and-a-half years' jail after being found guilty by the Sydney District Court of 13 fraud charges.

Despite the worries caused by the Bangaru case, I was able to keep my comeback on schedule, and I was back fully fit in the Australian team by the time we jumped on the one-dayer merry-go-round in August '04. After tournaments in Holland and England we arrived in India for the continuation of what was arguably the greatest rivalry in world cricket at the time. Australia hadn't won a Test series in India since 1969–70, and after the epic 2001 series there was a lot of excitement and talk about the prospect of more thrillers.

We won the four-match series 2–1. Ricky Ponting missed the first three matches with a broken finger, and by the time he returned, the Adam Gilchrist-led side had already ensured the Border–Gavaskar Trophy was in Australia's hands. However, the tour began a period of incredible frustrations for me; I didn't play one Test and wouldn't play my next for another nine months.

I went into the series knowing it was going to be tough to win a spot. After all, my last Test nine months earlier at the SCG had been so forgettable for me, yet in the minds of the selectors it was all too unforgettable. I knew I was unlikely to play the first Test in Bangalore. Glenn McGrath had returned from injury, Jason Gillespie had been a consistent performer, and Michael Kasprowicz deserved a position because his form in recent one-dayers had been outstanding. Despite all of that, I did expect to play a role at some point in the series.

After I was overlooked for the Bangalore match I vowed to myself that I'd use the time on the outer to train as hard as I could. If I wasn't going to have a chance to get wickets, at least I could get fitter. I was well on the way to being in the best shape of my career after my rehabilitation. And then, our stint in England for the Champions Trophy a fortnight earlier had further motivated me. Australia's conditioner, Jock Campbell, had given us some hell sessions; in some London gym workouts I wore a few shirts, a tracksuit and a beanie in a bid to replicate the sweat I could lose on the subcontinent. When we arrived in India, I came stocked with boxes and boxes of Weet-Bix. I didn't want to get sick or put on weight which could be easy to do if I wasn't playing. For much of the tour I ate Weet-Bix two meals a day. I just shoved them down. I suppose I became obsessed with training: gym work, boxing, sprints and jogs, both before and after play at all the grounds.

That devotion took some unusual twists. In Bangalore I was due to have a run with the other guys on the outer, Cameron White and Brad Hodge. However, we couldn't find a suitable place until Jock Campbell rang the race club near our hotel. Next thing you know the club's officials had suspended trackwork, and we were running down the home straight clapped on by punters who'd gathered to bet on a meeting at another venue.

I was 12th man for the whole series. Twelfth man is a position of contradictions. You can think it's embarrassing because you're not good enough to be in the team, yet in the same breath it's an honour to be part of the XII. Obviously a player would rather be 12th man than not on tour, but once you've played a Test, it is bloody hard to take a step back. I considered 12th man a shit job, but I still tried my best to be a team player. Throughout the series I geed up and congratulated players, and was at my busiest running drinks to the bowlers, and keeping an eye on all the players to make sure they kept their fluids up. I can't deny how tedious it all became and how I struggled to maintain interest in what was happening on the field, primarily because I've never been a good cricket watcher.

At times my frustrations got the better of me. After we won by 217 runs in Bangalore – the highlight being a century on debut by Michael Clarke – I wanted to make sure the guys were well equipped to celebrate when they came into the dressing room. So, earlier in the day I gave some money to one of our baggage guys, an Indian, to go and get some beer and spirits. I did this out of my own pocket. I loaded up some eskies with ice, put in the beers, and waited. When the guys came off they were really appreciative. I tried to look after them as much as I could by being their waiter. I also put some music on; I can't remember what, but it was probably something pretty standard for the team, like Powderfinger or Jimmy Barnes. However, Damien Martyn didn't like it and told me to 'put something decent on'. At the time I was getting someone else a beer, but that didn't stop Marto.

'Change the music and get us a beer,' he said bluntly.

'Please!' I replied.

'Just get us a beer!'

His rudeness pissed me off. Marto hadn't made many runs in the Test, which meant he could be tough to be around. But that was no excuse for treating me the way he did, so I told him: 'You're allowed to use your manners, you know.' Marto again told me to get him a beer and put on a decent song. And that's when I snapped and said: 'Stuff that! If you want another song do it yourself, and get your own bloody beer. I've always been nice to you, Marto, but you treat me like shit.' I then walked out of the room and was fired up for the rest of the night.

The next Test started in Chennai four days later. On match eve Marto and I still hadn't spoken to each other since the blow-up. I thought it was getting ridiculous, so I penned Marto a letter. I waited until he went to bed, and then slipped it under his hotel door. I wrote that I wouldn't apologise for what I'd said because I'd meant it, but I acknowledged we'd have our differences from time to time. Although I felt let down by the way I was treated, I stressed that Marto had my full support and I wished him the best for the Test. I finished by predicting he'd go out and get a hundred. In the morning, he came down to breakfast, thanked me for the letter, and apologised.

'What's happened has happened. Let's move on,' I said.

I say with tongue in cheek that I actually helped Marto. Not only did he get 104 in the second innings, but in the third Test in Nagpur he scored 114 and 97. When he was at his best he was in the same class as VVS Laxman and Mark Waugh for silky timing.

The episode with Marto showed a side of touring life that's often overlooked: it can be a real challenge, even a pain in the arse, living in each other's pockets for weeks, if not months on end. Potentially a player may be on tour for 250 to 300 days of the year. That means a lot more time is spent with your team than your family and mates. Think about it: you have 14 or so guys strung together in close quarters. Some you may have known for years, but others arrive – who you've never met or only know vaguely – and suddenly have to find their way as quickly as possible. How can you instantly be best friends with these people? You do strike up some close mateships in the team, but to expect every single player in a touring party to have good, friction-free relationships with everyone else all the time is a fantasy. It just doesn't and won't happen.

I found that being in the Australian team was like being a piece in a Rubik's Cube. There were times when we were all red on one side, blue on the other and so on, but there were other occasions when there would be a jumble of colours because of poor form, personal issues, injuries, personality clashes, and so on. In the early 2000s when we were on the record-breaking run of winning 16 Tests in a row, I reckon the cube was complete and didn't need any twisting at all; everyone knew their place and there was a great harmony through the whole squad. Compare that with the 2010 Australian team that had lots of changes, a fair few losses and personal disappointments, and it's fair to say the cube was very confused. I don't think it has been stable since Steve Waugh retired.

The best team environment I've heard of belonged to the NSW 1992–93 Sheffield Shield winning team. When I was on my way up through the Blues' ranks, players spoke about the 1992–93 squad in almost reverential terms. Perhaps I'm biased because Shane made his debut that season although he didn't play in the final. The team had some of the greats of NSW and Australian cricket: the Waughs, Mark Taylor, Mike Whitney, Phil Emery, Adam Gilchrist, Greg Matthews, Michael Bevan, Glenn McGrath, Michael Slater. From all I was told, they enjoyed the good times but they also stuck together during the bad times. I enjoyed hearing talk about that environment, and the bond of the Blues players left a tremendous impression on me while I was making my way in the game.

Cricket has changed now. There's still friendship and loyalty between players, but unfortunately there are also jealousies. For example: I know times when players have got together and discussed what other players are doing away from the game, especially in relation to endorsements and sponsorship deals. Jealousy can arise when belief grows that players may be more committed off the field than on it. At times I'm sure that was a talking point about me, and in fact one player even confessed to me he envied what I'd achieved away from cricket.

What I've just said strays some way away from the 2004 Indian tour, but it's important to mention it because so many people on the outside consider touring to be a wholly glamorous lifestyle. Yes, cricketers do get to stay in some amazing hotels, and yes there can be some fun times, and we're looked after in a way the man on the street isn't, but it still has its problems.

On the 2004 tour I spent long hours by myself. If ever there was a time for music to help me, that was it. At the end of most days I went back to my room and strummed my guitar. It was a lonely place to be, yet I chose to be there because it offered me an escape. I was lucky I had such a distraction. Over the years I've known guys who've been that intense about their cricket that they almost live and die by their performances every single day. Good or bad, they go back to their rooms, turn on the TV, watch the highlights, and analyse how they played that day. I couldn't think of anything worse; that sort of behaviour would do my head in.

For me, it was much better to play a few tunes, have a sing, and lose myself. There were times when I did that, while in the room next to me I heard someone tapping a ball on their bat, even at 11.30 at night! That shows how different the characters in a team can be. It's also why I've rarely kept in touch with my teammates when I'm not on tour with them. It's so refreshing to come back and spend time around my tight-knit circle of friends and family, knowing that cricket wouldn't be part of the conversation.

Now, back to the India series. After winning the first and third Tests and drawing the second, Australia lost the fourth by 13 runs on a dodgy deck at Mumbai's Wankhede Stadium. The ball turned square from the start, and the match lasted only three days; 20 wickets fell on the last day when Australia was rolled for only 93.

My tour was summed up by something that happened in our hotel gym in Mumbai. Throughout the trip I did a lot of boxing with Justin Langer. When JL stepped into a ring his eyes started to spin. He was a madman! On this particular day we were smoking each other with some good hits in the ribs, but then we clashed heads. Actually JL still reckons it was a head clash, but I think he might have sneaked one in on me.

Whatever the true reason, I recall the vision in my left eye suddenly went smoky. I didn't know what had happened until I looked in the mirror and saw blood running down my face; I'd split open an eyebrow. Luckily, there was a little makeshift hospital across the road, so I walked over to it holding an ice-pack against my head. In another stroke of good fortune there was a visiting plastic surgeon working there that day. He happily told me: 'I can fix it, Mr Lee!' He stitched me up, and for the next three days I had a weird fold of skin hanging over my eye that began to worry me. It eventually disappeared and there was barely a scar after the stitches were taken out. When it happened, I initially thought: 'How can this tour get any worse?'

The trip was extremely disappointing for me. Because I'd become so popular in India I was desperate to show the fans what I could do, and I also wanted to repay the faith my various Indian sponsors had shown in me. All the hype made it worse because wherever I went, people were asking me: 'You're the world's fastest bowler, why aren't you playing?' I would try to say with a smile: 'Tell that to the selectors.' I also had to accept that the bowlers in front of me did a great job, and I returned to Australia knowing I was going to have to fight as hard as I could to win back my spot.

20

While on the 2004 tour of India I couldn't stop thinking about someone I'd met a party in Sydney earlier in the year. She told me we'd first crossed paths at the Buena Vista Hotel at Mosman in Sydney's inner-north, but I can't recall that. We hit it off, and for a period after the party we caught up from time to time, but it wasn't anything serious. Her name was Liz Kemp.

Towards the end of the Indian tour I texted Liz out of the blue. The message was simple: 'Are you still on this number?' She replied that she was, and that set everything in motion. I went and saw her the day I returned from India, 7 November, the day before my 28th birthday. Perhaps it was a bit old fashioned, but I asked her: 'I don't know how they do it these days, but do you want to be my girlfriend?' With her answer came the end of a single man's life. Some of my close mates, such as Maxi, had been encouraging me to think about settling down, but it had never appealed to me until I got to know Liz.

While that was happening, I was trying to fight my way back into the Test team. I'd trained so fiercely on the Indian tour that I returned to Australia seven kilograms lighter. I was ready to roll, but was hampered by a farcical lack of opportunities;

240

when I began my season with a game for NSW against New Zealand at the SCG, I'm glad I didn't know it would be my last first-class outing for the season! Throughout the summer I did little more than fill the position of contradictions, 12th man for Australia.

At one stage, NSW made special applications to Cricket Australia in a bid to get me some game time. This included a request to change the date of a Pura Cup match against Tasmania, so it wouldn't coincide with a Test in Perth, but I still couldn't get a release from my responsibilities as the world's highest-paid drink's waiter! The inflexibility of the rules was a joke. My best chance of making a selection bid was by getting results in matches, but how could I when all I could do was bowl in the nets?

I tried to stay upbeat and impress whenever I could; at one net session in Perth I put the message across by hitting both Adam Gilchrist and Matthew Hayden in the gloves with balls that kicked. Despite the fact Australia won all five Tests for the summer – two against New Zealand and three against Pakistan – I felt I should have been chosen at some stage. However, I couldn't begrudge those in front of me: Pidgey, Dizzy and Kasper were all doing their jobs.

If there was one blessing to come out of my lack of cricket, it was my freshness for the one-day series against Pakistan and the West Indies. I warmed up with a couple of matches against the Windies in Hobart, and felt I was at my quickest since the 2003 World Cup. The signs were good, although in renewing acquaintance with Brian Lara I was monstered for a six that ended up in the front yard of a house opposite Bellerive Oval.

I played in all eight of Australia's matches in the tri-series, which we won by beating Pakistan 2–0 in the best of three final. I finished the leading wicket-taker with 16 scalps at

21-ish. I'd been quick and had got both the new and old ball to move around. My best haul came against the Windies when I took 4-38 in Adelaide after I'd belted 38 not out in a useful partnership with Dizzy. Although I wasn't one to bask in awards, I was rapt when I won Player of the Series.

I'd done everything I possibly could to improve my chances of Test selection. With a tour of New Zealand beginning two weeks after the tri-series, I was confident I'd soon be back wearing the baggy green. Before I left I asked Trevor Hohns what I had to do to further improve my chances. Collectively the message from the selectors was: 'Keep bowling fast and taking wickets.' Understandably there was still some concern about how well my ankles would last, but I hadn't had any pain for months, not even a niggle.

Our trans-Tasman campaign began at Auckland's Eden Park with what we thought was nothing more than a complete novelty: the very first Twenty20 international. We played in retro gear, the shocking body-hugging uniforms from the 1980s. The New Zealanders really got into the spirit of it; some grew moustaches, and Hamish Marshall looked like a B-grade porn star with a cloud of fuzzy hair and a headband. Australia won, but neither team treated the match seriously. How times would change.

We then moved into a five-match one-day series, my last chance to stake a claim before three Tests. Again I finished with the most wickets – 10 at about 17 – and had also clocked my fastest-ever delivery, 160.8 kays (99.9 miles per hour) in the final match at McLean Park, Napier. I had no doubt I was only getting better and better. However, a controversy in the third game at Eden Park outweighed talk about my form. It took only one ball to cause a storm that I believe was a good example of a story blown out of proportion by the media.

Significantly, the incident happened in the evening and late in the match when Australia were well on top. I was striving for some extra pace against Brendon McCullum when I slipped at the crease, which was covered in dew, and delivered a chest-high beamer that Brendon fended away with his gloves. He had every right to be angry, and stormed down the pitch and said a few words to me. I apologised straight away, but Brendon was still fired up. Off the field we were mates, but this wasn't a time to swap yarns and a beer.

I knew how he felt; during a match against Pakistan earlier in the season Abdul Razzaq had fired a couple of beamers at me in the one over. It was frightening. What made matters worse was that I then bowled Razzaq a beamer in the same match, and suddenly there was talk in the media of a square-up. So, after Brendon copped the one at Eden Park some journalists went to town on me, suggesting I wasn't only a repeat offender but had bowled the balls on purpose. New Zealand coach John Bracewell also implied this, and recalled other times when I'd strayed against the Kiwis.

I wasn't at all perturbed by Bracewell because I didn't value his opinion at all, but it was upsetting to have my sportsmanship questioned by others. I'm not making excuses for myself, but I don't think many of the critics realised how difficult it can be for a fast bowler to have sure footing on a pitch affected by evening dew. In addition to that, the footmarks on the pitch can be uneven, and the ball can be slippery. All told, there are enough ingredients to force a mistake. Basically, we're talking about a matter of centimetres in positioning of feet, body and hand being the difference between bowling a yorker and a beamer. Imagine asking an Olympic javelin thrower to run in on a wet surface, land in a hole, and throw a javelin without some margin for error. I swear on my life I've never meant to bowl a beamer.

243

Perhaps there was already some extra feeling going around Eden Park because earlier in the innings I'd hit opener Michael Papps flush on the side of the helmet with a bouncer. He got a bit wobbly but didn't fall, so I walked back to my mark. Meanwhile Ricky Ponting went over to check on him.

'Are you alright, mate?' asked Punter.

'Yeah, why?' said Papps.

'Because you just got filled in.'

'No I didn't. Brett was running in to bowl but lost his run-up so he pulled away.'

The poor bloke had no recollection of being hit. He took his helmet off and discovered an egg-sized lump on his head. He retired hurt and was taken to hospital.

When the Papps mishap was added to the McCullum beamer controversy and the hit-wicket incident involving Adam Parore at Carisbrook in 2000, I suppose some Kiwi fans thought I was after blood. Later in the tour I was driving with Michael Clarke in Wellington when a car full of Maoris pulled up next to us at an intersection. One of the passengers looked over at me and said angrily: 'Hey Lee, you better watch out for that bean ball, hey bro!'

Showing all the lack of intelligence that fast bowlers are renowned for, I egged him on by saying: 'Yeah, well you better watch your bumper bar because I'm coming over, bro!' I actually didn't mean to say it; the words just came out! Anyhow, we took off quickly after the lights changed and got back to the hotel. To this day I still think: 'Shit, did I really say that?!'

By that stage of the tour, I admit I was frustrated, pissed off! I'd been overlooked for the first two Tests and had realistically no chance of playing the third. Pidgey, Dizzy, Kasper and I had come to be known as the 'FBC', the fast bowlers' cartel. We were mates, and we looked after each other, but I couldn't help feeling I should have been in the team at either Dizzy's or Kasper's expense. They were class players in a winning team, but because of the form I was in I thought I would have only improved the make-up. This was an incredibly difficult period for me, but I'm proud to say there were never any problems between us quicks. No matter how I felt, I had to keep telling myself that my time would come again. However, the unknown was, as I told the media: 'Each time a problem has come up throughout my career I've managed to find a solution, but this time around I don't have any straightforward answers.'

The lowest of lows for the whole tour came before the second Test in Wellington, when NSW officials considered ways of getting me to Brisbane to play in the Pura Cup Final against Queensland. Although both games started on the same day, there was initially some hope that because of the three-hour time difference between New Zealand and Queensland I could stay for the first ball of the Test, and then, if Cricket Australia granted permission, I could fly to Brisbane and help the Blues. We worked on several different scenarios. Alan Jones even offered to get a private Learjet to pick me up. If AJ had his way I would have landed on the Gabba or been parachuted straight to third man! I'd never thought of marking out my run from 30,000 feet!

Eventually it all seemed too hard, and the night before the matches I was told by NSW officials that I hadn't been selected. I was gutted, but I understood the Blues selectors' point of view. They'd stuck with a team for much of the season and it was fair to be loyal to the players who'd served them well. However, I couldn't comprehend Cricket Australia's reluctance for me to go. I thought they were being one-dimensional; I assumed they believed it wouldn't have been in Australian cricket's or my best interests. Considering how little cricket I'd played, I'll argue against that.

The Blues ended up winning the final by a wicket in a thriller, while the Wellington Test was a rain and fog-affected draw. After the disappointments and boredom of being a spectator, I had some quiet nights with Liz in my room eating spaghetti bolognese and playing Green Day songs.

As had become the norm, music was my therapy, and it also gave me an opportunity that literally sent tingles along my spine. A few months earlier at a hotel bar in Hobart I was playing my guitar in a group sing-along. We were belting out the Crowded House classic 'Better Be Home Soon' when a photographer, William West, asked me: 'So, you like Crowded House, do you?' 'Mate, I love them! They are unbelievable!' I replied.

I told him the band's music had been a big influence on me. William then revealed that he'd lived for a while with Crowded House's famous Kiwi brothers, Neil and Tim Finn, in Melbourne. After more of a chat he promised he'd try to arrange a meeting between Neil and me while I was in New Zealand.

It turned out much better than that because Neil invited Liz and me to dinner at his Auckland home just before the third Test. When we arrived he greeted us wearing jeans, a T-shirt and no shoes. He was so casual. We met his wife, Sharon, and one of their two sons, Elroy, who was about 16. Their other boy, Liam, wasn't home. Sharon's parents were also there. Over dinner, we swapped stories about music and cricket: how the ball swings, what it's like to do a concert in front of tens of thousands of fans, how much of a role nerves played . . .

Afterwards, Neil said to me: 'My dad is a massive cricket fan and loves the way you play. Do you reckon if I get him on the line, you could say g'day to him?'

It's those sorts of moments that I absolutely love. It can be easy to forget how such simple things can bring great pleasure to the people around you. I chatted with Neil's dad for several minutes, and then asked Neil for a return favour. You may remember me earlier mentioning Mick Vawdon, the lead singer of Funhouse, a band Six and Out came to know when we were first starting out. Since then Mick had become one of my closest mates, and we had plans to work together in a band. Mick had been performing on the Sydney pub circuit for years. One night I asked him what would be his perfect day. He replied: 'If I could have a few beers and sing a few songs with Neil Finn I'd die a happy man.' I told Neil that, and before I'd even asked if he'd speak to Mick on the phone, he was saying: 'Let's ring him.'

I stood close to Neil while he made the call. There were a few rings before there was a quiet 'hello' at the other end.

'Is that Mick?' asked Neil.

'Yeah, speaking.'

'Mick, it's Neil Finn.'

Silence followed, and I had the biggest grin on my face imagining Mick in a state of shock. It was just another of those great moments.

It turned out that Mick was about to go on stage to do a gig, but he held off for 20 minutes to chat to his idol. He reckons he ended up playing Crowded House and Split Enz songs just about all night.

The evening with Neil only got better because after dinner we went downstairs into his studio. Neil picked up his electric guitar, sat on a speaker box, and joked: 'So do you know any Crowded House songs?'

He began with 'Fall at Your Feet'. It seemed so surreal that I kept thinking: 'Gee that sounds like the original!' For a while I couldn't convince myself I was hearing the real thing. And what gave me the tingles down the spine? I was playing bass.

Then we changed over and launched into 'Better Be Home Soon'. It was a night I didn't want to end.

We stayed for a few hours, after which I took home some signed CDs, including one for Mick and another for me, on which Neil wrote: 'Take it easy on the Kiwis.'

The next day he took me and Elroy to a warehouse that he was going to turn into a studio. I gave Elroy my Australian kit and the three of us had an impromptu match. It was another surreal moment: one day I was singing with Neil Finn and the next I was sniffing him up with a half-taped tennis ball. If only I could have had the chance to do the same thing with a cricket ball to some other Kiwis at Eden Park. Australia won the Test to claim the series 2–0. Next stop, the Ashes. And to me, 12th man wasn't an option.

21

I took a wicket with the very first ball I bowled in a match on the 2005 Ashes tour. In the context of all that happened over the following months, it wasn't at all important: New Zealand captain Stephen Fleming caught by Ricky Ponting at second slip in a Twenty20 match against an invitational XI at Arundel. However, I hoped it was an omen. In my situation, every wicket and every ball counted.

The early games of the tour were basically shockers for both me and the Australian team. We beat Leicestershire in a one-dayer, and then England hammered us by 100 runs in a T20 match in which Andrew Flintoff drilled me with short stuff. One ball smacked into my right shoulder, and I was still feeling some pain two days later when I left the field after bowling only four overs in an embarrassing loss to Somerset.

Our fortunes didn't improve when the limited overs tri-series with England and Bangladesh got underway. In our first two games, which I didn't play, we were beaten by both teams. The Fleet Street journos had a field day, especially after they found out Andrew Symonds had been dropped from the game against Bangladesh because of an off-field incident. Many of us had gone out the night before to celebrate Shane Watson's birthday, but unfortunately Symo kicked on longer than he should have. He was fined about $20,000 and suspended for two games.

We turned our fortunes around with a 57-run win over England in the third match of the series at Durham's Chester-le-Street ground. I replaced Michael Kasprowicz and knew how important it was to claim a few points over him in our battle for Test spots. I finished with 2-27 off 10 overs, a pleasing return. But that's enough stats for the moment because our visit to Chester-le-Street was much more memorable for what happened away from the match.

We stayed at Lumley Castle, a beautiful old building dating back to the 1300s that had been converted into a hotel. Apparently, there were rumours it was haunted by a girl who'd died after falling down a well hundreds of years earlier. After the team bus first pulled up, some of us noticed two women and a bloke in a kangaroo suit loitering nearby. Suddenly, the women flashed their breasts and a photographer was handy, ready to take any shots of us having a good look. It was the typical tabloid stitch-up that we'd already been warned about. A security guard quickly took care of them, and we were soon in the castle checking in.

As I was settling into my room in the early evening, there was a knock on my door. It was Shane Watson who looked pretty shaken up.

'I can't stay up there. This is bullshit!' he said.

'You can't stay where?' I asked him.

'In my room. I can't sleep in my room.'

'Why not?'

'Because it's haunted!'

'Watto' insisted I go with him to have a look in his room, so we walked down a long corridor that had a row of stone busts that gave the impression they were looking at us as we went past.

We walked up a couple of staircases and along another corridor before we arrived at his room. It was tiny in comparison with mine. It also had no windows, just a big mirror.

'Ghosts love mirrors,' said Watto.

I had to fight back laughter when I asked him if he was serious. He was.

'I can't stay here,' he said again.

'Well, what do you want to do?'

'I'll sleep on your floor.'

And that's what he did, with a doona and pillow that he brought from his room.

The next day Watto got his room changed, but for the rest of his stay he had all his lights and television on, because he was adamant ghosts didn't like brightness and noise. He was 100 per cent serious; he reckoned he wouldn't have been at all safe in the dark.

Not surprisingly, the rest of the team had a field day with him. One night, Ricky Ponting and I were in a taxi with Watto when we were heading home from a restaurant. I looked out at Lumley Castle; it looked stunning with the moon behind it.

'Oh no!' said Punter.

'What?' asked Watto.

'Binga, it's a full moon tonight. We're in trouble now!' continued Punter.

'What do you mean?' said Watto.

'A full moon. The ghosts, mate. Everything comes out on a full moon. That's when it all happens.'

Watto knew he was being wound up. Then again, this was a bloke who once asked if *Planet of the Apes* was a documentary.

While all this was happening, at some point I'd mentioned Watto's stay in my room to our team's media officer, Belinda Dennett. It was too good a story not to get out, so next thing it was in the papers. The best part came when we played the day–nighter at Chester-le-Street, and some of the English fans came dressed in long, white sheets. But nothing could top when Watto came out to bat and Darren Gough put his fingers up to the side of his head in clichéd fashion and went 'Boo!' in Watto's face. It was priceless.

The win at Chester-le-Street changed our fortunes and form. We went through the rest of the series unbeaten, including a tie in a low-scoring final against England at Lord's. In that match I was again in the spotlight for the wrong reasons when opener Marcus Trescothick copped a beamer. Umpire David Shepherd gave me an official warning that was justified, yet it embarrassed me. I don't want to sound like a cracked record, but again I was struggling with my footing on a wet pitch. I even tried changing my spikes, bowling around the wicket, and putting sawdust down in a bid to help me. Considering my recent history, I could understand there being some heat from rival teams, but thankfully Marcus, one of the nicest blokes ever to play the game, accepted my apology and played down the incident afterwards. It was best to move on, although I did hate the fact I'd had a bad run with what is undoubtedly the worst type of delivery in cricket. It affected me for the rest of the game, and I was conscious I couldn't afford to keep doing it.

Despite that controversy, I'd bowled well throughout the tri-series and continued my good run in three further matches against England in another one-day series. Australia won 2–1. I was pumped after returning the best limited-overs figures by an Australian at Lord's in the second game. Punter bowled me in short bursts, and it worked. I didn't get any wickets in my first four-over spell, but worked up good pace and late swing. In my second spell I bowled Kevin Pietersen, the former South

African who was getting huge wraps, including from himself, although he was still to play a Test match. We'd already seen enough of him to know he'd be a real threat during the Ashes. I also claimed another danger man, Andrew Flintoff. By the time Punter took a screamer in the covers to get rid of Ashley Giles, I'd taken 5-41.

Although I played down the haul, I knew I was surely close to a Test comeback. In what can be a bitter-sweet part of professional sport, my chances were helped by the lean returns for my mate Jason Gillespie. He'd only taken one wicket on tour, but he wasn't bowling badly, he just wasn't getting wickets. I really felt for him, and yet his form was opening the door for me.

The Lord's match was significant for reasons that made personal performances seem so unimportant. Three days earlier, four suicide bombers linked to Al-Qaeda killed 52 people in a series of explosions on London's trains and a double-decker bus. The Australian team heard about the attacks after we played a game against England at Headingley, Leeds. At a team meeting we discussed what we should do. As was originally scheduled, we travelled to London that night, but there was lots of chat on the way down about whether we'd made the right decision. After all, if we were in Pakistan would we have travelled to Karachi if there were bombings? I was comfortable continuing the trip, but if anything else had happened, I would have been putting my hands up to go home. Playing a game is not worth risking your life over. I thought about that during the minute's silence that was held before the Lord's match.

After the one-dayers finished we only had one match before the first Test. It was a three-dayer against Leicestershire, and Dizzy, Kasper and I were all playing in what had come down to a bowl-off for two Test spots behind Glenn McGrath. The

Foxes (Leicestershire) won the toss and batted. Luck was on my side from the very first ball of the match when I trapped Darren Robinson plumb in front. I took three more wickets, and a fourth batsman, John Sadler, retired hurt after he copped a blow.

Gilly and Punter saw the funny side to that when I told the trainer who'd run out to attend to the batsman: 'He's been hit on the clavicle.' A number of guys cracked up, because my correct use of terminology came from years of knowing the aches and pains from my own body. I took 4-53, Dizzy claimed 2-40, and Kasper 1-43. In the second innings we all got tapped about a bit by Western Australia's Chris Rogers, who hit a double century. When the team was announced for the first Test at Lord's, I summed up what I heard in one word: relief. Kasper was the unfortunate one to miss out.

It's hard to explain how I felt after being on the outer for 18 months and 17 Tests. In some articles written about my impending return, stats were mentioned. In my first seven Tests, I took 42 wickets at 16.07. In my next 30, I got 97 at nearly 39. Had I lost it? Was I yesterday's man? I didn't care. All I knew was that I'd been given another chance, and deserved it. This was a new beginning for me in a series surrounded by incredible hype. There was a lot of talk in the media, by the public, and the English players themselves, that their time had come. The Ashes had been in Australia's hands since 1989. This was the Poms' moment to wipe away all their bad memories.

But someone forgot to tell Pidgey McGrath who made the first Test his own. Initially, we were in all sorts of trouble after Punter won the toss and chose to bat on a greenish wicket. Forty-one overs later, we were all out for 190 after Steve Harmison had taken 5-for. He pinned a couple of batsmen along the way, including Punter who had his cheek cut. It was obvious England were out to intimidate us, and they'd done a very good job. Harmison was quick, but just as crucially his height allowed him great bounce and he made batting very uncomfortable.

England's players could pat themselves on the back, but that feeling didn't last long: by the end of the day they were 7-92. Pidgey had 5-for, and I had two. There are few grounds in the world where it's better to hear individual responses from the crowd than at Lord's. When I heard people ooh-ing and aah-ing and saying things like, 'How would you fancy facing Lee? My Lord, he's quick,' I knew I was bowling well. After 18 months of waiting, I felt I was back where I belonged.

And how much fun was it to be opening the attack again with one of the greatest bowlers of all time! We bowled unchanged for 17 overs, by the end of which Pidgey had 5-11 off nine overs, and I had 0-10 off eight. Pidgey ended up bowling 13 overs straight but didn't pick up any more wickets for the innings. The next day England were rolled for 155. I took 3-47; happy days, and I allowed myself to think: 'This is my time.'

Half centuries by Michael Clarke, Damien Martyn and Simon Katich, who batted brilliantly with the tail, steered our second dig to 384. I was run out for eight, but not before the big fella 'Harmy' Harmison hit me with a ripper to the back of my left hand. I initially thought it was broken, and it was still very sore when I bowled again.

As England's openers walked out, I wished Andrew Strauss good luck. He and I had built a good friendship based on Straussy's stint for my club, Mosman, in Sydney grade cricket. But that meant nothing when I began my spell. If England had plans to intimidate Australia, well, I had no thoughts of taking it without giving it back with interest. Straussy and Marcus Trescothick put on 80 in a really gutsy partnership before

Straussy tried to pull a short one off me, but only managed to sky it towards a short cover. I sprinted after it and took a sliding catch, but as I came to ground my left hand, which still had little feeling in it, rolled over and the ball touched the ground. It didn't matter because I already had the ball well under control. Later, an article in an English paper implied I'd cheated. The accusation angered me so much that I asked Neil Maxwell to take legal action. We received quite a substantial amount in an out-of-court settlement. If there's one thing I've detested more than anything else during my career, it's being labelled a cheat.

Soon after Straussy's wicket, I bowled the captain Michael Vaughan. By then England were 4-112 and Australia were heading for a big win. Pidgey and Warnie each took four wickets, the match was over on the fourth day, and I thought: 'This is the same old story. We're going to smash the Poms. This is going to be a walk in the park.'

My arrogant view was reflected by what the Australian team did at the ground hours after the match finished. England's players had long left, but we were still in a party mood, so we took the liberty of inviting ourselves into the Poms' dressing room and having a beer. It was a way of saying: 'You guys talked it up but couldn't deliver, so we're going to have a drink on your turf and say stuff you!' We had a look around and cracked a few jokes. We shouldn't have gone in there, but we were swept away by the moment. All these years later, I look back at our behaviour and wonder if we put the mocker on ourselves.

Two weeks later, the second Test at Edgbaston would turn out to be the subject I've most spoken about of all the things that have happened during my career. It began terribly, even before play got underway. In our warm-up on the first morning, Pidgey accidentally trod on a ball and rolled his ankle. He knew he was in trouble straight away. McGrath out, Kasprowicz in.

The next problem – although it was generally a good problem to have – was that Punter won the toss and chose to bowl on a slightly damp pitch. I can't remember if there was much team discussion about what we should do. This was only my second Test under Punter's captaincy, and as time went along I'd discover he was like Tugga when it came to tosses. Players could have their say, but in the end it came back to the captain, and everyone else just backed the decision, even though we may have disagreed with it.

In hindsight it was probably the wrong decision. Although we dismissed England by the end of the first day, we got pumped, especially me! Marcus Trescothick took it to me right from the start, and by the time the innings was over I had 1-111 off only 17 overs. 'Tres' top-scored with a punchy 90. He looked good. So did Pietersen and Andrew 'Freddie' Flintoff, who both smoked their ways to half-centuries. England finished with 407. In reply, we folded for 308.

Our team talk between innings stated the obvious: 'Boys, we're under the pump here. We better pull our fingers out!' I was determined to make up for the disappointment of the first innings when I knew I'd let the team and myself down. I arrived at the ground on day three feeling excited. Sometimes I just knew when I was going to do well, and this was one of those times. Resuming at 1-25, England slipped to 4-31 after I got Trescothick, Michael Vaughan and nightwatchman Matthew Hoggard out in the space of 10 balls. Vaughan's dismissal was great – as a fast bowler it's a fantastic sight when a ball nips through the gate and sends a stump or two flying.

Then Warnie took over and started knocking over batsmen for fun. Before we knew it, the Poms were 9-131, and I felt we'd hauled the game back our way. But I'd forgotten about Freddie

Flintoff. At six foot plenty and with shoulders you could park a truck on, he could hit a ball as hard and far as anyone I've ever seen; the sight of former England captain Graham Gooch, a spectator, picking up one of my balls off the pavilion roof was testament to that. Freddie hit me for two massive sixes, and also took to Kasper in a 51-run partnership with Simon Jones. It didn't seem that Freddie actually hung around too long, but by the time Warnie bowled him, he'd made 73. Although I was his opponent, I loved the way Freddie played. Hold onto that thought because I'll come back to it in a while.

We rissoled England for 182. Warnie got 6-for (10 for the match) and I finished with the other four. Our target: 282. Time wasn't a problem because we began the chase only halfway through day three; in other words, we were only halfway through the Test match. But by the end of the day we were shattered: 8-175. We'd made a decent start, but then Freddie did it again. In his first over he got rid of Justin Langer and Punter. From that moment on we lost wickets steadily against all of England's quicks. The one that hurt most was the final ball of the day when Steve Harmison cleaned up Michael Clarke with a slower ball. We had no excuses; the pitch had no tricks to it, but the bowlers, especially Jones, were getting the ball to swing.

The mood on the bus going back to the team hotel was really flat. Although I wasn't normally one to analyse happenings at the end of play, a lot of questions were running through my mind. Had we taken England too easily? How much did we let them off the hook with our first innings bowling? And most of all, how had we got ourselves into so much trouble? I hadn't lost hope, but I did know victory for us would be a monumental task, especially because I'd join Warnie at the crease the next morning, and I'd hardly scored a run all tour. Before the bus had stopped, I tormented myself about facing Jones. I thought: 'If he bowls me an outswinger in the right spot I'm going to nick it every time.' I had next to no confidence in my batting.

The next morning we arrived at the ground to find a bumper crowd there already – a sell-out, I think. There were people lined up down the street, and TV news crews were filming and interviewing people who couldn't get in. It was an amazing reaction considering the match could have lasted only two more balls. 99.9 per cent of the crowd wanted to see England win, no matter how short the day was. The sight overwhelmed me, and confirmed my view that we'd stuffed up.

I didn't feel any more at ease when I went out for a hit in the nets, which were only a matter of metres away from where the public walked past. Some of the fans didn't muck about giving it to me, saying: 'You cocky bastards are going to lose. Two more wickets. It's going to be finished in an over, and you're first, Lee!'

Our coach, John Buchanan, threw me a few balls. For the first dozen or so, the pattern was: bowled, nick, nick, play and miss, bowled . . . Punter and Pup (Michael Clarke) watched on and joked: 'We're gone. Binga can't even hit a straight throw down! What's he gonna do against Freddie?' They actually started laughing at me. That made me angry. So I slapped the next ball as hard as I could, and nearly cleaned up Buck; I was trying to land one near Punter and Pup to shut them up. I eventually smoked one that went straight past them. I didn't say anything to them when I walked out of the nets, but although I didn't know it at the time, I could have been grateful they'd helped me get my eye in.

I still had the shits when I walked out to bat. We needed 107. Warnie said he was going to have a go. That was one thing I loved about him: no matter what the context of the game, he always backed himself. For me, it was a matter of survival in more ways than one, as I got hammered with short stuff. I decided I'd take as much as I could on the body rather than risk popping up a catch. Freddie and Harmy battered me; in what wasn't the greatest psychological tactic, I wondered what would happen if I got hit on the head at 90-plus miles per hour. I honestly stressed myself to the point that I thought I could be killed. Because of their size both bowlers gave the impression they were quicker than they were, and the pitch seemed a lot smaller. There was no sledging, but there was a lot of 'eye language'. After bowling a ball Freddie would glare at me before returning to his mark. It was intense cricket.

Somehow I managed to stay there long enough to start ticking over a few runs. Even though some came through nicks through slips, I was more than happy to take whatever I could get. I followed Warnie's lead and decided that if the ball was up I'd really unwind. Forget the situation of the match, this was good fun. We were beginning to have an absolute ball, knowing at any time the game could be over, but there was no pressure on us because no-one expected us to win.

I lost track of time until left-arm orthodox spinner Ashley Giles came on to bowl. We needed 62 runs. It was only at that point I began to think: 'We're going alright here.' I noticed for the first time a couple of pockets of Aussies in the crowd. I was only drawn to them because they were becoming vocal, or perhaps I'd allowed myself to relax and was taking in more around me. I also remember looking at Andrew Strauss and Michael Vaughan having a chat, and I got the feeling Vaughan was worried.

I reckon Warnie's presence started to play on England's minds *and* nerves. Considering all the things he'd done to the Poms over the years, it shouldn't have surprised anyone if he was able to produce a batting miracle. But when he was on 42 he tried to whip a ball down the leg side off Freddie's bowling and moved back so far he trod on his stumps. What a way to go; any way but that! A sinking feeling went through my whole body. Plus, I was in a world of hurt. My arms and ribs throbbed, and my left hand remained sore from where it was hit in the first Test. We still needed 62. I didn't think it was possible.

Kasper walked in to bat. Even from a distance I could tell he looked really nervous. He was stiff and awkward. When we got together I told him nothing was wrong with the pitch. It was also one of those times when it was worth a batsman telling his partner what was going on, something which – as I've mentioned – I considered unnecessary most times I batted. I told Kasper to play straight and take the ball on the body if he had to. I also said: 'Mate, watch the ball like a hawk.'

That sentence became our trademark line, and the further our partnership lasted, the more I went down the pitch between deliveries and said it. England didn't bowl well to us; they spent too much time trying to bounce us out. The runs came surprisingly easily and quickly, and by the time we needed about 30 to win, the Aussie fans had really amped it up. I didn't need to look at the scoreboard because they were singing every single run off the target: '39 runs to win, 38 runs to win, 36 runs to win . . .' I got great vibes from them. I still didn't think we could steal the match, but my hopes were getting stronger.

With 15 needed, Kasper cut Freddie and the ball flew high to third man. It was one of those moments that seemed to go in slow motion. I watched Simon Jones run in, and I thought the match was over. But either the ball dipped or Simon misjudged it and he was forced to dive forward at the last moment. He dropped it, his head went down, and I was thinking for the first time that Australia could win.

We got down to four to win when Harmison bowled a full toss outside off stump and I hammered it to deep point where I think the fielder was Giles. He took two steps to his right and stopped it. He was the only one outside the ring preventing singles. If the ball was another metre away from him it would have been a boundary, and game over. If that had happened, I reckon no-one would talk about the 2005 Ashes series as they do today. It would have been 2–0, and I wholeheartedly believe we would have gone on to win 5–0. But, there's no use thinking about 'if and buts'.

Two balls later, the infamous delivery – or famous, depending on which way you look at it – was bowled: Harmy came in, pitched short, the ball rose, Kasper tried to avoid it but it flicked his glove, and Geraint Jones took a fantastic diving catch down the leg side. It seemed the whole ground, minus one team and a few groups of Aussies, appealed. Umpire Billy Bowden put up his bent finger, and the Test match was over. We'd lost by two runs.

I looked over at Vaughan who was clenching his fists and yelling. Geraint Jones had thrown the ball up, and someone knocked his cap off in all the excitement. England's players were hugging and jumping on top of each other. Instantly, I went down on my haunches. Moments later, I felt this big hand on my shoulder. It was Freddie. I still don't know exactly what he said, but it was something like: 'Awesome game, bad luck, I thoroughly enjoyed it.' This happened in the space of a few seconds, but it seemed a moment trapped in time. That moment was caught by a photographer, and the image has since become one of the Ashes' most famous photos.

I thanked Freddie and told him to go and celebrate with his team. We shook hands as I stood up, then I went down and hugged Kasper. I could only say: 'Bad luck, mate.' Kasper was really upset. He blamed himself, but shouldn't have. He'd batted out of his skin, and shown true Australian spirit. Putting the result aside, he had every reason to be proud of what he had done.

We walked off the field too empty to say much. I'm not embarrassed to say that by the time we reached the dressing room, I was tearing up for the first time after a game. I went straight through the change area and headed for the showers. I can't recall if any players had commiserated with me on my way through; at that stage I was in my own little world.

I stayed in the shower block without having a shower for a considerable time, maybe 20 or so minutes, but again I couldn't say for sure. I was by myself. I still had my gloves on; I'd taken them off to shake the English players' hands, but felt more comfortable with them on back in the dressing room. I sat and cried. I'd finished with 43 runs, as good an innings as I've ever played, but I would have swapped them all for a win. I couldn't believe what had happened. A few of the guys came in and hugged me or slapped me on the back and said: 'Bad luck, great job.' None of their words really registered.

Now, we return to Freddie. Remember how I said earlier I loved the way he played? The reason for this was simple: although I didn't know him too well heading into the series, he gave the impression he was the type of guy whose attitude I'd like to think I had as well. That is, he played as hard as anybody, but afterwards he'd be ready to shake your hand and have a chat and a beer. He'd already shown that on the field, and then, in the privacy of the Australian dressing room, he displayed it again when he was the first English player to walk in. He poured me a beer and threw his arm around me. Half an hour or so earlier he'd been on the field trying to pin me. Both the 'before' and 'after' were sport at its best. It was a really, really special moment which cemented a great bond between us. We had incredible respect for each other and an understanding of what pressure each of us was under. We played for different teams but we belonged to the same club.

A while later, some talk began circulating about the controversy of Kasper's dismissal. Apparently he had his hand off his bat when the ball hit his glove, and that meant he wasn't out. But to the naked eye, I thought there was no doubt about the wicket, and that was good enough for me. No-one could deny England had played better and deserved to win. The result stirred huge interest for the rest of the series, while the match itself was a good boost for cricket at a time when there was concern that Australia's domination wasn't good for the sport.

The second Test had been a reality check for the Australian team. We'd gone from being too cocky to realising the rest of the series was going to be hard work. There was such a mental shift that England suddenly believed they could win more than us. By this stage the biggest difference between the teams was unity. From the outside looking in, I thought England were a really tight-knit bunch of mates who were willing to go through thick and thin for each other. The Australian squad didn't have that.

Imagine your own workplace where people walk through the door at nine o'clock, they go to their desk, do their stuff, have a few chats with colleagues during the day, take a meal break, go to a meeting or two, then they pack up at five and say to their colleagues, 'See ya tomorrow,' and then they're off. I felt the Australian squad was doing exactly that. The cricket field was our workplace, while outside of hours we split into groups and did our own things, whether they were social outings, sponsorship obligations, or even sitting in our rooms alone. That isn't to say there was huge disunity among us, but we were certainly fragmented.

The WAGS – wives and girlfriends – contributed to the problems. Not all of them, including Liz, saw eye to eye. Put bluntly, there was some bitchy stuff going on. Different personalities caused different groups to form, and this meant players were torn different ways as well. For example, simple pastimes like going out to dinner weren't only a matter of deciding what restaurant to go to, but working out what people got along with each other. Did the issues with the girls affect the way the guys played? I'd probably say 'no'; however, it definitely affected the relationships between the guys for a period. I mean, if you're close to a playing mate, but your partners don't get on, you can be put under incredible strain, especially in a team environment. Because of the rumblings on this tour, Cricket Australia began inviting the WAGS to Australia's annual pre-season camps in Coolum so they could be better guided about touring life and team protocols.

Leading up to the third Test at Old Trafford, Manchester, I had another worry. When I caught and bowled Andrew Strauss in the first Test I grazed my knee. I didn't think anything more about it until it became tender and puffy after the second Test. The end result was that I spent a couple of nights in hospital being dosed up on antibiotics to treat cellulitis. There was media talk that I was in doubt, but I was fine.

The third Test turned out to be just as fantastic as the second. Again we were on the back foot after England won the toss and made 444. The early signs were good for us when I bowled Strauss with a slower ball for a milestone moment: my 150th Test wicket. With some help from dropped catches Michael Vaughan returned to form with 166 to ensure England gained control. I took 4-100 off 27 overs and thought I'd bowled well.

Meanwhile, England's bowlers were in sensational form. Simon Jones wrecked our first innings, taking six wickets. He got tremendous swing with the old ball, and questions were raised about why Australia's bowlers weren't doing the same. There were queries over the Poms' use of saliva generated from mint lollies, but I don't believe anything untoward happened. Plain and simple, Jones and his teammates knew what they had to do with the Duke ball. I think their skills ultimately proved the main difference between the two teams.

After leading by 142 on the first innings England declared at 6-280 in their second dig, thanks mainly to a century by Strauss, who wore a plaster on his ear after I'd pinned him with a bouncer. We were set 423 to win. Entering the final day we were 0-24, and full of belief we could pull off the unlikely on a wearing pitch. Punter led the way. He was brilliant. But whenever it looked as though he was building a match-winning partnership with someone, a wicket fell. When I got to the crease, Punter was 150, and we were 83 runs short with just under 10 overs to go and two wickets in hand. No chance. And yet Punter told me: 'Let's just bat. I'm not saying we're going for the runs or we'll shut up shop. We'll just bat.' It was good advice because it stopped me from thinking too much about the pressure of the situation. It was the old cliché: treat every ball on its merits.

But then Punter brushed a short ball down the leg side to the keeper off Harmison. He didn't want to walk, but I could see on his face he knew he'd hit it. The appeal was more of a roar from both England's players and the crowd. Pidgey walked in with 24 balls to go. He'd taken 5-for in England's second innings, a gutsy effort considering his ankle wasn't 100 per cent, and he'd surprised many people by playing. I stated the obvious to him: 'Mate, we've gotta try and hold these guys out here.' Maybe it was our day because I'd already survived a close LBW off Freddie, and then I got hit again by a big inswinger from him.

I thought I was plumb, but thankfully umpire Steve Bucknor disagreed. Replays confirmed he'd made a good decision.

Freddie's and Harmy's main tactic was the yorker. I was already batting a foot outside my crease to reduce the chances of getting LBW. I'd even told the umpires where I was standing. I suggested to Pidgey he do the same thing, so he did. However, it did open up another type of dismissal that England didn't pick up on. There were a couple of balls off Harmy that Pidgey played to Ian Bell at short leg. Pidgey didn't even think about getting back in his crease, but Bell didn't even think of having a ping at the stumps either.

With seven balls to go I wanted to get on strike for the last over. Freddie bowled a full one on my legs and I hit it through midwicket; for the only time in my batting career I prayed the ball would pull up short of the boundary, so we could stroll through for a single. I actually yelled at the ball: 'Pull up, get a cramp!' But it trickled over the line, and in between overs some of the English guys joked they would have kicked the ball over the line if it hadn't made it. So, six balls to go and Pidgey was on strike. Stuart MacGill came out with a message from the dressing rooms. It was a reminder to get back in his crease between deliveries.

It was really tense; the crowd was a strange mix of shouts and silence. Ball one, down leg side; ball two, a play and miss outside off stump; ball three, a single to the leg side. Well done, Pidgey! Now, my turn. I kept telling myself: 'I don't care how, but I'm not getting out.' Ball four, way down leg side; ball five, left alone outside off. One ball to go. I tried not to think about what it could be; it was best to adopt Punter's strategy of 'just bat'. Thankfully, Harmy made it easy for me; a full toss that I whipped to fine leg for four. I punched the air and looked across at the Australian team on the pavilion balcony. The guys were celebrating as though we'd just won the Ashes. As Pidgey and I walked off, the greatest number 11 batsman in the world never to make a Test century joked: 'Never in doubt!'

To have played two spine-tingling matches back to back was unbelievable. Realistically, I don't think anyone could have expected a third, but it happened. Again we had some bad luck before the game when Pidgey pulled out with a crook elbow. Dizzy was also dropped. South Australia's Shaun Tait was selected to make his debut. Following on from what Gilly had done for me before my first Test, I gave 'Taity' a 'good luck' gift, which from memory was a bottle of Scotch. I was excited about the prospect of bowling with him. He was seriously quick, and the fact that he had a slinging action prompted talk in the media that Australia was unveiling another Jeff Thomson.

The Poms again batted first and put us under the pump after making 477. Guess who did most damage? Freddie scored 102. By this stage of the series I understood his true value. He wasn't the greatest all-rounder I played against – South Africa's Jacques Kallis takes that honour – but Freddie had a presence that lifted others around him to greater things. If presence was a statistic, he'd have an average of 100-plus. He inspired others simply by being there. That is the rarest of qualities in any athlete, or human being for that matter.

In reply, we had a shocker against Simon Jones and Matthew Hoggard, who continued to embarrass us by swinging the ball prodigiously. Our innings was so poor that I top-scored with 47 off 44 balls. I wasn't many when we lost our ninth wicket and Taity came out to bat. No offence to Taity, but I thought our best chance of getting a few runs was by 'teeing off'. I smashed Harmy out of the ground twice, and also hit Jones for a six. I was eventually caught at third man going for an up-and-under off Jones.

We were all out for 218. If that wasn't ordinary enough, we were asked to follow on, and finished up with 387. That left England 129 to win. Small totals can be harder to chase than you think because of the tricks the mind can play on you. Although you should be confident, the loss of a couple of quick wickets can create doubts that multiply with every other wicket that falls. And that's what happened to England. They were cruising at 0-32, but all of a sudden they were 4-57 after Warnie grabbed the top three and Ian Bell holed out to Kasper at fine leg off me. Kevin Pietersen and Freddie looked on the right track until I came back for a second spell and Gilly took a diving catch to get rid of Pietersen. Then, I beat Freddie with a jaffa that cut back and hit the top of off stump. You beauty! At that moment, all the pressure I felt under, all the emotion, and all the relief exploded together and I did something that I now look back at and think: 'What an idiot!' I impersonated Freddie's trademark celebration with arms stretched out and back arched. It wasn't planned; it just happened. Five runs later Warnie removed Geraint Jones and the Poms were in trouble: 7-116.

Throughout England's innings we knew we could win. It was a belief that Steve Waugh had instilled in many of us during his captaincy and had passed on to Punter. I was certainly in the mood to play to the death. But it wasn't to be. Ashley Giles and Matthew Hoggard saw England home, and Australia's players had their tails between their legs. We were devastated. England played exceptionally well and were very humble in victory. Although they were our so called 'enemies', I found it impossible not to like the guys.

We needed to win the fifth Test at The Oval to retain the Ashes, but the match was an anti-climax: a rain-affected draw. There were some great individual performances on both sides. Warnie bagged six wickets in each innings, Freddie got a 5-for and Justin Langer, Matthew Hayden and Andrew Strauss all scored centuries. But the match belonged to a cocky bastard who was easy to dislike, if not hate on the field. Kevin Pietersen was his own man. Although I got on well with him throughout the series, I understood he could rub people up the wrong way. Yet he was great to play against; in fact, he was one of my favourite players to take on because he fancied himself and took risks. To this day he remains one of the few players in any team I'd jump the turnstiles to go and watch.

I'd had a fair bit of success against Pietersen throughout the series, and was desperate to mark up another notch in England's second innings. If we knocked him over early and grabbed some other quick wickets we thought we still had some – albeit small – chance of winning. It was just before lunch on the final day, and the Poms were looking to bat out time after leading by six runs on the first innings. Pietersen had hardly got started when he went hard at a ball from me outside off stump. The edge flew to Warnie in the slips, but he grassed it. England were only about 100 ahead at the time. It was a catch Warnie should have taken, and 99 times out of 100 he would have, but how could anyone blame him? He'd had an awesome series, and was bowling at the other end, trying his hardest to produce the match-winning magic only he could.

Pietersen took full advantage of the chance and blasted the game away from us. He and I had a great contest. I pushed above 150 kays and landed a couple into his ribs and hands. He also once nearly fell onto his stumps as I peppered him with the short ball while we had a leg gully in place. Like when bowling to Lara and Tendulkar, this was a moment I dug deep for that extra effort. I hope everyone watching appreciated it.

After lunch Pietersen was unbelievable. In my first over I bounced him and he hooked me about 15 rows back. An over later I put a man back for the trap and launched again. This time I was hit about 20 rows back! It was a sensational shot. After that, Pietersen gave me a look, almost a wink, as though he was saying: 'I'm the cat and you're the mouse. Is that the best you can do?' Next ball I bent my back even more. Whack, another four, and another one after that. After a couple more the following over, I was out of the attack.

Pietersen ended up with 156. By the time we got England out we could only bat for an over. The realisation slapped me straight away: we'd lost the Ashes. From an Aussie point of view, yes, you get over losing a series, but not the Ashes. In the dressing room there were feelings of emptiness, bitterness, frustration, and also the belief that we'd lost the series as much as England had won it. But as time passed, we realised we were outplayed by a more united and hungrier team. Then again, just a couple more runs, or a couple more wickets and the series could have been very different. To me, that was fantastic.

I initially took the loss hard because I was desperate to make an impact after 2001 and lead the attack as well as I could, especially when Pidgey was out. I finished with 20 wickets at 41.10, the third-best return behind Warnie (40) and Freddie (24). Again people might look at the stats and say I was expensive. Again I say: 'Look behind the numbers.' I also managed to contribute a few times with the bat. Overall, it was the best series I ever played, and was also the best series I ever played in. I must admit, though, I can't believe the Poms got OBEs for winning. What would they have got if they'd won 5–0? A room each in Buckingham Palace? Ah well, good luck to you guys. It was a great series with great memories. Thank you, England.

22

On one of my many promotional visits to India, I teamed up with Sachin Tendulkar to be ambassadors for Boost Energy drinks. After we'd finished shooting a television commercial we arranged to have dinner with Liz and Sachin's wife, Anjali, at Sachin's own Mumbai restaurant. Indians eat notoriously late, so it was about midnight when we finished our meals, and as we prepared to say our goodbyes Sachin asked me in his typically quiet way: 'Would you like to go go-karting?'

'Yeah, that sounds great. Let us know what time tomorrow and we'll link up,' I replied.

'No, no, I mean *now*,' said Sachin.

I was surprised, but why not? Soon afterwards we arrived at a track; I'm not sure if it was Sachin's own facility, but there were certainly a lot of people making sure he had everything he needed as soon as we got there. There must have been 30 or more pumping petrol, starting karts up, checking tyres, polishing helmets, dusting the track. Someone wheeled out Sachin's kart which had 10, his cricket number, on it. Another one was wheeled out for a friend of Sachin's, and I was given one that didn't look as flash as the others; I'm sure Sachin stitched me up! We all got fitted in the proper clothing, including gloves, but when it came to getting into our machines, my fast bowler's backside was too big for the seat. Sachin laughed; I had no choice but to accept I was like an elephant driving a Mini. About half-a-dozen workers at the track jumped into other karts to swell the race number, and before I knew it I was on pole at the start line swallowing smoke and waiting for the lights to change.

Before I go any further, I must tell you that one of the reasons Sachin has had so much success on the cricket field is because he wants to win; in fact, he *has* to win. And he was the same behind the steering wheel of a kart.

Red, orange, green, and racing! We floored it, and headed into the first bend of a figure eight circuit. Straight away Sachin flew up on my inside, but I didn't see him in my little putting machine. I took a different line and in doing so bumped another driver coming through, who in turn crashed into Sachin. That triggered a pile-up after only 10 seconds of the race. I looked over and there was a wheel spinning next to Sachin's head. The world's best batsman got out and cracked up laughing. He was just a big kid having fun.

We ended up having another race which Sachin won. By the time we'd finished mucking about it must have been about two or three o'clock in the morning. I was exhausted. Then Sachin asked me: 'Do you want to go for a drive tomorrow?'

'Yeah, what time?'

'I'll pick you up at half past five.'

That sounded a good plan to me. I didn't know exactly what he meant by going for a drive, but since it was Sachin I expected there'd be some surprise involved. I told him I'd rest up throughout the day and see him in the evening, but he shook his head and said, 'No, no, I meant 5.30 this morning.'

273

Not wanting to disappoint him, I went back to my hotel, had a couple of hours' sleep, and woke up like a bear out of hibernation. At right on 5.30 a red Ferrari pulled up at my hotel. *Vrroooom!* Everywhere else, there was quiet. But within a minute or two there were 50 or more people crowded around the car saying to each other: 'Sachin and Brett Lee!' Many were ringing their friends and telling them. I got in the car, and then Sachin spun around and sped off. It was dead quiet on the road, and it was only then that I realised this was the only possible time Sachin could drive without either traffic jams or the hassles of his own popularity, which would cause even bigger traffic jams.

We flew along roads for more than an hour. I'm not saying that Sachin didn't obey the law, but I reckon he had what I'd call an 'access-all-areas pass' to Mumbai. I doubted he would ever get booked, and if he ever got pulled over I'm sure a police officer would only be chasing his autograph. By the time we headed back to my hotel there was a convoy of tuk-tuks giving chase. None of them caught us. We arrived back at the hotel at about seven o'clock. I think I slept for much of the day.

It was fascinating to see how Sachin lived. I'd heard rumours that he'd even been known to dress up in disguises in a bid not to be recognised by people on the street. He was cricket's biggest superstar who'd achieved just about everything his sport could offer. Unfortunately, there was one honour he missed: he was injured when an ICC World XI played Australia at home in three one-dayers and a Test at the start of the 2005–06 season. There isn't much that needs to be said about those games. Originally they were planned to be a showdown between Australia, a team that was dominating world cricket, against the ultimate team of the world's best players. But since we'd lost the Ashes a month earlier, and the World XI was missing someone like Sachin, the games were a bit of a non-event even before they began. Australia won every match, and as much as anything, I liked getting another baggy green cap specifically made for the Test. In reality, the contests were like exhibition matches, but I still treated them as I did any other game when I was representing my country.

When the season began I was nearly 29 years of age, and I think I was finally maturing mentally as a fast bowler. For much of my career I'd primarily been a two-length bowler: yorkers and bouncers. That isn't to say I had no other deliveries, but full and short were undoubtedly my 'go-to' weapons, as they'd been ever since I'd worked my way up from the junior ranks. But growing older and hopefully wiser, and with 43 Tests under my belt, I knew it was time to evolve. Neil Maxwell and I spoke about this, and Maxi recommended I talk with former Australian captain Mark Taylor.

Maxi considered Mark a very 'intelligent cricket thinker' who wouldn't only analyse me from a captain's perspective, but also from the viewpoint of an opening batsman, a first slip, and a television commentator who'd looked straight down the wicket at my bowling since I'd first played a Test. Mark was only too happy to help, so over a beer at the Bayview Hotel in Gladesville, Sydney, we sat down and worked out what I could do differently to help my bowling. He was really up-front and honest. He believed that sometimes I was a little too impatient with my bowling. Even though Glenn McGrath and I were different types of pacemen, he suggested I try to emulate Pidgey more. He said I had to hit better lines and lengths consistently and use change-ups of pace rather than bowling stock standard balls. Overall, I had to get the ball going through to the keeper over off stump off a nicking length 29 times out of 30.

The advice was a significant turning point for me. I went back to cricket with the mindset of being really patient rather than shocking batsmen out or jagging them with unplayable balls. A few days later I took five wickets in a Pura Cup win for the Blues over South Australia at the SCG. Throughout my spells I kept repeating Mark Taylor's words: 'Be patient, the rewards will come.' I was so grateful for his advice. I'd been told similar things by others, but for me it was really beneficial to hear it from someone removed from the day-to-day team environment, yet who understood the workings of it all. Add to that, the out of the blue text messages full of support that Steve Waugh sent, and I was in a really good mood leading into a three-Test series against the West Indies.

The first Test in Brisbane was one that reflected the transitional phase my bowling went through. In the first innings I sent down a fair amount of crap; the media term would be 'erratic deliveries'. Ricky Ponting and I had a long talk at the halfway point of the game that further consolidated my approach. He told me he wasn't going to bowl me in long spells that would affect my pace, as had happened in England. He wanted me to steam in, bowl as fast as I could, and he'd back me by giving me the fields I wanted. However, I was very conscious of the 'patience and consistency factor'. So I bent my back but also paid more attention to my lines than I previously had. The end result was 5-30 off 14 overs, my best haul in Test cricket and my first 5-for in four years.

That match also saw me hit the biggest six of my career. In the first innings Daren Powell pitched one up outside off stump and I launched into a shot over cow corner. I couldn't have hit it any harder; the sound was so sweet. The ball kept going up and up. Afterwards there was debate in the media over whether it had landed on, or actually gone over, the top of a grandstand. For mine, it definitely went over. The funny thing was it nearly hit former Australian bowler Carl Rackemann, who was walking along with his family outside the stand. Hitting a six off another fast bowler gives me as good a feeling as getting a hat-trick. It is the ultimate display of arrogance.

Australia made a clean sweep of the series, and I finished the leading wicket-taker with 18 poles at about 20. I was confident I had indeed entered a new stage of my career, and was 'finding myself' as a Test bowler. It wouldn't have mattered if Steve Waugh, Ricky Ponting, Adam Gilchrist, Michael Clarke or anyone else had been captain; I would have been comfortable under the lot of them because I was comfortable with myself. My success was a result of what was happening off the field too. I was in a great relationship with Liz, and that contributed to me being comfortable in my whole life. If a player is settled on all fronts outside the game, his cricket definitely comes a lot easier. I had a new sense of responsibility and stability. I was content. I was happy. I was growing up.

In what was a hectic summer, the Australian team travelled to New Zealand to squeeze in three one-dayers before returning for a Test series against South Africa. As had become the norm for me across the Tasman, I couldn't escape controversy. In the first game in Auckland, which we won, I took 3-5 from six overs and then had an apple thrown at me by someone in the crowd. I tried to laugh it off by telling the media I loved fruit, but not when it was hurled at my head at 120 kilometres an hour.

In the second match at Wellington there was a touch of deja vu when I lost grip of a wet ball and bowled a beamer. And guess who faced it yet again? Brendon McCullum. I copped a lot of booing and jeering from the crowd, but this time there was no long-lasting media story. Instead, my nose became more of a news angle; I contracted an infection in the nasal passages and flew home after the match. There was some medical opinion that it was the same type of problem I had when I'd infected my knee a few months earlier during the Ashes. A doctor told me I could have carried the offending bug in my body for months. Despite some jokes from my teammates that I was going home for a 'nose job', it didn't turn out to be too serious, and I was ready to take on the South Africans.

I had another pleasing series including a 5-for in the drawn first Test in Perth. However, the memories of a battle I had with Jacques Kallis in the second Test in Melbourne stand above all others from the series. I think Jacques is the complete cricketer because he can win and save matches with both bat and ball, not to mention his catching with his meat-plate-sized hands. I regarded his wicket as a 'top-shelf scalp' every time I played him.

This particular duel in Melbourne happened at a critical stage of the match. Australia had made 355 after batting first, but we were under the pump heading into day three when South Africa resumed at 2-169, with Jacques and Herschelle Gibbs well set. Pidgey and I opened up and concentrated on drying up the runs. With Pidgey keeping his end so tight, I managed to get 20 balls in a row against Jacques. During that time he didn't score one run. The ball was nearly 70 overs old and I was starting to get it to go 'spit rock', but I resisted the temptation to bowl a yorker, and instead just concentrated on that 'patience and consistency' tactic of line and length with the occasional bouncer.

On the 19th delivery I sniffed him up and hoped he'd have some doubts in his mind about whether I was going to give him some consistent 'chin music'. Then, I finally thought the time was right for the glory ball, the yorker. It came out perfectly and swung in. Jacques went forward but played too late and the ball crashed into his off stump. 'Kallis bowled Lee 23' was one of the most rewarding and clinical dismissals of my career. Furthermore, the whole duel was similar to the one I'd had with Brian Lara in Trinidad a few years earlier. It was another moment that defined the sport, the characters, and the power of being part of an intense contest. Give me those over an easy victory any day. Wickets fell steadily after that and we took a small first-innings lead, which, thanks to a Matthew Hayden century and great bowling by Pidgey and Warnie in the second dig, was converted into a strong win.

Jacques was also involved in another battle I had during the third Test in Sydney. But this time he only played a small role in what turned out to be a highly publicised dispute between me and Pakistani umpire Aleem Dar. It was after Aleem had turned down my appeal for LBW against Jacques early in South Africa's innings on the first day. As I walked back past Aleem to my mark, I asked him: 'How come that wasn't out?'

Players know they have the right to question an umpire about any decision he makes. It's up to the umpire as to how he answers. He may give a reason or simply choose to say it just wasn't out. Aleem told me he would tell me at the end of the over. When the over finished I took my hat and I asked Aleem again. He didn't say anything. That frustrated me, so I told him: 'This is bullshit!' I wanted to push him further but Adam Gilchrist pulled me away. I don't think I crossed the line, but at a hearing that night I was reprimanded by match referee Chris Broad for 'showing dissent at the umpire's decision by action or verbal abuse'. I had to cop it but I didn't think it was fair, and I certainly didn't agree with the well-worn excuse of officials that behaviour like mine looked bad for the kids watching.

Punter, Warnie and Pidgey also had disagreements with either Aleem or the other umpire, Billy Bowden, and as a result, Australia were criticised in the media for our 'ugly behaviour'. I thought that was unfair; it seemed to me that everyone could be held accountable for their actions, except the umpires.

To me, an umpire is like a ground. There are grounds on which I played well and there were umpires I played well in front of. One who springs to mind was South African Rudi Koertzen. I thought he was a fantastic umpire. There were many times after he turned down my appeals he told me why. For example: 'In my opinion, Binga, it was going down leg.' Yes, he even called me Binga! I would never get the shits with Rudi, even if he made a blatantly wrong decision, because I respected him as a person. There was no fuss about him. We always said hello to each other, as I did with all the umpires, but unlike some others, he was friendly and willing to have a chat.

My relationship with umpires varied. I got on really well with Rudi, Australia's Simon Taufel, and England's David Shepherd. Shep was brilliant. He was a no bullshit bloke. Whenever I even looked like getting out of line he simply said: 'Just go back and bowl. It wasn't out, and that's that!' I also got on tremendously with Asad Rauf. Even though he was a Pakistani, he understood Hindi, which made for some interesting exchanges between us. There were times when I'd hand him my hat at the start of an over and swear at him in Hindi as a joke, and he'd hit back with interest!

West Indian Steve Bucknor was another I generally got on well with. I remember the little exchanges we'd have when I'd be fielding somewhere near Steve at square leg and I'd sing a bit of 'No Woman, No Cry' or 'Buffalo Soldier'. Steve would bop away, oh so cool, in his West Indian way. I started doing those little bursts after Steve once saw me playing the piano at a hotel bar in Hobart, and he asked me if I knew any Bob Marley songs. He was a massive fan.

I've no doubt I conned some umpires into favourable decisions for me. Schmoozing the umpire is part of the game, and I knew if I got on their right side I was more likely to get luck going my way in 50/50 decisions. However, I wasn't as good as Warnie who I considered the king in that department. I'm sure there were also batsmen who got good and bad decisions depending on their relationships with the umpires.

Aleem Dar and Billy Bowden were the two I had more run-ins with than anyone else. I'm not saying they weren't nice blokes, but for some unknown reason we just didn't get on. I'll mention more about Aleem later.

Australia won the Test after Punter scored a century in each innings. We then went on to claim the one-day series with South Africa and Sri Lanka. In our first preliminary match against the South Africans in Brisbane, Jacques Kallis well and truly left his mark on me. He was bowling decent wheels when he put a little extra on one delivery that I went to pull until I realised it was coming on to me too fast. I only succeeded in being hit flush underneath the helmet grill on the left side of my jaw. My legs turned to jelly and I felt as though I'd been knocked out. For several weeks afterwards my jaw hurt on the right side; apparently the whole bone had been shunted across in what is known as a 'boxer's jaw'. Despite being hit, I managed to go on and get my highest-ever one-day international score: 57 off 70 balls.

The day before our next game I did something I'd never done before: I took myself away for additional bowling practice after Australian team training was over. I'd been concerned I wasn't hitting my yorker well, and since it was such a vital weapon for me, I wanted to work on it. However, it was always hard to do so against my teammates because if I overcompensated I could hit someone with a beamer. Instead, I waited until all the batsmen had gone, and I then went back to schoolboy coaching basics: I put a pair of shoes where a batsman would stand, and three empty Gatorade bottles that acted as mini-stumps on the popping crease. Ball after ball I tried to blow the bottles away. I did that for at least an hour, which came after at least an hour at team training. It was muscle memory: *bang, bang, bang*. I went into the game at Melbourne's Docklands Stadium, again against South Africa, with a plan to keep the ball as full as I could for the entire time. It worked because I finished with my best one-day international bowling figures: 5-22 off 10 overs, including four batsmen I clean bowled.

Two weeks later, I was named the best one-day bowler in the world under the ICC rankings. At the time it didn't mean much, but now it's good to look back and think there was a period when I was regarded so highly. It was a nice pat on the back to remember, especially considering I'd had so many up and down moments.

The highs and lows of cricket were never more obvious than when we finished our home summer and left straight for South Africa to play a T20 game, five more one-dayers and three Tests. Some of you will no doubt remember one extraordinary contest in Johannesburg.

Ever since I'd come into the Australian one-day team John Buchanan had always said: 'Guys, one day a side is going to get 400. It's not impossible. It's achievable.' I didn't believe him. But then came the game at Wanderers Stadium. It was the last and deciding contest in the series. Punter won the toss and batted on what was a strip of highway that had been chiselled from somewhere outside the ground and transplanted onto the cricket field. It was an absolute belter. Punter led the way with one of the most ridiculous one-day innings I've ever seen: 164 off 105 balls. All the batsmen smashed the ball around, and by the finish we were laughing in the dressing room at our total: 4-434. Buck was right after all.

We were amazed at the score, and I reckon most, if not all of the team, assumed we had the match in the bag. I pretty well thought we could have gone out and bowled left-handed and won. But strange things happen in sport. If Punter's innings was ridiculous, Herschelle Gibbs's knock was pure fantasy. Coming in at number three in the second over, he played one of the best innings I've seen in any form of cricket: 175 off 111 balls. Gibbs remains one of the most dangerous and exciting batsmen in the world. He reads the ball so quickly that he's hardly ever out of position. He also has magical timing and slaps the ball on the up as well as anyone. He was so dominant that he rattled up his runs with 18 overs still to go.

At that stage the South Africans needed 136 to win at nearly eight runs an over. I thought we were still going to win. But all the following batsmen did their bit, and the result came down to the last over. *My* over. South Africa required seven runs, we needed two wickets. Five came off the first two balls before Andrew Hall holed out to mid-on. Makhaya Ntini then hit a single and Mark Boucher drilled me over mid-on for a four and the win.

When we got back to the dressing room a few shoes and other pieces of gear were thrown, and both Punter and Buck were fuming. I kept thinking: 'How embarrassing! How could we lose that?' But soon I realised we'd been part of one of the most incredible games in history, and there was an odd feeling that I was lucky to have been involved. However, that didn't stop me from being really upset for Victorian paceman Micky Lewis. He was humiliated. Punter shouldn't have kept bowling him, and his eventual figures, 0-113 off 10 overs, were obviously painful but they could have happened to anyone. Micky never played for Australia again.

Heading into the Test series, I put added pressure on myself. Although I'd done well in recent series, this was another new start for me because Glenn McGrath had stayed at home to be with his wife, Jane, whose cancer had returned. Considering I'd overtaken Jason Gillespie and Michael Kasprowicz in the selectors' 'pecking order', I was the leader of the pace attack. In the first Test at Newlands, Cape Town, it was a new name that upstaged us all. My NSW teammate Stuart Clark had an unforgettable debut when he took 5-for in the first innings and nine wickets for the match, which we won comfortably. In many ways Stuey was a Glenn McGrath clone who bowled in the channel ball after ball after ball. It's one of the mysteries of Australian cricket that he only played 24 Tests.

I snared five scalps, and although the return continued a healthy time for me, I had a much greater achievement to be proud of: 50 Test matches. That milestone showed my longevity performing the toughest role in Test cricket. The fact I'd overcome years of strain and pain meant more to me than wickets and runs because it showed I was able to fight through all the down times, as well as riding the ups. Reaching 50 Tests was a statistic I was immensely proud of.

Another great moment came in the second Test at Kingsmead, Durban, when I bowled Mark Boucher to take my 200th Test wicket. The match was also significant from a personal viewpoint because I wore a brand new baggy green after I'd retired my old frayed one following the Cape Town match. That was no simple matter because I had to fill out a report stating that my cap was in poor condition and request a replacement. I gave the report to team manager Steve Bernard, who sent it through to Cricket Australia. Once the appropriate people said 'yes', I had a new cap. Unlike others, most famously Steve Waugh, whose original cap underwent some repair work, I didn't want my original one fixed because its condition reflected what I'd been through. Nowadays, it takes pride of place in a glass case in my home.

Kingsmead was one of my favourite Test grounds to play on. Forget the fact that I took 5-69 in the first innings and six wickets for the match in another win; the real fun came from soaking up the atmosphere of a happy crowd. Kingsmead had a unique identity where one grassy section of the ground, Castle Corner, was filled with wooden huts full of spectators getting smashed. The whole area smelled of spilt beer and meat cooking on *braaie*, the South African equivalent of barbeques. Sometimes when playing in the huge arenas like the MCG, it was hard, if not at times impossible, to have individual exchanges with fans because there were just too many people.

But at Kingsmead it was as though I was playing park cricket, albeit on the big stage. There was plenty of interaction and both men and women didn't mind hopping in and sledging me. That's why I decided to learn a few sentences in Afrikaans. So, after one bloke had a crack at me, saying he could bowl faster than I could, I told him he was too fat because he'd had too much *brandewyn* (brandy) and Coke and eaten too much *potjiekos* (stew). He was surprised when he heard me use a few of his words. He laughed, raised his beer to me and sat down. After that I was a hero in that area. Each time I'd field there, I'd be offered sausages and sips of Castle beer because: 'It'll help you bowl faster!'

In the final Test in Johannesburg, I had one of my best all-round matches, taking 3-for in each innings, and scoring

64 in the first dig. But it was the second innings that I really remember. Needing 292 to win, Australia resumed on the final morning at 6-248. Damien Martyn was in his 90s and I was in single figures. Marto ended up falling for 101, and when Stuey Clark got out we still needed 17. Michael Kasprowicz walked out to join me; the last remaining batsman was Justin Langer playing his hundredth Test. Poor JL had been filled in by an Ntini bouncer from the first ball of the match. He was badly concussed and retired hurt and hadn't batted again since. He was desperate to play his part, but Buck, Punter and the medical team overruled him. If he'd been hit again, who knows what would have happened to him. So, Kasper and I got together, knowing the match rested with us.

Kasper was really nervous, so I tried settling him down with something out of left field. I said: 'I saw this movie last night about two blokes caught in an ice cave. No-one was there to help them but somehow they managed to find their way out. We're stuck in an ice cave here as well, and we're going to find our way out too. I can guarantee it's not going to be the same result as Edgbaston. We're going to knuckle down and get these runs.' And we did. However, I can't remember anything about our partnership. I can't even tell you who got the winning runs, but I do clearly remember my ice-cave ramble. It's strange, isn't it? There are no rules to the things I remember in cricket.

A look at the records shows I had a handy summer. Since having the conversation with Mark Taylor, I'd taken 48 wickets at 23.54. Only the crystal ball would know what lay ahead, but at least I had every reason to be confident. The tour to South Africa also continued the happy parallel between my on-field and off-field happenings. Before the second Test I made the biggest decision of my life when I proposed to Liz. We decided we'd only have a short engagement, but before our wedding I had yet another tour to go on in what seemed a never-ending period of being on the road. Apart from a three-week break after the Ashes, Australia's players who were in both the one-day and Test teams had enjoyed little time off for 10 months. Although I felt strong and fit, I was exhausted and admitted to the media there were times when I'd been 'running on fumes'; I couldn't wait until the end of a short trip to Bangladesh that immediately followed the South African tour.

As expected, we won both Tests and all three one-dayers, but the clean sweep wasn't one-sided. It was only centuries by Gilly and Punter that saved us from an embarrassing loss in the first Test at Fatullah. The second Test at Chittagong is remembered because of another century maker. In what would have to be one of the more unbelievable achievements in the modern era, Jason Gillespie went in as a first-drop nightwatchman late on day two and not only did he do his job by hanging around until stumps, he came out and batted all of day three and into day four. He scored 201 not out, sharing a fourth-wicket partnership of 320 with Mike Hussey. Along the way he bettered the highest-ever Test innings of Huss, the Waughs, David Boon and Michael Clarke, among many others. It was an innings that nearly never happened because I was initially going to be the nightwatchman until Dizzy volunteered to do it. It was very generous of me to step aside.

My contributions throughout the series were small, although I doubt Aleem Dar will forget them. Unfortunately for me – and maybe for Aleem too – he was umpire in both matches. That led to trouble between us in, I think, the second Test.

The match should have been a mini-celebration for me because I'd just been named one of *Wisden*'s five cricketers of the year for 2005, which was another satisfying accolade to look back on after I finished playing. However, my focus soon turned to Aleem.

At the start of my first spell from each end in a match, I usually took four steps back from the stumps, scratched a mark, and asked the umpire to stand there; this was generally the point I jumped from for my last stride before delivery. However, Aleem said 'no' to me against Bangladesh. I asked him why and he told me he felt he was too far away. In reply, I said every other umpire didn't have a problem doing it. However, he still refused. I argued I wouldn't be able to bowl, because if he stood further forward, it was likely I'd hit him on my way through. Remember how New Zealand's Danny Morrison used to come in and bowl right over the top of the umpire? It was similar for me, so the umpire's positioning was crucial.

After Aleem said he still wouldn't budge, I called Punter over and quietly told him about my problems. Punter took up the argument with Aleem, but he also had no success. As a result, I ended up having to modify my approach. I had the shits and was put off my game. Later, I took a catch right in front of the sightscreen and my celebratory ping of the ball to the middle smacked into Aleem's back. It looked bad but I honestly didn't mean to do it.

Because of the issues, Aleem and I were called in to try to sort out our differences in front of the match referee, Jeff Crowe. Jeff asked if there were language barrier problems, but I said I understood Aleem fine; he was simply someone I couldn't seem to get on with. Off the field I thought he was a nice man who always said hello to me in passing.

By the end of the Bangladesh tour any type of bowling was the last thing on my mind. In the previous nine months I'd bowled nearly 900 overs in 17 Tests and 23 one-dayers. It was time to put my feet up and prepare for my life as a married man.

23

The invitation was unbelievable: England's singing superstar Robbie Williams wanted me to play in a charity soccer match he was organising. What a dream opportunity! I'd never met Robbie but was a huge fan of his music. He and his songwriter and producer, Guy Chambers, were two blokes I'd definitely invite over for the ultimate 'If you could have anyone to dinner, who would it be?' party. So, the soccer match was irresistible. Or normally it would have been. However, it overlapped with a much more important occasion for me: 3 June 2006, Liz's and my wedding day.

The morning of the wedding went in a blur, although I do remember ironing shirts with my best man, Adam Rainford, and brothers Shane and Grant, who were my groomsmen. I also recall spending time alone going through my speech at Mum and Dad's new home at Yellow Rock, about 15 minutes' drive from Mount Warrigal, and not far from a farm I'd bought a few years earlier.

The wedding was to be held nearby on Alan Jones's farm at Fitzroy Falls in the NSW southern highlands. When Liz and I first told Alan of our marriage plans, AJ immediately offered his place, and in the weeks leading up to the wedding he organised everything from marquees to floral arrangements. He even managed to tee up a priest to officiate, which was no easy job considering we weren't getting married in a church.

Unfortunately, it was also necessary to have security. In addition to guards, farm manager Shayne Stanton did laps of the property on his quad bike to make sure no photographers or journalists sneaked in. When I drove up to Alan's front gate a number of media were waiting. My cousin Luke who was with me joked he could shield me with a Weet-Bix towel. We laughed, and then I pulled a windscreen visor down, dropped my head, and drove past the pack. At the same time, a police vehicle arrived, and the media was so distracted by it that only one photographer managed to take a grainy shot of me.

It was at that point I realised how much my cricket profile had turned me into public property. I'd always hoped my private life would remain private, but that wasn't to be. It would have been so nice to have been like normal couples and not had a care in the world about who did what. Instead, I entered an area that even had helicopters flying overhead carrying paparazzi with telephoto lenses. AJ had actually tried, without luck, to get the air space protected. When it came time for the wedding ceremony, the weather favoured us. After bursts of sun throughout the day, the clouds dropped in the late afternoon, meaning the choppers couldn't get close enough for a shot.

The location was stunning. One marquee had been set up for the reception and another was placed on AJ's tennis court for the ceremony. It was a relatively small occasion. Shane Watson, and Michael Kasprowicz and his wife, Lindsay, were among the few cricket connections there. Other than them, most of the guests were family and close friends. After the formalities we swung into party mode. AJ arranged some surprise acts: Lee Kernaghan and classical and jazz performer Kane Alexander.

Without getting too carried away, I can only say it was a good, fun night.

The honeymoon was amazing. Again, AJ showed his kindness by contacting his 'pick-and-stick' media mogul mate, James Packer, who invited Liz and me to spend a few days aboard his luxury boat, the *Arctic P*, in Fiji. It was just me, Liz, and 27 staff! However, there was an additional person on the way. Liz was about three months pregnant; the baby was due in November near the start of the Ashes series.

As was the way with my lifestyle, I was soon again into the swing of business and cricket commitments. Although the 2006 winter was meant to give Australia's players a solid couple of months away from the game, we returned to duty sooner than we needed to when John Buchanan organised a five-day military-style boot camp in August. Apparently Buck thought it would be good for team bonding and help us get primed to win back the Ashes. What followed was one of the most exhausting, outrageous, controversial, yet fun things I ever did in the name of Australian cricket.

All 25 CA-contracted players and our support crew met in Brisbane, and after a night of yarn-swapping and catch-ups, we were taken early the next morning by bus to a warehouse on the city's outskirts. When we arrived, a bloke got on board and yelled at us. He said from that moment until the end of the camp, we were only to be known by numbers not names. I think I was '35'. Also, we could only address the bloke yelling at us as 'Sir'. He said he was the co-ordinator and soon introduced us to a handful of his workmates, who were all apparently ex-services men employed by the multi-purpose employment training company BLP.

We got off the bus and had to hand in our watches and mobile phones. We were then led blindfolded into the warehouse where we were divided into groups of either five or six; my group was called 'Foxtrot' and had Adam Gilchrist, Mike Hussey, Michael Clarke and the team's IT specialist, Richard McInnes. All the groups were lined up and had to stay straight-faced and silent while the co-ordinator walked slowly past and inspected us; it was hilarious, like a scene straight out of the movies.

I wondered how Warnie was going to go with it all. He'd never been a fan of Buck, and had protested when our coach first told us about his plans for a boot camp, while we were on the Bangladesh tour. I knew it was going to be really interesting to see how Warnie and some of the other guys would cope outside their comfort zones. I was looking forward to it; when I was a boy I loved going camping and hunting with Dad, so I imagined the boot camp would be an extension of things I'd already experienced and enjoyed doing.

Suddenly the co-ordinator shouted: 'Right, strip to your undies now! Underwear only!'

Although we were meant to keep our eyes to the front I sneaked a look along the line and had to stop myself cracking up when I saw all these fit bodies and then Warnie's 'roof' hanging over his elastic. He took the piss out of himself after we were each given a sleeping bag, a hootchie (a piece of tarpaulin that could be tied between trees to use as shelter), and a backpack that we were told to fill with a couple of pairs of socks, undies, shoes, pants, T-shirts and a rain jacket. Warnie made us all laugh – the players, not the army grunts – when he flashed around some Playboy undies; they were the same ones he'd been filmed wearing only a few weeks earlier when he'd been caught in a British tabloid stitch-up with two women in a hotel room. Warnie's actions relaxed us all; it was obvious he was quite happy to play the rebel during the camp.

He did it again moments later after the guys with health issues were asked to present medication for approval. 'Huss' (Mike Hussey) was allowed to put in his asthma puffer, but when Warnie tried to sneak in some of his treasured packs of Benson & Hedges and a lighter, the co-ordinator wasn't impressed. Warnie told him: 'Mate, if you don't grant me these, I'm walking out now and quitting cricket!' Of course he wasn't serious, but he got his way and he surely remains the only elite sportsperson in history who's had cigarettes medically approved! He wasn't the only one to stretch the rules; when no-one was looking I sneaked some bike pants into my pack because I thought they'd stop me chafing during what I expected to be some long days of exercise.

We were then bundled into mini-vans and driven for an hour or so. I wasn't sure if our spirits were high, or whether we were trying to stay upbeat to hide our fears of what was going to happen. There were plenty of comments flying around like: 'Boys, we're going to get smashed here'; 'We're going to get nailed'; 'We're cooked'; 'We've got five days of this shit!'

We eventually drove off a main highway and pushed through some bush before we reached a clearing in a plantation-like area where more BLP grunts were waiting. As soon as we got out of the vehicles, one of them yelled: 'Righto, 50 push-ups on your knuckles, now!' As we were doing them I heard a few whispers: 'Who does this prick think he is?' It didn't help that there were pieces of broken glass on the road near where I did mine. Although it was winter, the day was hot and humid. Many of us were already sweating in drill pants, boots, and T-shirts with our respective numbers. It was dreadful.

We copped a lot of push-ups during our first exercise when each group had to carry a 20-litre jerry can up a hill. Each group had to fan out in a straight line and stay 10 steps behind the nearest group both in front and behind them. If the lines or distances were broken, we'd hear the yell: 'Right, 20 push-ups!' We did these wearing backpacks that must have weighed 12 or more kilos. After that we had a small map exercise, and then we had to push a car along a track for about an hour, or roughly eight kilometres. There were other activities throughout the day, but there's no need to go into them all; I'm sure you get the idea.

It was just after dark when we finally rested and had some food; I think each group was given two cold cans of Chunky soup, five slices of bread, and we were allowed to fill our water bladders from the jerry can we'd carried all day. Some of the guys were really hurting; they were chafed and walking around lifting their balls! I was really thankful I had my bike pants.

That night, we didn't have long to recharge the batteries before we went out on a bush navigation exercise. Afterwards, the groups were put in different sleeping locations. Warnie's mob was near to Foxtrot, and as we tried to settle down I heard our great leg spinner complaining about the mosquitoes: 'Bloody hell, it's like Formula One!' There was a fair bit of whingeing coming from all the groups: 'What are we doing this shit for?'; 'My legs are cooked!'; 'How is this going to help me get runs?' I sat back laughing and loving it.

We had to camp under the stars. I got into my sleeping bag nude and tried to get some rest. I reckon I'd only been asleep for about 10 minutes when I was woken by a massive BOOM! It was a stun grenade being let off, the loudest thing I'd ever heard. One of the grunts yelled out: 'We're getting attacked! Everyone up! You've got two minutes.'

It was pitch black. There I was, starkers and struggling, until Gilly helped me get some of my gear that I'd left on a tree to dry. Lots of swearing went on around us. Everyone was buggered. We then had to walk another six or seven kilometres before we were allowed to sleep on a fire trail for the rest of what turned out to be a chilly night.

Just before dawn I woke up and felt warm and snug in my sleeping bag, complete with a hood over my head. I looked over at Warnie and was surprised to see he hadn't zipped up the bottom of his bag, leaving his lower legs and feet lying in dew. His socks were soaked, and he was shaking. But what took most of my attention was the red light that came and went each time he sucked back on his 'medication'. He told me afterwards he'd smoked to try to keep himself warm.

We did similar exercises for the next few days, including some dangerous climbs up mountain faces and hikes along steep ridges. We also had a bit of fun with some paintball games. On the last day we had boxing rounds against a mountain of a bloke who was some sort of kick-boxing or cage-fighting champion. He was amazing; he took on 18 of us one at a time in the morning, and another 18 after lunch. The first minute-and-a-half of each bout was a wrestle, before it was an open slug-fest for 30 seconds. We all wore boxing gloves and headgear. Some of the guys really did well; Andrew Symonds actually got a good clean hit away, but he was drilled back quick smart.

I was one of the last to go in, and after analysing all my teammates' approaches, I decided I'd be a bit cagey. I reckoned the wrestling was used to tire each player out so he'd have little energy left to throw any good punches. So my plan was to pretend I was going hard during the wrestle by grunting and screwing up my face, and then I'd go in for the kill with the boxing. At first it worked because I landed a quick one on the Mountain's chin, but that didn't turn out to be a good thing to do, because in a heartbeat I had four or five punches laid into my stomach.

'You've been resting, you've been cheating!' shouted the Mountain.

After that, I got pummelled.

At least I wasn't our media manager, Philip Pope. The poor bloke had had a tough few days, but he wanted to finish on a high, so he went in swinging right from the start of his fight. Popey was built like a wine glass, and even if he'd connected with a punch there wouldn't have been much force behind it. But he only threw haymakers. The Mountain just watched and weaved, and then went *tap*, *tap*, *tap*, *bang*, *bang*, and Popey went arse over.

We were all relieved when the camp finished. I thought the whole experience had been great for team bonding, working together, solving problems and overcoming fears. I loved the challenges and sense of adventure. It certainly wasn't for everyone, especially Stuart MacGill, who twisted his knee on the first night and reckons the injury affected him for the rest of his career. By the time we'd had a few beers back at our training base at Coolum, I got the feeling most of the guys saw some advantages in doing the camp, but I doubt if many would be in a hurry to ever put themselves through it again.

A month later we returned to the cricket roundabout with victory in a one-day tournament against India and the West Indies in Pakistan. I took 12 wickets in three matches and was named Player of the Series. It followed my selection in the one-day Team of the Year at the ICC annual awards. Again it was a nice honour, but one I wouldn't crack open a Champagne bottle for.

We continued in the one-day mode for the Champions Trophy in India. That tour opened up an exciting opportunity for me away from cricket. On a previous trip to India – I think in 2004 – I was interviewed by popular television host

Simi Garewal on her program *Rendezvous*. I sang a few songs, including 'Muqabla', the tune I'd first heard in the tuk-tuk way back on the 1994 academy tour. Afterwards, Neil Maxwell was approached by some representatives of recording companies who were keen to produce something with me for the local market. I thought nothing more about it until I met with another recording company representative, Shamir Tandon, in Mumbai before the Champions Trophy.

Shamir revealed he was working on a compilation with Asha Bhosle, one of the most famous Indian singers in history. She was in her 70s and had sung thousands of songs for Bollywood movies, and had countless albums. She was the Aretha Franklin of Indian music. Shamir said the compilation would involve a number of high-profile musicians and Bollywood actors. He rattled through a list of names, and my ears pricked up as soon as I heard one of them: Robbie Williams.

'If Robbie's in, I'm in!' I said straight away.

Before we could take the proposal any further, I had to prove I could sing; I passed the test by doing a couple of songs in a room that had been booked in the team hotel. Shamir seemed happy with the result. I was told a song for the compilation would be chosen for me, then I'd learn it, and get together with Asha at some point during the Champions Trophy for the recording. I couldn't believe it was happening; what a tremendous opportunity to work with an absolute legend. There was only one thing I wanted to change.

'Is is possible to write my own song?' I asked.

Shamir said 'yes', so straight after the meeting I went to my room and worked on an idea that I already had. I wrote the entire song in half an hour. It was a cheesy piece called 'You're the One for Me', which was about a guy trying to catch the attention of a pretty girl; nothing unusual there! I wanted the song to be a sing-off between languages, with me doing English and Asha Hindi, until the very last part of the song when we'd reverse roles. I rang up Shamir, read him out the lyrics, and played a few chords. Again he was happy. In part, the lyrics were:

Can you tell a girl you don't know that
You're the one for me
Do you walk right up or play it cool
Or simply let her be

I know I'm different, I'm not from here
I am just another guy
With blond hair, though, it's hard to hide
I think I caught your eye

My attention then shifted to cricket. We beat the West Indies, England and India, which qualified us for a semifinal against New Zealand in Mohali. A day or two before that game I went to a studio in Chandigarh, near Mohali, put down a guitar track and a guide vocal, then hurried to team training before going back to the studio to put down the main vocal. All the bits and pieces were then 'flown' via email to a studio in Mumbai where Asha did her vocals the following day.

Then the pressure was on because the only window to do the film clip with Asha was in Mumbai where the final of the Champions Trophy was to be played. That meant I had extra incentive to help Australia beat New Zealand. We won by 34 runs and I took 2-31 off eight overs. So, luckily, everything went according to plan.

The final against the West Indies was three days later, but before then I squeezed in a four-hour shoot with Asha. She was a lovely gentle woman with a wonderful sense of humour. The clip was primarily set in an office. The concept was that I was lovestruck and had to make advances to a really hot-looking girl; to add a comical twist, I also day-dreamed about her only to find a much older woman, Asha, standing in front of me. If you want to have a laugh you'll find the clip on YouTube. Although I didn't have much of an idea about what I was doing, I had great fun. I didn't tell any of my teammates what I was up to; when I went for the shoot I told them I was going for a look through the streets.

After the shoot it was back to cricket mode. We beat the Windies in a rain-shortened match to claim the Champions Trophy for the first time. It wasn't the only success of the tour; 'You're the One for Me' went on to become a number-one hit in India after making its chart debut at six. It also did well in South Africa. Four months after that whirlwind recording experience, I caught up with Asha when she visited Sydney to perform at the Opera House. She gave me her compilation album with a personal signed message. It will always be one of my treasures.

At the time of my recording experience I'd already discovered I felt more comfortable writing material than recording it. To me, songs are poems. Some of the things I've written about over the years have come from personal experiences, while other songs have been made up or have been a mixture of fact and fiction. Above all, my entire musical journey has taught me that music has no boundaries. In sport there are always rules in place: you can't step over the front line; you can't be out LBW if hit outside the line of leg stump; you have to restrict the number of bouncers, and so on. But in music, you can do whatever you want. Unlike the constraints of cricket, where administrators may frown at individuals who don't conform, such as Andrew Symonds, music allows people to express themselves. It's freedom.

The best example of the boundaries I faced while playing for Australia was just before the first Ashes Test, which was to begin at the Gabba on 23 November 2006. Give or take a day, that coincided with the anticipated birth of Liz's and my baby. Although we already knew it was a boy, we kept this quiet from the public. About a month earlier interest started building in the media about what my priorities were. If the birth and Test did happen to clash, what event would I miss? I said I could definitely do both.

Liz and I had already decided she'd be induced about a week before the Test if the baby hadn't come by then. If that hadn't been possible, I would have missed the Test, but I didn't reveal that decision to anyone. Regardless of the realities, after a chat I'd had with John Buchanan several months earlier I was comfortable I'd be given some flexibility by team management. When I told Buck of the prospective clash, he'd said: 'Whatever you need to do, we'll work around you because we need you there for the first Test. Even if that means flying you up the afternoon of the day before the match, we'll grant that.' I walked away feeling relieved and comfortable that everything had been ticked off well in advance.

As it turned out, Preston Charles Lee didn't want to muck up the old man's schedule and was born at 3.28 am, Thursday 16 November at Sydney's North Shore Private Hospital. Soon afterwards, I sent a group text announcing the great news that both mum and bub were doing well. Later that day Buck texted back his congratulations. I then received another text from him – I'm not sure how long after the first one – saying that we needed to speak.

I think Buck's call came through in the late afternoon – he congratulated me again and then said I had to link up with the team on Saturday night, which was four days before the Test would begin on the following Thursday. I adamantly said that wasn't possible, because I wanted to take Preston and Liz home on the Monday. I told Buck I'd fly to Brisbane straight after that, but he knocked back the idea. That made me angry.

'When's the first training session?' I asked him.

'Monday.'

'Well, why do you need me there before that?'

'I want to get everyone settled into camp on the Saturday. Then we'll have a team walk on Sunday and a meeting at night. Everyone has to be there.'

I asked again if I could have leave until the Monday and reminded Buck of our conversation months earlier. But he wouldn't change his mind, saying: 'We need you Saturday night. This is the start of a big series. We need you as part of the team.'

I couldn't believe what I'd heard. Buck had turned on what he'd initially said. I was in the hospital at the time and told him firmly that I wasn't going to leave Liz and Preston to get home by themselves while I went for a walk and a chat with my teammates. I put my foot down and said I'd be there for the first training session, but not a moment before it.

We argued, but neither of us would budge, so I hung up. I got off the phone and said to myself: 'This is bullshit!' I was really stressed. There and then, I contemplated throwing everything in. Stuff playing Tests, stuff the one-dayers, stuff Cricket Australia, and stuff Buchanan; family came first, end of story.

About five minutes later, Buck rang again and asked me if I'd changed my mind about the Saturday night. I said I hadn't.

We hung up again. He then rang about an hour later and said at the top of the conversation: 'Look, I suppose we can have the team meeting on Monday night.' I'd won; rightfully so, I believe.

After that episode, Buck lost my support. Right at the start of my career we'd got on, but the more time passed, the more I didn't agree with many of his analytical methods. I'm sure he over-complicated things. At one stage every player had to do a multiple-choice questionnaire that determined different personality types. These were: mossie, thinker, enforcer and feeler. I was classed as a mossie, which meant I acted on instinct and buzzed around going from one activity to another without serious planning.

For example, if I went to the shops I wouldn't take a list with me; instead, I'd determine what I needed on the run. Whereas a thinker, such as Mike Hussey, would work out everything he needed and write a list before he left home. Of the others, an enforcer was more of a leader who had good communication skills and got on well with people, while a feeler was someone whose behaviour could be heavily influenced by wondering what others thought about him. It was possible for every person to have a blend of personality types that could be more or less prominent depending on the situation.

Buck got the results of all these tests to find out what we were like, and yet he still treated everyone the same. That didn't make sense to me; it should have been a case of 'different strokes for different folks'. In other words, I didn't think he knew how to best tap into each individual. His rigid approach didn't work with me. There were times when we'd have conversations like the following at the start of a training session:

Buck: 'You have to bowl 48 balls today.'
Me: 'I don't feel like bowling that many today.'

303

Buck: 'Well, you have to.'

Me: 'Well, I can't. My body is too sore and I need more time to recover.'

Then we'd have a blow-up. As time went on, these got worse. I eventually got to the stage where I did my own thing, which I reckon really annoyed him because he lost some control. He governed by the clipboard, and we had way too many meetings. Alan Jones best summed up my attitude one day when he said: 'Winners have parties and losers have meetings.'

The fact that Buck and I didn't get on in my final few years under him was as much a reflection on me as it was on him. Maybe I should have bent more. I don't know. We were just different people who didn't gel. Did he help my bowling? Not one little bit. Did he help my batting? He did at the start of my career.

When I became frustrated with him I spoke to other players who said he was just trying to get the best out of me. However, in doing so, his approach worked the opposite way and made me go into my shell around him. He probably got the worst out of me in many ways. But even though I didn't agree with his methods, he was great for some people, like Huss, Steve Waugh and Justin Langer. However, for guys who needed more slack, like me and Andrew Symonds, it was very difficult. We didn't need to be that structured or caged up, but unfortunately Buck was 'my way or the highway'. Also, I thought he was a great family man, which made his treatment of me during Preston's birth all the more disappointing. He let me down when I needed his support the most. But I accept he was under a lot of pressure leading into a very important series.

Despite the conflict with my coach, nothing could take away the ecstasy I felt when Preston was born. When Liz told me she was pregnant I was so excited. I'd always wanted five children, so this was the first of the batch! I knew it was meant to happen and at no stage over the months before the birth did I ask myself: 'What have I got myself in for?' It was a weird feeling knowing that we were going to have a little person in our lives, a person who'd change our lives. I knew I was ready for it, and when Preston arrived, I didn't think it could have happened at a better time.

The whole birth process was surreal. After watching Liz's stomach grow, and seeing all the changes that came with it, I still didn't feel it was going to happen until Liz told me: 'We'd better get to hospital.' As we drove away from home I kept thinking: 'This is it. This is real. This is actually happening!'

There was a mix of anxiety and excitement in the hours that followed. During Liz's labour it was impossible not to want the process to be over as quickly as possible so we could meet our 'little man'.

And then it happened. What can I say? When you're with a partner you grow to love them, but with a child it's instant love. From the moment I first saw Preston I knew I'd do anything for him and be there to protect him. I'm sure most parents feel that way. The first time I held him I smothered him with kisses. The birth was the best moment of my life . . . ever. All the staff at the hospital, headed by the CEO, Greg Brown, were fantastic, and I thank them publicly now. You guys did an amazing job.

When I drove Liz and Preston home, I don't think I've ever been slower behind the wheel of a car. I'd liken it to having hundreds of eggs on the back seat, and trying to be careful enough not to crack one. I felt every single bump. I was 'Mr Overcautious'. That trip home was the start of a journey that would definitely change me for the better. When a child is born, it's important to realise parents are also 'born'. Although

I didn't want to go, hours later I was on a plane to Brisbane to link up with the Australian team. A few days after that, Andrew Flintoff played and missed a ball against me in the first Test. At the end of the over he tapped the wicket and thanked me.

'What for?' I asked.

'It's nice of you to name your first son after the place where I was born, but it's going to be bloody hard to call my next son Wollongong,' Freddie replied.

It was the wrong time to tell him I'd first heard the name, Preston, when introduced to my host on a barramundi fishing trip in Darwin a few months earlier. I liked the name straight away. It was strong and manly. Liz agreed. I didn't know when I'd get around to telling Freddie the story. At that time I had a one-week-old son, and in the years ahead I wanted to be able to tell him how Australia won back the Ashes in 2006–07.

24

The day before Preston was born I had to shoot a television commercial for 3mobile. The ad went like this: I was reading messages on my phone while standing on a balcony several storeys up in a block of flats. I then accidentally dropped the phone over the edge, and in a sudden state of panic I sprinted to the nearest elevator only to find it was taking too long to arrive, so I bolted down the stairs and caught the phone before it smashed into pieces. The end caption was: Brett Lee, paceman.

The final product came together well, although those TV tragics who looked closely enough would have realised that I was replaced with a 'double' for the running scene; just a week out from the first Test in Brisbane, Cricket Australia and I didn't want to take any risks with me getting an injury. I hoped that commercial would be the only time all summer that a replacement was called for me.

I doubt I'd ever been in a home series with more hype and build-up than the 2006–07 Ashes. It didn't sit right with any Australian player or fan that England held the famous urn, and it seemed even less conceivable that the Poms could retain the trophy by winning on Aussie soil. Such had been Australia's dominance in the modern era that I was only 10 years old when the Poms last won a series down under in 1986–87. Like my teammates, I didn't want to be in a side that couldn't extend that run, and in doing so, be sledged for dropping the bundle two series in a row.

As a result, there was a lot of tension around the squad in the days leading up to the Gabba Test. Everyone was confident, especially Ricky Ponting. One of Punter's strengths as a captain was his ability to charge everyone up and have them ready to go. His basic message was: 'We've done the work. We know we're good enough. We know what we have to do. So, let's go and do it and thrash these blokes.' I reckon the series had become personal for Punter because of what happened in 2005; being the Aussie captain to give back the Ashes didn't go over well with such a competitive person.

Apart from the obvious discussions about plans for each batsman and bowler, Punter made one surprising tactical demand: on the field we weren't to call any of the English players by their nicknames. After the 2005 series, criticism had come from various sections of the media and ex-players that Australia had been too friendly with the Poms and that that may have affected our performances.

I still disagree and use my friendship with Andrew Flintoff as an example. Our relationship off the field was formed because of how hard we played on the field. Even though he had become a mate – or perhaps because he was a mate – I wanted to beat him every time I came up against him, and I know he thought the same way. Freddie summed it up well at a benefit dinner for him in Sydney during a match England played against NSW at the SCG in the build-up to the first Test. I was the only Australian player to go to the function, and as a way of acknowledging that, he told the room:

'It's funny how Brett and I have been sitting next to each other and having a chat over a good steak and wine, but tomorrow he'll be trying to knock my bloody head off.'

Freddie wasn't the only one to have a sense of humour about our rivalry. Some Aussie fans created a stir with the Barmy Army by penning words for the first Test to be sung to the tune of Queen's 'Bohemian Rhapsody'. One of the lines was: 'Brett Lee just killed a man, bowled a ball around his head, hit his temple, now he's dead.' The batsman was, of course, Freddie. I'm sure he didn't mind. It was all meant in good fun.

Just like Ricky, there was a lot of pressure on Freddie. He was named captain after regular skipper Michael Vaughan had been ruled out because of ongoing knee problems. Although Freddie would never have wanted to let England down, he gave me the impression he was a bit reluctant to be in charge. Considering the hopes of England's fans that Freddie would pick up the way he left off in 2005, the added weight of captaincy must have been monumental.

Meanwhile, I had my own pressures to take care of: the pressures of distraction. The day before the Test series began, Liz flew up with Preston so we could all be together. I could sit here now and say my mind was 100 per cent focused on cricket, but I wouldn't be telling the truth. I just wanted to spend as much time as I could with the little guy. As opposed to previous series, I was learning how to strike the balance between responsibilities to my family and my cricket team. I didn't discuss this with anyone; it was something I knew I'd work out as time went along.

The first Test was a strange match. After all the excitement of the build-up, the game was a fizzer. Perhaps the omen came when Steve Harmison bowled the very first ball straight to

Freddie at second slip. A hundred and fifty-five overs later, Australia declared at 9-602, led by Punter's epic 196. I took first points in my 'mini-battle' with Freddie when I *drilled* him for four after I ducked a bouncer but left my bat up like a periscope. The ball hit the bat's toe and looped over the keeper's head on the way to the boundary. I smiled, but Freddie wasn't impressed. I finished 43 not out. Freddie was also my first wicket of the series when he edged a ball to Adam Gilchrist. My scalps were rare: I took only one in each innings, Kevin Pietersen being the other on a surface I struggled to gain good footing on.

After our first innings England were never in the game. Justin Langer got a second innings century, Glenn McGrath, Stuey Clark and Warnie all took bags, and we were off and running with a good win. Afterwards I had a chat with Freddie about the coincidence of my son sharing the same name as his birthplace. Months later, I received a gift from him in the mail: a 00 size blue, yellow and white uniform of his home-town football club, Preston North End.

After my small return in Brisbane, it was reported in the media that I was no certain starter for the second Test in Adelaide. There was a push to include Stuart MacGill as a second spinner and Shane Watson as an all-rounder who could act as a third seamer. With Pidgey and Stuey Clark in form, I would have been the obvious casualty. However, Watto failed a fitness test on a hamstring injury and Australia went in with an unchanged team.

In contrast to the Gabba Test, Adelaide produced one of the most ridiculous games I've ever played in. How could a team score six declared for 551 in the first innings and still lose? Well, that's what England did. They won the toss on a very flat deck and batted and batted and batted. Paul Collingwood scored a double century, and Kevin Pietersen belted 158. Stuey Clark was the only bowler who got any sort of success with a 3-for.

I got 1-139 off 34 overs. If that wasn't bad enough I was also fined $3125, a quarter of my match fee, for excessive appealing. The incident happened early on the second day after I was convinced I had Pietersen caught behind. I did the wrong thing to begin with by running towards the slips before turning to appeal. When I did turn, I saw that umpire Steve Bucknor had a blank look on his face. To give this some perspective it's important to know each umpire has his own distinct way of giving a batsman out. For Rudi Koertzen it was the really slowly drawn finger, for Billy Bowden it's a crooked finger, and for Steve Bucknor it was generally a nod of the head followed by a casual raised finger. By the time I looked at Steve, I assumed he hadn't yet made his decision, so I appealed and kept on appealing. I didn't know he'd already shaken his head. Because of my actions he was forced to shake his head again.

It wouldn't have looked good, and I wore my punishment without complaint. But I do believe I was innocent; I'd made a mistake, not broken a law. In my defence here's a hypothetical. Put the average Joe Public on the field in hot weather and ask him to bowl his fastest. He's under stress to begin with because he's playing for his country. Then let's add the crowd, the emotion, and the self-induced pressure that comes when he tries so hard for a vital breakthrough. Then finally he thinks he gets it. So he's happy. But then the umpire deflates him. How does he react? I reckon under such circumstances a fair few Joe Publics wouldn't be Mr Perfects, or Mrs Perfects for that matter. Why can't they show some emotion and colour? Why can't they kick the ground to express their disappointment? I know we have to respect officialdom, but we also have to respect the fact we need to show our personalities. It would be very boring if we all walked back past the umpire and said: 'Sorry for the appeal, thank you very much for considering it.' I acknowledge there were times when I crossed the line, such as my send-off of Shane Bond at the WACA, but let's be realistic *and* reasonable.

The incident highlighted something I just didn't – and still don't – get in cricket. Australia's players are constantly told by Cricket Australia's General Manager, Michael Brown, that television images of anyone 'having a word' to a batsman, over-appealing, or venting frustration with a decision, don't send the right messages to the public. However, a viewer can flick the channel and see some footy or boxing where blokes are belting the crap out of each other all in the name of sport. And yet cricketers get criticised for over-appealing! There were times I knew full well that the cameras were on me, so I would purposely say something to the batsman or glare at him. Why? It was the performer in me. I thought it helped make good TV, a good show.

Perhaps if administrators want colour and emotion out of the game, they could include umpires in their directives to get everyone to behave the same way. Imagine if we didn't have Rudi Koertzen's slow finger or David Shepherd's superstitious jumps on 111 or Billy Bowden's exaggerated signals for six.

Now, back to the Adelaide Test. Another ton by Punter and one to Michael Clarke helped us to 513 and within reach of the Poms. Matthew Hoggard finished with 7-for, a gutsy display on such a batting-friendly wicket. By stumps on day four England were 1-59. Even the most one-eyed of supporters would have expected a draw.

But on day five, the ridiculous happened. When we got to the ground Warnie was as amped-up as I'd ever seen him. He was making sure everyone knew we could win the game. Buck also thought we could do it, and told us all we needed were some early breakthroughs to make England's players doubt themselves.

Warnie and Stuey Clark opened up, and England played right into our hands by being ultra-defensive; it was obvious that a draw was the only thing on their minds. Because of this, Australia's players kept the chat up, making sure Andrew Strauss and Ian Bell heard. We kept saying things like: 'Come on, boys. We can win this. England doesn't want it.' With Stuey keeping it tight, Warnie took the rock-star role as only he could. In a three-over spell he got Strauss, helped run out Bell, and bowled Pietersen with a huge turner round his legs. Punter then brought me on, and I have my brother Shane to thank for what followed.

After the disappointments of my first innings bowling, I rang Shane to see if he'd noticed anything I was doing wrong. He was always a great mentor and motivator for me; at times throughout various series I received texts from him offering advice. Shane knew my bowling as well as anyone, plus he had a great cricket mind; whatever he said, I listened to. Assessing my first innings efforts Shane thought I'd used the 'hero ball' too often. That is, the old ball that swung in, which generally happened with my action. He thought it was too predictable. He told me not to forget about the ball that went away; if I could get a few to hold their line by holding the ball across the seam, I was going to create more uncertainty.

Shane's advice was in my thoughts when I began a spell against Freddie. The ball was 30-odd overs old, the right time for it to reverse swing at the Adelaide Oval. My tactic right from the start was to work 'spit-rock' inswingers at a knee-roll length to try to bring LBW into play. If I bowled yorkers, they could be seen out of the hand a fraction earlier, but if I hit the track back a couple of metres, balls skidding in with my trajectory could be harder to play on a fifth-day pitch. I did that for much of my first two overs, until with the final ball of my second I went for an away swinger. Seconds later I was hugging Gilly; Freddie had followed the ball and nicked it. The wicket was exactly how I pictured it would happen. I later got Geraint Jones out when he sliced a ball to Matthew Hayden in the gully. Pidgey came back to help Warnie clean up the tail and England were rolled for 129. I finished with 2-35 off 18 overs. The stats would suggest a solid performance, but it was much more than that to me; that last-day spell was one of my best-ever efforts with the old ball.

Our target was 168 in 36 overs. Not an easy get on a last-day pitch, but Punter and Michael Hussey batted superbly to ensure the win. Huss top-scored with 61 and fittingly hit the winning runs, but that moment wasn't the one that left an impression on me. The telling one belonged to Damien Martyn, one of the most extraordinarily gifted players I've ever seen. Marto had been going through a tough period, and there were whisperings in the team that he was contemplating retiring at the end of the season. After he backed away off Freddie in the second innings, played a loose cut and got caught, I immediately thought: 'Nah, he's had enough, he's going to walk away from Test cricket right here.' And that's what happened. After a big night of celebrations we all went back to our respective states before linking up for the third Test in Perth. Marto, however, went missing, and it soon hit the media that he'd retired. I admired what he did; why bother hanging on if he wasn't enjoying himself? I hoped I'd also know when the time was right to give the game away.

In what was an anti-climax for the series we reclaimed the Ashes before Christmas when we won the third Test by 206 runs in Perth; all the bowlers contributed, especially Warnie with 4-for in England's second dig. Every Aussie bowler was lucky he wasn't on the other side in this match. In our second innings Gilly went berserk, scoring a century off only 58 balls. What more can I say other than, he was a freak!

After the game, the Australian team sat on the floor of our dressing room with our feet up on our bags. It was early afternoon on the final day, and there was a lot of relief that the Ashes were back in our hands. I can't recall much about that night's celebrations, apart from going to The Deen pub with former England and West Australian bowler Alan Mullally. The place was packed full of Poms when we arrived, and Alan asked me if I was sure I wanted to go in. I didn't mind at all.

I was invited up on stage by the band that was playing, and all I could say to the crowd who were razzing me was: 'Unlucky, guys, but it was a good game. Now let's forget about that and play some music.' They cheered, and with the help of a beer or 10 everyone was rocking. I played a few songs on bass – 'Brown Eyed Girl' and 'Sweet Home Alabama' come to mind – then I got down and chatted with some of the crowd. In elite sport it's often difficult for players to spend the time they should with the fans who support them; this was a rare occasion when we could. I hope players continue to do that forever and a day.

In the lead-up to the Boxing Day Test, Australian *and* world cricket were on the brink of a telling change because Glenn McGrath and Shane Warne announced they'd retire at the end of the series. Their announcements were added incentives for the team to complete a 5–0 whitewash and give two legends the send-offs they deserved. Personally, I also wanted to show I was ready for life after McGrath and Warne. Although I'd headed the attack without them at various times, their retirements were confirmation I simply *had* to perform from that moment on. Punter said as much in a pre-match presser when he stated that

I 'might have to stand up a bit more as a real strike, wicket-taking option'.

My returns to that point of the series had been lean: eight wickets at 58. But I wasn't worried. Apart from a couple of spells, I didn't think I'd bowled anywhere near as badly as the stats implied. In some ways, the series began again for me in Melbourne because of the added responsibility that waited just around the corner.

There are few moments in cricket that match bowling the first ball of the Boxing Day Test. The nerves, excitement and anticipation are all wrapped up in the crowd's roar when the bowler charges in for the first time. Coming in from the Southern Stand end, I was given the new rock. The buzz was magnified by the honour of knowing my partner in crime at the other end was Pidgey McGrath. When he walked up from fine leg and gave his cap to the umpire, I heard one of the loudest cheers I ever have on a cricket field; it was beaten later by the only possible bloke who could have done it. When Warnie took his 700th Test wicket, bowling Andrew Strauss, I could have sworn the whole stadium was going to lift off.

The occasion gave me goose bumps; 80 or so thousand people, both English and Australian supporters, cheering for two of cricket's all-time superstars. I was rapt to get an early wicket when Alastair Cook edged a ball to Gilly. Throughout the innings I bowled much better, taking 2-36, but the undoubted hero – surprise, surprise – was Warnie. With his soap-opera lifestyle he always knew how to pick his moment; he took 5-39 and the Poms were rolled for 159. The match was already ours for the taking.

Australia had to face about a dozen overs before stumps. Pleased with my bowling I was content to put my feet up and relax, but all that changed when Punter said: 'Put the pads on.' I was to be nightwatchman. Justin Langer and Matthew Hayden got away to a flier and looked to be handling things so comfortably that my hopes grew that I wouldn't be needed; but in the 10th over JL fell to Freddie and I was soon out in the middle taking guard. One ball later I was trudging off after I edged a jaffa straight to the keeper, Chris Read. You have no idea how big the MCG is until you have to walk off it with a golden duck next to your name!

That night I got a number of texts from friends who wrote: 'Stiff ball to get first up!' I was in good company because Punter, Huss and Michael Clarke all went cheaply the next day before Haydos and Andrew Symonds scored centuries to give us a 260-run lead. Pidgey, Warnie, Stuey Clark and I then shared England's second-innings wickets around and we won by an innings and plenty. I took 4-47 and along the way had a lot of fun with the Barmy Army, who didn't mind throwing the old 'You're a chucker' line at me. Perhaps in another frame of mind I might have become annoyed, but with wickets to my name and Australia on fire, it was a case of 'sticks and stones'.

On the eve of the fifth Test in Sydney, Australia was given yet another reason to win when Justin Langer announced he'd be playing his last game. We thrashed England again to finish with the desired 5–0 result. I finished with three wickets in each innings, but the dismissal that meant most to me was when Jimmy Anderson hit a simple catch to Huss at midwicket to end England's second dig. The bowler was Pidgey; how fantastic and fitting that he'd taken a wicket, his 563rd, with his final ball in Test cricket.

In the laps of honour that followed the match, Symo and I put Pidgey on our shoulders. All the photos showed me smiling, but in the dressing room afterwards I felt sad because we'd lost members of a family. Apart from Pidgey being my bowling partner, he was a good mate. It goes without saying that he, Warnie and JL represented an incredibly successful era of Australian cricket. Their influence was much greater than runs, wickets, catches and wins.

They all had different personalities that helped make the Australian cricket team such a colourful and enjoyable mix of characters. Pidgey was so often the court jester or serial pest, JL was the tough-as-nails competitor who inspired everyone to fight, and Warnie was just Warnie. With their retirements, Australian cricket not only lost great players but great individuals. On the heels of Marto's sudden exit, the signs were there that while Australian cricket wasn't necessarily breaking apart, it was facing some tremendous challenges if it was to be as successful in the future.

While reflecting in the dressing room, I felt slightly daunted about what lay ahead. That didn't stop me being involved in some raucous celebrations. If my memory serves me correctly, Prime Minister John Howard came into the room after the match and swigged some beer that had been poured into a trophy. I went for a long scull after him. Yet again, being an Australian cricketer made me feel very privileged.

25

In the lead-up to the 2006–07 Ashes, up-and-coming fast bowler Mitchell Johnson said in an interview that he considered me one of his mentors. It was a role I cherished; I was happy to pass along what I'd learnt for myself and also the lessons taught to me by others I'd played with along the way. Pidgey, Bich, Flem, Dizzy, Kasper and all the other members of the Fast Bowlers' Cartel shared a bond to help each other out. We were teammates *and* mates. Any advice wasn't only cricket related, but there were life tips as well, such as how to deal with increased public scrutiny and so-called celebrity status. The most important thing I believe I told Mitch was cricket focused; I said there'd come a point in his career, as had happened to me, when he'd realise he couldn't bowl every single ball flat out. My turning point came at about the time of my conversation with Mark Taylor before the 2005–06 season. I told Mitch that the day I realised I could still bowl extremely fast at 90 per cent effort but preserve my body better was the day I knew I really could have a long career in the game.

Australia suffered a post-Ashes hiccup when England beat us in the finals of the one-day tri-series with New Zealand in February. My own form had been solid, and I had no reason to believe I couldn't maintain – if not improve – my returns at the World Cup in the West Indies, beginning in March. As part of Australia's preparation we went to New Zealand to play the Chappell–Hadlee series over three matches. The day before the opener we had a fielding session at Wellington's Basin Reserve. The ground was quite wet and I was 'iffy' about taking part. As a precaution I wore my bowling boots that had longer spikes for extra grip; I usually did fielding drills with shorter spikes. It was a disastrous decision that would put me out of the World Cup.

It all happened so quickly. When I attacked the ball in a simple drill, my spikes caught in the turf and my left foot twisted one way, my knee went the other, and I felt my ankle snap. I immediately thought I'd broken it. I was in agony on the ground for about 10 minutes. The next day I was back knocking on the door of Kim Slater's consulting room in Sydney.

I'd ruptured two-and-a-half ligaments. Initially I hoped I'd make a quick recovery, but that wasn't realistic. So that hope surrendered to disappointment and anger. There was no way we should have been training on the ground that day; it wasn't up to standard. But what could I do? It was no use complaining. It was best to look to the future.

The injury didn't need surgery, but after further consultation with Kim, Australian physio Alex Kountouris and team doctor Trefor James, it was decided I'd go under the knife for the regulation clean-out of floating bone in my ankle. I turned the situation around by convincing myself the injury had its upside, because with a sensible recuperation I could prolong my career.

Australia went on to win the World Cup, although I couldn't bring myself to watch one single ball of the tournament. Instead, I went to India with Neil Maxwell for business meetings, including discussing offers to act in Bollywood. Over the years various movie agents had offered me a number of roles, some of which were hilarious. In one I was asked to play a James Bond type character, but after looking at the script that had me jumping out of buildings and playing the real action man, it only took me a second to realise the part wasn't quite me.

There was also a Bollywood head honcho in charge of about 30 big-budget productions a year who offered me a part and said we could start filming the very next day. I asked him: 'But don't you want to know if I have any acting experience?' He brushed that off as a minor detail. We didn't go any further with negotiations after he said he needed me for 60 days, which just wasn't possible with my cricket commitments. Finding time was generally the main problem with saying yes to any offer. However, thinking long term (after my cricket career had finished), Maxi and I wanted to find out more about the industry, so we thought a meet and greet was a good idea.

Around the time of my recuperation, I also went to Las Vegas with Alan Jones. Preston, Liz and Liz's mum, Eugenie, also came. AJ always had a habit of surprising me with amazing experiences. On one occasion back in Sydney, he invited me to his home to meet English singer Russell Watson, who's known as 'The People's Tenor'. After I played a few contemporary tunes on the guitar which Russell sang along to, he suggested we go to the Opera House where he was to perform the following night. Within a few minutes, there was AJ saying to Opera House security: 'Look, we've got the world's fastest bowler and a world-famous singer here. We'd like to go inside, please.' We were allowed into the concert hall, and for the following 45 minutes, Russell and his piano player, who stayed at Russell's request after a rehearsal, gave AJ and me a very personal performance covering everything from classical to Elvis Presley. There was no-one else there.

AJ loved big performers, so it wasn't surprising when he said he wanted to go and see the master illusionist David Copperfield when we were in Vegas. Liz wasn't keen, so she stayed in our hotel looking after Preston, while her mum went with AJ and me. Not long after the show began, Copperfield threw out Frisbees into the crowd. AJ kept saying, 'Don't catch them, don't catch them,' and after one landed at my feet he turned his back as though to say: 'You're on your own here!' I picked it up and Copperfield came over and introduced himself. When he heard my accent, he said: 'Oh, I think you're an Australian from down under!' He then asked me some questions, including: 'When was the last time you played your didgeridoo?' I joked that it was 24 hours ago.

After Copperfield spoke with a few other audience members, we were all invited up on stage. The master illusionist then gave me keys to a glass box that had been in plain view of us all. I opened it and found an audio cassette and a piece of paper. I was asked to put the cassette into a player, and press play. The words that came out blew me away: 'Hi, I'm David Copperfield. I recorded this tape before tonight's show. I knew tonight I'd meet a guy from Australia who last played his didgeridoo 24 hours ago.' He also mentioned correct snippets about every other person he'd brought up on stage. All the information was also in his handwriting on the piece of paper that I'd pulled out of the box.

If that wasn't enough to spin the head, I was then asked to stay on stage and hold two steel poles with another audience member. Each was about a foot in diameter and six feet high. There was nothing around them or above them.

'Keep your heads down and hold on tight,' said Copperfield.

He threw a big sheet over the poles and us, and moments later I felt a strange weight come on. The sheet was ripped off and there above us, balancing on the poles, was a motor car. Copperfield climbed up a ladder, got into the car, and waved at everyone while pretending he was driving. After he hopped down again, the sheets were tossed back on and within seconds the car had gone. There are lots of things I don't have answers for in my life, and this is one of them. I know it was all smoke and mirrors, but how? Perhaps some things are best left unknown.

On the same trip, I met Australian tennis player Mark Philippoussis, who was based in Vegas. In a case of 'It's a small world', Mark was friends with Gavin Rossdale, the British lead singer of the former rock band Bush. In turn, Gavin was married to American singer Gwen Stefani. The short story is that Gavin arranged front-row tickets for Liz, Mark and me to go to one of Gwen's concerts at the MGM Grand. Afterwards we met Gwen backstage. I was impressed how interested she was in us. She asked Liz and me how long we'd been married, and she was keen to know about Preston. Later that year, Liz and I caught up with her when she was in Australia on a world tour. One of the first things she asked us was: 'How's Preston?' That alone ensured I'd be a fan of hers for life.

Although cricket was out of sight during my winter, it was far from out of mind because I was determined to be firing for the inaugural Twenty20 World Cup in South Africa in September. By July, five months after hurting my ankle, I was 100 per cent fit after a solid rehabilitation that included gym sessions and runs at Sydney's Balmoral Beach. By the time the T20 cup began, I was hard to hold back, like an unbroken colt. I'm sure my energy and attitude were boosted by T20 itself. It was hard to believe that I'd played in the very first international game against New Zealand only two-and-a-half years earlier.

Looking back, I don't think the T20 World Cup meant as much to the Australian team as the 50-overs World Cup, and we didn't take it as seriously as we should have. I for one thought it needed less preparation. After all, bowlers only had to bowl four overs each, a walk in the park. This was a welcome change from the other forms of the game; I used to pull up as sore from bowling 10 overs in a one-dayer as I would from delivering 20 or more in a Test match innings, because the shorter form was more rushed and urgent.

There were lots of discussions about the tactics needed to succeed in T20. From a bowling point of view, no-one really knew what good figures for four overs should be. In one-dayers, economy rates around four-and-a-half to five an over were generally considered good, but in T20s were you being expensive if you went for eight or more? Furthermore, were the best weapons the same that were used in 50-over games? That is, change-ups of pace and yorkers. When batting, was it best to go hard from ball one? Or should a team build up a platform for 10 overs and then go crazy?

It wasn't until after the World Cup when scores regularly pushed beyond 160 and higher that every team knew it needed guys at the top of the order who'd try their best to put their foot down from the get-go. If a team was 3-90 after 10 overs it was in a good position. However, most sides were more conservative during the World Cup.

Australia didn't gain any great momentum during our campaign. We played our five preliminary games at Newlands, undoubtedly one of the most stunning cricket grounds in the world. After Zimbabwe beat us with one ball remaining in my comeback game, we downed England comfortably before having a good win over Bangladesh in a match in which I became the first bowler to take a T20 international hat-trick.

Sure it was an honour, especially since I'd already claimed a hattie in the 50-over World Cup, but it wasn't something I dwelt on. In fact I was more excited about upholding a pledge I'd made to a bloke I'd quickly become good mates with after first meeting him a year earlier at a Weet-Bix function in Sydney. I told him if I got a few wickets in one of the matches, he should watch out for some unique celebrations. So, after I took my first two scalps against Bangladesh, I lived up to my word by taking a free swinging kick and a hop at the side of the pitch. I forgot to do it after I got my hat-trick – I was too busy standing in the Freddie Flintoff arms-horizontal pose – but I hoped the earlier two actions hadn't been wasted.

It was some time later that my mate returned the gag by impersonating my trademark 'chainsaw' celebration after he scored a goal for Everton in England's Premier League. It was a nice in-house joke between me and Australian soccer superstar Tim Cahill. Since our first meeting, we've always followed each other's progress and have become very close. After he was married in 2010 in Las Vegas, I was really humbled when he invited me to sit next to him on his bridal table at an additional ceremony that he and his wife, Bec, hosted in Sydney on their return. My music mate Mick Vawdon and I also played a few songs at the function.

After beating Bangladesh, we continued our up-and-down World Cup with a loss to Pakistan, and a win over Sri Lanka. Despite our inconsistency, we qualified for a semifinal in Durban where we were beaten by India, who went on to defeat Pakistan in the final.

When assessing the tournament, the disappointment I felt with losing was outweighed by the excitement the World Cup had generated. T20 was growing fast, and it was obvious that it was only going to become more popular. It had risen at a time when there was considerable concern about the long-term health of both one-dayers and Test matches. To my way of thinking, the future could be summed up by the following: parents take their kids to watch Test cricket, whereas kids take their parents to watch T20 games.

The World Cup signalled another hectic period for Australia's cricketers. Those involved in all forms of the game faced 11 months on the go with few breaks. The schedule reinforced the hidden blessing of my ankle injury; I'd gone through the World Cup without a twinge, and felt I was as well prepared as I could be to cop the fast-bowling punishment that lay ahead.

After playing in all seven matches of a one-day series in India, I returned home and fronted up for NSW in a drawn Pura Cup match against Queensland at the SCG. Although I went wicketless, I was in a positive frame of mind heading into Test series against Sri Lanka and India.

The first Test against Sri Lanka in Brisbane started on my 31st birthday and the second Test in Hobart began on Preston's first birthday. If there is such a thing as cricket gods, the Lee family must have done something to please them, because in the four innings of the series I finished with 4-26, 4-86, 4-82 and 4-87. We won both matches, I took home the dust-collectors for best player in each game, and I also claimed Player of the Series.

That period wasn't necessarily the best I'd bowled, but it was the best I'd used my patience. In one very important way I'd won the battle against my own mind because throughout those matches there were times when I walked back to my mark and resisted the urge in my head to bowl bouncers and yorkers. I told myself it didn't matter if the ball went through to the keeper time and again; the rewards would come if I stuck to my plans to keep it tight and use the yorker and bouncer as shock balls.

Technically I hadn't changed anything. All the ingredients I needed for success were combining: I was confident; my body was strong and injury free; I was hitting the pitch hard at 150-plus clicks; and I was swinging both the new and old ball. Every time I went out to bowl I knew I was going to do well. It was one of those golden patches that every athlete strives for, and hopes to go through, when everything seems so perfect. I was further helped by having the chance to have good cracks at the tail, something I didn't have many opportunities to do when Warnie and Pidgey had played. My bowling gave every indication – not only to myself, but to the fans and critics – that Australian cricket could still be successful without two of the game's all-time greats.

During the Hobart Test I took one of my most memorable wickets when I bowled Mahela Jayawardene for a golden duck with reverse swing in the second innings. Perhaps it became one of my favourites because of what happened a few weeks later. It was a Thursday evening, and I was feeding Preston when my mobile rang. The call was from a private number, and being wary of any number that wasn't identified, I didn't answer. The phone rang again, then again. Each time I let it go through to voicemail, but no message was taken. On about the fourth time, I'd had enough and decided to answer it with a cautious 'hello'.

'Is that Brett?'

'Yes, speaking.'

'Brett, it's Elton John.'

My next words, which I still remember distinctly, were probably not the best ones I could have uttered: 'Are you shitting me?'

There was laughter at the other end of the phone. At this stage I thought it was a stitch-up, but Elton soon convinced me he was the real deal, and I was as close to being speechless as I'd ever been. Elton, who I'd never met – I still have no idea how he got my number – told me he was in New Zealand about to do a gig, but he was coming to Australia and wanted to meet me.

'I see you're playing in Sydney this Sunday against New Zealand,' he said. 'Are you busy for lunch on Saturday?'

'I'm not now!' I replied.

Two days later I went to his hotel at The Rocks. After reaching his floor I met two security guards sitting at a desk outside his door. They told me to go straight in. I walked through to find Elton standing in a tracksuit waiting to give me a handshake and a hug. We settled down for a coffee, and straight away Elton turned the conversation to the Hobart Test.

'That ball where you went wide of the crease, swung it in and bowled Jayawardene was the ball of the summer! They're coming out really well for you, aren't they?'

I was stunned, to say the least. Was this really happening? Here was one of the most identifiable and successful people on the planet wanting to have a yarn as though we were two old mates. Until I met him I didn't know he was an avid cricket fan. For two-and-a-half hours we spoke about many things: inswingers; Watford, the football club where he was once chairman; big gigs; training sessions; songs; and fans. He asked me about touring life, and what it was like to play Test matches. He told me he admired other players, especially Justin Langer, for his determination. It was an amazing time. After being very nervous and embarrassed for the first five minutes, I was able to relax, but I couldn't stop thinking about who was at the other end of the couch.

When arranging the meeting with Elton's personal assistant, I asked if it would be OK if I brought my guitar. There were no problems with that, and Elton was pleased when I asked him to sign it.

'If my mum was here right now, she'd be going crazy,' I told him.

Elton smiled and asked me my parents' names. He then got me four CDs and DVDs and signed them: 'To Helen and Bob, lots of love, Elton John.' They're now hung up at Mum and Dad's home. He also gave me some similar gifts, and in return I gave him one of my Test shirts.

I really can't put into words how fantastic the afternoon was. Afterwards, when I picked up my car, the hotel valet said: 'You're happy!' I then hopped in, turned on the radio and 'Candle in the Wind' was playing. I drove away in a daze, wondering if it had all happened. The next day I was still floating when we played New Zealand. I grabbed two quick wickets before rain wrecked the match; even if Don Bradman had been batting that day, I would have fancied my chances against him, because I was on such a high.

I was on a high in my whole life. My family life was wonderful, my cricket was powering, and other opportunities kept presenting themselves. Among them was confirmation I would appear in a Bollywood movie. The high-profile Indian businessman and cricket official, Lalit Modi, had also given me a handshake agreement that I'd produce and perform the theme song for the 2011 World Cup on the subcontinent. Everything was a dream.

26

After Australia beat New Zealand 2–0 in the Chappell–Hadlee one-dayers, our attention turned to a four-Test series against India. I couldn't wait for the show to begin because I had some important points to prove. I hadn't played a Test against India since the 4-201 outing in 2004 at the SCG, and my original successes in 1999–2000 seemed so far in the past that I wanted to show I still had the ability to shake up one of the world's most formidable batting line-ups. Perhaps in some eyes I was no longer the lightning quick, but I was still confident my 150 k plus speed, that I'd shown during the Sri Lanka series, was just part of the make-up of a vastly experienced fast bowler who'd matured over the years to become the spearhead of his country's attack.

I remember the first Test at the MCG well. India were rolled for under 200 and for the fifth straight Test innings I bagged a 4-for: 4-46. One of the traits of human nature is that the more you have, the more you want, and there's no doubt I was wondering: 'What do I have to do to get five?' However, I was still immensely satisfied, especially when I looked at the scoreboard to discover I'd taken my 250th wicket, Anil Kumble caught by Adam Gilchrist. I was playing my 62nd Test. Plenty more to come, I thought.

My stretch of four-wicket hauls came to an end in the second innings when I took 2-43. India again fell cheaply and we won by 300 and plenty on the back of a first innings century by Matthew Hayden.

We headed to Sydney for the second Test over the traditional New Year period. If we won, what a way it would be to ring in 2008, because we would have equalled the world record 16 consecutive victories set by Steve Waugh's side near the beginning of my career. Unfortunately, the match turned out to be full of controversy that will probably always overshadow a phenomenal contest.

After winning the toss Ricky Ponting did as expected and batted. What wasn't expected was the run of poor umpiring decisions by Mark Benson and Steve Bucknor, which built up a lot of tension between the teams. On the first day Punter edged a ball off Sourav Ganguly down the leg side and was caught but not given out; he then cut a ball in half into his pads and was marched LBW off his arch-rival, Harbhajan Singh.

The most blatant mistake happened when Andrew Symonds escaped after edging Ishant Sharma through to the keeper. Symo was on 30 at the time and ended up 162 not out. In his typical 'call a spade a shovel' kind of way, he didn't mind admitting in a presser that he'd nicked the ball. That really fired up the Indians. Symo's innings had held Australia together after a dodgy start. Brad Hogg batted brilliantly for 79 and I got 59 and shared a century stand with Symo. I'd never batted with a more laid-back bloke. His philosophy was so simple: use the bat in your hands, hit the ball and score runs. In this coaching age of over-analysis, such a view can unfortunately be overlooked.

We finished with 463. I took an early Indian wicket, but after that the batsmen dominated, with Sachin Tendulkar and Very Very Special Laxman hitting hundreds. Although I finally bagged the 5-for I'd been looking for (5-119), I was disappointed I couldn't do more to stop India reaching 532. At one stage it looked as though we'd take a first-innings lead but Harbhajan Singh came in and scored 63 to help Sachin take India past us. It was during their partnership that the shit hit the fan, although I didn't think it was a huge issue at the time.

I was in the second over of a new spell and wanted to try to unsettle Harbhajan. I'd already sniffed him a couple of times, and was being urged on by Symo saying: 'Come on, Binga, let's get a wicket here.' After the previous umpiring mistakes, I could feel a definite edginess and niggle between the teams. On my fourth ball I went for the inswinging yorker. Harbie just managed to keep it out and squeezed a single to midwicket.

As we passed on the pitch I said to him: 'Nearly got ya!' He then gave me a friendly pat on the backside and said: 'Well bowled.' It wasn't meant sarcastically or to aggravate me; there was no malice in it at all. I didn't have a close relationship with Harbhajan, but I knew him well enough to have the odd chat with him in hotels, or to walk past him and say a quick 'hi'. On the field, all the Australians knew him as an agitator who carried on; we actually thought he thrived on winding his opponents up. So, when Symo saw our exchange, he might have thought Harbie was being a smart arse. As he crossed to the other side of the pitch, Symo said a few words in passing to Harbie. I was heading back to my mark and heard nothing that was said, and to this day I still haven't asked Symo.

After I finished the over, I was halfway to fine leg when I heard the crowd chirping up. I turned to see a series of discussions involving Harbie, Symo, Haydos, the umpires, and Punter. It was obvious something serious had taken place, and I was glad I was out of the picture. That is purely and simply my recollection of my part in the incident.

Afterwards, the accusations came out that Harbie had triggered a racism row by calling Symo a monkey. The media grabbed hold of the issue and created an atmosphere that further affected the relationship between the teams for the rest of the Test. And then, with a few more umpiring controversies thrown in, it seemed some sections of the media were pumping up an all-out war between Australia and India.

The umpiring problems happened in India's second innings. Earlier, Haydos and Mike Hussey scored hundreds to set up a final-day declaration just before lunch. India's target: 333. I picked up Wasim Jaffer in the first over and Stuey Clark got rid of Tendulkar and Laxman. From then on it was a matter of India trying to hang on for a draw. And this was where the controversies began again.

The first was when Rahul Dravid was given out caught behind off Symo's off-spin. Replays showed Rahul had only hit his pad. Next, Ganguly edged a ball off me low to Michael Clarke who took a good catch in front of him at second slip. However, Ganguly didn't want to go. From my position it was a clean grab, although in hindsight I appreciate Ganguly's reluctance because replays suggested it was a very close call. But forget the television; the best person to judge was Ricky Ponting who was standing right next to Pup, and he had no doubt it was a fair take.

In the closing overs, Indian captain Anil Kumble led a gutsy fight. He didn't deserve to lose. Meanwhile, Punter threw in the changes, including bringing me back for one final shot at blasting them out when they were seven down. The pitch was still playing well, although as you'd expect, it was turning. I really tried to produce something out of the ordinary in my first over, but Harbhajan saw me out, and as I took my hat from umpire Benson I thought: 'Well, we've come close but this is going to be a draw.' Then I saw Punter having a chat with Pup. As a result of that, my final blast lasted only one over and part-timer Pup was given the ball. Around the ground I heard a few murmurs, and I presumed people were saying: 'What's going on!' But credit to Punter because he was backing his judgement, no matter how wild it seemed.

Pup's first over of left-arm orthodox was insignificant. But his next? Well, every Australian cricket fan – and probably Indian too – knows what happened: he took three wickets in five balls and we stole the win with only minutes to go. I was at gully when the final wicket fell, Ishant caught by Huss at first slip. I threw my hat into the air in a spontaneous release of tension and joy. Considering all the dramas of the Test, for Pup to come on and go *bang, bang, bang* was an awesome and fitting end to a gripping match.

But in the aftermath, our unbelievable record-equalling win seemed to mean little when compared with other issues. Although Harbhajan was suspended for three Tests, which was later changed to 50 per cent of his match fee on appeal, much of the focus was on the behaviour of the Australian team that parts of the media and public labelled as bad sportsmanship. First, our on-field celebrations after winning were considered excessive. Punter in particular copped it for running around pumping his fists. Yes, he was carrying on. We all were. But it was the emotion coming out, and there was no way we should have stopped that. Behaving like humans is better than the public watching robots. For anyone who criticised us, I'd ask them to take a look at some of the things they've done to express emotions in their lives. In the case of Australia's cricketers, a sequence of events and pressure throughout the whole Test led to the valve being released when we won. I say, fair enough.

What angered me more was the accusation that we'd cheated

in relation to the dismissals of Dravid and Ganguly. I felt especially sorry for Gilly, who'd appealed long and hard for the Dravid catch. He was labelled a hypocrite for having a bit both ways. That is, he was the 'goody two shoes' for walking when he nicked one while batting, but he was also the world's worst bloke because he apparently appealed for wrongful dismissals. What garbage! I never played with a fairer cricketer than Gilly. He played it hard, but that was the Australian way. In the post-match presser, Anil Kumble said Australia hadn't played in the spirit of the game. I didn't agree with him, but he was entitled to his opinion. In short, there were many unfortunate incidents that all spiced up conflict.

Relations between the teams were difficult for the rest of the series. I was closer to the Indian players than any other Australian, so I really made an effort – more than usual – to chat with the guys, say 'hi' to them when our paths crossed, or at the very least smile at them to let them know I still wanted to be their friend. It was a tough period for a few weeks, but by the end of the summer I'd like to think the teams got on at least reasonably well.

Some would say Australia got what we deserved when India beat us in the third Test in Perth, before we drew the last match in Adelaide. I picked up a further 11 wickets, taking my series tally to 24, the highest on either side. The haul also took me to 40 poles at 20.57 in the six Tests for the home summer; I hadn't taken less than a 2-for in any innings. Justifiably I'd had my knockers at times in the past, but for once no-one had reason to criticise me. In the world of international cricket, where every single delivery or shot can be replayed and analysed over and over and over again, it was a super place to be.

The wickets kept coming during the one-day series with India and Sri Lanka. I finished with 16, five behind the leading player Nathan Bracken. India gained some revenge by beating us in the finals. The two matches were Gilly's last before he retired. With that, Australian cricket took another step towards an uncertain future. They say no player is irreplaceable, but I reckon Gilly came close. He was the one who started to revolutionise shots in Test cricket, and his batting reshaped the role of modern-day keepers. He had a freak eye, amazing hands, and most importantly, he wasn't afraid to take risks. Although he was one of a kind as a player, it's as a person where his true qualities are. To this day he remains honest, caring and thoughtful; a genuine bloke. Of all the privileges cricket has given me, few have been more valuable than spending time with Adam Gilchrist.

At the time of Gilly's retirement, another player had already called it quits indefinitely, and I believe it's really important to mention him because his situation reflected the often overlooked effects of being a professional athlete. Not long after playing the Perth Test, which was only the third of his career – it also turned out to be his last – Shaun Tait decided to have a break from all forms of the game. The media cited his reasons as 'emotional breakdown'.

I felt immensely sorry for him, and in some ways I related to what he was going through, because he and I were both express fast bowlers. Public expectation can be horribly unfair. In the case of Taity, he came into Australian cricket with everyone expecting him to bowl rockets from the very start. That alone put considerable pressure on him. I remember watching him during the Perth Test and was amazed – shocked if you like – that his run-up was about 10 metres longer than mine; he struggled to get to the crease because it was so long. I could see all this nervous energy going through his body because he was so keen to bowl thunderbolts; it was his first Test in Australia and he didn't want to let anyone down. After a short while he looked exhausted, and unfortunately he was wayward and got pumped a bit on a flat pitch. I told him a couple of times: 'Just make sure you hit your lengths.'

In the back of his mind I reckon he was thinking that he *had* to bowl 155-plus kays every single ball because that's what he was in the team to do, and that's what the public, the media, even his teammates expected him to do. He was only 24 years old and feeling his way in the game. I don't know if he had other issues in his life that were troubling him at that stage, but I do know how low he could have felt after not doing as well as he would have hoped to in Perth.

In the televised world of professional sport there's nowhere to hide, and in the case of being an Australian Test cricketer who is rightly or wrongly considered to be public property, fans demand nothing less than success. If you don't succeed, you must prepare to wear some pretty ordinary attacks. That's one area in which I believe administrators could do better. Sure, it's fine to teach players about training techniques, fitness, diet and so on, but how much work has actually gone into preparing players for what they will go through mentally? It's an area that needs more attention, especially when you consider some players, from the time they are teenagers, are put into environments that are so cricket focused that little attention is given to the outside world. I know many cricketers who've led very sheltered lives.

After the international season had finished, Australia's players gathered in Melbourne for the premier presentation night on our calendar. By the end of it I was wearing the Allan Border Medal around my neck. I was really proud of being only the second bowler behind Glenn McGrath to have won the award since it began in 2000. To me, it wasn't so much a reward for good performances, but more so consistency, something

I'd really worked hard at achieving. Voting for the peer-based award stretched from February '07 to Feb '08. I finished with 125 points, 18 ahead of the runner-up, Matthew Hayden, who'd won the medal in 2002.

It's only now, a few years later, that I'm beginning to appreciate the honour, yet I still don't think it has really sunk in. Perhaps when I'm an old man whose name is surrounded by a few generations of winners will I realise how lucky I was. Of course by then I hope to be telling my grandchildren how good I was! For the moment, though, the richer accolades are the ones I receive from the public, such as being stopped at an airport in India by someone who simply wants to say: 'Mr Brett, I love watching you play cricket. You are always smiling.' Imagine how awful it would be to finish your career, have good stats, but no-one liked the way you played.

The final honour for the season came when I lined up for NSW in the five-day Pura Cup final against Victoria at the SCG. On the night of the third day, I received a text from my mate Mick Vawdon. By that stage the Blues were in control with a lead of more than 400 halfway through our second innings, and I was the next man in. Mick, a smoker for more than 20 years, said that if I went out and got a century he would give up the cigs.

I actually believed I could do it, and entered the next day really determined. I went in early after Dominic Thornely fell, and right from the start I felt very comfortable. At the other end Beau Casson was hitting the ball well, and we ticked over the runs pretty quickly. We both passed 50, and I started to think I really could get a hundred. That's when the pressure began because I started trying to play like a batsman instead of continuing in my own 'slap-it-and-see' way. Beau and I were neck and neck for most of our partnership until Bryce McGain bowled Beau for 89.

After that it felt as though I was in the 80s for ages. I don't think I was, but the nerves were starting to play tricks on me. When I was 93, I nicked a ball from Peter Siddle straight between first slip and the keeper for four. It should have been caught, but when it wasn't I allowed myself to think: 'Yep, you beauty, this is my day. Have your last puff, Mick!' Mick was in the stands with a few mates and had actually lit up because he was convinced he was about to give up. The next ball, though, Siddle bowled one that sat up and I hit it straight back to him. Caught and bowled 97. I was disappointed, but that feeling soon wore off. Fate said I wasn't meant to get a century; at least it allowed me to get bloody close.

We won the match by 258 runs, and the celebrations that followed were among the best I'd ever been part of. I found there was a different feeling between the NSW and Australian teams. In some ways the Blues were a lot closer. Perhaps that was because of the loyalties that developed along state lines, and also that many of the players had grown up together through junior teams and grade. I've always found mateship an amazing force in NSW cricket. The 'Bluebaggers' are a very powerful unit to be part of, and there's an incredible level of pride that is founded by great history. Considering this, it was no wonder the 2007–08 Pura Cup champions were all happy to sit in the dressing-room spa and get drunk. The occasion was made even more special for me because my brother Shane had been part of a winning NSW team, and to follow in his steps was an achievement that the whole Lee family, especially Mum and Dad, could look at proudly.

2007–08 was a brilliant summer for me. And I'm still to mention another story that I was involved in towards the end of the season. It was a story that has changed cricket forever: the Indian Premier League story.

27

It was mid-February 2008. I was at Sydney's Rushcutters Bay with Darren Lehmann and Nathan Bracken doing a promotional appearance for Cricket Australia. We were monitoring via text what was happening in India. One message stood out: India's one-day captain M. S. Dhoni had been bought for US$1.5 million by Chennai. We were stunned.

Later, I went home and waited. I was really nervous and couldn't help thinking: 'Does anyone want me?' Finally the phone rang. It was my manager Neil Maxwell.

'I've got your contract and it isn't great,' said Maxi.

My heart sank.

'What is it?' I asked.

'You only got US$900,000.'

'Bullshit! No way!'

Maxi laughed. So did I. Wow! This was just crazy; never had I even dared to dream that I'd get that much. Over the following days the cricket world was turned on its head by revelations of the millions and millions of dollars that were spent at the players' auction for the inaugural Indian Premier League (IPL) tournament scheduled for April: Andrew Symonds, $1.35 million; Sanath Jayasuriya, $975,000; Ishant Sharma, $950,000;

With a technique like this, I was always destined to be a fast bowler.

I loved the outdoors right from the start. Some of the greatest catches I remember have been well away from the cricket field.

The season that changed my life: 1999–2000. A trademark appeal for New South Wales against Queensland at the Gabba. A few days later, I was chosen in the Australian XII for the third Test against Pakistan at the WACA.
©Newspix/Glenn Barnes

Was this really happening? Seven wickets in my debut Test against India at the MCG. You beauty!
© Newspix/Phil Hillyard

Wearing the baggy green at the 'G. Not a bad Christmas present.
© Newspix

Those days of sibling rivalry at 8 Winter Avenue prepared us well. My international one-day debut versus Pakistan, Brisbane, January 2000. Shane was 12th man. We played our first game together three days later.
© *Hamish Blair/ALLSPORT*

Onya, Marto! Damien Martyn catches Saeed Anwar at the MCG in my debut international season.
© *Newspix/Phil Hillyard*

If I hadn't been a cricketer, no points for guessing what I would have wanted to be. The early days of playing the bass with Six and Out – it was hard to concentrate with Cheeks (Richard Chee Quee) belting out the lyrics next to me.
© *Newspix/Noel Kessel*

Two great people to hav in my corner. Captain Steve Waugh and Malcolm Speed, CEO of the Australian Cricke Board, during the medi conference in 2000 that announced I'd been reported for chucking.
© *Newspix/Brett Faulkner*

Taking the final wicket, Courtney Walsh LBW, against the West Indies, Perth, 2000. Our record 16th Test win in a row.
© *Newspix*

The other Brett Lee.
© *Newspix*

The launch of my clothing range with Shane and *Cleo* Bachelor of the Year, David Whitehall.
© *Newspix/Troy Bendeich*

With Shane Warne and Michael Slater as VIPs at a Bon Jovi concert during the 2001 Ashes Tour. Slats was in heaven!
© *Newspix/Brett Costello*

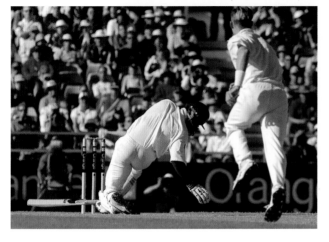

An ugly side of fast bowling. Alex Tudor cops a short ball in the face at the WACA during the 2002–03 Ashes.
© *Newspix/Paul Hutton*

I've rarely been fitter.
Putting in the hard yards
during the 2003 World
Cup.
© Newspix/Phil Hillyard

World Cup
champions 2003.
Moments like these
make playing a team
sport so special.
© Newspix/Phil Hillyard

What a great surprise to see
my cousin Luke Buxton
lob at my door before the
final against India. He
enjoyed celebrations with
the rest of us.

My baggy green, bowling shoes and guitar were the first things I packed on a Test tour.
Grenada, West Indies, 2003.
© *Newspix/Phil Hillyard*

Cricket has given me the good fortune to meet so many people from all walks of life.
Having a drink with Australian 'Invincible' Bill Brown was a privilege.
© *Newspix/Eric Harrison*

On my way to an unwanted double century against India at the SCG, 2004.
© *Newspix/Mark Evans*

My date for the 2004 Allan Border Medal night, Sarah Genuis. She is an inspiration.
© *Newspix/Wayne Ludbey*

Hitting a six at the SCG in a one-dayer in 2004 after a tough Test. This was the photo that inspired my manager, Neil Maxwell, to write: 'Remember what they said yesterday.' One day I was down and out, the next day, riding high. Cricket can be so fickle.
© *Newspix/Mark Evans*

Twelfth man, the position of contradictions. Such a frustrating place to be for 18 long months.
© *Newspix/Kerris Berrington*

My battles with
Freddie Flintoff in the
2005 Ashes cemented a
great friendship.
© *Newspix/Phil Hillyard*

Ouch! The epic second
Test at Edgbaston. In
between a lot of 'eye
language', Freddie extends
his hospitality on the
gripping final day.
© *Newspix/Phil Hillyard*

It's a question I often
get asked: What did
Freddie say to me
when this famous
snap was taken after
the Edgbaston Test?
© *Tom Shaw/Getty
Images*

Glenn McGrath and I hang on for a draw in the third Test at Old Trafford. Pidgey reckoned it was 'never in doubt'.
© *Newspix/Phil Hillyard*

Marcus Trescothick edges me for four in the fifth Test at The Oval. Thanks for the memories, England, both good and bad.
© *Newspix/Phil Hillyard*

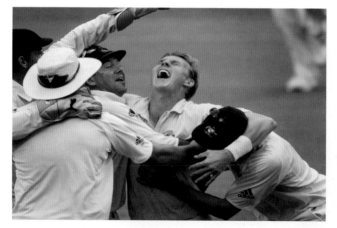

My first '5-for' in four years against the West Indies at the Gabba, 2005. A chat with Mark Taylor before the season helped me tremendously.
© *Newspix/David Kapernick*

Umpires are like grounds. You like some more than others. Here, Punter and I share a lighter moment with Asad Rauf.
© *Newspix/Graham Crouch*

It all began with a chat about a movie featuring two blokes stuck in an ice cave. Michael Kasprowicz and I help win a thriller in the third Test against South Africa, Johannesburg, 2006.
© *Hamish Blair/Getty Images*

Sharing trade secrets with Pidgey during the 2006–07 Ashes. How lucky was I to bowl with one of the all-time greats!
© *Newspix/Phil Hillyard*

Cause for celebrations. Andrew Strauss on his way in the fourth Ashes Test at the MCG.
© *Tom Shaw/Getty Images*

Revenge! After the disappointments of 2005 in England, our demolition of the Poms in 2006–07 was unforgettable. We reclaimed the Ashes after only the third Test in Perth.
© *Hamish Blair/Getty Images*

In the blink of an eye, or in this case the turn of an ankle, your fortunes can change. I'm out of the 2007 World Cup after a training mishap in Wellington, New Zealand.
© Newspix/Colleen Petch

There is a unique spirit in NSW cricket. Here, we celebrate winning the 2007–08 Pura Cup (Sheffield Shield). My close mate Dominic Thornely is to my left.
© Newspix/Phil Hillyard

My 300th one-day international wicket: West Indian Darren Sammy caught and bowled, Grenada, 2008.
© Stan Honda/AFP/Getty Images

The most sickening incident of my career. When a skidding bouncer hit Shivnarine Chanderpaul in the head, the cracking sound was heard as far away as the stands. First Test, Jamaica, 2008.
© *Timothy A. Clary/AFP/Getty Images*

I was in the wrong during the infamous blow-up with captain Ricky Ponting during the second Test in Mohali on the 2008 India tour. My off-field problems didn't have me in the right 'head space' at all.
© *Newspix/Graham Crouch*

Even now I can only say: 'How' the hell have I achieved this? My 300th Test wicket. Punter catches Jamie How in the first Test against New Zealand, 2008.
© *Newspix/Glenn Barnes*

On the comeback trail from ankle surgery in 2009. Injuries are an occupational hazard for fast bowlers.
© *Newspix/Sam Ruttyn*

Trying to prove my fitness during the 2009 Ashes tour. I felt I was ready to play.
© *Newspix/Colleen Petch*

A win every bit as sweet as an Australian victory. NSW winning the inaugural T20 Champions League final against Trinidad, Hyderabad, 2009. Dom Thornely (to my right) and Moises Henriques carry the load.
© *Mark Dadswell/GCV/ Getty Images*

Great to be back! Celebrating a wicket at the 2011 World Cup on the subcontinent. Fit and strong after conditioner Paul Haslam 'smashed' me in the gym for months.
© *Newspix/Phil Hillyard*

Jacques Kallis, $900,000 . . . the figures were unbelievable. But the big question was: could it work?

The 2008 IPL involved eight franchises that were owned by some of the biggest businesses and personalities in India. I was bought by the Mohali Kings XI Punjab, which was owned by businessman Ness Wadia and his girlfriend at the time, Preity Zinta, a Bollywood superstar. My signing fuelled media rumours that there was something going on between me and Preity. This all stemmed back to either 2002 or 2003 when I presented her with 'Leading Actress' at a Bollywood awards night in Singapore. At the time, when the Indian media asked me who my favourite actress was, I told them: 'Preity Zinta, because she's cute and has a dimple. And I love dimples.' It was all a bit of fun, but some journalists picked up on that, and when we reunited for the IPL, the two links years apart were enough to cause rumours. They simply weren't true.

Before the tournament I did a lot of publicity and media interviews with Preity. She was very hands-on with her business, but didn't know much about cricket. That didn't worry her, and right from the start she told me: 'I'm going to be asking a lot of dumb questions.' That approach continued even once the tournament began. She knew the game was all about scoring runs, and for the first couple of matches she wanted to tell our captain, Yuvraj Singh, to change the order.

I think it was the very first game when she came to the players' shelter and said: 'We need more runs. We need to send in a good batsman. Who is a good batsman here? Who can score runs quickly?' Our coach, Tom Moody, had to tell her: 'You're the owner, you take care of the financials and I'll take care of the cricket.' It was strange to have a Bollywood actress running a cricket team. When we won our first match, after opening with two losses, Preity threw a party at which celebrations were still going strong at four o'clock the next morning. Tom told her the gesture was great, but the players couldn't afford to do it every time they won a match. To her credit, Preity did a lot of homework, and quickly picked up a sound knowledge of cricket. She's a very smart person.

When I first arrived in Mohali for the competition I didn't know what to expect. I don't think any player did. Fireworks, cheerleaders and loud music were all gimmicks that westerners were used to, but how would they go in India? And would the most cricket-mad nation on the planet take to overseas players representing their own cities and regions? The whole concept of the IPL was the brainchild of Lalit Modi, the businessman and cricket administrator who pledged I could produce the theme song for the 2011 World Cup. He had no doubts the IPL would not only work but would have a long-term future, backed by the dollars from enormous television deals and the money coming from the increasingly wealthy middle and upper-class India. To Lalit, the IPL was an announcement that India had arrived on the international sports and business stage.

I was only able to play four games for the Kings XI before I had to link up with the Australian team for a tour of the West Indies. I experienced enough during those matches to be confident the IPL was going to help shape the future of international cricket. It was a pioneering T20 tournament that is now being mirrored by other countries across the world. T20 is definitely here to stay because it's what the crowd wants. It's full-on action with a party atmosphere under lights for three hours. It's fit for people of all ages, and there's no need to understand the intricacies of the game to enjoy it. You could say it is cricket's equivalent of going to the movies or a rock concert.

In this day and age, when more and more things are happening quickly in society, it makes sense that sport has to keep pace. T20 is what cricket needs. I only hope the world's administrators fully understand its significance. It's all part of our evolution. As a player, I love one-day cricket, but unfortunately I believe it could be approaching its use-by date. It is struggling. Now it's the turn of T20 to take the game forward and go hand-in-hand with Test cricket, which itself will need to bend with the times by experimenting with such things as night matches or four-day contests to survive.

Apart from playing, one of the things I loved about the IPL was the cross-section of cultures in the competition. My Kings XI teammates included: Australians Simon Katich and Shaun Marsh; Sri Lankans Kumar Sangakkara and Mahela Jayawardene; West Indian Ramnaresh Sarwan; and high-profile Indians Yuvraj Singh, Irfan Pathan and Shanthakumaran Sreesanth.

It was really interesting to see how the guys prepared. How did Sreesanth get ready to bowl? Did he listen to music? Did he go into his shell? Did he eat? The same questions people asked me about my preparations I was suddenly asking of others. Sitting next to Yuvraj was a revelation. He was so laid back we almost needed a cattle prod to get him up and going. It was a tremendous contrast to being in the Australian dressing room where Mike Hussey was so psyched up before batting that his feet would pump up and down on the floor like pistons; whereas Yuvie would lean back in his chair with his eyes shut and you'd swear he was asleep.

It was fantastic to spend time with guys I'd played against internationally yet didn't really know. I hope it doesn't sound strange to say it was wonderful to hug the guys when we celebrated wickets or wins. In bringing us together, the IPL also brought cricket together, which was timely considering the volatile series Australia and India had just played. Many of us became mates; Kumar Sangakkara and I, in particular, built a friendship that will last forever.

The funniest part about getting to know the guys was that we all discovered secrets about each other's games that could help us when we were rivals in international matches. For example, I heard chats between players about how they handled short balls or what their mindset was against particular types of bowling; I was like a spy locking pieces of useful information away for future reference.

The Kings XI went on to reach the semifinals before being knocked out by the Chennai Super Kings. The Rajasthan Royals, captain-coached by Shane Warne, won the competition. In the seasons since then, the IPL has had its highs and lows, most notably match-fixing allegations, and corruption accusations involving Lalit Modi that have threatened the future of teams including the Kings XI. I'm disturbed by what has happened, but believe the sheer weight of public and financial support for the IPL will ensure it continues to grow. As an aside, Lalit's demise meant my chance to produce the 2011 World Cup song disappeared.

For critics and fans alike, one of the biggest talking points of the IPL and T20 in general is the career choices players now have. In Australia, we're still at a stage where most players are driven by the desire to wear the baggy green, but the more time passes, the more there will be mercenaries who will use competitions like the IPL to make big dollars. Some critics may argue that is wrong, but point-blank it's the way cricket is heading. For argument's sake, there may be players who could earn more money freelancing around the world than signing up for contracts with their governing boards. Australia's David Warner is a good example.

A timely question for all concerned with the game is: do the players coming through now look at cricket as purely a way of making as much money as they can as quickly as they can, or do they look for more prestige and longevity by representing their country? It will be a tough question to answer for the next generation. Playing for your country is a great feeling and should always be the pinnacle, but how do you set yourself up for life as well? Of course, if you're a good player you can, but there are many others on the fringe who'll wonder if hard work for no guarantees is a sensible option.

I'm all for a player trying to make as much money as he can. Forget the jealousy that some former players and commentators have, like when we hear: 'Back in my day we played for the love of the game.' I reckon that nearly every single one of these critics would have their hands out if they were playing today. Look at it this way: in next to every other field of work, if a person is offered a position with more money – say, five times as much in a fifth of the time – would that person say ,'Oh, I think I'll just stay where I am because I'm doing this for the love of the job'? Sure, the occasional person mightn't move, but nine times out of 10 the response would be: 'Thank you very much – I'll take the new job. When would you like me to start?'

You also have to remember the big numbers mentioned in IPL contracts aren't always paid out. If you look at my situation, payment was based on a per-game rate. That is, I would have had to play every one of the 15 matches over the six weeks of the tournament to have earned the entire US$900,000. I didn't, so people who assumed the IPL had made me close to an instant millionaire were well off the mark.

While in India, I wasn't only involved with the IPL. Following an offer that was made earlier in the Australian summer, I agreed to play a small role as myself in a Bollywood movie called *Victory*. The fictitious story was about a cricketer, Vijay, who rose from obscurity to become a star before he fell from grace, only to rise again. Throw in a family illness and a love interest and it was enough to make a feature production. I was one of a number of real cricketers who had roles. Others included: Mike Hussey, Brad Hogg, Stuart Clark, Muttiah Muralitharan, Chaminda Vaas, Andre Nel and the Morkel brothers, Albie and Morne.

We squeezed in some filming in Sydney straight after our Test series with India. In my part, I helped Vijay come to Australia to receive treatment for a chronic back injury. We shot at the SCG and a set depicting a doctor's surgery, before the rest of the filming needed to be done in India. The movie's producers asked if I could source some 'Australian-looking guys in India', but Neil Maxwell suggested it would be easier to fly over a number of authentic Aussies. So, I invited a handful of mates – Mick Vawdon; former first-grade rugby league player Dennis Scott; Adam Rainford; Corey Richards, and Liz's brother, Christian Kemp – to come with me. Brad Hogg went as well. What followed was hilarious.

After arriving in the filming location, Jaipur, we prepared for a few days of shooting a mock one-day match. We were told the sessions would be seven o'clock to seven o'clock; the only problem was that it was evening to morning! As is the case with most filming, it was very stop-start. Bowl a ball. Cut. Action. Bowl another ball. Cut. Reposition. Bowl another ball. Cut.

On the first night we got to the stage where everyone hit the wall. It was about midnight. Someone, I can't remember who, suggested a few beers might help us through. So, a few longnecks were brought in, and the rest of the night, or should I say early morning, became a drinking session. That became the trend for the remainder of the shoot. We had a ball! We were signing autographs, playing guitars, drinking, and doing some very *creative* acting. I laughed every time I watched one of my mates fly around the boundary in an Australian uniform, swoop or dive on the ball, and fling it back to the stumps. In one scene we were asked to pretend to celebrate a wicket. We were pretty pissed, and guys started running around yelling and high-fiving like complete idiots. Then Mick Vawdon did a completely over-the-top crocodile roll similar to the one Harbhajan Singh did once after dismissing Ricky Ponting.

'Brilliant!' said the director.

In typical Bollywood style, it made the final cut.

One night, I asked a police officer if it was OK to get some fireworks to help pass the time. 'Of course, how many do you want?' he asked.

'Five or six would be enough,' I replied, thinking of individual crackers.

In the typical Indian way I'd become used to, the cop returned with about six bags full of crackers, more than you'd ever need for Sydney Harbour on New Year's Eve. Some of them were about a foot long, six inches in diameter, and sounded like bombs going off. We let them off between takes, and woke some of the movie staff who'd been sleeping. The cop lit them all using a long piece of wood so he didn't have to stand too close to some very short wicks. The scene was like something out of a *Tom and Jerry* cartoon.

One of the biggest crackers fell over on a 45-degree angle just as it was lit; it shot through the air like a tracer bullet, and nearly took off the heads of a couple of cameramen before it cleared a stand and exploded outside the ground. It was funny at the time, but looking back it was pretty dangerous. Maybe we were just rehearsing the climax of the movie that involved

Vijay hitting a match-winning six off the final delivery of the match, and sending the ball into an exploding light tower.

In the lead-up to that, I'd pretended to hit a batsman in the head and delivered the dramatic line of an angry fast bowler: 'This is not a tennis ball. These things crack skulls.' When that line was dubbed for the final cut, I think they used either a South African or New Zealand voiceover. It was as authentic as the fake blood.

The whole experience was a lot of fun, but I don't think Martin Scorsese or Steven Spielberg will ever come knocking on my door.

28

Of all the times I hit a batsman during my Test career, none made me feel sicker than when I drilled Shivnarine Chanderpaul during Australia's 2008 tour of the Caribbean. It happened in the first Test at Sabina Park, Kingston. Shiv was on top of us and holding the Windies' first-innings chase together. After bowling him a few bouncers I came around the wicket and banged in a ball that skidded on. Shiv ducked, turned his head away, and the ball smashed into the back of his head near the edge of his helmet. The crack was heard in the stands.

Shiv's knees buckled, and he dropped to the ground on his back. I ran straight to him. When I got there, I could only see the whites of his eyes, and he was convulsing. I went to undo his helmet strap but I heard a teammate say: 'Don't move him.' The convulsing stopped and Shiv didn't move a muscle. I thought I'd killed him. Not only was I worried sick, I was actually frightened. Medical staff, including Australian physio Alex Kountouris, sprinted onto the ground. A stretcher was carried on. I squatted down, stood up, walked around; I didn't know what to do.

After about a minute-and-half Shiv came to and began to move, and I doubt I've ever felt more relieved. The poor guy didn't know what had happened. He put an ice pack on his injury, and after several minutes he continued batting. He was 86 at the time, and went on to make 118. I wasn't the least disappointed that he'd made his century; it was a bloody gutsy knock.

Not surprisingly, I became a punching bag for the West Indian bowlers in our second innings and for the rest of the series. Fidel Edwards gave me a complete going-over and the crowd loved it. He got me out cheaply, but at least I could smile at the end when Australia won by 95 runs.

Despite the ugliness of the Chanderpaul incident, there was one thing I was pleased about: it showed I was bowling fast, and my good rhythm and form from the Australian summer was still with me. I picked up five wickets for the match, playing the support role to my new-ball mate Stuey Clark, who was magnificent with a haul of eight. His second innings 5-32 off 20 overs was straight out of the Glenn McGrath school of bowling.

We swapped roles in the first innings of the second Test in Antigua when I took 5-for. I was wicketless after 16 overs, but came back in the next five to produce my best-ever spell with the old ball. And it was a *very* old ball, 93 overs when I started. Up-front I admit there was an unusual touch of tampering involved. About 15 overs earlier Dwayne Bravo hit Stuart MacGill for a six that landed on some sharp rocks surrounding a crowd-control moat and fence. As a result, a couple of considerable chunks were taken out of one side of the ball.

So, we had natural scuffing, and immediately started working a shine into the other side of the ball. Not long after that, the ball started hooping for the first time since it had been new. By that stage Bravo was nearing 50 and Shiv Chanderpaul was closing in on another century; they were right on top of us, although still about 170 behind our first innings total. When I came on, the ball started bending long and late. I took three wickets in four balls: Bravo caught down the leg side; and Denesh Ramdin and Darren Sammy were both LBW to inswinging yorkers. Umpire Russell Tiffin may have been generous with all three of those decisions, but there were no doubts when I castled Jerome Taylor, and Daren Powell was plumb for the final wicket. Five for 59 off 21 overs: I never moved a ball more. Stuart MacGill still claims he helped me out; he reckons getting smacked for six was all part of his plan.

By stumps I didn't have as much of a glow after Edwards licked me up with a beauty. I watched the ball rise and keep coming until I made the mistake of turning my head. The ball busted my helmet grill right next to my jaw. I had a little taste of what I'd done to Chanderpaul because I went weak at the knees and got the wobbles. Some of the West Indians hurried over to me. One of them was my Kings XI teammate, Ramnaresh Sarwan, whose concern for me was a subtle example of how the IPL had strengthened the bond between players.

A few balls later Edwards had me out cheaply caught behind, although the ball had only flicked my armguard. I was really dirty because I'd been fighting hard to make it through until stumps, but then again, considering I'd had some luck with umpire Tiffin earlier in the day, I couldn't be too annoyed. Furthermore, I'd belted 63 not out in the first innings, so I'd already had my share of good luck.

We drew the Test, and I grabbed another three wickets to finish with my best match return to that point of my career: 8-110. I still had the mindset that I'd do well every time I bowled. I wrapped up the series with five more wickets in our win in the third Test at Bridgetown, Barbados. With 18 scalps,

I was again lucky enough to finish on top of the stats pile. However, there was a negative: I was exhausted.

In the nine Tests since the start of Australia's 2007–08 summer I'd averaged 46 overs a Test and had bowled nearly 60 overs more than Australia's second most used bowler, Mitchell Johnson. That was without taking into account the demands of the 11 one-dayers I played during that time. Ricky Ponting acknowledged I'd had a huge workload. For both of us it was a case of catch 22. I was bowling so well that I was happy to be the 'go-to' man, but that brought the pressures of added use. I was confident I could handle the stresses. After all, I would rather have been bowled into the ground than not bowled at all; the memories of my days on the outer in 2004–05 were major motivators.

I certainly didn't want to be rested for the five-match one-day series after the Tests. For one of the few times in my career, I was very aware of the statistical milestone I was approaching. It came in the third game at St George's, Grenada, but not before I'd made a fool of myself. I bounced Denesh Ramdin, who, in trying to hook, lobbed me back a simple catch. I took the ball and hurled it in the air to celebrate my history making moment, but then I realised the umpire had his arm out. I was shattered. Two overs later, there wasn't a no-ball in sight when I caught and bowled Darren Sammy. However, my response was low key; my achievement of becoming the fastest bowler in history to reach 300 one-day international wickets had been dulled by the embarrassment of my 'dress rehearsal' celebrations.

Australia won the series 5–0. The first half of 2008 had been one to remember for me. If I had nothing but form to worry about I could have banked on the second half of the year being just as successful. Unfortunately, I have to say the end of 2008 was the worst time of my life.

29

As I start this chapter, I have to stress that because of legal *and* personal reasons, there are many details I won't mention about my marriage break-up with Liz. However, I do hope to be candid enough to give you an insight into a period of my life that I never imagined would happen. From the time I was old enough to understand family values, I'd always pictured my life being like Mum's and Dad's. I planned to get married, have five children, and live 'happily ever after' on a farm. But life isn't always like that, is it?

On 18 August 2008, I launched my own underwear range at a function in Sydney's Double Bay. I didn't want to be there, but hid the reasons why: a couple of days before that, I'd broken up with Liz. Anyone who's been involved in the breakdown of a relationship knows how tough it can be. Until that point, pretty well my whole life had gone as I planned it would, but suddenly I just didn't know about anything anymore.

There were only a handful of people I turned to in confidence: my parents and brothers; Alan Jones; Neil Maxwell; my cousin Luke; and my close mates Adam Rainford, Corey Richards, Mick Vawdon and Dom Thornely. After I told Dom what had happened, we went fishing. It was one o'clock in the morning.

Actually, we weren't really fishing; we were just sitting and talking on the edge of a Drummoyne wharf with rods in our hands. We hadn't been there long when a water-police boat pulled up alongside us. After one of the officers told us we weren't allowed to fish where we were, he did a double take and said: 'You're Brett Lee, aren't you? No, mate, you'll be right. Keep fishing if you like.'

That incident was a hint of what would follow. Being an Australian cricketer I've accepted that I have a higher profile than the average person. I also acknowledge that I'm apparently a celebrity and have used this status to help my career, particularly in the business world. However, I don't accept that my personal life should be open to mass public exposure. Personal is personal. But when the media found out about the split the day after the clothing launch, Liz, Preston and I all became paparazzi targets.

The day after the news broke in the media, there were about a dozen photographers and journalists camped in their vehicles on the street outside my Sydney home. I was holed up for a couple of days with Mum and Dad who came to stay with me because they were so worried about what was happening. The media's presence made me feel vulnerable and violated. I thought I'd always done the right thing by them and had given them my time when they asked, so why couldn't they respect my right to privacy? Looking back, I can see they were just doing their jobs; I understand that rightly or wrongly there was interest in what was happening.

Eventually, I thought the best way to handle the situation was to confront it head-on, so I walked out my front door and straight up the driveway to the media huddle. This prompted a sudden *snap-snap-snap-snap* of cameras. I said: 'Guys, I appreciate you're doing your jobs, but I'm not going to say anything about what's happened. I can't and I won't. You're welcome to sit here as long as you want, but you're not going to get any quotes out of me about the situation. You can take photos now while I'm here – go for it.'

Then, before heading back inside I tried to add some *Beverly Hills Cop* levity to the situation by saying: 'And if you want me to send out some cookies, let me know.'

Many were still there past midnight. I remember looking out a window and seeing the glow of laptops in the backs of cars and vans. As soon as I'd go to walk out the front door, they'd hear the gate and they'd be up quick as a flash to take photos of me. I felt I was a prisoner in my own home. Then I thought: 'Well, if they're going to cage me in, I might as well have some fun with them.' So, I went upstairs, and looked out a window while I hit the remote button to my car. When the car's lights flicked on, all the pack sprang into action, and some of them spilt food and coffee. I hit the remote on and off for about an hour until I'm sure they realised what was going on.

Humour was one of the best coping mechanisms I had, but that couldn't overcome the loneliness I felt. I was very lonely. Of course I was. When you've been living with someone for three years, and then you come home at night and you're by yourself, well that's a tremendously dark hole in your life. Even playing music was tough for me, because so many songs I knew and liked were about relationships, heartache, love, and pretty well everything that could remind me of what I was going through.

My biggest escape was fishing with Dom, and occasionally Mick Vawdon. I went out most mornings. Although this gave me space, it wasn't good preparation for another part of my life that I couldn't ignore. Little more than a month after the break-up, Australia was to begin a four-Test tour of India. The squad got ready for it with a camp and three one-day matches against Bangladesh in Darwin. I was allowed to miss these, although I did attend the camp for one day just to get free of Sydney. At a media conference, where questions about my break-up were off-limits, I told journalists I couldn't wait for the India series. That was a lie. I wasn't ready for it at all. The last thing I wanted to do was bowl a cricket ball; the closest I came to cricket training before the tour began was catching flatheads and kingfish on Sydney Harbour.

We arrived in India towards the end of September. Once there, I had a talk with Ricky Ponting about my situation. He was very understanding. Even though Punter and I didn't always see eye-to-eye, we had shared some amazing experiences, and I had the utmost respect for him as a player, friend and family man. I really valued his opinions. Many other teammates also offered their support and told me they'd be there for me if I ever felt like unloading my worries. That sort of thing was lovely to hear, but in reality the team environment was too close, especially when some of the players' partners were friends of Liz, and I couldn't be sure what would be kept in confidence.

The first Test, only seven weeks after the break-up, was in Bangalore. At the time, if I had to describe myself in a player profile I would have said: 'Emotionally shot, physically out of shape.' Yet there was still part of me that was determined to do really well despite everything that was happening off the field. I still hadn't played a Test in India; this was an important moment in my career, and I hoped my love for the country and its people might somehow magically allow me to perform well and perhaps help me get on top of my private life.

However, playing Test cricket in India is tough. Really, really tough. It's a place that requires *all* your focus, otherwise you're going to fail. I remember next to nothing about the

Bangalore match. It was a draw, and I took one wicket in each innings. Apparently I bowled badly with the second new ball in India's first innings when we were in control. I honestly can't recall it.

We moved on to Mohali for the second Test. Still very distressed and distracted, I was grateful that Mick Vawdon flew from Sydney to be with me. He stayed for two Tests and offered me true mateship and support. Touring with a team can be so strange because you're living in close quarters with people you know as teammates, yet you may feel as though you have no-one to turn to. I definitely felt like that; in fact, in a country of more than a billion people I didn't think I had one friend until Mick came along. By that stage I'd been able to turn to music again, and Mick and I spent long hours playing our guitars and writing songs.

The Mohali Test was a shocker. We were thrashed by 320 runs, and I again grabbed only a wicket in each innings. I was far from my best: I was below pace, inaccurate, and rarely got the ball to seam or swing. I suppose that wasn't surprising considering all the negativity I was fighting off the field. It also wasn't surprising that my frustrations at not doing well collided with my off-field worries, and caused further problems.

On the fourth morning India resumed at a really strong position in their second innings, with an overall lead of 301. Shane Watson and Cameron White started the day's bowling. Then Mitchell Johnson and Peter Siddle had a go. I was fielding at deep point and wondering when I'd get a chance. Unfortunately, it hadn't been communicated to me that we were way down on our over rates, and that meant we were facing a considerable fine. I knew we were behind, but I didn't know by how much, and I assumed I'd be asked to bowl sooner rather than later.

Not long before drinks, I looked at Ricky and gestured, asking if I could have a roll, but he put a finger to his head as though he was saying: 'Use your brain!' I just didn't get it; I probably wasn't in the right frame of mind to be thinking as I should have been. At drinks I grabbed my bottle, and as I moved away from the team circle I said in general: 'Is there any fuckin' hope of getting a bowl?' Punter turned around and snapped at me, saying something along the lines of: 'Use your brain, we're six overs down!' I replied that I wasn't aware of that because I'd been on the fence. I then told him to 'Get stuffed!'

I walked away, but Punter followed me. He was pissed off, and had every right to be; looking at it from his point of view, he was not only under pressure for his team's performance, but had the added responsibility of dealing with a player, me, whose attitude was all over the shop. So there was a lot of emotion, other than that being caused by the situation of the match. Normally, we would have brushed it off and moved on. But on this occasion it was wrong place, wrong time, especially when Punter told me to use my brain. I got my back up. If it was all a matter of over rates, I could have bowled off three steps and been as quick as Mike Hussey, who was also used before me. I didn't understand. While Punter and I continued to argue, a photographer took some shots of us, ensuring the altercation would become a media issue.

I didn't bowl until straight after lunch. I had the shits with Punter for the whole day, but I apologised that night. By then, the media was on to the story. When I was questioned about it, I denied there was a problem; I hoped the issue would be seen as nothing but a beat-up. That was a lie, but I didn't want to upset the whole team environment. Sometimes in the world of media spin you have to twist the truth. That happens in everyday life as well. Thankfully the issue eventually passed, but not before coach Tim Nielsen also had to become involved.

In hindsight, I was in the wrong. Punter shouldn't have said what he did to me, but my reaction was exaggerated by all the other worries in my life. The fact we were in India didn't help either, because the tough playing conditions can combine with everyday annoyances to magnify many problems. For example, a bowler may be seen to be angry after having an LBW turned down, but his reaction might follow a morning when his laundry turned up three days late, he couldn't have a full warm-up before play because the team bus was caught in a traffic jam, and he's not feeling the best in the stomach after nearly having an accident when rushing to the toilet because he was stopped by a group of autograph hunters. I love India but there are times when even the smallest things can play on my nerves and grate me. It's such a tough tour, and when you're at the end of your tether it only needs something little to pull the rope that bit tighter until it snaps. My situation was made worse by being very sensitive to everything. I read stories about my poor form in the papers, and although I tried to shrug them off, they played on my mind until I was convinced of my own worthlessness.

For a few days after the incident with Punter, we put some self-imposed spin on the situation by making sure we were seen together talking, laughing and patting each other on the back. That wasn't a directive from team management; it was just us showing there was no problem. We actually didn't speak about doing it; we just knew what we should do.

Punter and I get on really well. He has his loves and passions away from cricket, and so do I. It's a simple fact of touring that you're going to have ups and downs with your teammates from time to time. I felt awful that I'd taken my frustrations out on Ricky.

Again I can't remember much about the third Test in Delhi, other than it was a draw on a belter. I added three more wickets, including my best return for the series, 2-48 off 17 overs in the second innings. If there was a glimmer of hope, I didn't see it. I was more worried about the wickets I wasn't taking. I'd let my own frustrations get the better of me; the more I didn't do well, the more the disappointment played on me and sent me further downhill.

The only high points came off the field. Early one morning Mick Vawdon and I sneaked out of our hotel with some Mohali Kings XI connections to go to a temple. I didn't tell Australian management because they would have quashed the idea. The team were in a security bubble, and players weren't allowed to even think about going outside the hotel without the appropriate protection. There has always been some rebel in me; sometimes when I'm told I can't do something, I don't mind pushing the boundaries. I didn't believe there was a security problem and thought there was more chance of something going wrong at an autograph session surrounded by hundreds of people than at a temple.

I did officially seek help on another occasion when I did a half-hour road run with fitness trainer Stuart Karppinen. We had a police car both in front of and behind us as we ran along a lane that had been specifically blocked off for us. It was as though we were running in an Olympic marathon, and provided me with a welcome distraction from thinking about my break-up.

The biggest highlight of the Delhi leg was after I received a message at the hotel to 'Please ring Mick Jagger'. Yes, *the* Mick Jagger. I called the number I was given and spoke to Mick's personal assistant, who invited me for a beer and a chat with Mick who was visiting India. All the arrangements were made and I took teammate Jason Krejza, who was an avid guitarist, with me. We went to a farmhouse about 40 minutes away where we met Mick and sat down and listened to a traditional Indian band playing. At the end, we got out a guitar and had a brief sing. I don't know if Mick knew of my separation, but he went out of his way to be the perfect host. I look back at those few hours as another extraordinary moment in my life. Sometimes I wonder why people like Mick and Elton John have contacted me. I just don't know. But I do know I've been incredibly lucky to have met the people I have.

At the final Test in Nagpur, Murphy's Law struck: when things go wrong, they really go wrong. Two days before the match I got sick with what medical staff thought was a typical stomach bug that would pass in a day or two. I was put on a broad spectrum antibiotic, but by the time the Test came round I still wasn't right. However, I convinced everyone I was OK. That was a huge mistake and I felt queasy for the whole Test. The hardest part was that I couldn't hold any food or liquid down. Between sessions I was attached to saline drips in the dressing room. Then I went out and bowled in heat pushing about 35°C, before coming back in to get needled up again. It was ugly. I reached 48 vomits, and then stopped counting them halfway through the Test. I lost five kilograms. At the end of every day I went back to the hotel and straight to bed. It was only when I got back to Australia that I was diagnosed with Giardia. It took three months to clear up.

We were thumped in the Test by 172 runs. I didn't get a wicket in the first innings, the first time in 36 Test innings and two-and-a-half years that I'd failed to grab a pole. I took 1-27 in the second dig to finish with eight wickets for the series at 61.62. This time the stats didn't lie. I'd had a miserable tour, the worst of my life.

We had only two weeks before we began the home summer with two Tests against New Zealand. I'm not 100 per cent sure of the exact timing, but it was around that period that I was involved in an incident that really got me in a huff. One day I took Preston to Sydney's Balmoral Beach. I was wearing shorts, a hat and sunnies, while Preston was in a swimming kit, and he had a little boogie board.

We were near the water's edge when, for some reason, I was drawn to look up. About 70 metres away I saw a guy holding a camera with a long lens by his side. He was looking straight at me. I pretended to look elsewhere, but watched out of the corner of my eye as the guy lifted the camera. I turned towards him and he immediately put the camera down. I didn't really care if he took a photo of me, but I wasn't comfortable with Preston being involved. Furthermore, we were on a beach and the snapping of kids is a sensitive issue.

The photographer left, and I thought that was the end of it. A short while later I needed to change Preston, so I put a towel around him and faced him towards the water. As I was doing that, I looked up and saw the photographer had returned wearing a backpack. He was definitely taking pictures of us, and his actions were a complete invasion of our privacy. I dressed Preston as quickly as I could, and took him off the beach to a footpath where I told him to wait. I then sprinted about 30 metres to the photographer and asked him what he'd been doing.

'Nothing,' he replied.

'What's in your backpack?' I challenged.

'Nothing.'

I grabbed the backpack, ripped it open, found the camera, and said: 'What's that? Show me the photos you've taken.'

'No.'

'Show me the photos, otherwise I'll call the police, because you're not allowed to take photos of minors on the beach!'

'No, I wasn't taking photos of . . .'

I turned the camera on and found the memory card had nothing but photos of me and Preston. I told the photographer to delete the images, but he refused. He also gave me a name and details that turned out to be false. I gave him a real spray, and walked away telling him he'd be hearing from me. With a few phone calls, Neil Maxwell and I were able to track down his true details. He was freelancing for a company that sold photos to various magazines and media. We sent him a legal letter and nothing was published.

The week after Preston turned two, I was in Brisbane for the first Test against the Kiwis. Although I'd tried to keep my personal and cricket lives separate, the Indian series showed how badly one affected the other. I knew recovering from the break-up would be tough, but I just didn't realise how incredibly tough it would be; I'd come to understand I couldn't put a time frame on my recovery. Nevertheless, I believed I was focused and ready for the first Test, not least because I was on the verge of another memorable milestone that would sit alongside my one-dayer dismissal of Darren Sammy earlier in the year.

I knew I was getting close to 300 Test wickets without knowing exactly how many I had to go, but as soon as it was mentioned in the media, there was no way I could simply forget about it. I entered the Gabba game with 297 scalps. That alone made me feel under more pressure than usual; think of a batsman in the 90s approaching his century. I moved to 299 after I got Jamie How and Ross Taylor out in the first innings, but my 2-38 only added to the pressure because I entered the Kiwis' second dig impatient to reach the mark and move on.

Thankfully I didn't have to wait long. With only my third ball, an outswinger on a full length, Jamie How went for the drive, nicked it, and Punter took a sharp catch right in front of his face. As I celebrated, I thought it was fitting that How was my victim because I spent a long time asking myself: 'How the hell have I achieved this?' For a bloke who paid little attention to stats, I knew all about this one: I was only the fourth Australian bowler – Shane Warne, Glenn McGrath and Dennis Lillee were the others – to join the exclusive 300 club. The moment proved one very important thing that I have no doubt some critics will disagree with: you can't take 300 Test wickets if you're injury prone. Yes, I'd had my battles with my body from time to time, but this was a reward for overcoming them. I was justifiably proud of my achievement.

Jamie How was the only wicket I took in the second dig while we went on to win easily. The Man of the Match, Mitchell Johnson, led the way with 5-39 following on from a first innings 4-for and Stuey Clark also bowled well, picking up six wickets. In the comparisons made in the newspapers I was considered the least impressive of the quicks. I wasn't worried because I knew I could return to my pre-India form.

In the second Test in Adelaide, one ball alone in the first innings was enough to give me even greater confidence. After failing to make breakthroughs with the new ball, I returned with the old one and got some 'spit rock' happening to clean up left-hander Daniel Flynn with a late inswinger from around the wicket. I got a lot of joy out of that. It's such a hard trade to learn to bowl with the old ball, yet I loved doing it. The general perception is that quicks need fast, green pitches that seam. But there are times when low and slow tracks that scuff up the ball can have advantages for someone who knows how to hoop it around. The fact the ball was moving for me was a great sign.

Helped by a couple of tail-end wickets, I finished with 4-66 and couldn't wait to get out and have another crack.

I entered the second innings with the most enthusiasm I'd had for months, and I finished the innings with 5-105, and my best-ever Test match return, 9-171. Australia won again. I was stoked, and not for the first time in my career I felt I'd answered my critics. Importantly, I'd bowled more than 50 overs, including one 10-over spell. Although Giardia was still playing games with my guts, I felt stronger and well on the way to returning to full fitness. I was also more comfortable with my personal situation. The break-up was still very much affecting me, but at least I was beginning to cope with it better.

The support I received during this time came from some unexpected areas. One evening I checked my mobile messages and was blown away to hear a familiar voice, yet it came from someone I'd never met.

'Hi, Brett, it's Jimmy Barnes – give us a call.'

What!

As with so many Aussie kids of the 1970s and '80s, I loved the way Jimmy sang. Cold Chisel will always be one of the greatest Aussie bands of all time, and Jimmy, whether fronting Chisel or going solo, is an icon. But what was he doing calling me? I rang him back straight away.

'What are you doing on Sunday?' he asked.

'Ooooh, I don't know,' I said nervously.

'Well, we're having a big dinner here and you're coming.'

He then told me he related to what I'd been through in my personal life. Over the years he too had had his problems. He insisted I'd find things easier to handle as more time passed, and I should gain strength from the people who cared about me and admired me. He said he was one of them. I was speechless.

A few days later I arrived at Jimmy's place. In the first surprise of the evening, Diesel, who'd played at my 27th birthday party, opened the door. He was Jimmy's brother-in-law. I walked in and met Jimmy, his wife, Jane, and a number of others, including Tex Perkins, the lead singer of The Cruel Sea. After dinner, Diesel said: 'Let's have a bit of a jam, eh?' They all got out their guitars and started singing and doing harmonies. And the best part? I was invited to join in. It's easy to think moments like that just don't happen. But they do!

That night, Jimmy and I struck up an instant friendship, and since then I've had some of the most amazing experiences of my life at the Barnes house. How will I ever forget the day Jimmy invited me over and greeted me with a cheeky grin?

'What's going on?' I asked.

'I just thought you might like to be a fly on the wall,' said Jimmy.

I followed him into his studio to find Steve Prestwich, Phil Small, Don Walker and Ian Moss all there: Cold Chisel had reunited for an afternoon. They played all the classics: 'Khe Sanh'; 'Flame Trees'; 'Standing on the Outside'; 'Cheap Wine'; 'Bow River' . . . I rang my brother Shane and told him to come over. What an incredible afternoon.

As with Elton John, I'm still not sure how Jimmy got my number before he first rang me. I've never asked him. I don't think he'll ever realise how timely his phone call was. I now consider him in my inner-circle of friends, and I'll always treasure how he reached out to me at such a vulnerable time in my life.

During this period he surprised me again when he invited me to see his mate Billy Joel in concert in Sydney. We were given backstage access and walked into the Green Room where we met Kylie Minogue. During the concert Billy dragged Jimmy up on stage to sing 'You May Be Right'. Afterwards at a private party, Jimmy introduced me to Billy. Forty minutes later we were still talking. Billy was genuinely interested in cricket, and we spoke in detail about the comparisons between fast bowling and pitching in baseball. After I told him I could bowl nearly 100 miles an hour he said: 'Wow, we'll get you back home playing for the Yankees.'

I met Billy only days before I flew to Perth to link up with the Australian team. The New Year was just around the corner, and after all I'd been through, I was more than happy to say goodbye to 2008. But before then, I had the first two of three Tests against South Africa. I told myself I had a lot to look forward to.

30

Any athlete knows the importance of setting goals. Heading into the series against South Africa I told a media conference I wanted to play Test cricket until at least 2013. Dennis Lillee's wicket tally of 355 was also in my sights. I thought achieving both was a definite possibility. But after the first Test in Perth, I suppose many people would have thought those aims were very ambitious.

Australia lost the match, I took only one wicket, and Ricky Ponting came out afterwards and said his team were carrying 'passengers'. The media and I both had no doubt he was pointing the finger at me. That really pissed me off. You didn't have to be Einstein to work out I didn't have a good game, but the thing that disappointed me was Ricky's lack of respect for what I was going through.

Although I was improving, I was still struggling through the toughest period of my life, and at a time when I needed people to stick up for me and back me, I was publicly criticised. If Ricky had spoken with me privately I would have been comfortable with that, but his decision to let every man and his dog know offended me. You just don't do that in a team. At no stage did he come up and talk with me about it, even after he mentioned it in the media. I can only think he hadn't cooled down after South Africa had scored 4-414 in their second innings to record the second-biggest successful run chase in Test history. Graeme Smith and A. B. de Villiers both scored hundreds, and J. P. Duminy, in his first Test match, looked really solid and composed on his way to an unbeaten 50. All three batted out of their skins. They were just too good for us.

My situation was made worse by two comparisons. The first was with my new-ball partner, Mitchell Johnson, who bagged 8-61 in the first innings and finished with 11 wickets for the match; the second was with myself, as reports came out that I wasn't as fast or dangerous at the WACA as I was at the start of my career. In my defence, the WACA pitch had changed and was no longer the bouncy strip that launched rockets. In fact, its batting-friendly nature, together with the changes of character of other Australian pitches, made me wonder if there had been a decision by administrators to deaden tracks in a bid to make matches last longer and therefore get better gate takings.

Throughout my career I'd become used to enough ups and downs to realise when my head was on the chopping block, and I accepted that going into the second Test at the MCG, but my confidence wasn't helped by the belief I didn't have the full faith of my captain. As a result, I had a bad attitude for the Boxing Day match. Instead of being focused, I was angry. My prime aim was: 'Well, Ricky, I'll fuckin' show you.' I felt no-one in the team was backing me, and if I didn't perform well, I was playing my last game for some time. That negativity was enhanced by my personal problems. When all things were considered, it was an ordinary place to be. I found it really hard to believe it was happening, considering only a game earlier I'd taken nine wickets.

My date with destiny was prolonged by a day after Punter won the toss and batted. He scored 101, and Australia managed 394. By then, another comparison with me was being made. Heading into the series, there'd been a lot of hype about South Africa's fast bowler Dale Steyn, who'd been clocking speeds similar to mine; he'd had an incredible year, taking 60 Test wickets before our series began. After starting slowly with two scalps in each innings in Perth, he stepped up a notch in Melbourne to take 5-87. So how would I fare in return?

In short, the answer was 'not well'. I took 0-68 off only 13 overs before I surrendered to pain in my left foot that kept me off the field for an entire day while South Africa piled up 459. I'd felt a little discomfort in the foot in Perth, but I thought it was just a niggle that could be overcome. However, early in my opening spell in Melbourne it began to hurt more, and only got worse as time went on. While my teammates struggled to get rid of century maker J. P. Duminy, who held the South Africans together, I went off to have scans and returned with the news that I had a 'hot spot', the precursor to a stress fracture in my fourth metatarsal. I managed to bat in our second innings but contributed only eight to our disappointing 247. Steyn impressed again with 5-67.

South Africa needed only 183 to win the Test and become the first touring team to win a series in Australia since the West Indies in 1992–93. I was determined to help stop that from happening, so I decided I'd bowl, even if that meant I'd make my injury worse. Before I went out, I had eight painkiller injections: four needles on top of the foot and four more underneath. Although my foot was initially numb, it wasn't long before the pain returned. Basically, every single step of my run-up and every single ball I bowled hurt like hell; it was the worst pain I'd ever had to endure while playing.

I should have left the field, but I wanted to prove to myself that I could go on no matter what the problem was. I was driven by stubbornness and the anger that remained towards Punter and his pre-match comments.

South Africa lost only one wicket in getting the runs. My return: 10-0-49-0. As I limped off the field at the end of the match, I didn't give a single thought to the possibility that I'd played my last Test. Instead, when team management announced I'd be out for six weeks and would miss the remainder of the home season, as well as a return Test and one-day tour of South Africa, I immediately adopted the comeback attitude.

I'd been in similar positions before, and knew I could fight back again. My biggest worry was being out of the game for too long, because experience had taught me the longer any player was absent, the more he was either forgotten, or the greater the speculation was that he'd never be able to make it back. The media talk began straight away. The general theme was that if I'd been in trouble before the Melbourne Test, how much greater were my challenges now? In *The Australian*, Peter Lalor summed up a popular train of thought when he wrote that I may have been 'hobbling into the sunset'. Alan Jones was yet again instrumental in stopping me from thinking about the negative angles surrounding me. It didn't matter what situation I was in, or what the media were saying, AJ always found ways to make everything seem OK; he never failed to give me confidence and self-belief.

My plan was simple. I had to recuperate, then get as fit as I could, and only after that point would I work on my bowling. I wanted to give myself every chance of being ready for the T20 World Cup in England, which was five months away. Immediately after that was the Ashes.

My first step was to have surgery in early January to have the regular clean-out of floating bones in my left ankle. While that was being done, it was discovered my fourth metatarsal was, in fact, broken, and it was highly likely it had been that way when I bowled in the second innings in Melbourne. No wonder I'd been in so much pain.

After the break was discovered, my foot was placed in a special boot, and for the following month or so I was extremely limited in what I could do. I still went to the gym, but it wasn't until after the boot was removed that my recovery really began. Each day was pretty well the same: physio, walking, massage. When I got more movement through my ankle I built up to jogging, then running, then bowling. The process took a few months, during which I worked with Paul Haslam, who I came to know as 'the Unit', a two-time Mr Australia and fitness trainer recommended by Alan Jones.

He developed the most specific program I'd ever had. A key element was strength training; bowling against both South Africa and New Zealand I'd felt weak and consequently down on speed. Paul got me in the best physical shape of my life. Training was intense: five days a week, two hours a day. I put on some bulk and felt really good for it; after my playing weight had been around 85 kilograms for much of my career, I worked up to about 95 kilos. I was driven by the need to make a statement to everyone – teammates, fans, opponents, selectors –that I wasn't too old or injury prone.

By April I was in good shape, and headed to South Africa for the second IPL series. The tournament had been moved from India because the country's general election was being held at the same time, and player security couldn't be guaranteed. I needed to show my worth ahead of the T20 World Cup, but I came across an unexpected hurdle: Cricket Australia said I couldn't play in the IPL unless I first proved my fitness to CA. For some strange reason, that meant I had to go to Dubai to play a one-off T20 match for Australia against Pakistan.

This led to some pretty angry exchanges between Neil Maxwell and CA's General Manager of Cricket, Michael Brown. Maxi argued that CA's stance was totally opposite to the one it had mandated for 10 years, whereby a player had to play a match elsewhere *before* being considered for Australian selection. But CA wouldn't budge, so farcically I flew to Dubai, bowled four overs, got 'signed off' and headed back to South Africa. Surely it would have been much easier for me to have simply played an IPL game? However, the Dubai match at least proved I was back in the swing of things. With my first ball I clocked 151 kilometres an hour. I took 1-22 and came off smiling. By that stage I'd been named in Australia's T20 World Cup squad.

I continued my comeback with a handful of IPL matches, which included a spell of 3-15 against the Delhi Daredevils in Bloemfontein. Five days after that I received the news I'd been hoping for: I'd been named in Australia's Ashes squad.

With doubts about my foot and fitness apparently gone, I flew to England for the T20 World Cup in June. After bowling well in warm-up games against Bangladesh and New Zealand, my campaign opener against the West Indies at The Oval was a disaster. Chris Gayle hit me for a four off my first ball, and everything went downhill from there. In my third over, Gayle smoked me for 26 runs, including three sixes, one of which landed in a schoolyard outside the ground. I finished with 1-56, but bowled better in the next game, taking 2-39 against Sri Lanka at Trent Bridge. That was the last chance I had because Australia lost both matches and were out of the tournament.

If there was a blessing to come from the T20 World Cup it was that I'd got through a couple of competitive matches unscathed. Of course, short bursts in 20-over innings were a long way short of stressing the body to the max in a five-day match, but I was happy with my progress. My comeback plan was nearly complete. All I had to do was get picked for the first Test at Cardiff.

I had only two games to prove my worth. The first against Sussex at Hove was six months after my Melbourne Test disappointments. In that time Mitchell Johnson had become the pace spearhead who reversed the home-season fortunes by leading Australia to a 2–1 Test win in South Africa. Peter Siddle and Ben Hilfenhaus played solid support roles. That meant I had a lot of work to do, especially when Stuey Clark was also thrown into the mix. Although we all took a few wickets, 'Sids' was considered the best bowler against Sussex, and Tim Nielsen all but said he was a certainty to join Mitchell in the first Test. In comparison, my hopes were shaky, especially after I'd chalked up 14 no-balls.

We moved on to Worcester to play the England Lions, a team of players considered to have Test potential, in a four-day match. I knew this was to be one of the most important matches of my career. Obviously I was under pressure. In particular I thought that News Limited journalist Ben Dorries was running a campaign against me. During my comeback, and before I'd been picked for either the T20 or Ashes squads, he wrote some stuff about me struggling for fitness that just wasn't true. That annoyed me. Once I'd been picked, I thought Ben continued to have an excessive interest in my progress; it was as though he couldn't write about anything else. I didn't handle his press or the overall pressure at all well.

Regardless of any perceived media slants, the bottom line was that I had to bowl bloody well against the Lions. Punter had pumped my chances up before the match when he said he'd never seen me train harder or look fitter. I went into the game feeling pretty good, but my fortunes quickly turned for the worse.

After Australia batted first, I got my chance to bowl early on the second day, sharing the new ball with Mitchell. In only my second over I felt a sharp sting low across the left side of my ribs. I knew I was in trouble immediately. Over a couple of balls the pain intensified and I was faced with two distinct choices: I could try to bowl through it and push for selection at the risk of making my injury worse, or I could go off the field and in all likelihood throw away my chances of selection. That moment turned out to be one of the most critical points in my career *and* my life because I felt I was screwed no matter what I did.

Weighing up my choices I considered what Punter, Tim Nielsen and the selectors had all said publicly at various times during my comeback. That is, above all else they wanted to see if I could bowl fast again and take wickets. To this day I firmly believe that if I'd walked off the ground as soon as I'd felt my injury, I wouldn't have played another international game in any form for Australia again, because I wouldn't have proven what I could do. So, I made the choice, one of my hardest and most painful decisions, to stay on and push through the injury.

After two wicketless spells I returned for my third when the ball was 40-odd overs old. The Lions openers were still in and I could tell Punter was getting annoyed. A few overs earlier, I'd been on the boundary having a few fun exchanges with some of the crowd who were telling me: 'You're shit, Lee, you can't bowl!' While this was going on, Punter yelled and gestured for me to look at him because he thought my mind wasn't fully on the game. That gave the crowd some more fuel for banter, and also fired me up. Not long afterwards, when he signalled for me to warm up, I thought: 'You want me to bowl? Yeah, I'll show you. Stuff the pain!'

I then went and took five wickets in 40 deliveries. The way the ball came out was unbelievable: late swing both ways and pace consistently pushing towards 150 kays. I went off the field that night but hid the full extent of my injury, telling only team physio Alex Kountouris that I had some stiffness. The next day I claimed another wicket to finish with 6-76, and the day after that I took 1-38 to be Australia's leading bowler in the drawn match. In all I'd bowled 35 overs, all but one of them in pain.

In the dressing room some of my teammates congratulated me, saying: 'Awesome, Binga, you're looking good for the Test.' It was only then that I came clean and revealed I was no hope of playing. When quizzed more, I told them I shouldn't have bowled at all, but I'd wanted to prove to the media and the team hierarchy that I could still do well, no matter what the situation.

There was a lot of surprise, but not as much as when I walked into the media tent for a presser and revealed I was injured and had to go for scans in Cardiff. Although I said I was uncertain what would happen, I already knew I was no chance of playing the first Test. I was gutted. It wasn't the worst thing that had happened in my career but it was shocking timing. A couple of days later it was revealed I had a large muscle tear under my rib cage, and was out for at least a month.

A look at the scorecards will tell you I missed the whole series, but it doesn't tell of the friction created by this, or the effect it had on my desire to continue playing Test cricket. After missing the first two Tests I was keen to play the third match but the team hierarchy told me not to rush back before I was fully fit. I was happy with that plan, but was definitely ready by the time the fourth Test at Headingley was due to start nearly five weeks after I'd suffered my injury. I'd had a couple of outdoor bowling sessions in front of Tim Nielsen, selector Jamie Cox and team bowling coach, Troy Cooley, to prove I'd recovered. With the way the ball came out I knew I could shake up the Poms. At that stage they led the series 1–0, and all the pressure was on Australia.

I was ready to play, and I believed I should have been in the team. Two days before the match I was surprised when Shane Watson told the media conference that I wouldn't be playing because I wasn't fit. I know he was incorrectly informed by the hierarchy, so it wasn't his fault. Watto and I spoke about it later that day; there wasn't an issue between us and there never has been.

It was either that day or the following one that Jamie Cox visited me in my hotel room. I knew straight away what he was going to say.

'What's up, mate?' I asked him.

'We've chosen the team and we've left you out. We don't feel like you're ready yet or fit enough to play,' said Jamie.

The conversation took place just before I was going to have a bowl by myself at an indoor facility. I got to the centre and Jamie, Troy Cooley and 'Vinnie' (Tim Nielsen) were there. Vinnie backed up Jamie's comments that I wasn't ready to play. He suggested I didn't need to train and could rest instead. That was enough to make me blow up. I told them I *was* ready and was also going to train. I was really pissed off, to say the least. It was a session filled with complete anger. Afterwards, when things calmed down a bit, I told my coach not to push my buttons at what was a sensitive time.

I then went back to my hotel room and made up my mind about my Test future. I was finished. I'd had enough. It wasn't being overlooked for the Test that made me quit; there were a lot of other factors too. But the incident at the indoor facility certainly didn't help. I felt let down. It was one of the toughest days of my cricket career.

Australia won the fourth Test by an innings, but that didn't change my feeling that I should have been in the team. Before the series-deciding fifth Test at The Oval, I was chosen to play a two-day match against another England Lions team at Canterbury. I was the most successful of the bowlers, taking 3-37 off 16 overs in our only innings.

When I wasn't picked for the Oval Test, the decision was the biggest knife in the back I'd ever received. I felt I wasn't wanted and that was that. I truly believed I'd given my all and had represented my country well, and had been a good ambassador for the sport and Cricket Australia, but now I was thinking: 'What's the point?' To this day I don't believe I got much support from the hierarchy throughout that period. If they'd said to me, 'Look, Brett, at this particular point of your career we don't believe you're up to the standard that we need you to be at,' I would have disagreed with them but I would have accepted it. But they didn't say that; they simply told me I wasn't fit. How would they know? I knew my body, knew what I was capable of, and knew I deserved to be picked in the team.

My views at the time were obviously affected by what was happening in my home life. Since Preston's birth I no longer wanted to be away for 300 days every year. It just wasn't the life I wanted to live. Right now, at the time of doing this book,

I honestly believe I could play Test cricket for another two years, but I don't want to, and why bother?

My only highlight of the Ashes tour came during the second Test at Lord's when the whole Australian squad, including the support staff, met the Queen. We were all dressed in Brett Lee label suits. That was as close as I came to making my mark for the entire series.

At least I had a belated chance to show what I could do during the following one-day series against England. After picking up two wickets in a warm-up against Scotland, I grabbed another 12 scalps to be the best performer in either team in Australia's 6–1 win. My best was 5-49 at Lord's, the second time I'd taken 5-for in a one-dayer at cricket's home. That made me happy. To be perfectly blunt, there was a lot of 'Stuff you!' in my bowling throughout the series. I hoped to leave everyone in the entire Australian squad thinking: 'Gee, what would have happened if we'd chosen Brett for the Tests?' That wasn't my primary motivation; above all else I just wanted to play and have a good time. However, my emotions and anger certainly played their part. The fact there has been a lot of swearing in this chapter reflects my state of mind at the time.

There was one other issue on the tour that I must mention. One night I was at the bar of London's Royal Garden Hotel with Mitchell Johnson, Shane Watson and Stuey Clark, when we were approached by an Indian man who was all 'blinged up'. He tried putting on a cool American accent: 'Hey, Brett. I met you in a lift in Johannesburg. Nice to see you again.'

He asked if he could buy us a drink. That wasn't unusual because we were used to being approached by random people, but there was something about this guy that didn't feel right. He gave the impression that all he wanted to do was splash his cash around. We politely refused his offer and then went and reported what happened to our team manager, Steve Bernard. It was exactly the type of incident we'd been warned about by both Cricket Australia and ICC anti-corruption officials. Although our reports were meant to have been confidential, the news eventually made the media with stories that the guy was a suspected gangster who was linked to illegal Indian bookmakers. I was annoyed that our names had been made public, and said so when the Australian team was next officially addressed by John Rhodes from the ICC anti-corruption unit.

Looking back, the whole Ashes episode was a sad way for me to end what I knew afterwards was my final tilt at Test cricket.

31

After the one-day series in England, Australia went straight to South Africa for the Champions Trophy. We won, and I was happy with the way I bowled. By then I had a lot to weigh up. After the Ashes I kept my thoughts close to my chest, and it wasn't until I returned from South Africa that I shared my feelings with someone. Alan Jones was the first person I turned to. I told him I had 'Harvey Norman' – no interest – in Test cricket. I'd treasured every single moment of playing, but the combination of frustration and anger had affected me. Being overlooked for the last two Tests in England made me the most pissed off I'd ever been in the Australian cricket environment, and I didn't want to put myself through any more torment. AJ told me not to rush anything. With that in mind I went to India to play for NSW in the inaugural Champions League Twenty20 tournament involving the leading domestic teams from around the world.

In contrast to the Ashes, I really felt I was wanted in the Blues team. It was a young squad with the likes of Phil Hughes, Steve Smith, Moises Henriques and Dave Warner mixed in among older heads like me and Stuey Clark. Our captain was Simon Katich. If circumstances were different, he would have made a great Test skipper. His leadership was brilliant. Plus, he remains a top person. If you can't get on with 'Katto', you must be an ordinary bloke. Period.

The tournament came at a great time for me because I fed off all the youthful energy, and in return I loved playing a leadership role in which I gave advice and hopefully inspired the new generation of stars. But it came at a price that further affected decisions about my future.

In the second over of our first game against South Africa's Diamond Eagles, there was some deja vu when I snapped a ligament off the bone near my right elbow. With extensive treatment from team physio Ryan Murray, I managed to play the whole tournament. I could throw with minimal pain, but the first two or three balls I bowled in every spell were excruciating. It got worse every game, but thankfully the nature of T20 saved me from the lengthy spells that would have destroyed me.

Against the odds, the Blues made the final in Hyderabad. We took on Trinidad and Tobago, the only team that had beaten us during our five preliminary games. There were a lot of nerves, especially with the added incentive of each player netting about $60,000 if we won. That was a lot of money for the young guys coming through, and I could tell it played on their thoughts.

Everything went wrong for us at the start, and we soon felt as though we'd tripped at the last hurdle. Sent in to bat we collapsed to be 6-83 in the 12th over. I went in having barely batted or scored a run in the tournament. Steve Smith was at the other end and he was very edgy. I told him: 'Just watch the ball. If it's in our zone, slap it!'

We put on 50 in six overs, the Blues ended up making 159 and I top-scored with 48 off 31 balls. At the innings change-over there was tremendous hype in the camp.

'Boys, we're right in this match! We get some early wickets and let's back ourselves here,' I said.

We then went out and blitzed it. I got a wicket with only my second delivery, and by the time I got my second, Trinidad and Tobago were 3-21. More than anyone on the field, Katto went berserk. But we had a long way to go, especially since we still had to get rid of Kieron Pollard, who'd smashed us in our preliminary match with 54 off only 18 balls! Again he looked in the groove and took to Doug Bollinger and Nathan Hauritz with some huge sixes.

But credit to 'Haurie', because he threw out more carrots until Pollard skied one into orbit towards me at long-on. The ball hung in the air for an eternity; it was later timed by television commentators as being eight seconds. I was near the boundary rope and right in front of the Blues camp. While the ball was coming down I had time to think: 'If I drop this we could lose the match.' But I didn't, and we didn't! I threw the ball as high as I could, not giving a second's thought to my arm. Behind me, Blues coach Matthew Mott jumped up and cheered. I've had many great moments on the cricket field, and this was up there with any of them. The guys rushed towards me. The look on their faces was magic.

Stuey Clark wrapped up the tail: Trinidad and Tobago all out 118, and victory to the 'Baby Blues' by 41 runs. After the final wicket I sprinted into the team huddle. It was an amazing feeling, comparable to winning the World Cup. It wasn't only the victory, but the whole tournament that counted. The way the team had grown together was a great example of working together, all mates, all in. I got Man of the Match and Player of the Series, but the satisfaction came from achieving as a team, and seeing the excitement of every single player, including my close mate Dom Thornely.

Throughout the tournament we'd been playing the song 'I've Got a Feeling' by the Black Eyed Peas. That was our theme song. How fitting. We got back to the dressing room and turned the volume up really loud; then we drank and hugged and went crazy. Later, back at the hotel bar, a few of the team wore budgie smugglers. No-one cared. We'd won. Everyone was over the moon.

The Champions League tournament had stopped me thinking about my Australian future, but I soon faced that head-on when I joined the national one-day team for a seven-match series against India. I bowled only six overs in our opener at Vadodara before my injury became too painful. I went off and had a painkiller straight into the elbow joint. My whole arm went numb, at which point I knew I was kidding myself.

I flew home and although I talked up my chances to the media of making a quick recovery without surgery, the reality was I had no choice but to go under the knife. Sydney surgeon Jeff Hughes reattached my ligament and also removed a bone spur. Afterwards my arm was so sore I couldn't even lift a coffee cup. It was November 2009, and the time had come to make some serious decisions.

32

When I got back to Australia after my aborted one-day campaign in India, I told Neil Maxwell I was almost sure I was going to retire from Test cricket. After I had elbow surgery, I was even more certain. The recovery was expected to take eight to 12 weeks, ruling me out of the 2009–10 home series against the West Indies and Pakistan. After that, my date of return was a lottery.

Although I'd begun weighing up my options as long ago as the Ashes series, it was only from November onwards that I sat down and assessed my position carefully. I spoke to many people whose opinions I valued, including Maxi, my family and Alan Jones. Despite media reports to the contrary, at no stage did I talk with Andrew Flintoff about my future; I don't know where that rumour came from.

The more I thought about it, the more I realised it made sense to quit the longer forms of the game. Apart from reducing the stress on me physically, it also made financial sense: if I wanted to look after my monetary future it was better to concentrate on the dollars I could earn from the IPL and other T20 possibilities. In a nutshell, if I could play less cricket, earn the same if not more money, and have more time with Preston, then why wouldn't I quit Tests?

I also looked at the mental and emotional toll that playing – or trying to play – Test cricket had taken on me. Until I was about 27 I'd been absolutely carefree when doing my best for Australia; I'd trained my arse off, played my arse off, and at the right time and place partied my arse off. But after that, I started to think about the game a lot more, which was both a good and bad thing for me. I understood a lot more about the politics that went on, and that did affect me. I was never one to suck up to someone although I saw others do it; if I was wanted in the side it was because I was a good bowler, not because I was a friend of the hierarchy. I hated that garbage.

Furthermore, I became disillusioned with cricket as a merry-go-round. I hopped on it when I was 23 years old. There I was, riding the horse, hanging on and doing well. But then suddenly I fell off because of injuries and poor form. I dusted myself off and got back on, but the merry-go-round was going faster. I hung on for a while and then got flung off again. And that was the pattern for the rest of my career on a ride that only ever got quicker and quicker.

So, all things considered, I decided I could do without such hassles. Yes, cricket had been very good to me, but I also believed I'd paid it back with integrity and commitment. It was time to move on.

On 24 February 2010, I announced my immediate retirement from Test cricket at a media conference in the Members' Bar at the SCG. I was 33 years old. I told the gathering of reporters and friends I'd had a wonderful career, and was so blessed and lucky to have been given a gift that allowed me to achieve some truly special things that I could share with so many people. Ricky Ponting, who was at my side, praised the way I'd played the game. I was genuinely touched by his words.

In the days and months following my announcement, I received lots of phone calls, texts, emails and letters from both friends and strangers from across the world. I only wish to single out one here. Allan Donald said: 'Congratulations on a wonderful Test career.' The 'White Lightning' took 330 Test wickets. I finished with 310. I think it's fitting I didn't go past my childhood hero.

After my announcement, relief flooded over me. It was like closure that I'd been waiting on for so long. I didn't intend to reflect too much on my career; that would be left for many years down the track when I was only capable of bowling in my memories. Instead, I told myself my Test retirement was just the end of one part of my cricket life, and I still had one-dayers and T20 to look forward to.

But then, more injuries struck that made me think again. After working hard to be fit for the third season of IPL, I broke my thumb trying to take a return catch off Sachin Tendulkar, and worse followed when I was ruled out of the T20 World Cup in the West Indies after straining a muscle in my right arm while bowling in a warm-up game against Zimbabwe.

So, what to do? There were some media reports that my career was over. Deep down, I knew I wasn't finished, but at 33 years of age and having injury after injury after injury, I couldn't stop some self-doubt from creeping in. That was only natural. I decided I wouldn't make a call on my playing future until I was fully fit again.

After beginning my rehabilitation in Sydney, it didn't take long for me to realise I still had the hunger to play. By then there were probably only two people who thought I could get back into the Australian team: me and my trainer Paul Haslam, who smashed me in the gym for two to three hours a day, five days a week, for six months.

The training wasn't all cricket-specific; there was significant 'cosmetic' work because we both knew the importance of perception. We felt I'd get people talking if I came out after a winter away from the spotlight and showed that I at least looked fit, buffed, brown, and ready to roll. Whether I'd withstand other injuries was an unknown but I at least wanted to make people think, 'Binga is having a real crack!'

My goal was to be selected for Australia's one-day squad to play the World Cup in India, Sri Lanka and Bangladesh in early 2011. I took the first step when I played a few games for Mosman at the start of the 2010–11 season. In some ways I felt as though I was starting all over again; it was exciting, yet daunting, being with a young group of players I didn't know. I then linked up with the NSW team for some T20 and one-day matches.

I started with some reasonable returns that were enough for me to receive some calls from journalists and Cricket Australia officials, who were keen to know how my body was going. I gave the stock-standard answer: 'I've never felt better.' Their interest kept me going, but I received a setback when I wasn't chosen in the Australian team for a T20 match and three one-dayers against Sri Lanka in early November. That really deflated me, and I wondered if I'd ever get picked again, no matter what I did.

There were some references in the media to my age. I was now 34. I hate how much attention is paid to age. If you're good enough to play cricket, or work in an office, or climb a mountain, or do whatever you want, age should never come into it. Being overlooked for the Sri Lankan series soon made me more determined: I was going to make the World Cup, and that was that. And when it happened, I hoped Australia would win and I'd then retire. That was my plan.

In my first chance to impress after Sri Lanka beat Australia 2–1 in the one-dayers, I took 5-47 for the Blues against Western Australia in Perth. I knew I was on track. In a further boost I was chosen for the Prime Minister's XI to play against England in Canberra. The team announcement happened a month before the actual match, so I tried to keep the momentum going by playing other games, most notably across the Tasman where I lined up for Wellington in New Zealand's T20 competition. Initially, Australian selector Andrew Hilditch had some concerns, but he eventually saw the advantages of me getting more game time. The deal with the Kiwis had an unusual clause that is probably a first in this day and age of professionalism. Instead of being paid, I happily played for wine. Yep, that's not a misprint, and my cellar is now very full.

By early January I was on top of the Blues' one-day wicket tally with 15. It was time for the nerves to set in as I started playing over in my mind: 'Will I or won't I get picked?' On the final day of the fifth Ashes Test in Sydney – which we all know ended a disappointing series for Punter and the boys – I was doing a Weet-Bix commercial with Australia's world champion surfer, Stephanie Gilmore. I hadn't been able to concentrate all day. As soon as the shoot finished, I walked out the studio door and turned on my phone. A minute later, I bolted back inside to find my mate Dominic Thornely, who'd helped organise the filming. My cheering and leaping gave it away. Andrew Hilditch had left a message: I was in the Australian team for two T20 games and the start of a seven-match one-day series against the Poms. The hard work had paid off, but the pressure had only just begun.

The day before the first T20 game at the Adelaide Oval, I turned to a seemingly small cosmetic detail to help show I was ready. I got my hair styled in a way that a guy in his early 20s would wear. It was a touch I hoped would make people think that I looked young and fresh, not an old bloke who'd patched himself up. Despite this appearance, I definitely had doubts about my body but I didn't want to think about that, because any further injuries simply weren't part of the script. Nor did I think too much about making an international comeback 15 months after I'd last played for Australia in a one-dayer. Instead, I went in with the mindset that I'd come off a 5-for in a game only a couple of days earlier and I was just preparing for the next match.

I took one wicket in the drawn T20 series, and headed into the one-dayers with the specific aim of becoming the team's number-one bowler. There was no definitive point in the series when I knew I was back. However, when I saw the ball swinging and I hit the 152-plus k mark a few times early on, I confirmed my own belief that I still had a lot to offer at the top level. In game three at the SCG I took 3-27. It was the best I'd bowled in a long, long time. The other matches were just a blur; once again I was back trying to cling on to the merry-go-round. Australia won 6–1 under Michael Clarke, the stand-in skipper for Punter, who was recovering from a broken finger. I finished on top of the series bowling stats with 11 wickets.

Throughout the summer I worked hard on some new deliveries that were especially important when bowling at the death of an innings, one of my favourite yet pressure-filled roles in cricket. In addition to fine-tuning a slower bouncer, a ball that evolved from the T20 format, I spent time developing a delivery from around the wicket that swung back into left-handers, as opposed to my usual habit of moving the ball away. In the nets I also had a special drill for bowling to right-handers, where I'd try to hit the base of a stump placed at the junction of the wide line and the popping crease, an area where it's obviously difficult to play an aggressive stroke. I was able to use all these deliveries successfully during the series. They were part of my development as a fast bowler, and moving with the times.

Although I thought I'd done more than enough to get picked for the World Cup, there was still that period of uncertainty when the 'what if's played with my mind. Given that, it was a great relief when I was named in the tour squad. My selection, or more precisely the choice of three front-line fast bowlers, was controversial. The media questioned why Mitchell Johnson, Shaun Tait and I would all be needed on the slow pitches of the subcontinent. Furthermore, we had Shane Watson and John Hastings as medium pace back-ups, while we only had one specialist spinner, Jason Krejza, and all-rounder Steve Smith. Were the selectors gambling too heavily on the quicks? No. I believed if we all got the ball in the right areas we'd be a handful, because of our different styles and angles.

Unfortunately, the team had an ordinary start. We lost warm-up games in Bangalore against India and South Africa. Back home I heard there was a lot of negative media about us: not only shouldn't we have chosen three quicks, but Punter was under pressure both as a batsman and captain, our middle order was struggling, and questions were raised over our skill against spin. Everything seemed up against us.

We spoke about the issues in team meetings, and although we were in a decent head space I don't think we were in a great one. For the first time I sensed throughout the team that we were questioning whether we were good enough to go all the way. In previous World Cups we had Gilly, Warnie, Pidgie and others who could be banked on to do something special. If one failed, another stepped up. But this time we didn't have the luxury of having blokes like that.

Our opening match against Zimbabwe in Ahmedabad reflected one of our downfalls during the tournament: we were too timid with the bat. Shane Watson and Brad Haddin reached only 32 off the first 13 overs. Admittedly spin helped tie them down, but if an aggressive game-breaker like Virender Sehwag had been playing, he would have been murdering the ball into the stands. That's probably spoken like a true fast bowler, and I'm the first to admit there were times when we didn't do our job with the ball either. Overall, I wondered if guys were worrying about their spots too much to play normally. Our tentative approaches, and at times lack of initiative, certainly put us under pressure.

The game against Zimbabwe was an interesting one for me. A couple of days before we played, Punter told me Taity was going to bowl the first over and I'd come on at the other end. I actually didn't think I'd heard him right. I thought the decision showed I wasn't considered the number-one strike bowler. I could see Punter's point of view because he reckoned Taity's extreme pace and ability to swing the ball back in was most likely to get a wicket. However, I still felt I should have had the honour, and when it came time to charge in off my mark for the first time, I didn't have the right attitude.

I was hit for 13, including a six, after only two overs. Stupidly, I was angry with Punter and I sulked at fine leg. It was only at the start of my third over that I pulled myself together and concentrated on what I had to do. I quickly got a wicket, my only one for the innings in a 91-run win. Afterwards Punter said to me: 'You had the shits with me, didn't you?' We laughed about it, but that didn't stop it happening again later in the tournament against Canada. Looking back, it was nothing more than a slap to my ego.

After beating Zimbabwe, we had wins against New Zealand and Kenya, and we drew a rain-abandoned match against Sri Lanka. I took a wicket in each game before grabbing a 4-for against Canada. At that point we knew we weren't playing well enough, either individually or as a team, to be a real threat when the competition heated up. There was some anxiety in the squad and it was obvious we weren't enjoying playing as much as we should have been.

Before our final preliminary game against Pakistan in Colombo, a couple of the players asked me if I thought it was strange we didn't have any beer in the dressing room after matches. I said it wasn't only strange, it was ordinary as well. I don't want to give the impression that we were really keen to get smashed, but I do think the fun had been taken out of our team culture. I acknowledge we had to adhere to warm-down practices, such as ice baths, but in my opinion, and it may be my opinion only, we weren't relaxing together as a group. It made me wonder what we were playing cricket for; it almost seemed that we were too afraid to have fun. When Tim Paine, who I believe will be a great leader for Australia at some stage, asked me if he should get some beers, I jumped up at the idea. Tim wasn't playing, so he had some time to arrange the post-match activities, which we decided would go ahead win, lose or draw.

The match turned out to be a shocker for us. We lost by four wickets. After winning the toss and batting we were rolled for only 176. Our bowlers tried really hard to fight back, and if there was a personal positive to come out of the result, it was my 4-28 off eight overs. I felt in the groove and mostly landed the ball where I wanted to in my best display since returning to Australian colours. The satisfaction I got from that was overshadowed by our team performance. The loss ended Australia's record run of 34 unbeaten World Cup matches that stretched back to 1999 in England. Some of the guys were devastated, but I preferred to think that we'd qualified for the quarterfinals and needed to concentrate on what lay ahead. And, importantly, I hoped some team bonding would help us.

The players looked happy when they saw the beers. We sat in the dressing room, and after a couple of drinks we started to relax and tell a few stories; it was like the old days. I found it really interesting watching some of the younger guys in the team; they kept their eyes on Punter, and it wasn't until he had a beer and chilled out that the others followed suit. Then, our batting coach, Justin Langer, said a few words. He told us we'd displayed a lot of character to keep the game as close as we did, and that showed we had what it took to win the tournament. It was stirring stuff.

Our fielding coach, Mike Young, followed. Youngie, an American with a baseball background, is fantastic for team morale. He is always up-beat and full of energy. Before speaking, he told me the gist of what he was going to say. It was a little different, but I thought it would be a great way to get the guys together. So, Youngie got up and read from a piece of paper he was holding.

'Listen to this. Win, win, win, win, win, win, win, win, win, win . . .' he said, making reference to our unbeaten run.

He compared Australia's record against other champion teams such as the Chicago Bulls, and various baseball and Premier League soccer clubs. No-one came close to Australia's record. Youngie continued by asking everyone to link arms before he said: 'All you have to do is yell "Yeah, man!" after each line I say.'

He then launched into a verse, supported by every other guy in the room coming together as one: 'I went down to the river.'

'Yeah, man!'

'And I started to drown.'

'Yeah, man!'

'When I heard about Australia.'

'Yeah, man!'

'I couldn't go down.'

'Yeah, man!'

'So I went to the railroad.'

'Yeah, man!'

'Put my head on the track.'

'Yeah, man!'

'When I heard about Australia.'

'Yeah, man!'

'I pulled it right back.'

'Yeah, man!'

'So I went to a bar.'

'Yeah, man!'

'And they started a fight.' (At that moment Mike pointed to Pakistan's dressing room.)

'Yeah, man!'

'They should've heard about Australia.'

'Yeah, man!'

'Because we'll fight all night.'

'Yeah, man!'

'It takes Elvis to rock.'

'Yeah, man!'

'It takes a cricket ball to roll.'

'Yeah, man!'

'It takes a team like Australia.'

'Yeah, man!'

'To soothe my soul-l-l-l-l.'

We finished with a huge 'Woop, woop!' and high-fived each other. Everyone was pumped; the mood was fantastic and was exactly what we'd been missing. Most of us decided we'd head out that night and have a few drinks at a bar just down the road from the team hotel. It was a Saturday night, and we had no team commitment until Monday afternoon when we'd travel to our next venue ahead of our quarterfinal on the Thursday, still five days away. This was the perfect time to gather as a group and lift morale; it was much more important than having a drink when everything was rosy after we'd smashed an opponent.

However, team management decided it wasn't the right time to unwind and we should already begin concentrating on our next match. The players were stunned. It was like someone had deflated a massive balloon filled with our energy. It was a huge letdown. I heard one player say, 'What are we, Under-17s?' Punter, to his credit, told us to grab some beers for the road. I took about six and shoved them in my bag.

By the time we got back to the hotel, there were whispers the order had come from higher up at Cricket Australia, and our security had been instructed to report back to management the names of any players who went out. Punter asked me what I was planning, and after I told him I wanted to go out he warned me to 'just be careful'. Over the next while, a handful of players came to my room at different times to seek my advice. They said they felt that, as a senior player, I was in a different position and didn't have as much to lose as them. That swayed me to stay in. It was a case of 'one in, all in'.

However, no-one said we still couldn't have a good time. So, some of the guys gathered in my room and we stayed up until about 4 am, having a few drinks. Nothing untoward happened, and no harm was done to anyone.

I think it's important to mention the incident because I really want the outsider to have an idea of what being in a team environment can be like. I can understand where management was coming from, but then again, we were all grown men who were capable of making our own decisions. I believe that the incident had a negative effect on the squad. It's all too easy for such decisions to snowball. If a player is told he can't do something that he considers to be quite reasonable, it's possible resentment can develop. Or alternately, the player becomes so worried about doing something wrong that suddenly he thinks twice about taking a chance in a match, for fear that his action might be seen as irresponsible. I reckon that guys in our squad became scared of doing everything from having a beer or two to playing a daring shot.

So, the signs weren't great heading into our quarterfinal against India in Ahmedabad. I have two distinct and different memories about the day before the game. The first involved a Skype call I had with Preston in Sydney. At one stage my son said to me: 'Daddy, can you lose tomorrow so you can come home and see me?' How do you answer that?

The second happened when I asked to see Punter alone in our hotel team room. He'd been copping a lot of bad media and questions were growing over whether or not he should retire if Australia were to lose. He didn't deserve that crap. I'm sure he thought I wanted to chat with him about my bowling, but instead I wanted to talk about his batting. I told him he was the one person in Australian and world cricket who'd stood up when needed in the past decade.

'If you go out tomorrow and snick the first ball, but have the right mindset, I won't care,' I said.

I added that I thought he was trying too hard, and all he needed to do was 'just go out and bat, mate. Just go out and hit the ball. Don't be scared about getting out. Nothing has changed. You're still our number one batsman.' I think Punter appreciated it.

The next day he scored 104 in our 6-260. He was brilliant, returning to his form of the 2003 World Cup when he hit the ball over cover, taking on the spinners and the quicks. I could see how much he wanted to get runs; he was dying to get them for the team. I was really proud of him.

But it wasn't enough. We didn't bowl consistently well enough, and in the end, India got the runs with five wickets and 14 balls in hand. My Kings XI mate Yuvraj Singh steered his team home with an unbeaten 50-odd. I'd bowled OK in patches to finish with 1-45, including having the winning runs hit off me. My day, and perhaps Australia's as well, was summed up when I dived for a ball on the boundary, only for it to bounce up and smack into my right eye. Then I felt something dripping on me. Blood. I went off, got patched up, and returned for the final overs of our tournament, and the last World Cup match of my career. I couldn't believe we'd lost. How? What? Why? I just couldn't comprehend it at all.

Back at the team hotel, the disbelief made way for one of the true joys of playing sport, when some of the Australians joined the Indians for a drink. I took my guitar and soon players from both teams were having a sing-along. There was no need to be tough Aussie bastards any more. It was time to relax and renew friendships. While this was happening I realised I'd soon be seeing Preston again. His request on Skype had come true, although he later told his mum that he thought Australia's loss was his fault; the poor little man.

We came back to Australia to find most of the media focus on Punter. Within a week he stepped down as captain of both the one-day and Test teams. I believe he still has the drive and ability to follow Sachin Tendulkar, who is batting as well as ever after surrendering the Indian captaincy a while ago. Time will tell.

As for me? Well, my plan to retire at the end of the World Cup has been shelved. I'd now love to go past Glenn McGrath's Australian record of 381 one-day wickets and become the first Aussie to reach 400. At the time of writing, I'm on 348. I wish I could press the fast-forward button and find out what will happen. But it's also nice to be challenged by the uncertainty of the future. I'll continue to play for as long as I enjoy it and feel as though I'm contributing to the team. Of course, that's if my body allows it. If I start hurting too much, I'll quit. Simple as that.

Within days of my arrival home from the World Cup, I discovered a paparazzi photographer lurking in my street. After I was able to lose him in traffic when he was following me, I later found him back near my home. I confronted him. Initially he denied he was looking for me, but he soon admitted he was hoping to take a picture of me and Preston. Instead, I took a photo of him on my mobile phone and reported him to the police. It was just another day for me as an Australian cricketer.

33

The following story sums up how I've had a far from normal life, and it's a life I'll be forever grateful for. The day after NSW won the Champions League in India, I had to fly across the country to link up with the Australian team. I was hungover and keen for sleep when a polite, well-dressed man approached me. He said his name was Rohit, the personal assistant of Mr Venky, who requested my company in the first-class cabin. Presuming it was just an autograph or photo request, I said I'd see Mr Venky at the end of the flight. Rohit went away, but came back again a few minutes later and insisted I was to swap seats with him and go and sit with Mr Venky. I still didn't want to do it, and tried to put an end to the issue by going to the toilet, but when I returned Rohit was sitting in my seat.

So I went to the pointy end of the plane and found Mr Venky. At first his name didn't register, but then I realised it had been on the uniforms of the Trinidad and Tobago team that we'd beaten in the Champions League final. Mr Venky had sponsored the team because he was looking at ways to increase his business's exposure and cricket was the ideal avenue. Mr Venky ran the biggest commercial poultry operation in India. We got on well right from the start, and after some basic chat I said half-jokingly that I should be the 'face of Venky's', to which Mr Venky replied without hesitation: 'Done!' From that moment on, I've been the brand ambassador for Venky's chickens.

We parted as the best of friends with a promise from me that I'd arrange a private box for Mr Venky to watch Australia play India in Mumbai just a few days after my 33rd birthday. Unfortunately, by the time of the match, I was back in Sydney nursing my elbow injury. It was at that point Neil Maxwell received a phone call that stunned us both.

'Can you remember Rohit?' Maxi asked me. 'Well, he's coming to Australia, and you'll never guess why.'

'Why?'

'Because he says he has to deliver you a birthday present from Mr Venky.'

Sure enough, a couple of days later Rohit arrived in Sydney. Maxi and I took him to dinner at the revolving restaurant at Australia Square. Before the meal began, he presented me with a gift-wrapped box. I opened it to find another box. I opened that one to find a watch. A $45,000 Rolex watch!

'Happy birthday from Mr Venky,' said Rohit.

Rohit flew back to India the next morning; he'd been in Australia for less than a day.

I realise not everyone has this kind of thing happen to them – I've been incredibly lucky in a profession that, rightly or wrongly, allows such luck. While putting this book together, I've been blown away by looking back at what has happened in my life. I would never have thought in my wildest dreams that I would have done what I have. I'm immensely proud to have played for Australia. Some people may think that I had a sad farewell from Test cricket, but I don't consider limping off the field at the MCG as my last game. I prefer to consider my final outing as being against the England Lions at Worcester in 2009 when I took a bagful of wickets. That was the last time I wore my greatest personal Australian cricket treasure: the baggy green cap.

I've surprised myself a lot in my cricket career. I look back now and wonder how I played with various injuries. How did I bowl when my arm wasn't joined or when I had a broken foot? Those questions and their answers are little wonders to me. I also ask myself: 'How did I hit that six? How did I take that wicket? How did I speak at that media conference?' The broad answer is that I was very fortunate to have been given the chance to do any and all of it.

I also look at the people I've played with and against. There are too many names to mention here. I need only say that I've played in an incredible era with some of the all-time greats of the game. I'm grateful for the friendships I've made, and feel privileged that I'm a member of the international cricket family. I'll leave it to others to judge me, but I hope enough fans and players alike will remember me as a player who gave everything he had on the field, and gave mateship off it. I like to think I played with the utmost determination, but was, for much of the time, able to smile too.

It's essential not to understate – or overstate – the financial gains I've made from cricket. I have benefited tremendously. Money is very important to me, but it's not everything. To this day I'd give it all back if I could have a perfect family life.

Preston is my greatest joy. I remember the first time I saw him roll over, and the first time he walked. When I took him to his first swimming lesson, I held him in my arms while standing in a circle of mothers singing nursery rhymes that I didn't know; if I was to be a good dad I realised I had to learn them quickly! I also remember when the little man started saying a few words, just mumbles really; I'd sneak into his room when he was trying to sleep and I'd hear him struggling to get his mouth around the syllables. It was so cute.

Preston has always made me laugh. When he was about two, he saw me on a television commercial and immediately went round the back of the TV to see if I was there. Not so long ago, I flew him over to Fiji in his very own business class seat. His legs didn't reach the ends of the cushions and his arms couldn't reach the arm rests. He looked like a child prince. He waved at every passenger who passed us, and oh so politely asked the stewardess for a 'water, please'. It was a simple moment, yet a precious memory. There was also the time he came and watched me and Tim Cahill shoot an ad for Weet-Bix in which we had to be astronauts. I'm sure Preston actually thought we went into outer space. My proudest moment is when I go to pick Preston up from pre-school and he pops his head up from whatever he's doing and says: 'That's my daddy!'

I look at Preston now as though we're the best of mates. I'm best mates with my dad as well, so I hope Preston and I have the same relationship all the way through his life. Obviously my break-up with Liz means we don't have the perfect set-up for raising a child, but Preston will never be short of attention. Liz and I both love him dearly and that will never change; we'll always strive to be the best possible parents.

Every age and stage of Preston's life has been great, and it will only get better and better. I look forward to growing up and growing old with him, and making him very much a part of the whole Lee family. He couldn't have better teachers than H and the Doctor, who have loved me, Shane and Grant every day of our lives. Mum and Dad devoted their lives to us; they are the most amazing parents ever. Welcome to a very special club, Preston. That club also extends to my close friends. They know who they are. My life would be totally different without their love and support, and their sledges when I'm getting too far ahead!

So what about my future? That's a difficult question to answer because I've never been much of a planner; I prefer to be spontaneous. However, I do know that music will play a central role in my life. A couple of years ago I formed a band with Mick Vawdon and his girlfriend, Mel. We called it White Shoe Theory, a name we thought of while we were sitting in a pub one night wondering why so many people were wearing white shoes. Since then, we've produced a number of songs that we want to develop further. In late 2010, Mick and I went on a six-gig tour of India with two full-time musicians, Kere Buchanan and Jak Housden. It was great fun, and something Mick and I want to do a lot more of in the future. I realise there are so many musicians with a million times more talent than me, but how many of them are too frightened to have a crack? I never want to be one of those people. It's best to have a go and fall flat on your face than not have a go at all.

In wrapping this all up, I'll share one final story with you. In mid 2010, I was in Byron Bay on the far-north coast of NSW. Mick and I had just finished playing at a Sanitarium sales conference. It had been a 1960s theme, so I got dressed up as John Lennon, complete with a wig, glasses, tight slacks, the works. Afterwards, I decided to leave the full kit on when we went to a bar for a beer. It was fantastic because no-one recognised me. People were coming up and saying: 'Hey, John, I love the Beatles!' Finally, a little Indian man approached me, gave me the once-over, and said with a really serious voice: 'You're Brett Lee. I know it's you. I can tell it's you.' I smiled and told him not to tell anyone. Then he shook my hand, walked off, and kept the secret between us. If I wound the clock back 20 or so years I was just a boy from Mount Warrigal who wanted to play cricket for Australia and be on TV. To pinch a word from a Lennon classic, imagine.

ACKNOWLEDGEMENTS

BRETT LEE

My life has been made up of various parts: family, mates, mentors, music, injuries and, of course, cricket, both on and off the field. In each part I've been blessed to have great people around me who've had a tremendous impact on me. They've brought me back from the pits of non-selection and injury, they've been there to share my joy, they've counselled me, and they've kept me in touch with reality. Above all else, they've always been there. So, there are many people to thank.

Firstly, to Mum and Dad. You've given me endless love and support, and taught me about the real meaning of life and how to respect and treat others. Thank you too for those thousands of hours driving and watching cricket so I could achieve my dream. I love both of you very much. To my brothers, Shane and Grant, thank you for also helping to shape me into what I am today. And to my little man, Preston, you're my best friend. You're so kind and caring, you make me laugh and inspire me every single day. Thanks for being the best boy in the world, I love you so much!

To Maxi, Rachel and the kids (Lachie, Sophie and Olivia are all great friends of Preston's), I am so lucky to have you all in my life. Maxi, your guidance and friendship has been my rock since this all began. Nothing is ever too hard for you; you are forever honest and have taught me about life away from cricket. Professionally you are brilliant at what you do, and your integrity and loyalty are the reasons why you're so well respected and successful in the corporate world. You're a true friend.

I also owe so much to my other close mates. AJ (Alan Jones), you are not only a friend, but my guardian and mentor who is always there to advise me. You are a 'one-off' because of your wish to always help people; I feel privileged I am a part of the very small and exclusive 'pick-and-stick club'. And to Luke Buxton, Corey Richards, Adam Rainford, Mick Vawdon (and Mel) and Dom Thornely (and Katie), thank you for all you've done, and I look forward to our journeys together as we grow older.

There are so many others on my thank-you list:

- All the team at Insite, especially Judie Andersen who does the hard work day in and day out. Jude, you are my 'go-to' person. Your work ethic is unquestionable. You are amazing.
- Richard and Julie Bowman for providing me with my first break and being great friends.
- Mick Vawdon for showing me the joy of music.
- Dennis Lillee for being 'the master'.
- Allan Donald for exciting me about fast bowling.
- Basil Sellers and the MRF Pace Foundation.
- Steve Rixon for being a great coach and believing in me.
- Patty Farhart for getting me on the field when no-one else could.
- Paul Haslam for the many hours in the gym.
- Oak Flats, Campbelltown and Mosman cricket clubs.
- Cricket NSW, Cricket Australia and all my teammates.

My partners at Sanitarium, especially Rick Wilson, Derick Frere and Christina Hawkins; Vodafone, in particular Nigel Dews; Nine Network; Jupi; Castrol; Podar Enterprises, in particular Rajiv Podar; Pearls India, the chairman Mr N. S. Bhangoo and my little mate Rikhab Jain; Venky's India, in particular Mr Venkatesh and Mr Balaji; Timex, especially Mr Kapil Kapoor.

Thank you also to Jane Burridge for helping to make this book happen. To Alison Urquhart, Patrick Mangan and all the team at Random House, a big pat on the back to you all. I think the book looks great. And last but by no means least, James Knight. Thanks, Knighty, for putting this into words and for following me around the world to get them.

JAMES KNIGHT

In addition to those mentioned above, thank you to Caite Nguyen who administers the official website: brett-lee.net. The information you provided was invaluable. A big thank you as well to Mark Raisbeck, the most organised 'band manager' I've ever known. To Philip Gregson and Dave McCredie, I appreciate you having the time to read sections of the manuscript. To Clare and Mum, thanks for putting up with me.

To my late dad, thank you for being proud of me and my brother, Lewis, and I'm sorry we can't add this book to your special shelf. To Raymond and Michelle, thank you for listening to the never-ending driveway conversations about the book, and to my other close friends, especially Tombsy and Pete, I can never repay you for 'being there'.

And to 'B' Lee. Mate, thanks for your tolerance when I pushed you. We had our moments, but mostly it was good fun. Now, let's get out and go for a run somewhere. Maybe Goa would be nice!

CAREER STATISTICS

FIRST-CLASS CAREER

	M	Inn	NO	Runs	HS	0s	50	100	Avrge	Ct	St	Balls	Mdns	Runs	Wkts	Avrge	5	10	Best
Test cricket	76	90	18	1451	64	14	5	–	20.15	23	–	16531	547	9554	310	30.82	10	–	5–30
Sheffield Shield	21	29	4	422	97	8	2	–	16.88	9	–	4590	166	2543	97	26.22	7	2	7–114
Other first-class games	19	20	3	247	79	5	1	–	14.53	3	–	3072	94	1650	80	20.63	3	–	6–25

Opponents	M	Inn	NO	Runs	HS	0s	50	100	Avrge	Ct	St	Balls	Mdns	Runs	Wkts	Avrge	5	10	Best
BANGLADESH	4	3	–	67	29	–	–	–	22.33	5	–	578	20	376	8	47.00	–	–	3–23
Central Districts	1	1	–	0	0	1	–	–	0.00	–	–	156	4	61	2	30.50	–	–	2–35
ENGLAND	18	21	5	334	47	4	–	–	20.88	4	–	3921	101	2518	62	40.61	1	–	4–47
England Lions	1	1	–	6	6	–	–	–	6.00	–	–	210	7	114	7	16.29	–	–	6–76
Essex	1	1	–	79	79	–	1	–	79.00	–	–	42	1	41	1	41.00	–	–	1–41
Hampshire	1	2	–	24	22	–	–	–	12.00	–	–	156	8	71	5	14.20	–	–	3–17
Indian Board President's XI	1	1	–	0	0	1	–	–	0.00	1	–	216	5	121	2	60.50	–	–	1–60
Indians	1	2	1	11	11*	1	–	–	11.00	–	–	312	13	133	7	19.00	–	–	4–77
INDIA	12	16	3	192	59	5	1	–	14.77	2	–	3028	93	1695	53	31.98	2	–	5–47
Jamaica Select XI	1	1	–	1	1	–	–	–	1.00	–	–	150	5	85	2	42.50	–	–	1–33
Leicestershire	1	1	–	6	6	–	–	–	6.00	–	–	162	5	131	5	26.20	–	–	4–53
Matabeleland Invitational XI	1	1	–	10	10	–	–	–	10.00	–	–	106	5	39	9	4.33	1	–	5–26

Opponents	M	Inn	NO	Runs	HS	0s	50	100	Avrge	Ct	St	Balls	Mdns	Runs	Wkts	Avrge	5	10	Best
Mumbai	1	1	–	21	21	–	–	–	21.00	–	–	126	4	53	2	26.50	–	–	2-53
Northern Districts	1	1	–	39	39	–	–	–	39.00	–	–	210	7	111	4	27.75	–	–	2-50
NEW ZEALAND	8	10	1	169	61	1	1	–	18.78	2	–	1662	63	928	44	21.09	3	–	5-67
New Zealand Cricket Academy	1	1	1	0	0*	–	–	–	–	–	–	156	2	119	4	29.75	–	–	3-71
New Zealanders	1	1	–	33	33	–	–	–	33.00	–	–	196	7	89	5	17.80	–	–	3-52
PAKISTAN	3	4	–	27	12	–	–	–	6.75	–	–	401	13	234	5	46.80	–	–	2-15
Queensland	4	7	1	80	34	1	–	–	13.33	–	–	792	28	460	9	51.11	–	–	3-77
South Australia	5	6	1	26	17*	3	–	–	5.20	2	–	1090	39	638	30	21.27	2	1	7-114
SRI LANKA	2	–	–	–	–	–	–	–	–	1	–	568	23	281	16	17.56	–	–	4-26
SOUTH AFRICA	14	19	4	314	64	4	1	–	20.93	2	–	3122	104	1732	50	34.64	2	–	5-69
Sri Lankan Board President's	1	1	–	2	2	–	–	–	2.00	–	–	64	1	47	5	9.40	–	–	4-29
South Africa A	2	3	–	6	6	2	–	–	2.00	1	–	252	6	124	8	15.50	–	–	4-37
South Africans	1	1	1	9	9*	–	–	–	–	–	–	246	9	115	2	57.50	–	–	1-42
Sussex	1	–	–	–	–	–	–	–	–	–	–	198	3	144	2	72.00	–	–	2-27
Tasmania	6	6	–	102	37	2	–	–	17.00	3	–	1474	61	742	31	23.94	4	1	5-53
Victoria	4	7	2	213	97	–	2	–	42.60	3	–	786	23	450	16	28.13	1	–	5-42
Western Australia	2	3	–	1	1	2	–	–	0.33	1	–	448	15	253	11	23.00	–	–	4-55
WEST INDIES	12	14	4	338	63*	–	2	–	33.80	6	–	2705	110	1472	64	23.00	3	–	5-30
WORLD XI	1	2	–	4	3	–	–	–	2.00	1	–	108	3	96	2	48.00	–	–	1-42
Zimbabwe Cricket Academy XI	1	–	–	–	–	–	–	–	–	1	–	114	2	52	8	6.50	1	–	6-25
ZIMBABWE	2	1	1	6	6*	–	–	–	–	–	–	438	17	222	6	37.00	–	–	3-48

	Inn	NO	Runs	HS	0s	50	100	Avrge	Ct	St	Balls	Mdns	Runs	Wkts	Avrge	5	10	Best
First Innings	43	7	752	74*	7	4	–	20.89	12	–	5777	195	3257	133	24.49	8	–	6–25
Second Innings	57	8	760	64	13	2	–	15.51	11	–	7928	262	4575	143	31.99	4	–	7–114
Third Innings	27	6	397	97	3	2	–	18.90	7	–	3723	115	2111	74	28.53	3	–	5–30
Fourth Innings	12	4	211	46	4	–	–	26.38	5	–	6765	235	3804	137	27.77	5	–	5–26

Team	M	Inn	NO	Runs	HS	0s	50	100	Avrge	Ct	St	Balls	Mdns	Runs	Wkts	Avrge	5	10	Best
AIS Cricket Academy	3	2	1	10	10	–	–	–	10.00	1	–	376	9	210	21	10.00	2	–	6–25
Australia A	1	1	1	9	9*	–	–	–	–	–	–	246	9	115	2	57.50	–	–	1–42
AUSTRALIA	76	90	18	1451	64	14	5	–	20.15	23	–	16531	547	9554	310	30.82	10	–	5–30
Australian XI	13	14	–	184	79	4	1	–	13.14	2	–	1942	56	1103	45	24.51	1	–	6–76
New South Wales	23	32	5	466	97	9	2	–	17.26	9	–	5098	186	2765	109	25.37	7	2	7–114

How Dismissed:	Inns	NO	Bwd	CFd	CWk	LBW	Stp	RO	HW
	139	25	19	52	26	13	1	3	–

Wickets Taken:	Wkts	Bwd	CFd	C&B	CWk	LBW	Stp	HW
	487	116	154	8	131	78	–	–

Batsmen Dismissed:	Wkts	1/2	3	4	5	6	7	8	9	10	11
	487	121	60	51	39	44	41	42	26	40	23

411

Brett Lee

Highest Score: 97   New South Wales v Victoria, Sydney, 2007–08

Best Bowling: 7–114   New South Wales v South Australia, Sydney, 2002–03

Wkts	Team	Opponent	Venue	Season
5–53	New South Wales	Tasmania	Hobart	1998–99
5–26	AIS Cricket Academy	Matabeleland Invitational	Bulawayo	1998–99
6–25	AIS Cricket Academy	Zimbabwe Cricket Academy	Harare	1998–99
5–47	Australia	India	Melbourne	1999–00
5–77	Australia	New Zealand	Hamilton	1999–00
5–42	New South Wales	Victoria	Richmond	2000–01
5–61	Australia	West Indies	Perth	2000–01
5–56	New South Wales	South Australia	Sydney	2001–02
5–67	Australia	New Zealand	Brisbane	2001–02
5–63	New South Wales	Tasmania	Sydney	2002–03
5–86	New South Wales	Tasmania	Sydney	2002–03
7–114	New South Wales	South Australia	Sydney	2002–03
5–124	New South Wales	Tasmania	Sydney	2003–04
5–30	Australia	West Indies	Brisbane	2005–06
5–93	Australia	South Africa	Perth	2005–06
5–69	Australia	South Africa	Durban	2005–06
5–119	Australia	India	Sydney	2007–08
5–59	Australia	West Indies	North Sound	2007–08
5–105	Australia	New Zealand	Adelaide	2008–09
6–76	Australian XI	England Lions	Worcester	2009

TEST CAREER

Debut: 1999–00, Australia v India, Melbourne

Season	Opponent	Venue	M	Inn	NO	Runs	HS	0s	50	100	Avrge	Ct	St	Balls	Mdns	Runs	Wkts	Avrge	5	10	Best
1999–00	India	Australia	2	1	–	27	27	–	–	–	27.00	–	–	414	19	184	13	14.15	–	–	5–47
1999–00	New Zealand	New Zealand	3	4	1	20	8	1	–	–	6.67	1	–	604	26	314	18	17.44	1	–	5–77
2000–01	West Indies	Australia	2	2	2	103	62*	–	1	–	–	–	–	355	21	177	11	16.09	1	–	5–61
2001	England	England	5	4	–	24	20	2	–	–	6.00	–	–	725	18	496	9	55.11	–	–	2–37
2001–02	New Zealand	Australia	3	3	–	119	61	–	1	–	39.67	–	–	605	19	352	14	25.14	1	–	5–67
2001–02	South Africa	Australia	3	3	–	64	32	–	–	–	21.33	1	–	630	27	314	9	34.89	–	–	3–77
2001–02	South Africa	South Africa	3	4	2	27	23*	2	–	–	13.50	1	–	572	10	416	10	41.60	–	–	4–82
2002–03	Pakistan	Sri Lanka	3	4	–	27	12	–	–	–	6.75	–	–	401	13	234	5	46.80	–	–	2–15
2002–03	England	Australia	3	3	–	87	46	1	–	–	29.00	–	–	868	26	536	13	41.23	–	–	3–78
2002–03	West Indies	West Indies	4	4	–	58	20	–	–	–	14.50	4	–	867	33	491	17	28.88	–	–	4–63
2002–03	Bangladesh	Australia	2	1	–	23	23	–	–	–	23.00	2	–	296	10	190	6	31.67	–	–	3–23
2003–04	Zimbabwe	Australia	2	1	1	6	6*	1	–	–	–	–	–	438	17	222	6	37.00	–	–	3–48
2003–04	India	Australia	2	2	–	8	8	–	–	–	4.00	–	–	605	17	476	8	59.50	–	–	4–201
2005	England	England	5	9	3	158	47	–	–	–	26.33	2	–	1147	25	822	20	41.10	–	–	4–82
2005–06	World XI	Australia	1	2	–	4	3	–	–	–	2.00	1	–	108	3	96	2	48.00	–	–	1–42
2005–06	West Indies	Australia	3	3	–	74	47	–	–	–	24.67	–	–	687	26	377	18	20.94	1	–	5–30
2005–06	South Africa	Australia	3	4	1	72	32	2	–	–	24.00	–	–	798	29	421	13	32.38	1	–	5–93
2005–06	South Africa	South Africa	3	4	1	88	64	–	1	–	29.33	–	–	696	29	332	17	19.53	1	–	5–69
2005–06	Bangladesh	Bangladesh	2	2	–	44	29	–	–	–	22.00	3	–	282	10	186	2	93.00	–	–	1–35
2006–07	England	Australia	5	5	2	65	43*	1	–	–	21.67	2	–	1181	32	664	20	33.20	–	–	4–47
2007–08	Sri Lanka	Australia	2	–	–	–	–	–	–	–	–	1	–	568	23	281	16	17.56	–	–	4–26
2007–08	India	Australia	4	7	2	86	59	2	1	–	17.20	1	–	1121	33	542	24	22.58	1	–	5–119
2007–08	West Indies	West Indies	3	5	2	103	63*	–	1	–	34.33	2	–	796	30	427	18	23.72	1	–	5–59
2008–09	India	India	4	6	1	71	35	2	–	–	14.20	1	–	888	24	493	8	61.63	–	–	2–48
2008–09	New Zealand	Australia	4	7	–	93	29	–	–	–	13.29	–	–	879	27	511	13	39.31	1	–	5–105
Total			76	90	18	1451	64	14	5	–	20.15	23	–	16531	547	9554	310	30.82	10	–	5–30

Brett Lee

Opponents	M	Inn	NO	Runs	HS	0s	50	100	Avrge	Ct	St	Balls	Mdns	Runs	Wkts	Avrge	5	10	Best
Bangladesh	4	3	–	67	29	4	–	–	22.33	5	–	578	20	376	8	47.00	–	–	3–23
England	18	21	5	334	47	4	–	–	20.88	4	–	3921	101	2518	62	40.61	–	–	4–47
India	12	16	3	192	59	5	1	–	14.77	2	–	3028	93	1695	53	31.98	2	–	5–47
New Zealand	8	10	1	169	61	1	1	–	18.78	2	–	1662	63	928	44	21.09	3	–	5–67
Pakistan	3	4	–	27	12	–	–	–	6.75	–	–	401	13	234	5	46.80	–	–	2–15
Sri Lanka	2	–	–	–	–	–	–	–	–	1	–	568	23	281	16	17.56	–	–	4–26
South Africa	14	19	4	314	64	4	1	–	20.93	2	–	3122	104	1732	50	34.64	2	–	5–69
West Indies	12	14	4	338	63*	–	2	–	33.80	6	–	2705	110	1472	64	23.00	3	–	5–30
World XI	1	2	–	4	3	–	–	–	2.00	1	–	108	3	96	2	48.00	–	–	1–42
Zimbabwe	2	1	1	6	6*	–	–	–	–	–	–	438	17	222	6	37.00	–	–	3–48

	Inn	NO	Runs	HS	0s	50	100	Avrge	Ct	St	Balls	Mdns	Runs	Wkts	Avrge	5	10	Best
First Innings	30	5	580	63*	4	3	–	23.20	7	–	3881	134	2200	87	25.29	6	–	5–47
Second Innings	37	5	535	64	7	2	–	16.72	7	–	5097	163	2993	87	34.40	1	–	5–77
Third Innings	15	5	176	32	–	–	–	17.60	5	–	2899	90	1614	46	35.09	1	–	5–30
Fourth Innings	8	3	160	46	3	–	–	32.00	4	–	4654	160	2747	90	30.52	2	–	5–61

Venue	M	Inn	NO	Runs	HS	0s	50	100	Avrge	Ct	St	Balls	Mdns	Runs	Wkts	Avrge	5	10	Best
in Australia …																			
Adelaide	5	5	1	68	32	–	–	–	17.00	2	–	1449	37	787	26	30.27	1	–	5–105
Brisbane	6	6	2	224	62*	–	2	–	56.00	–	–	1188	53	625	29	21.55	2	–	5–30
Cairns	1	–	–	–	–	–	–	–	–	2	–	174	3	133	2	66.50	–	–	1–45
Darwin	1	1	–	23	23	–	–	–	23.00	–	–	122	7	57	4	14.25	–	–	3–23
Hobart	3	2	–	59	41	–	–	–	29.50	1	–	656	22	351	13	27.00	–	–	4–82

Venue	M	Inn	NO	Runs	HS	0s	50	100	Avrge	Ct	St	Balls	Mdns	Runs	Wkts	Avrge	5	10	Best
Melbourne	8	9	1	82	27	2	–	–	10.25	–	–	1840	71	968	34	28.47	1	–	5–47
Perth	8	10	2	205	41*	1	–	–	25.63	1	–	2118	61	1165	40	29.13	2	–	5–61
Sydney	9	11	2	170	59	2	1	–	18.89	3	–	2006	75	1257	38	33.08	1	–	5–119
in Bangladesh ...																			
Chitragong	1	1	–	–	–	–	–	–	–	2	–	120	5	71	1	71.00	–	–	1–35
Fatullah	1	2	–	44	29	–	–	–	22.00	1	–	162	5	115	1	115.00	–	–	1–47
in England ...																			
Birmingham	2	3	1	49	43*	1	–	–	24.50	1	–	324	4	301	7	43.00	–	–	4–82
Leeds	1	1	–	0	0	1	–	–	0.00	–	–	228	7	168	2	84.00	–	–	2–103
Lord's	2	3	–	31	20	–	–	–	10.33	1	–	331	12	192	7	27.43	–	–	3–47
Manchester	1	2	1	19	18*	–	–	–	19.00	–	–	234	6	160	5	32.00	–	–	4–100
Nottingham	2	3	1	77	47	–	–	–	38.50	–	–	353	3	242	6	40.33	–	–	3–51
The Oval	2	1	–	6	6	–	–	–	6.00	–	–	402	11	255	2	127.50	–	–	1–30
in India ...																			
Bangalore	1	1	–	27	27	–	–	–	27.00	–	–	222	9	90	2	45.00	–	–	1–26
Delhi	1	1	–	8	8	–	–	–	8.00	–	–	282	5	167	3	55.67	–	–	2–48
Mohali	1	2	–	35	35	1	–	–	17.50	1	–	228	5	147	2	73.50	–	–	1–61
Nagpur	1	2	1	1	1*	1	–	–	1.00	–	–	156	5	89	1	89.00	–	–	1–27
in New Zealand ...																			
Auckland	1	2	1	12	6*	–	–	–	12.00	1	–	114	8	55	4	13.75	–	–	2–19
Hamilton	1	1	–	8	8	–	–	–	8.00	–	–	250	10	123	8	15.38	1	–	5–77
Wellington	1	1	–	0	0	1	–	–	0.00	–	–	240	8	136	6	22.67	–	–	3–49

Brett Lee

Venue	M	Inn	NO	Runs	HS	0s	50	100	Avrge	Ct	St	Balls	Mdns	Runs	Wkts	Avrge	5	10	Best
in Sri Lanka ...																			
Colombo	1	2	–	14	12	–	–	–	7.00	–	–	150	4	112	2	56.00	–	–	1–49
in South Africa ...																			
Cape Town	2	2	–	0	0	2	–	–	0.00	–	–	419	11	248	8	31.00	–	–	3–37
Durban	2	3	1	23	23*	2	–	–	11.50	1	–	474	14	291	10	29.10	1	–	5–69
Johannesburg	2	3	2	92	64	–	1	–	92.00	–	–	375	14	209	9	23.22	–	–	3–40
in United Arab Emirates ...																			
Sharjah	2	2	–	13	12	–	–	–	6.50	1	–	251	9	122	3	40.67	–	–	2–15
in West Indies ...																			
Bridgetown	2	2	1	34	23*	–	–	–	34.00	3	–	484	19	294	8	36.75	–	–	3–64
Georgetown	1	1	–	20	20	–	–	–	20.00	1	–	147	5	98	2	49.00	–	–	2–41
Kingston	1	2	–	13	9	–	–	–	6.50	1	–	300	13	144	5	28.80	–	–	3–63
North Sound	1	2	1	67	63*	–	1	–	67.00	–	–	252	12	110	8	13.75	1	–	5–59
Port-of-Spain	1	–	–	–	–	–	–	–	–	–	–	252	8	137	5	27.40	–	–	4–69
St John's	1	2	–	27	18	–	–	–	13.50	1	–	228	6	135	7	19.29	–	–	4–63

Country	M	Inn	NO	Runs	HS	0s	50	100	Avrge	Ct	St	Balls	Mdns	Runs	Wkts	Avrge	5	10	Best
Australia	41	44	8	831	62*	5	3	–	23.08	9	–	9553	329	5343	186	28.73	7	–	5–30
Bangladesh	2	2	–	44	29	2	–	–	22.00	3	–	282	10	186	2	93.00	–	–	1–35
England	10	13	3	182	47	2	–	–	18.20	2	–	1872	43	1318	29	45.45	–	–	4–82
India	4	6	1	71	35	2	–	–	14.20	1	–	888	24	493	8	61.63	–	–	2–48
New Zealand	3	4	1	20	8	1	–	–	6.67	1	–	604	26	314	18	17.44	1	–	5–77
Sri Lanka	1	2	–	14	12	–	–	–	7.00	–	–	150	4	112	2	56.00	–	–	1–49
South Africa	6	8	3	115	64	4	1	–	23.00	1	–	1268	39	748	27	27.70	1	–	5–69
United Arab Emirates	2	2	–	13	12	–	1	–	6.50	–	–	251	9	122	3	40.67	–	–	2–15
West Indies	7	9	2	161	63*	–	1	–	23.00	6	–	1663	63	918	35	26.23	1	–	5–59

Dismissals:	Inn	NO	Bwd	Cgt	CWk	LBW	Stp	RO	HW	HB
	90	18	9	32	17	10	–	3	–	–

Wickets:	Ttl	Bwd	Cgt	CWk	LBW	Stp	HW
	310	65	109	91	45	–	–

Highest Score: 64   Australia v South Africa, Johannesburg, 2005–06

Best Bowling: 5–30   Australia v West Indies, Brisbane, 2005–06

Wkts	Team	Opponent	Venue	Season
5–47	Australia	India	Melbourne	1999–00
5–77	Australia	New Zealand	Hamilton	1999–00
5–61	Australia	West Indies	Perth	2000–01
5–67	Australia	New Zealand	Brisbane	2001–02
5–30	Australia	West Indies	Brisbane	2005–06
5–93	Australia	South Africa	Perth	2005–06
5–69	Australia	South Africa	Durban	2005–06
5–119	Australia	India	Sydney	2007–08
5–59	Australia	West Indies	North Sound	2007–08
5–105	Australia	New Zealand	Adelaide	2008–09

Brett Lee

SHEFFIELD SHIELD CAREER

Debut: 1997–98, New South Wales v Western Australia, Sydney

Season		M	Inn	NO	Runs	HS	0s	50	100	Avrge	Ct	St	Balls	Mdns	Runs	Wkts	Avrge	5	10	Best
1997–98	New South Wales	1	1	–	0	0	1	–	–	0.00	–	–	198	7	114	3	38.00	–	–	2/15
1998–99	New South Wales	5	4	1	21	9*	–	–	–	7.00	3	–	825	32	420	14	30.00	1	–	5/53
1999–00	New South Wales	5	9	2	100	34	3	–	–	14.29	3	–	1155	46	575	24	23.96	–	–	4/55
2000–01	New South Wales	2	3	–	48	26	1	–	–	16.00	1	–	443	19	234	9	26.00	1	–	5/42
2001–02	New South Wales	1	2	–	8	8	–	–	–	4.00	1	–	138	5	97	6	16.17	1	–	5/56
2002–03	New South Wales	2	3	1	15	14	1	–	–	5.00	1	–	565	23	329	21	15.67	3	2	7/114
2003–04	New South Wales	2	3	1	114	74*	–	1	–	57.00	1	–	570	14	343	10	34.30	1	–	5/124
2005–06	New South Wales	1	1	–	0	0	1	–	–	0.00	–	–	192	5	103	5	20.60	–	–	4/77
2007–08	New South Wales	2	3	–	116	97	–	1	–	38.67	1	–	504	15	328	5	65.60	–	–	4/72
Total		**21**	**29**	**4**	**422**	**97**	**8**	**2**	–	**16.88**	**9**	–	**4590**	**166**	**2543**	**97**	**26.22**	**7**	**2**	**7/114**

Opponents	M	Inn	NO	Runs	HS	0s	50	100	Avrge	Ct	St	Balls	Mdns	Runs	Wkts	Avrge	5	10	Best
Queensland	4	7	1	80	34	1	1	–	13.33	5	–	792	28	460	9	51.11	–	–	3/77
South Australia	5	6	1	26	17*	3	–	–	5.20	2	–	1090	39	638	30	21.27	2	1	7/114
Tasmania	6	6	–	102	37	2	–	–	17.00	3	–	1474	61	742	31	23.94	4	1	5/53
Victoria	4	7	2	213	97	–	2	–	42.60	3	–	786	23	450	16	28.13	1	–	5/42
Western Australia	2	3	–	1	1	2	–	–	0.33	1	–	448	15	253	11	23.00	–	–	4/55

	Inn	NO	Runs	HS	0s	50	100	Avrge	Ct	St	Balls	Mdns	Runs	Wkts	Avrge	5	10	Best
First Innings	9	2	117	74*	3	1	–	16.71	5	–	1248	40	724	23	31.48	3	–	4/72
Second Innings	10	1	166	37	2	1	–	18.44	2	–	1654	63	933	32	29.16	3	–	7/114
Third Innings	8	1	138	97	2	1	–	19.71	1	–	670	21	397	21	18.90	2	–	5/42
Fourth Innings	2	–	1	1	1	–	–	0.50	1	–	1018	42	489	21	23.29	2	–	5/53

Venue	M	Inn	NO	Runs	HS	0s	50	100	Avrge	Ct	St	Balls	Mdns	Runs	Wkts	Avrge	5	10	Best
Brisbane	2	4	–	46	34	1	1	–	11.50	–	–	366	12	186	6	31.00	1	–	3/95
Hobart	2	2	–	26	26	1	–	–	13.00	2	–	590	23	281	10	28.10	–	–	5/53
Melbourne	1	2	1	77	74*	–	1	–	77.00	1	–	264	5	152	4	38.00	–	–	3/83
Perth	1	2	–	1	1	1	–	–	0.50	1	–	250	8	139	8	17.38	–	–	4/55
Richmond	1	2	–	22	14	–	–	–	11.00	–	–	168	9	77	6	12.83	1	–	5/42
Sydney	14	17	3	250	97	5	1	–	17.86	4	–	2952	109	1708	63	27.11	5	2	7/114

How Dismissed:

Inns	NO	Bwd	Cgt	CWK	LBW	Stp	RO	HW	HB
29	4	7	10	6	2	–	–	–	–

Wickets Taken:

Wkts	Bwd	Cgt	C&B	LBW	Stp	HW
97	23	58	2	14	–	–

Batsmen Dismissed:

Wkts	1/2	3	4	5	6	7	8	9	10	11
97	25	11	10	8	8	9	8	6	8	4

Highest Score: 97   New South Wales v Victoria, Sydney, 2007–08

Best Bowling: 7/114   New South Wales v South Australia, Sydney, 2002–03

Wkts	Team	Opponent	Venue	Season
5/53	New South Wales	Tasmania	Hobart	1998–99
5/42	New South Wales	Victoria	Richmond	2000–01
5/56	New South Wales	South Australia	Sydney	2001–02
5/63	New South Wales	Tasmania	Sydney	2002–03
5/86	New South Wales	Tasmania	Sydney	2002–03
7/114	New South Wales	South Australia	Sydney	2002–03
5/124	New South Wales	Tasmania	Sydney	2003–04

INTERNATIONAL LIMITED-OVER CAREER

Debut: 1999–00, Australia v Pakistan, Brisbane

Season	Event	Team	M	I	NO	Runs	HS	0s	50	100	Avrge	Stk/Rt	Ct	St	Balls	Mds	Runs	Wkt	Avrge	Best	Stk/Rt	RPO
1999–00	CUB Series	AUS	9	2	–	3	2	–	–	–	1.50	50.00	1	–	487	4	320	16	20.00	5/27	30.44	3.94
1999–00	New Zealand v Aust.	N.Z	5	1	–	3	3	–	–	–	3.00	42.86	1	–	198	1	170	5	34.00	3/21	39.60	5.15
1999–00	South Africa v Aust.	SAF	3	2	1	25	24*	–	–	–	25.00	73.53	–	–	180	4	121	8	15.13	3/32	22.50	4.03
2000–01	Australia v S.Africa	AUS	2	1	1	6	6*	–	–	–	–	60.00	–	–	120	1	107	3	35.67	3/56	40.00	5.35
2000–01	ICC Trophy	KYA	1	1	–	31	31	–	–	–	31.00	110.71	–	–	60	–	39	2	19.50	2/39	30.00	3.90
2000–01	Carlton Series	AUS	4	1	–	2	2	–	–	–	2.00	40.00	–	–	198	3	215	6	35.83	4/33	33.00	6.52
2001	Natwest Series	ENG	5	5	1	10	10	–	–	–	10.00	55.56	–	–	288	4	264	10	26.40	3/63	28.80	5.50
2001–02	VB Series	AUS	5	5	1	79	51*	2	1	–	19.75	101.28	–	–	273	4	223	8	27.88	3/43	34.13	4.90
2001–02	South Africa v Aust.	SAF	4	3	1	44	28	–	–	–	22.00	107.32	1	–	205	1	199	9	22.11	4/45	22.78	5.82
2001–02	Australia v Pakistan	AUS	3	1	–	3	3*	–	–	–	–	50.00	–	–	60	–	44	2	22.00	2/44	30.00	4.40
2002–03	TriNation Tournament	KYA	4	1	1	6	6*	–	–	–	–	150.00	1	–	192	6	108	8	13.50	4/32	24.00	3.38
2002–03	ICC Champions Trophy	S.L	3	2	1	22	18	1	–	–	22.00	53.66	–	–	120	1	100	5	20.00	3/38	24.00	5.00
2002–03	VB Series	AUS	9	3	–	38	20	–	–	–	12.67	90.48	–	–	483	5	338	18	18.78	5/30	26.83	4.20
2002–03	World Cup	SZK	10	3	1	23	15*	1	–	–	11.50	65.71	8	–	499	9	394	22	17.91	5/42	22.68	4.74
2002–03	West Indies v Aust.	W.I	6	3	–	24	14	–	–	–	8.00	53.33	–	–	292	7	246	11	22.36	3/50	26.55	5.05
2003–04	Aust. v Bangladesh	AUS	2	–	–	–	–	–	–	–	–	–	–	–	102	3	49	4	12.25	4/25	25.50	2.88
2003–04	VB Series	AUS	8	4	2	27	12*	–	–	–	13.50	93.10	6	–	396	4	285	12	23.75	3/22	33.00	4.32
2003–04	Sri Lanka v Aust.	S.L	3	1	1	1	1*	–	–	–	–	100.00	2	–	138	2	122	2	61.00	1/31	69.00	5.30
2004–05	TriNation Tournament	NED	2	1	1	1	1*	–	–	–	–	100.00	–	–	42	1	29	1	29.00	1/29	42.00	4.14
2004	Australia v Pakistan	ENG	1	–	–	–	–	–	–	–	–	–	1	–	60	–	67	1	67.00	1/67	60.00	6.70
2004	ICC Champions	ENG	2	1	–	15	15	–	–	–	15.00	88.24	1	–	81	3	86	3	28.67	2/65	27.00	6.37
2004–05	Chappell–Hadlee	AUS	2	2	1	18	10*	–	–	–	18.00	112.50	–	–	102	1	88	4	22.00	2/40	25.50	5.18
2004–05	VB Series	AUS	8	4	2	87	38*	–	–	–	43.50	82.86	2	–	446	4	341	16	21.31	4/38	27.88	4.59
2004–05	New Zealand v Aust.	N.Z	5	1	–	4	4*	–	–	–	–	133.33	1	–	258	4	169	10	16.90	3/41	25.80	3.93
2005	Natwest Series	ENG	5	2	1	24	21*	–	–	–	24.00	104.35	–	–	234	4	174	8	21.75	2/27	29.25	4.46
2005	Natwest Challenge	ENG	3	1	1	15	15*	–	–	–	–	78.95	–	–	174	2	135	6	22.50	5/41	29.00	4.66
2005–06	Australia v World XI	AUS	3	1	1	26	26*	–	–	–	–	152.94	–	–	147	5	108	7	15.43	4/30	21.00	4.41
2005–06	Chappell–Hadlee	N.Z	2	1	–	0	0	1	–	–	0.00	0.00	1	–	96	4	90	4	22.50	3/5	24.00	5.63

Season	Series		M	I	NO	Runs	HS	0s	50	100	Avrge	Stk/Rt	Ct	St	Balls	Mds	Runs	Wkt	Avrge	Best	Stk/Rt	RPO
2005–06	VB Series	AUS	11	5	1	85	57	–	1	–	21.25	71.43	2	–	606	6	439	15	29.27	5/22	40.40	4.35
2005–06	South Africa v Aust.	SAF	5	5	3	60	38*	–	–	–	30.00	120.00	1	–	269	2	281	7	40.14	4/48	38.43	6.27
2005–06	Bangladesh v Aust.	BAN	2	1	1	12	12*	–	–	–	–	40.00	3	–	96	2	63	4	15.75	2/29	24.00	3.94
2006–07	TriNation Tournament	MAL	3	2	1	8	7	–	–	–	8.00	88.89	1	–	163	1	108	12	9.00	5/38	13.58	3.98
2006–07	ICC Championships	IND	5	2	–	5	5	1	–	–	2.50	83.33	–	–	256	4	204	5	34.00	2/31	42.67	4.78
2006–07	Commonwealth Bank	AUS	7	4	2	32	20*	1	–	–	16.00	59.26	4	–	408	3	322	12	26.83	3/41	34.00	4.74
2007–08	India v Australia	IND	7	6	4	24	17	1	–	–	12.00	113.21	6	–	298	4	240	6	40.00	3/37	49.67	4.83
2007–08	Chappell–Hadlee	AUS	3	1	1	0	0*	–	–	–	–	0.00	1	–	132	–	107	7	15.29	3/47	18.86	4.86
2007–08	Commonwealth Bank	AUS	8	7	1	73	37	1	–	–	12.17	58.82	2	–	430	5	356	16	22.25	5/27	26.88	4.97
2007–08	West Indies v Aust.	WI	5	3	3	19	12*	–	–	–	–	134.75	2	–	264	3	204	7	29.14	3/64	37.71	4.64
2009	Scotland v Australia	SCO	5	1	–	5	5	–	–	–	5.00	166.67	1	–	48	–	36	2	18.00	2/36	24.00	4.50
2009	England v Australia	ENG	6	3	–	0	0	3	–	–	0.00	0.00	–	–	319	5	275	12	22.92	5/49	26.58	5.17
2009–10	Champions Trophy	SAF	5	2	1	37	25	–	–	–	37.00	86.05	1	–	222	1	162	6	27.00	2/45	37.00	4.38
2009–10	India v Australia	IND	1	1	1	0	0	–	–	–	0.00	0.00	–	–	36	–	28	1	28.00	1/28	36.00	4.67
2010–11	Australia v England	AUS	6	4	2	41	39*	2	–	–	20.50	102.50	1	–	300	–	264	11	24.00	3/27	27.27	5.28
2010–11	World Cup	ISB	7	1	–	5	5	–	–	–	5.00	62.50	2	–	326	6	235	13	18.08	4/28	25.08	4.33
2011–11	Bangladesh v Aust.	BAN	2	1	–	–	–	–	–	–	–	–	1	–	108	2	73	1	73.00	1/36	108.00	4.06
2011–12	Sri Lanka v Aust.	S.L	4	1	1	14	14*	–	–	–	–	175.00	2	–	203	1	145	8	18.13	4/15	25.38	4.29
Total			**205**	**98**	**40**	**957**	**57**	**14**	**2**	**–**	**16.50**	**81.69**	**52**	**–**	**10415**	**130**	**8173**	**357**	**22.89**	**5/22**	**29.17**	**4.71**

Opponents	M	I	NO	Runs	HS	0s	50	100	Avrge	Stk/Rt	Ct	St	Balls	Mds	Runs	Wkt	Avrge	Best	Stk/Rt	RPO
Bangladesh	9	1	1	12	12*	–	–	–	–	40.00	4	–	444	8	306	15	20.40	4/25	29.60	4.14
Canada	1	–	–	–	–	–	–	–	–	–	1	–	52	–	46	4	11.50	4/46	13.00	5.31
England	34	17	6	149	39*	7	–	–	13.55	78.42	5	–	1831	20	1447	64	22.61	5/30	28.61	4.74
India	30	16	6	115	31	3	–	–	11.50	82.56	9	–	1435	15	1080	51	21.18	5/27	28.14	4.52
Kenya	4	1	1	6	6*	–	–	–	–	150.00	–	–	180	7	78	6	13.00	3/14	30.00	2.60
New Zealand	28	13	5	79	27	2	–	–	9.88	85.78	7	–	1369	17	1091	52	20.98	5/42	26.33	4.78
Namibia	1	–	–	–	–	–	–	–	–	–	–	–	36	–	36	1	26.00	1/26	36.00	4.33
Pakistan	21	10	3	84	22	–	–	–	12.00	70.00	6	–	1144	12	881	38	23.18	4/28	30.11	4.62
Sri Lanka	24	9	3	114	37	–	1	–	19.00	65.14	10	–	1208	11	975	30	32.50	4/15	40.27	4.84
South Africa	20	16	8	249	57	1	2	–	31.13	97.65	2	–	1107	14	946	40	23.65	5/22	27.68	5.13
Scotland	1	1	–	5	5	–	–	–	5.00	166.67	1	–	48	1	36	2	18.00	2/36	24.00	4.50
United States of America	1	–	–	–	–	–	–	–	–	–	–	–	30	–	21	1	21.00	1/21	30.00	4.20
West Indies	21	10	5	107	38*	1	–	–	21.40	80.39	4	–	1072	17	832	41	20.29	4/24	26.15	4.66
World XI	3	1	1	26	26*	–	–	–	–	152.94	–	–	147	5	108	7	15.43	4/30	21.00	4.41
Zimbabwe	7	3	1	11	6*	–	–	–	5.50	84.62	3	–	312	2	300	5	60.00	1/29	62.40	5.77

Brett Lee

Best Bowling: 5/22   Australia v South Africa, Melbourne, 2005–06

Wkts	Team	Opponent	Venue	Season
5/27	Australia	India	Adelaide	1999–00
5/30	Australia	England	Melbourne	2002–03
5/42	Australia	New Zealand	Port Elizabeth	2002–03
5/41	Australia	England	Lord's	2005
5/22	Australia	South Africa	Melbourne (Docklands)	2005–06
5/38	Australia	India	Kinrara	2006–07
5/27	Australia	India	Brisbane	2007–08
5/58	Australia	India	Sydney	2007–08
5/49	Australia	England	Lord's	2009

AUSTRALIAN DOMESTIC LIMITED–OVER CAREER

Debut: 1997–98, New South Wales v Australian Capital Territory, Canberra

Season	Team	M	I	NO	Runs	HS	0s	50	100	Avrge	Stk/Rt	Ct	St	Balls	Mds	Runs	Wkt	Avrge	Best	Stk/Rt	RPO
1997–98	New South Wales	1	1	–	–	–	–	–	–	–	–	1	–	60	–	50	1	50.00	1/50	60.00	5.00
1999–00	New South Wales	3	1	–	12	12	–	–	–	12.00	120.00	–	–	174	2	111	6	18.50	2/28	29.00	3.83
2000–01	New South Wales	5	2	1	18	14*	–	–	–	18.00	66.67	1	–	288	5	207	8	25.88	3/41	36.00	4.31
2001–02	New South Wales	3	1	1	44	44*	–	–	–	–	151.72	–	–	168	2	109	2	54.50	1/31	84.00	3.89
2002–03	New South Wales	1	1	–	0	0	1	–	–	0.00	0.00	1	–	60	–	49	2	24.50	2/49	30.00	4.90
2003–04	New South Wales	1	1	1	0	0*	–	–	–	–	0.00	–	–	60	2	41	–	–	–	–	4.10
2004–05	New South Wales	3	3	2	18	9*	–	–	–	18.00	72.00	–	–	156	1	114	2	57.00	1/24	78.00	4.38
2005–06	New South Wales	2	2	1	14	13	–	–	–	14.00	87.50	–	–	114	2	91	5	18.20	3/30	22.80	4.79
2007–08	New South Wales	1	1	–	11	11	–	–	–	11.00	84.62	–	–	55	1	57	–	–	–	–	6.22
2009–10	New South Wales	1	1	1	19	19*	–	–	–	–	135.71	–	–	54	1	42	–	–	–	–	4.67
2010–11	New South Wales	7	3	1	1	1	1	–	–	0.50	14.29	3	–	454	5	375	15	25.00	5/47	30.27	4.96
Total		**28**	**16**	**8**	**137**	**44***	**2**	**–**	**–**	**17.13**	**95.74**	**6**	**–**	**1643**	**22**	**1246**	**41**	**30.39**	**5/47**	**40.07**	**4.55**

Opponents		M	I	NO	Runs	HS	0s	50	100	Avrge	Stk/Rt	Ct	St	Balls	Mds	Runs	Wkt	Avrge	Best	Stk/Rt	RPO
Australian Capital Territory		1	–	–	–	–	–	–	–	–	–	1	–	60	–	50	1	50.00	1/50	60.00	5.00
Queensland		5	1	1	–	1*	–	–	–	–	100.00	–	–	276	3	199	10	19.90	3/30	27.60	4.33
South Australia		5	4	2	71	44*	1	–	–	35.50	129.09	1	–	306	1	264	7	37.71	2/49	43.71	5.18
Tasmania		6	3	1	31	19*	1	–	–	15.50	119.23	–	–	366	6	270	9	30.00	3/51	40.67	4.43
Victoria		8	6	3	33	11	–	–	–	11.00	59.89	3	–	445	9	327	6	54.50	3/41	74.17	4.41
Western Australia		3	2	1	–	–	–	–	–	1.00	16.67	–	–	190	2	136	8	17.00	5/47	23.75	4.29

Highest Score: 44* — New South Wales v South Australia, Adelaide, 2001–02

Best Bowling: 5/47 — New South Wales v Western Australia, Perth, 2010–11

Wkts	Team	Opponent	Venue	Season
5/47	New South Wales	Western Australia	Perth	2010–11

TWENTY20 CAREER

Debut: 2004–05, Australia v New Zealand, Auckland

Season	Team	M	I	NO	Runs	HS	0s	50	100	Avrge	Stk/Rt	Ct	St	Balls	Mds	Runs	Wkt	Avrge	Best	Stk/Rt	RPO
2004–05	Australia	1	1	–	–	–	–	–	–	–	–	–	–	24	–	26	1	26.00	1/26	24.00	6.50
2005	Australia	1	1	1	15	15	–	–	–	15.00	75.00	–	–	18	–	31	–	–	–	–	10.33
2005–06	Australia	1	1	1	43	43*	–	–	–	–	204.76	–	–	18	–	15	–	–	–	–	5.00
2007–08	Australia	8	5	2	37	13	–	–	–	12.33	142.31	4	–	180	–	206	8	25.75	3/27	22.50	6.87
2007–08	Australia	1	1	1	0	0*	1	–	–	–	–	–	–	19	–	35	3	35.00	1/35	19.00	11.05
2007–08	Australia	2	1	1	0	0*	–	–	–	0.00	0.00	1	–	42	–	30	3	10.00	2/17	14.00	4.29
2007–08	Kolkata Knight Riders	4	3	2	17	16*	1	–	–	17.00	130.77	3	–	96	–	112	4	28.00	1/9	24.00	7.00
2007–08	Australia	1	1	–	–	–	–	–	–	–	–	–	–	12	–	26	–	–	–	–	13.00
2008–09	Australia	1	1	–	0	0	1	–	–	0.00	0.00	–	–	24	–	22	1	22.00	1/22	24.00	5.50
2008–09	Kolkata Knight Riders	5	4	2	28	14*	–	–	–	14.00	82.35	1	–	120	1	111	5	22.20	3/15	24.00	5.55
2009	Australia	3	2	1	16	15	–	–	–	16.00	266.67	–	–	54	–	98	4	24.50	2/39	13.50	10.89
2009–10	New South Wales	10	6	3	59	48	1	–	–	19.67	140.48	4	–	213	3	228	8	28.50	2/10	26.63	6.42
2010–11	New South Wales	1	–	–	–	–	–	–	–	–	–	–	–	24	–	44	–	–	–	–	11.00
2010–11	Wellington	4	3	2	35	15	–	–	–	35.00	175.00	1	–	84	–	114	4	28.50	2/29	21.00	8.14
2010–11	New South Wales	3	1	–	–	–	–	–	–	–	–	2	–	66	–	90	1	90.00	1/41	66.00	8.18
2010–11	Kolkata Knight Riders	12	4	1	5	2*	–	–	–	1.67	55.56	2	–	272	1	338	5	67.60	1/12	54.40	7.46
2011–12	Australia	2	1	1	4	4*	–	–	–	–	133.33	–	–	48	–	77	4	19.25	3/39	12.00	9.63
Total		**60**	**32**	**16**	**259**	**48**	**3**	–	–	**16.19**	**130.81**	**18**	–	**1314**	**5**	**1603**	**49**	**32.71**	**3/15**	**26.82**	**7.32**

Opponents	M	I	NO	Runs	HS	0s	50	100	Avrge	Stk/Rt	Ct	St	Balls	Mds	Runs	Wkt	Avrge	Best	Stk/Rt	RPO
Auckland	1	–	–	–	–	–	–	–	–	–	1	–	18	–	33	1	33.00	1/33	18.00	11.00
Bangladesh	1	1	–	1	1*	–	–	–	–	100.00	–	–	24	–	27	3	9.00	3/27	8.00	6.75
Bangalore Royal Challengers	2	1	–	1	1*	–	–	–	–	150.00	–	–	42	–	79	1	79.00	1/31	42.00	11.29
Central Districts	3	1	–	15	15	–	–	–	15.00	–	–	–	24	–	31	–	–	–	–	7.75
Chennai Super Kings	3	1	–	6	6	–	–	–	6.00	85.71	1	–	72	–	59	1	59.00	1/35	72.00	4.92
Deccan Chargers	3	2	2	14	14*	–	–	–	–	93.33	–	–	72	–	85	2	42.50	1/24	36.00	7.08

Opponent	M	I	NO	Runs	HS	0s	50	100	Avrge	Stk/Rt	Ct	St	Balls	Mds	Runs	Wkt	Avrge	Best	Stk/Rt	RPO
Delhi Daredevils	3	2	1	2	1*	1	–	–	2.00	50.00	2	–	72	1	72	4	18.00	3/15	18.00	6.00
Eagles	1	1	–	0	0	1	–	–	0.00	0.00	–	–	24	1	14	1	14.00	1/14	24.00	3.50
England	5	1	–	15	15	–	–	–	15.00	75.00	1	–	96	–	135	3	45.00	1/3	32.00	8.44
India	3	1	–	2	2	–	–	–	2.00	100.00	2	–	61	–	73	2	36.50	1/13	30.50	7.18
Kolkata Knight Riders	1	1	1	7	7*	–	–	–	–	140.00	–	–	24	–	39	–	–	–	–	9.75
Kochi Tuskers Kerala	2	2	1	1	1	1	–	–	1.00	40.00	–	–	48	1	75	1	75.00	1/33	48.00	9.38
Kings XI Punjab	6	4	2	29	16*	–	–	–	14.50	111.54	–	–	24	–	27	–	–	–	–	6.75
Mumbai Indians	6	1	1	11	11*	–	–	–	–	275.00	–	–	135	–	170	3	56.67	1/9	45.00	7.56
Northern Districts	3	1	1	9	9*	–	–	–	–	128.57	–	–	18	–	21	1	21.00	1/21	18.00	7.00
New Zealand	1	1	1	9	9*	–	–	–	–	150.00	1	–	72	–	64	4	16.00	2/17	18.00	5.33
Otago	1	1	1	2	2*	–	–	–	–	33.33	–	–	24	–	29	2	14.50	2/29	12.00	7.25
Pakistan	2	–	–	–	–	–	–	–	–	–	1	–	48	–	52	1	52.00	1/22	48.00	6.50
Pune Warriors	1	1	–	0	0	1	–	–	0.00	0.00	–	–	24	–	28	–	–	–	–	7.00
Rajasthan Royals	3	–	–	–	–	–	–	–	–	–	1	–	62	–	76	2	38.00	1/12	31.00	7.35
South Australia	1	–	–	–	–	–	–	–	–	–	–	–	18	–	20	–	–	–	–	6.67
Sri Lanka	4	2	1	19	15	–	–	–	19.00	237.50	3	–	96	–	143	8	17.88	3/39	12.00	8.94
South Africa	2	2	1	54	43*	–	–	–	54.00	186.21	–	–	30	–	29	–	–	–	–	5.80
Sri Lankans	1	–	–	–	–	–	–	–	–	–	–	–	24	–	44	–	–	–	–	11.00
Somerset	1	–	–	–	–	–	–	–	–	–	–	–	24	–	15	1	15.00	1/15	24.00	3.75
Sussex	1	–	–	–	–	–	–	–	–	–	–	–	24	–	8	1	8.00	1/8	24.00	2.00
Trinidad & Tobago	2	1	–	48	48	–	–	–	48.00	154.84	2	–	30	1	27	3	9.00	2/10	10.00	5.40
Victoria	1	1	1	0	0*	–	–	–	–	0.00	–	–	24	–	15	2	7.50	2/15	12.00	3.75
West Indies	2	1	1	1	1*	–	–	–	–	100.00	–	–	36	–	82	1	82.00	1/56	36.00	13.67
Zimbabwe	1	1	–	13	13	–	–	–	13.00	185.71	–	–	24	–	31	1	31.00	1/31	24.00	7.75

Team	M	I	NO	Runs	HS	0s	50	100	Avrge	Stk/Rt	Ct	St	Balls	Mds	Runs	Wkt	Avrge	Best	Stk/Rt	RPO
Australia	23	12	6	115	43*	1	–	–	19.17	143.75	6	–	487	1	636	23	27.65	3/27	21.17	7.84
Kolkata Knight Riders	12	4	1	5	2*	1	–	–	1.67	55.56	2	–	272	1	338	5	67.60	1/12	54.40	7.46
Kings XI Punjab	13	10	6	56	16*	1	–	–	14.00	100.00	6	–	303	–	372	9	41.33	3/15	33.67	7.37
New South Wales	8	3	1	48	48	–	–	–	24.00	145.45	3	–	168	3	143	8	17.88	2/10	21.00	5.11
Wellington	4	2	1	35	15	–	–	–	35.00	175.00	1	–	84	–	114	4	28.50	2/29	21.00	8.14

Highest Score: 48 — New South Wales v Trinidad & Tobago, Hyderabad (RGIS), 2009–10

Best Bowling: 3/15 — Kings XI Punjab v Delhi Daredevils, Bloemfontein, 2008–09

INDEX

drugs 112, 179
Dubai 373
Duke ball 139–40, 266
Duminy, J. P. 369, 370
Durban 183, 284–5
Edgbaston 138, 142, 256, 286
Edwards, Fidel 168, 350
Eime, Andrew 44
Emery, Phil 27, 53, 237
England 116, 132, 145, 177, 208, 233,
    234, 249, 299, 319, 389
  Ashes *see* Ashes
  Lions 374–6, 378, 402
  World Cup (50-overs) 2003 182
  World Cup (Twenty20) 371
fame 1–4, 67, 69, 91, 100, 148, 157–8,
    291, 319, 337, 399, 404
  India, in 198–206, 274
Farhart, Pat 56, 128, 134, 407
fashion 32–3, 47–8, 128–31, 226, 379
Feroz Shah Kotla 140
Fink, Eric 49
Fink, Jacqui 49
Finlay, Ian 47
Finn, Elroy 246, 248
Finn, Neil 246–8
Finn, Tim 246
fireworks 35, 137–8, 198, 342, 347
fishing 10, 306, 353–6
fitness test 163–4
Fleming, Damien 'Flem' 30, 67, 77–9,
    135, 139, 319
Fleming, Stephen 103, 149, 182–3,
    249
Flintoff, Andrew 'Freddie' 249, 253,
    257–64, 266–9, 271, 306, 308–10,
    314, 317, 325, 385
flying 5, 33, 132–3
Flynn, Daniel 364
Freedman, David 53
Frere, Derrick 93
Funhouse 106, 247
Gandhi, Devang 88
Ganga, Darren 120
Ganguly, Sourav 187, 215, 217, 218,
    223, 331, 333, 335
Garnaut, Matthew 53
Garner, Joel 117
The Gas 166
Gatorade Sports Science Institute 163

Gavaskar, Sunil 114–15
Gayle, Chris 373
Genius, Sarah 224–8
Gibbs, Herschelle 278, 283
Gilchrist, Adam 'Gilly' 53, 55, 66, 73,
    83, 124, 158, 160, 168, 174, 217,
    233, 237, 241, 277, 279, 287, 336,
    391
  Ashes 2002–2003 174, 175–6
  Ashes 2005 254, 268, 269
  Ashes 2006–2007 310, 314, 315, 316
  Australia–India 2003–2004 214, 216,
    222
  Australia–India 2007–2008 330,
    335–6
  Australia–West Indies 2000–2001
    118–19
  boot camp 293, 295
  Boxing Day Test 1999 74–6, 79
  England 2001 139, 142, 143
  New Zealand–Australia 2000 100, 103
  World Cup (50-overs) 2003 180,
    183–6, 187
Gilchrist, Mel 74–5, 217
Giles, Ashley 253, 260, 262, 269
Gillespie, Jason 'Dizzy' xi, 33–5, 39–40,
    68, 135, 139, 143, 169, 172, 190–1,
    194, 208, 227, 229, 233, 241, 244–5,
    284, 287, 319
  Ashes 2005, 253, 254, 268
  Australia–India 2003–2004 214–17,
    224
  World Cup (50-overs) 2003 181–2
Gilmore, Stephanie 389
go-karting 272–4
Gordon Cricket Club 27
Gough, Darren 145–6, 147, 252
grade cricket 25–6, 29, 38, 87
Gregan, George 132
Greig, Tony 222
Grenada 189, 352
guitar ix, 59–60, 63, 146, 163, 167, 189,
    202, 217, 238, 246, 299, 321, 328,
    347, 357, 361, 366, 398
Haddin, Brad 44, 72–3, 213, 392
Hadlee, Sir Richard 110
Hair, Darrell 152
Hall, Andrew 103, 283
Hall, Wes 15–16
Hamilton 99, 102